The European Sovereign Debt Crisis

I0885331

The European Sovereign Debt Crisis: Breaking the Vicious Circle between Sovereigns and Banks explains why the euro area's progress towards reining in the risks arising from the well-documented bi-directional financial contagion transmission mechanism that links sovereigns to commercial banks has been more prominent compared to the channel of contagion moving from banks to sovereigns.

Providing an analysis of the legal and regulatory measures that Europe and the euro area have taken to mitigate the exposure of sovereigns to financial crises generated by commercial banks, this book draws attention to areas where improvements to the arsenal of tools hitherto introduced are either desirable or necessary. Chapters further explain – with recourse to economic and legal arguments – why the channel of contagion moving from sovereigns to commercial banks has proven harder to close, and explores ways in which progress could be made in the direction of closing it so as to avert the risk of future banking sector crises.

This work provides essential reading for students, researchers and practitioners with an interest in sovereign debt crises and the euro-area banking system.

Phoebus L. Athanassiou (LLB, LLM, PhD) is Senior Lead Legal Counsel with the Legal Services of the European Central Bank, a published author of works on banking and financial law, and a member of the Academic Faculty of the Institute of Law and Finance at the Goethe University of Frankfurt, Germany.

Angelos T. Vouldis (MEng, MSc, PhD) is an Economist at the European Central Bank, with year-long policy experience in financial crises and the stress testing of financial institutions. He has published extensively in leading journals on banking, financial stability, business cycles and institutional change.

Routledge Research in Finance and Banking Law

Housing and Financial Stability
Mortgage Lending and Macroprudential Policy in the UK and US
Alan Brener

Conceptualizing the Regulatory Thicket
China's Financial Markets after the Global Financial Crisis
Shen Wei

Banking Bailout Law
A Comparative Study of the United States, United Kingdom and the European Union
Virág Blazsek

Public-Private Partnerships in Emerging Economies
Augustine Edobor Arimoro

Regulation and the Global Financial Crisis
Impact, Regulatory Responses and Beyond
Daniel Cash and Robert Goddard

Discrimination, Vulnerable Consumers and Financial Inclusion
Fair Access to Financial Services and the Law
Edited by Cătălin Gabriel Stănescu and Asress Adimi Gikay

The European Sovereign Debt Crisis
Breaking the Vicious Circle between Sovereigns and Banks
Phoebus L. Athanassiou and Angelos T. Vouldis

For more information about this series, please visit: www.routledge.com/Routledge-Research-in-Finance-and-Banking-Law/book-series/FINANCIALLAW

The European Sovereign Debt Crisis

Breaking the Vicious Circle between Sovereigns and Banks

Phoebus L. Athanassiou and Angelos T. Vouldis

Routledge
Taylor & Francis Group
LONDON AND NEW YORK

First published 2022
by Routledge
2 Park Square, Milton Park, Abingdon, Oxon OX14 4RN

and by Routledge
605 Third Avenue, New York, NY 10158

Routledge is an imprint of the Taylor & Francis Group, an informa business

British Library Cataloguing-in-Publication Data
A catalogue record for this book is available from the British Library

Library of Congress Cataloging-in-Publication Data
Names: Athanassiou, Phoebus, author. | Vouldis, Angelos T., author.
Title: The European sovereign debt crisis: breaking the vicious circle between sovereigns and banks/Phoebus L. Athanassiou and Angelos T. Vouldis.
Description: Abingdon, Oxon; New York, NY: Routledge, 2022. |
Series: Routledge research in banking and finance law |
Includes bibliographical references and index.
Identifiers: LCCN 2021006886 (print) | LCCN 2021006887 (ebook) |
ISBN 9780367523466 (hardback) | ISBN 9781032030555 (paperback) |
ISBN 9781003186434 (ebook)
Subjects: LCSH: Debts, Public–Law and legislation–European Union countries.
Classification: LCC KJE7085.A84 2022 (print) | LCC KJE7085 (ebook) |
DDC 343.24/037–dc23
LC record available at https://lccn.loc.gov/2021006886
LC ebook record available at https://lccn.loc.gov/2021006887

ISBN: 978-0-367-52346-6 (hbk)
ISBN: 978-1-032-03055-5 (pbk)
ISBN: 978-1-003-18643-4 (ebk)

Typeset in Bembo
by Deanta Global Publishing Services, Chennai, India

Contents

Main legal instruments and sources

Treaty on European Union
Articles 3(4), 4(1), 5(2), 5(3), 5(4), 6(1), 13(1), 48(6)
Treaty establishing the European Community
Articles 230, 235
Treaty establishing the European Stability Mechanism
Recital (2)
Articles 4(3), 4(4), 11, 12(1), 12(3), 13(1), 15
Annex 1
Treaty on the Functioning of the European Union
Articles 4(2), 5, 50, 114, 115, 118, 120–123, 125, 126, 127(5), 127(6), 136, 143, 212, 263(1), 263(4), 277, 296, 311, 326–334, 340, 352
Article 8 of Protocol (No 2) on the application of the principles of subsidiarity and proportionality
Article 3(3) of Protocol (No 4) on the Statute of the European System of Central Banks and of the European Central Bank
Council Regulation (EU) 407/2010 of 11 May 2010 establishing a European financial stabilisation mechanism [2010] OJ L118/1
Recital (7)
Council Regulation (EU) 1024/2013 of 15 October 2013 conferring specific tasks on the European Central Bank concerning policies relating to the prudential supervision of credit institutions [2013] OJ L287/63
Recitals (28), (30), (35), (37), (61)
Articles 1, 4(1), 4(3), 6(3), 6(4), 6(5)(a), 6(5)(b), 6(5)(c), 6(5)(e), 6(6), 6(7), 7, 9(1)(a), 10–15, 22
Decision ECB/2012/3 of the European Central Bank of 5 March 2012 on the eligibility of marketable debt instruments issued or fully guaranteed by the Hellenic Republic in the context of the Hellenic Republic's debt exchange offer [2012] OJ L77/19
Article 20
Decision ECB/2014/16 of the European Central Bank of 14 April 2014 concerning the establishment of an Administrative Board of Review and its Operating Rules [2014] OJ L175/47

Directive 94/19/EC of the European Parliament and of the Council of 30 May 1994 on deposit-guarantee schemes [1994] OJ L135/5 (*no longer in force*)

Directive 98/26/EC of the European Parliament and of the Council of 19 May 1998 on settlement finality in payment and securities settlement systems [1998] OJ L166/45

Directive 98/43/EC of the European Parliament and of the Council of 6 July 1998 on the approximation of the laws, regulations and administrative provisions of the Member States relating to the advertising and sponsorship of tobacco products [1998] OJ L213/9

Directive 2013/36/EU of the European Parliament and of the Council of 26 June 2013 on access to the activity of credit institutions and the prudential supervision of credit institutions and investment firms, amending Directive 2002/87/EC and repealing Directives 2006/48/EC and 2006/49/EC [2013] OJ L176/338

Directive 2014/49/EU of the European Parliament and of the Council of 16 April 2014 on deposit guarantee schemes [2014] OJ L173/149

Directive 2014/59/EU of the European Parliament and of the Council of 15 May 2014 establishing a framework for the recovery and resolution of credit institutions and investment firms and amending Council Directive 82/891/EEC, and Directives 2001/24/EC, 2002/47/EC, 2004/25/EC, 2005/56/EC, 2007/36/EC, 2011/35/EU, 2012/30/EU and 2013/36/EU, and Regulations (EU) 1093/2010 and (EU) 648/2012, of the European Parliament and of the Council [2014] OJ L173/190
Articles 32(4)(d)(iii), 43, 44(5)(a)

Directive 2015/849 of the European Parliament and of the Council of 20 May 2015 on the prevention of the use of the financial system for the purposes of money laundering or terrorist financing, amending Regulation (EU) 648/2012 of the European Parliament and of the Council, and repealing Directive 2005/60/EC of the European Parliament and of the Council and Commission Directive 2006/70/EC [2015] OJ L141/73

European Council Decision 2011/199/EU amending Article 136 of the Treaty on the Functioning of the European Union with regard to a stability mechanism for Member States whose currency is the euro [2011] OJ L91/1

European Financial Stability Facility Agreement
Article 7
Annex 2

Guideline ECB/2014/60 of the European Central Bank of 19 December 2014 on the implementation of the Eurosystem monetary policy framework [2015] OJ L91/3
Articles 5, 9, 13

Headquarters Agreement of 18 September 1998 between the Government of the Federal Republic of Germany and the European Central Bank concerning the seat of the European Central Bank
Article 10

Regulation (EU) 575/2013 of the European Parliament and of the Council of 26 June 2013 on prudential requirements for credit institutions and investment firms and amending Regulation (EU) 648/2012 [2013] OJ L176/1
Articles 114(4), 150

Regulation (EU) 806/2014 of the European Parliament and of the Council of 15 July 2014 establishing uniform rules and a uniform procedure for the resolution of credit institutions and certain investment firms in the framework of a Single Resolution Mechanism and a Single Resolution Fund and amending Regulation (EU) 1093/2010 [2014] OJ L225/1
Recital (10)
Articles 14, 18(5)

Regulation (EU) 909/2014 of the European Parliament and of the Council of 23 July 2014 on improving securities settlement in the European Union and on central securities depositories and amending Directives 98/26/EC and 2014/65/EU and Regulation (EU) 236/2012 [2014] OJ L257/1
Articles 1(4), 3(2), 10–20, 22–24, 27, 28(6), 30(4), 46–47, 54–60

Regulation (EU) 468/2014 of the European Central Bank of 16 April 2014 establishing the framework for cooperation within the single supervisory mechanism between the European Central Bank and national competent authorities and with national designated authorities (SSM Framework Regulation) (ECB/2014/17) [2014] OJ L141/1
Articles 3(1), 25(1), 25(2), 31–33, 48, 67–69

Regulation (EU) 472/2013 of the European Parliament and of the Council of 21 May 2013 on the strengthening of economic and budgetary surveillance of Member States in the euro area experiencing or threatened with serious difficulties with respect to their financial stability [2013] OJ L140/1

Cases

European Union courts

Alessandro Accorinti and others v. European Central Bank [2014] ECLI:EU:T:2014:611

Amministrazione delle Finanze dello Stato v. Simmenthal SpA [1978] ECLI:EU:C:1978:49

Andrea Francovich and Danila Bonifaci and others v. Italian Republic [1991] ECLI:EU:C:1991:428

Asia Motor France v. Commission of the European Communities [1990] ECLI:EU:C:1990:230

Berlusconi and Finanziaria d'investimento SpA (Fininvest) v. Banca d'Italia et al. [2018] ECLI:EU:C:2018:1023

Brasserie du Pêcheur SA v. Bundesrepublik Deutschland and The Queen v. Secretary of State for Transport, ex parte: Factortame Ltd and others [1996] ECLI:EU:C:1996:79

Caisse Régionale de Crédit Agricole Mutuel Alpes Provence and others v. European Central Bank [2018] ECLI:EU:T:2018:219

Crédit Mutuel Arkéa v. European Central Bank [2017] ECLI:EU:T:2017:902

Criminal proceedings against Massimo Romanelli and Paolo Romanelli [1999] ECLI:EU:C:1999:71

Dineke Algera, Giacomo Cicconardi, Simone Couturaud, Ignazio Genuardi, Félicie Steichen v. Common Assembly of the European Coal and Steel Community [1957] ECLI:EU:C:1957:7

European Central Bank v. Sven A. Von Storch [2016] ECLI:EU:C:2016:846

European Central Bank v. Trasta Komercbanka and others [2019] ECLI:EU:C:2019:923

Federal Republic of Germany v. Council of the European Union (Product Safety) [1994] ECLI:EU:C:1994:306

Federal Republic of Germany v. European Parliament and Council of the European Union (Tobacco Advertising) [2000] ECLI:EU:C:2000:544

Federal Republic of Germany v. European Parliament and Council of the European Union [1997] ECLI:EU:C:1997:231

Foto-Frost v. Hauptzollamt Lübeck-Ost [1987] ECLI:EU:C:1987:45

Heinrich Weiss and others v. Deutscher Bundestag [2018] ECLI:EU:C:2018:1000
Iccrea Banca SpA Istituto Centrale del Credito Cooperativo v. Banca d'Italia [2019] ECLI:EU:C:2019:1036
Krohn & Co. Import-Export GmbH & Co. KG v. Commission of the European Communities [1986] ECLI:EU:C:1986:85
Laboratoires pharmaceutiques Bergaderm SA and Jean-Jacques Goupil v. Commission of the European Communities [2000] ECLI:EU:C:2000:361
Landeskreditbank Baden-Württemberg – Förderbank v. European Central Bank [2019] ECLI:EU:C:2019:372
Landeskreditbank Baden-Württemberg – Förderbank v. European Central Bank [2017] ECLI:EU:T:2017:337
Ledra Advertising Ltd and others v. European Commission and European Central Bank [2016] ECLI:EU:C:2016:701
L'Étoile commerciale and Societé Comptoir National Technique Agricole (CNTA) SA v. Commission of the European Communities [1987] ECLI:EU:C:1987:337
Meroni & Co., Industrie Metallurgiche, società in accomandita semplice v. High Authority of the European Coal and Steel Community [1958] ECLI:EU:C:1958:7
Oleifici Italiani SpA and Fratelli Rubino Industrie Olearie SpA v. Commission of the European Communities [1998] ECLI:EU:T:1998:204
Panagis Pafitis and others v. Trapeza Kentrikis Ellados A.E. and others [1996] ECLI:EU:C:1996:92
Peter Gauweiler and others v. Deutscher Bundestag [2015] ECLI:EU:C:2015:400
Peter Paul, Cornelia Sonnen-Lütte and Christel Mörkens v. Bundesrepublik Deutschland [2004] ECLI:EU:C:2004:606
Philip Morris Brands SARL and others v. Secretary of State for Health [2016] ECLI:EU:C:2016:325
Private Equity Insurance Group SIA v. Swedbank AS [2016] ECLI:EU:C:2016:851
Société civile immobilière Parodi v. Banque H. Albert de Bary et Cie [1997] ECLI:EU:C:1997:345
Steinhoff v. European Central Bank [2019] ECLI:EU:T:2019:353
The Queen v. Minister of Agriculture, Fisheries and Food and Secretary of State for Health, ex parte: Fedesa and others [1990] ECLI:EU:C:1990:391
The Queen, on the application of Vodafone Ltd and others v. Secretary of State for Business, Enterprise and Regulatory Reform [2010] ECLI:EU:C:2010:321
Thomas Pringle v. Government of Ireland, Ireland and the Attorney General [2012] ECLI:EU:C:2012:756
Trasta Komercbanka v. European Central Bank [2017] ECLI:EU:T:2017:623
Unión de Pequeños Agricultores v. Council of the European Union [2002] ECLI:EU:C:2002:462
United Kingdom of Great Britain and Northern Ireland v. Council of the European Union [1996] ECLI:EU:C:1996:431
United Kingdom of Great Britain and Northern Ireland v. European Parliament and Council of the European Union [2014] ECLI:EU:C:2014:18
United Kingdom of Great Britain and Northern Ireland v. European Parliament and Council of the European Union (ENISA) [2006] ECLI:EU:C:2006:279

United Kingdom of Great Britain and Northern Ireland v. European Parliament and Council of the European Union (Smoke Flavourings) [2005] ECLI:EU:C:2005:743

National courts

Italy

HVST (Cass 3 Marzo 2001, n. 3132)
Cassa di Risparmio di Prato (Cass 27 Ottobre 1994, n. 8836)
Banca Popolare di Fabrizia (Cass 22, Luglio 1993, n. 8191)

France

Conseil d'Etat, Assemblée du 30 novembre 2001, 219562, Ministre de l'économie et des finances c/ M. Kechichian et autres (recueil Lebon)
Conseil d'Etat, Assemblée du 29 décembre 1978, 96004 (recueil Lebon)

Germany

Order of 5 May 2020 (Beschlüsse der EZB zum Staatsanleihekaufprogramm) 2 *BVerfGE* 859/15
Order of 30 July 2019 (Europäische Bankenunion) 2 *BVerfGE* 1685/14, 2 *BVerfGE* 2631/14
Order of 21 June 2016 (Gauweiler) 2 *BVerfGE* 2728/13, 2 *BVerfGE* 13/13, 2 *BVerfGE* 2731/13, 2 *BVerfGE* 2730/13, 2 *BVerfGE* 2729/13
Order of 18 March 2014 (Stabilitätsmechanismus und Fiskalpakt) 2 *BVerfGE* 1390/12
Order of 12 September 2012 (Stabilitätsmechanismus und Fiskalpakt) 2 *BVerfGE* 1390/12
Order of 7 September 2011 (Griechenland-Soforthilfe und Euro-Rettungsschirm) 2 *BVerfGE* 987/10
Order of 30 June 2009 (Lissabon) 123 *BVerfGE* 267
Order of 12 October 1993 (Maastricht) 89 *BVerfGE* 155
Order of 22 October 1986 (Solange II) 73 *BVerfGE* 339
Order of 29 May 1974 (Solange I) 37 *BVerfGE* 271
Herstatt (Urteil vom 12.07.1979), BGHZ 75, 120
Wetterstein (Urteil vom 15.02.1979), BGHZ 74, 144

United Kingdom

Three Rivers DC v. Bank of England (No.3) [2003] 2 A.C. 1; [2000] 2 W.L.R. 1220
Three Rivers DC v. Bank of England (No.3) (Summary Judgment) [2001] UKHL 16

Abbreviations and acronyms

AML	anti-money laundering
AMLD4	Fourth Anti-Money Laundering Directive
APP	Asset Purchase Programme
BMF	*Bundesministerium der Finanzen*
BRRD	Bank Recovery and Resolution Directive
CAC	collective action clause
CET1	Common Equity Tier 1
CJEU	Court of Justice of the European Union
CRD IV	Capital Requirements Directive IV
CRR	Capital Requirements Regulation
CSD	central securities depository
CSDR	Central Securities Depositories Regulation
DCs	debt certificates
DGD	Deposit Guarantee Directive
DGS	deposit guarantee scheme
DMO	debt management office
DRI	Direct Recapitalisation Instrument
DSGE	Dynamic Stochastic General Equilibrium
EBA	European Banking Authority
ECAI	external credit assessment institution
ECB	European Central Bank
ECCL	enhanced conditions credit line
ECSD	European Central Securities Depository
EDA	European Debt Agency
EDIS	European Deposit Guarantee Scheme
EFSF	European Financial Stability Facility
EFSM	European Financial Stability Mechanism
EIB	European Investment Bank
ELA	Emergency Liquidity Assistance
EMF	European Monetary Fund
EMU	European Monetary Union
ESBies	European Safe Bonds
ESCB	European System of Central Banks

ESCF	Eurosystem Collateral Framework
ESM	European Stability Mechanism
ESRB	European Systemic Risk Board
ESRB HLTF	European Systemic Risk Board High Level Task Force
EZB	Euro Zone Basket
FSB	Financial Stability Board
GDP	Gross Domestic Product
GGB	Greek Government Bond
IGA	intergovernmental agreement
IMF	International Monetary Fund
IRB	internal ratings-based (approach)
IRI	Indirect Recapitalisation Instrument
JST	Joint Supervisory Team
LCG	Legal Certainty Group
LCR	liquidity coverage ratio
LOLR	lender of last resort
LSI	less significant institution
MoU	memorandum of understanding
MREL	Minimum Requirements and Eligible Liabilities
NCA	national competent authority
NCB	national central bank
NFC	non-financial corporation
NPL	non-performing loan
NRA	national resolution authority
NSFR	net stable funding ratio
OMT	outright monetary transaction
PCCL	precautionary conditions credit line
PEPP	Pandemic Emergency Purchase Programme
PIA	public interest assessment
PSI	Private Sector Involvement
PSPP	Public Sector Purchase Programme
RWA	risk-weighted asset
SA	standardised approach
SBBS	sovereign bond-backed security
SBS	sovereign-backed security
SGP	Stability and Growth Pact
SI	significant institution
SRB	Single Resolution Board
SRF	Single Resolution Fund
SRM	Single Resolution Mechanism
SRMR	Single Resolution Mechanism Regulation
SSM	Single Supervisory Mechanism
SSMR	Single Supervisory Mechanism Regulation
TEC	Treaty establishing the European Community
TEU	Treaty on European Union

TFEU	Treaty on the Functioning of the European Union
TLAC	Total Loss Absorption Capacity
UK	United Kingdom
US	United States
VAT	value added tax
VLTRO	very long term refinancing operation

Preface

Thomas Jefferson, one of the Founding Fathers of the United States Constitution and Third President of the United States, famously stated in a private letter to John Taylor Monticello that 'banking establishments are more dangerous than standing armies.'[1]

Although it has confirmed Jefferson's foreboding, the euro-area sovereign debt crisis of 2010–2015 has also served as a stark reminder of the *two way* nature of the interdependency between sovereigns and their domestic commercial banks: if banks can be a threat for sovereigns (as Jefferson feared, and as the case of Ireland, between 2008 and 2011 confirms), then sovereigns are no less capable of proving a menace for their banks (as demonstrated by the case of Greece, from 2010 to 2015), with some scope in-between for mixed scenarios, testifying to the bi-directional nature of the feedback loop between sovereigns and their banks.[2] Considering the deterioration, in recent years, in the public finances of many countries around the world, the attendant rise in their indebtedness and the impact of this rise on debt sustainability,[3] the risk

1 Thomas Jefferson, *The Works of Thomas Jefferson*, Vol. 11: Correspondence and Papers 1808–1816 (New York and London, G.P. Putnam's Sons 1905).

2 A case in point is that of the Republic of Cyprus, between 2012 and 2013, where both the sovereign and the domestic banking sector shared equally in the blame for the near sovereign default episode of March 2013. The case of Portugal would also fit into this intermediate category, as the Portuguese financial crisis was attributable, on the one hand, to an expansionary budgetary policy, which increased the need for government funding, and, on the other hand, to the drying-up of the regular (interbank) liquidity sources that Portuguese banks could draw on, pushing them towards more expensive (and, ultimately, unaffordable) funding options (see Anabela Sérgio and António Rebelo de Sousa, 'The Impact of the Financial Crisis on Portuguese Banks: The Problem of Portuguese Sovereign Debt' in Anabela Sérgio (ed.), *Banking in Portugal* (Palgrave MacMillan 2016)).

3 According to May 2020 projections of the Organisation for Economic Co-operation and Development, wealthy countries around the world (many of them, euro area Member States) were expected to take on upwards of $17 trillion in extra public indebtedness to fund the stimulus measures necessary to counter the fallout of the COVID-19 pandemic. Public finances were set to suffer further on account of the sharp drop in tax revenues resulting from the slowdown of economic activity between March and June 2020 (Organisation for Economic Co-operation and Development, *Sovereign Borrowing Outlook for OECD Countries 2020* (Special COVID-19 Edition) <https://www.oecd.org/daf/fin/public-debt/oecdsovereignborrowingoutlook.htm> accessed 30 September 2020).

that sovereigns represent for their banks (especially those that hold sovereign debt in their portfolios) is likely to only increase with time. Even if the current interest rate environment is supportive, the urgency of addressing contagion risks effectively, in order to avert future crises, remains.

The creation of the European Banking Union, and the euro area's radical transition from a national-only model of micro-prudential banking supervision and resolution to an elaborate, pan-European set-up – equipped with a powerful single banking sector supervisor and with a centralised bank resolution mechanism – bear testimony to the great lengths to which the European Union and, in particular, the euro area have gone so as to break the channel of contagion moving from commercial banks to sovereigns. However, progress with closing the reverse channel of contagion – the one moving from ailing sovereigns to commercial banks – has been sparse, with no clear prospect of effective preventive action in the foreseeable future, and with most hopes seemingly placed primarily on fiscal discipline, complemented by central bank interventions when the risk of fragmentation, apt to impair the monetary policy transmission mechanism, materialises. Even if it is not the lack of technical astuteness that has allowed the doom-loop to fester, the authors see merit in approaching the issues it raises from a technical perspective, exploring the root causes of the doom-loop problem and examining technically sound ways of mitigating and, eventually, resolving it, preferably without the need for (fundamental) changes to the Treaties.

The aim of this work[4] is twofold. It is, first, to examine the measures that Europe and, notably, the euro area have taken in recent years in order to mitigate the exposure of sovereigns to commercial bank-generated financial crises, drawing attention to areas where legal, institutional and other improvements to the arsenal of tools hitherto introduced are either desirable or necessary to stem future banking sector crises. A second and, in some respects, more central aim of this work is, on the one hand, to explain, mostly through recourse to economic theory, why the channel of contagion moving from sovereigns to commercial banks has proven harder to close, and, on the other hand, to explore ways – additional to the domestic adoption of fiscal adjustment measures – through which progress could be made in the direction of closing the second channel of contagion, so as to forestall a future crisis of the type that affected the banks of some of the less fiscally sound euro-area Member States between 2010 and 2015. Although it is prompted by the euro-area sovereign debt crisis, and despite the fact that it is more specifically geared towards addressing the specificities of the feedback loop between sovereigns and commercial banks in the particular legal and economic context of the euro area, the analytical

4 The authors' work draws on an earlier, more limited scope study by the first author (Phoebus Athanassiou, *Κρίση Δημοσίου Χρέους και Τραπεζικό Σύστημα στη Ζώνη του Ευρώ* [*The Sovereign Debt Crisis and the Euro Area Banking System*] (Athens, Nomiki Bibliothiki 2018)).

component of this work will also apply, mutatis mutandis, outside the euro area, whether to other currency unions or to purely domestic situations.

What emerges from the analytical component of this work is that the reason why only limited progress has so far been made in the euro area towards closing the second channel of contagion is because of the considerably greater degree of complexity involved in addressing it, compared to the channel of contagion moving from banks to sovereigns. What the authors of this work argue is that, although helpful, fiscal discipline and the promotion of greater diversification in the portfolios of sovereign bonds held by euro-area commercial banks (for instance, through changes in the regulatory treatment of sovereign bonds) are unlikely to prove sufficient to break the second channel of contagion, unless complemented by other policy options. Therefore, the authors see a need to consider anew certain policy options explored in the wake of the euro-area sovereign debt crisis but not yet acted upon (certainly not in the form proposed in the present work). These options include the issuance by the European Union Member States of some form of common, euro-area safe asset or Eurobonds, which would be more liquid and, by necessary implication, more credible compared to the debt of individual sovereign issuers, as well as the creation of a euro-area-wide stability support mechanism, to ensure that there is a potent structure in place to stand by troubled sovereigns, both *ex ante* and *ex post*. Regarding the first of these policy options, the authors of this work consider the creation of good collateral to be the main justification for the issuance of a common, euro-area safe asset or Eurobond, and expect such issuance to have a decisive contribution to make towards closing the second channel of contagion.[5] The authors also explore the parameters of a European debt issuance mechanism for the joint issuance of debt, contributing to the debate through a concrete proposal on how to address the operational challenges posed by the eventual issuance of a safe asset, presented, by some, as an inhibiting factor for the pursuit of this particular policy option. Regarding the second policy option, the authors of this work consider its implementation advisable, also as a means of equipping the European Union with a lender of last resort, the creation of which would remove the need for the European Central Bank to regularly intervene in the market through asset purchase programmes.

There is a tendency in the hitherto public but also academic debate to consider the various policy options in isolation from one another, without regard for their complementarities. The authors' analysis in this work suggests that many of these options are mutually reinforcing, and that, unless their complementarities are understood, their isolated implementation would risk yielding poorer results compared to their combined activation. For instance,

5 As explained in this work, commentators have tended to treat the creation of good collateral resulting from the issuance of a common safe asset as a positive side-effect thereof, rather than as its main policy justification. It is the latter that the authors of this work consider as being the main utility of the issuance of a common safe asset.

the authors consider that the much-vaunted review of the regulatory treatment of sovereign debt (which, incidentally, could pave the way for the eventual creation of a pan-European Deposit Guarantee Scheme, to help alleviate the fiscal fallout of eventual bank defaults) presupposes the existence of a safe asset (or, alternatively, a Eurobond). This is because, without it, banks may well be prompted to improve on their portfolio diversification but only at the price of greater risks for their balance sheet (in the case of banks in fiscally healthier jurisdictions, forced to hold debt issued by fiscally weaker sovereigns) or at the risk of creating contagion channels across countries (because of common exposures). To the authors' eyes, the main added value of a safe asset is that it would simultaneously facilitate the transition to a new regulatory regime on the treatment of sovereign debt while at the same time helping to address the trade-off between portfolio diversification and risk-taking.[6] In addition, a common safe asset would call for a revision in the regulatory treatment of sovereign debt, and for an induced rebalancing of banks' sovereign debt portfolios, in order to effectively avert destabilising capital flights within the monetary union. Last but not least, the authors argue that the revision in the regulatory treatment of sovereign debt and the issuance of a safe asset would complement micro-prudential supervision, thereby reinforcing its effectiveness.

In formulating their proposals, the authors of this work have sought to stand critically against some of the perceived shortcomings of policy options advocated and debated over the last several years. For instance, whilst agreeing that moral hazard concerns are legitimate and need to be addressed, the authors could not help but notice that such concerns have, at times, also been raised against proposals that feature embedded mechanisms to counter them, as in the case of some of the safe asset and Eurobond proposals. To the extent that it may be possible to further refine these proposals so as to help address legitimate moral hazard-driven concerns, it makes sense to do precisely that, rather than to reject them outright, for the wrong reasons. The moral hazard and public risk sharing-related concerns raised by the prospect of a Eurobonds' issuance do not, in the authors' view, amount to insurmountable obstacles to achieving progress on this front, as effective mechanisms exist to address those concerns.

The authors deem the grave human and economic cost of the COVID-19 pandemic, and the lessons drawn from it, to greatly reinforce the case for action along the lines proposed in this work, not only in order to help overcome the consequences of endogenous shocks, attributable to fiscal profligacy or excessive risk-taking by the euro-area banking sector but, also, as instruments through which to manage crises triggered by exogenous factors, such as the outbreak of a pandemic, which, even if building on latent weaknesses at the level of individual sovereigns or banking institutions, cannot be attributed to their culpability. At the same time, and however welcome, the temporary

6 Although this trade-off features prominently in most proposals for changing the treatment of sovereign debt, none of them consider the contribution that a safe asset could make to alleviate it.

and targeted 'European Recovery Fund' finally agreed upon by the European Council at around the time of the finalisation of the manuscript, would differ from the policy options discussed later in this book (see the author's discussion of safe assets and Eurobonds), meaning that its eventual establishment would not detract from the need for decision-makers to explore the policy options of safe assets and Eurobonds.[7] It is recalled that, on 21 July 2020, the European Council empowered the European Commission to borrow funds on the capital markets on behalf of the European Union up to the amount of €750 billion, for the sole purpose of addressing the consequences of the COVID-19 crisis. Of the abovementioned amount, up to €360 billion would represent loans, whilst an amount of up to €390 billion would represent grants.[8] Significantly, the common debt to be issued for the purposes of the European Recovery Fund would differ in several fundamental respects from earlier safe asset proposals, including in terms of the *purpose of its issuance* (which would not be to break the sovereign–banks feedback loop by substituting sovereign bonds with a European safe asset but, rather, to fund the costs of combatting the COVID-19 pandemic), its *duration* (which would be limited), the *scope of its beneficiaries* (which would include all EU Member States, not just the euro area 19), and the *degree of its mutualisation* (which would only be indirect, as its issuance on the capital markets by the EU Commission would be guaranteed by the EU budget rather than, directly, by the EU Member States). Be that as it may, it remains the case that 'the (legal) framework underpinning *Coronabonds* could become the basis for a genuine Eurobond,'[9] which is why Europe's

7 Under a competing proposal for a 'European Union Recover Instrument' presented by the European Commission on 27 May 2020, on the basis of Article 122 of the Treaty on the Functioning of the European Union, the European Recovery Fund (referred to as 'Next Generation EU'), would amount to €750 billion, as a top-up to a revamped Multiannual Financial Framework (i.e. the European Union budget), consisting of €500 billion in grants and €250 billion in loans to Member States, funded by debt issued by the European Commission on the capital markets under guarantees of the Member States. Under an earlier European Recovery Fund proposal presented by German Chancellor Angela Merkel and French President Emmanuel Macron on 18 May 2020, the European Commission would borrow €500 billion on the capital markets and distribute it, as grants (as opposed to loans), to the beneficiary Member States to fund short-term budgetary expenditure associated with addressing the impact of the COVID-19 pandemic. The resulting indebtedness would increment the European Union budget by the amount of the borrowing to which the Member States contribute in accordance with the size of their economies and prosperity. The borrowings would be repaid gradually, through several future European budgets, in the course of a seven-year budget cycle (Bundesregierung, *A French-German Initiative for the European Recovery from the Coronavirus Crisis* (Press Release 173/20, 18 May 2020) <https://www.bundesregierung.de/resource/blob/973812/1753772/414a4b5a1ca91d4f7146eeb2b39ee72b/2020-05-18-deutsch-franzoesischer-erklaerung-eng-data.pdf?download=1> accessed 30 September 2020).

8 European Council, Special Meeting of the European Council (17, 18, 19, 20 and 21 July 2020), 'Conclusions' EUCO 10/20.

9 Sebastian Grund, 'The Quest for a European Safe Asset – A comparative Legal Analysis of Sovereign Bond-Backed Securities, E-bonds, Purple Bonds, and Coronabonds' (2020) 6 *Journal of Financial Regulation* 223, 244.

COVID-19 pandemic could serve as an unexpected catalyst for developments in directions that the authors of this work consider worth exploring in order to break the second channel of contagion.

The observations made and the views expressed in this work are those of its authors, and they should not be attributed to the European Central Bank (to which the authors were affiliated at the time of writing) nor to the Eurosystem. The authors are grateful to Jochen Andritzky, International Monetary Fund Economist and former Secretary General of the German Council of Economic Experts; Alicia Hinarejos, Reader in European Union Law and Director of the Centre for European Legal Studies (University of Cambridge); Nicolas Véron, Senior Fellow at Bruegel and at the Peterson Institute for International Economics (Washington, DC); Patrick Sandars and Caroline Willeke, Head of Section and Deputy Director General, respectively, at the Directorate General Statistics, European Central Bank (Frankfurt); and, last but not least, to Professor Chiara Zilioli, Member of the Academic Faculty at Johann Wolfgang Goethe Universität (Frankfurt) and Director General of the Legal Services at the European Central Bank (Frankfurt) for their review of, and comments on, earlier drafts of this work. The authors also owe a debt of gratitude to Klaus Masuch, Principal Adviser in the Directorate General Economics of the European Central Bank for discussions related to the content of this work, and to Andra Florian, for her generous editorial support. All remaining errors are those of the authors.

References to the relevant economic and legal doctrine and literature take into account their status up to, and including, 30 September 2020, and the law is stated as it stood at the same cut-off date. However, the authors have made every effort to countenance future developments of which they had public knowledge by the above cut-off date.

Phoebus L. Athanassiou and Angelos T. Vouldis
Frankfurt am Main, 30 September 2020

Introduction

One of the features of the global financial system that both contributed to the outbreak of sovereign debt crises in the aftermath of the collapse of Lehman Brothers, and exacerbated their effects, was the interconnectedness between sovereigns and commercial banks.[1]

The interconnectedness between sovereigns and banks has continued to be strong in the euro area (see Chart 0.1), even after the sovereign debt crisis of 2010–2015. The reasons for this include the prudential regulation-driven sovereign debt bias of euro-area banks in the composition of their investment portfolios (and the attendant lack of diversification in their sovereign debt exposures);[2] the practical, balance sheet-related difficulties that euro-area commercial banks would face when disposing of the large stock of government bonds accumulated in their portfolios in the run-up to the euro-area sovereign debt crisis (see Chart 0.2); the politics of bank boards in the euro area, which have encouraged the accumulation by commercial banks of substantial amounts of sovereign debt, including debt issued by troubled sovereigns;[3] and

1 In this regard, see Helge Berger, Giovanni Dell'Ariccia and Maurice Obstfeld, 'Revisiting the Economic Case for Fiscal Union in the Euro Area' (2018) *International Monetary Fund Research Department Departmental Paper* 18/03 <https://www.imf.org/en/Publications/Departmental-Papers-Policy-Papers/Issues/2018/02/20/Revisiting-the-Economic-Case-for-Fiscal-Union-in-the-Euro-Area-45611> accessed 30 September 2020.

2 It has aptly been argued that, '[E]ven if it is likely that this bias has decreased with the introduction of the Euro, which rendered cross-border investment easier and safer, the pattern still persists and, interestingly, has contributed to reinforcing the sovereign domestic bank loop in the Euroarea' (Chiara Angeloni, Silvia Merler and Guntram B. Wolff, 'Policy Lessons from the Eurozone Crisis' (2012) 47 (4) *The International Spectator: The Italian Journal of International Affairs* 17, 26). We explore, later in this work, how a shift in regulatory (and other) incentives could contribute towards a reduction in the stock of (mostly domestic) government bonds that euro area commercial banks hold in their portfolios, and whether this would be sufficient to address the second channel of contagion.

3 In this regard, see Filippo De Marco and Marco Macchiavelli, 'The Political Origin of Home Bias: The Case of Europe, Finance and Economic' (2016) Board of Governors of the Federal Reserve System, Finance and Economic Discussion 2016-060 (De Marco and Macchiavelli (2016)) <https://www.federalreserve.gov/econresdata/feds/2016/files/2016060pap.pdf> accessed 30 September 2020. These authors have shown that government-owned banks or banks with politicians in the board of directors displayed higher home bias in sovereign debt compared to privately-owned banks

Chart 0.1 Holdings of debt securities issued by euro-area General Government reported by monetary financial institutions excluding the European System of Central Banks in the euro area (EUR billions) *Source*: European Central Bank Data Warehouse

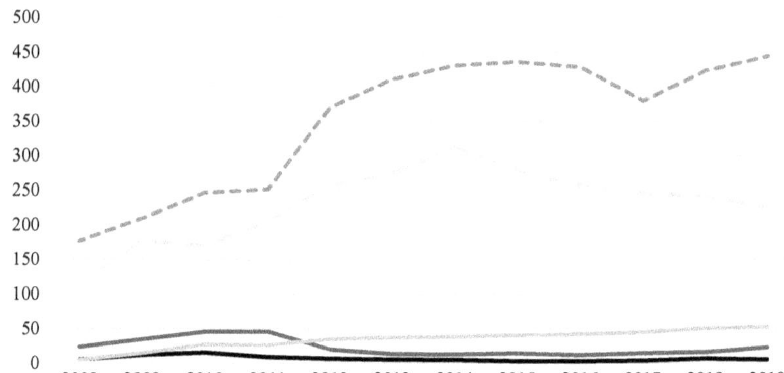

	2008	2009	2010	2011	2012	2013	2014	2015	2016	2017	2018	2019
Cyprus	5.5	12.1	15.6	9	6.4	5.3	4.6	3	2.7	3.5	6.2	5.4
Greece	24.2	35	46.1	46	19.6	13	12.6	14.1	11.9	14.4	16	22.6
Italy	177.1	209.7	246.8	251.6	370.1	410.9	430.5	436	428.2	379.4	422.9	444
Portugal	5.4	15.1	27	26	34.9	37.4	38.2	40.6	41.8	45	50.3	52.6
Spain	116.9	177.9	170.1	205.1	256.8	274.1	312.1	278.8	256.7	246.4	241.8	223.9

Chart 0.2 Holdings of debt securities issued by euro-area General Government reported by monetary financial institutions excluding the European System of Central Banks in selected countries (EUR billions) *Source*: European Central Bank Data Warehouse

the incentives that the low interest rates environment may create for commercial banks in the euro area to invest in sovereign debt, for risk management and profit-seeking considerations alike. These (and other) reasons, and their precise parameters, are explained in greater detail in Chapter 1 of this work.

An *increase* in the euro-area commercial banks' holdings of sovereign debt in the short to medium term appeared, at the time of writing, probable, not least because of the increasing pressure on public finances across the euro area in response to the likely impact of the COVID-19 pandemic).[4] As a result, and although the current low interest environment supports the sustainability of sovereign debt, the materialization, in the short to medium term, of tail risks due to the nexus between sovereigns and commercial banks in the euro area, cannot be excluded.

Through its concerted efforts, reflected in an impressive programme of legislative reforms adopted within a record short period of time, the euro area has made considerable progress towards addressing the channel of contagion moving from troubled commercial banks to sovereigns (referred to, in this work, as the 'first channel of contagion'). The far-reaching institutional reforms introduced since the outbreak of the euro-area sovereign debt crisis to address the first channel of contagion have included, first, the creation of a (partially) centralised system of micro-prudential banking supervision, in the form of the Single Supervisory Mechanism ('SSM'), with the policy aim of overcoming the pre-crisis supervisory home bias and regulatory capture phenomena deemed co-responsible for its outbreak; second, the introduction of a harmonised bank recovery and resolution framework, in the form of Directive 2014/59/EU[5] ('the Bank Recovery and Resolution Directive' or 'BRRD'), which implements the Financial Stability Board's ('FSB') *Key Attributes of Effective Resolution*

throughout 2010–2013, and that only government-owned banks increased the home bias during the sovereign crisis (pointing to moral suasion).

4 In a report released in April 2020, the International Monetary Fund forecasted a massive increase in borrowing by governments on account of COVID-19 pandemic. Concretely, the International Monetary Fund predicted a global net public debt increase from 69.4% of GDP in 2019 to 85.3% in 2020 (see Gita Gopinath, 'The Great Lockdown: Worst Economic Downturn Since the Great Depression' (*International Monetary Fund Blog*, 14 April 2020) <https://blogs.imf.org/2020/04/14/the-great-lockdown-worst-economic-downturn-since-the-great-depression/> accessed 30 September 2020).

5 Directive 2014/59/EU of the European Parliament and of the Council of 15 May 2014 establishing a framework for the recovery and resolution of credit institutions and investment firms and amending Council Directive 82/891/EEC, and Directives 2001/24/EC, 2002/47/EC, 2004/25/EC, 2005/56/EC, 2007/36/EC, 2011/35/EU, 2012/30/EU and 2013/36/EU, and Regulations (EU) 1093/2010 and (EU) 648/2012, of the European Parliament and of the Council [2014] OJ L173/190.

Regimes for Financial Institutions,[6] including the 'bail-in' tool, to ensure that the losses and recapitalisation costs associated with bank resolution are not borne only by tax payers but, also, by banks' shareholders; third, the establishment of a centralised resolution mechanism, in the form of the Single Resolution Board ('SRB'); and fourth, the proposed (but still elusive) creation of a pan-European Deposit Guarantee Scheme ('EDIS'), to help alleviate the fallout of an eventual bank default, if neither enhanced banking supervision nor harmonised bank recovery and resolution should suffice to avert a banking crisis. The adoption and activation of these measures, subsumed under the label of a 'European Banking Union', represent, jointly, core policy achievements on the path to European (and, more notably, euro-area) integration, arguably the most important and far-reaching since the launch, in 1999, of the Economic and Monetary Union ('EMU'), to which they are complementary. The combined effect of centralised supervision and centralised resolution (featuring a bail-in tool) is to transfer a large share of banks' risks (including their resolution costs) from the shoulders of taxpayers to those of investors and, ultimately, depositors,[7] thereby weakening the sovereign–banks nexus.

At the same time, Europe's progress with closing the channel of contagion moving from ailing sovereigns to healthy commercial banks (hereafter, the 'second channel of contagion') has been very limited, and precious little had been done, at the time of writing, at an institutional level, to address the risks inherent in its possible re-activation. The conclusion to which Europe's inaction could lead the casual observer is that there are no obvious top-down solutions to complement the national fiscal austerity programmes pursued in the countries of the euro-area periphery (those worst hit by the crisis), and that fiscal crises apt to prejudice domestic banks can only be avoided through budgetary discipline measures. As explained in this work, the limited progress achieved in closing the second avenue of contagion may not so much be attributable to complacency as it is to objective considerations, which make the task harder compared to the task of closing the first channel of contagion. However, as also explained in this work, in order to close the second channel of contagion, a number of non-fiscal discipline-driven options should also be explored. Although these have been considered in the extant literature, but also by policymakers, no decision had yet been taken, at the time of writing, to actually pursue them through concerted, European-level action, similar in rigour to the action taken with a view to closing the first channel of contagion. And yet, unless the second channel of contagion can be closed, there is every

6 Financial Stability Board, *Key Attributes of Effective Resolution Regimes for Financial Institutions* (FSB (2011)) <https://www.fsb.org/wp-content/uploads/r_141015.pdf> accessed 30 September 2020.

7 On the issue of the treatment of bank deposits as (bail-inable) investments (see Phoebus Athanassiou, 'On the Legal and Economic Treatment of Bank Deposits as Investments: Some Reflections' (2014) 29 (12) *Journal of International Banking Law and Regulation* 715.

probability of future episodes of financial instability in the euro area and, in particular, of the recurrence of a 'Greek scenario,' which can summarily be described as that of a reasonably well-managed and supervised domestic banking sector, brought down by a profligate public sector, operating subject to the vagaries of the political process and the changing fortunes of the electoral cycle.

Three observations are apposite. The first observation is that although the literature recognises the existence of a two-way, mutually reinforcing link between sovereigns and their commercial banks, each of the two channels of contagion (or interdependence) will, for analytical purposes, be explored separately in this work, starting with the channel of contagion that moves from banks to sovereigns. It has been argued, not implausibly, that it is artificial to examine the two channels of contagion in isolation from one another.[8] And yet, the authors of this work consider that unless an attempt is made to segregate the two channels of contagion, and to explore their particularities, there is a risk of erroneously assuming that efforts to address any one of them will necessarily contribute towards addressing both, because of their interconnectedness: this may in some respects be true, but it need not be so across the board.

The second observation is that because the issues at stake present both a legal/institutional and an economic interest, it is from both of these perspectives that they need to be assessed if the multi-faceted challenge of addressing the feedback loop between sovereigns and banks is to be genuinely understood and tackled. Accordingly, the authors of this work pursue a twofold objective. On the one hand, they seek to present and explain the economic arguments accounting for the hitherto imbalance in Europe's efforts to address both channels of contagion, evaluate the efficiency of measures so far taken in order to close the first channel of contagion and explore the merits of different policy responses to the challenges thrown up by the relationship of interdependency that connects banks to their sovereigns. On the other hand, they seek to bring to the fore the legal and broader institutional dimensions of the debate, assessing, from both a legal and an institutional perspective, the feasibility of some of the technical proposals put forward to counteract the feedback loop between sovereigns and commercial banks, and testing alternative solutions for their legal viability and practicability.

The third observation is that this work assumes the continuing existence, going forward, of a banking system such as we know it in 2020, with banks continuing to perform their central functions in the transmission of monetary

8 It has, for instance, been argued that 'most papers exclusively focus on one channel of transmission, either quantifying the effects that banking crises have on public finances or analysing when banking crises may cause sovereign debt crisis or vice versa' (Clara Galliani and Stefano Zedda, 'Will the Bail-in Break the Vicious Circle Between Banks and Their Sovereign?' (2015) 45 (4) *Computational Economics* 597, 597)).

policy and financial intermediation, their key role as guardians of deposits and their preponderant role in the transmission of funds for payment purposes. Some of the observations and remarks made in this work and many of its conclusions would need to be revisited in a scenario where the size, role and function of banks would diminish or fundamentally change on account of policy decisions aimed at re-calibrating the financial system, changing the prevailing concepts of 'currency' and 'money,' and revolutionising the ways in which money is held and transferred to discharge debts. Whether and how soon such changes are likely to materialise can only be the object of speculation at the present juncture. That said, discussions were underway, and reflections were ongoing, at the time of writing, around the future of money, banks and the financial system at large, which the reader may want to take cognisance of and, also, keep in mind while perusing this work.[9] This is not because shifts are bound to occur but, rather, because should they eventually occur, these would inevitably have an impact on the assumptions underlying this work and on the real-world relevance of the issues treated in its pages.

This work is organised into five chapters. Chapter 1 examines the reasons why banks choose to hold domestic sovereign debt and provides an account of the triggers and transmission mechanisms of the sovereign–banks nexus. Chapter 2 explores, on the one hand, the effects of commercial bank crises on sovereigns, illustrating the risks of contagion by reference to the near-collapse of the Irish and Cypriot[10] banking sectors during the sovereign debt stage of the financial crisis and, on the other hand, the effects of sovereign debt crises on their domestic banking sectors, drawing on the example of the near-collapse of the Greek banking sector, early into the sovereign debt stage of the financial crisis, as well as on the dramatic events in Cyprus, in March 2013. Chapter 3 explores the extent to which the European Banking Union constitutes an optimal policy response from the perspective of breaking the vicious circle connecting banks to their sovereigns; it enquires into the role of enhanced fiscal surveillance as a means of closing the second channel of contagion, in particular, it examines the challenges posed by a possible revision of the regulatory treatment of commercial banks' sovereign debt holdings; and it explains how safe assets and Eurobonds could contribute to breaking the sovereign–banks loop. Chapter 4 examines in detail the concrete measures so far taken in the European Union ('the Union' or 'EU') and the euro area with a view to addressing the first channel of contagion, focusing on their legal and

9 See, *ex multi*, Bank of Canada, European Central Bank, Bank of Japan, Sveriges Riksbank, Swiss National Bank, Bank of England, Board of Governors Federal Reserve System, Bank for International Settlements, *Central Bank Digital Currencies: Foundational Principles and Core Features* (2020) <https://www.bis.org/publ/othp33.pdf> accessed 20 November 2020.

10 As used in the remainder of this book, the terms 'Cyprus' and 'Cypriot' shall refer to the Republic of Cyprus (16 August 1960).

institutional shortcomings, and on the extent to which those have an impact on the ability of the European Banking Union to deliver on its objectives. Finally, Chapter 5 explores the options, both *ex ante* and *ex post*, through which to close the second channel of contagion, their legal shortcomings, and the likelihood of their implementation in the short to medium term.

1 The sovereign–banks nexus

An economic analysis

1.1 Introductory remarks

This chapter explores the sovereign–banks nexus from the perspective of economic theory and with the benefit of relevant empirical evidence. Its first analytical section seeks to explain why commercial banks choose to hold national domestic debt. The aim of its second analytical section is to analyse the feedback loop between sovereigns and their banks, triggered by the direct holding, by the latter, of sovereign debt but, also, by a number of other complementary transmission mechanisms. The analytical component of this chapter is preceded by an introductory section, which traces the history of the funding of sovereigns by banks, with a view to adding some historical context to our discussion of the current state of affairs. The focus of this chapter is on elements that are of particular relevance for countries participating in a monetary union, such as the EMU.

1.2 Brief historical overview

The direct funding of sovereigns by banks was already widespread in the Italian city-states of the 12th century, often in the form of compulsory lending repayable by tax revenues.[1] The public debt holdings of the members of the governing élites of the Italian city-states has been considered as a credibility mechanism against default,[2] as it reinforced the incentives of governing officials to follow a sound public policy. Later, the public banks that appeared in 15th-century Europe, especially in commercial centres, were often subject to 'fiscal exploitation' by their respective cities or republics, more often than not in order to finance wars or military adventures.[3] Indeed, it was in order to facilitate the

1 Michele Fratianni and Franco Spinelli, 'Italian City-States and Financial Evolution' (2006) 10 *European Review of Economic History* 257.

2 Reinhold C. Mueller, *The Venetian Money Market Banks, Panics and the Public Debt, 1200–1500* (Baltimore, Maryland, The John Hopkins University Press 1997), Ch. 12.

3 William Roberds and François Velde, 'Early Public Banks' (2014) *Federal Reserve Bank of Chicago Working Paper* 2014-03 <https://ideas.repec.org/p/fip/fedawp/2014-09.html> accessed 30 September 2020.

government lending necessary to finance the war effort against France (1689–1697) that the Bank of England was established in 1694. According to the seminal analysis of North and Weingast,[4] the aim of the constraints placed by the new institutional set-up on the Crown's ability to borrow from the Bank of England (only possible with the explicit consent of Parliament) was to underpin the credibility of public finances and to mark a break with the past, when 'forced loans' were the norm. The new set-up resulted in lower capital costs for entrepreneurs, thereby supporting the incipient Industrial Revolution.[5]

Recurring cycles of sovereign debt increases were observed during the 20th century, especially during the two World Wars. These were followed by a clear downward trend during the 1950s and the 1960s and by a gradual increase after the 1970s. The aftermath of the global financial crisis of 2007–2009 has seen a further increase. In addition, there is evidence, in advanced economies, of heightened sovereign debt holdings by domestic commercial banks during crisis periods, such as the two World Wars and the economic crises of the 1970s.[6]

What this very brief historical overview shows is that the link between banks and state finances is hardly a novelty and that a pattern of banks holding increased amounts of sovereign debt, especially at times of crisis, is discernible throughout history, although the reasons for it may well differ from one case to another.

1.3 Why do banks hold domestic sovereign debt?

1.3.1 Discrimination and selective defaults

In trying to explain why banks may choose to hold domestic sovereign debt, a line of research has focused on the desire of banks to earn a price subsidy on them, as their holding may entail lower credit risks compared to those that foreign investors face as holders of the same domestic sovereign debt. The assumption is that, in the event of default, the sovereign issuer will discriminate against the foreign holders of its debt by choosing to pay domestic holders instead. In other words, it is assumed that sovereigns will prefer to selectively default on the foreign holders of sovereign debt in order not to

4 Douglass C. North and Barry R. Weingast, 'Constitutions and Commitment: The Evolution of Institutions Governing Public Choice in Seventeenth-Century England' (1989) 49 *Journal of Economic History* 803.

5 There are criticisms of this view, see, for example, Nathan Sussman and Yishay Yafeh, 'Institutional Reforms, Financial Development and Sovereign Debt: Britain 1690–1790' (2006) 66 (5) *Journal of Economic History* 906.

6 S.M. Ali Abbas, Laura Blattner, Mark De Broeck, Asmaa El-Ganainy and Malin Hu, 'Sovereign Debt Composition in Advanced Economies: A Historical Perspective' (2014) *International Monetary Fund Working Paper* WP/14/162 <https://www.imf.org/en/Publications/WP/Issues/2016/12/31/Sovereign-Debt-Composition-in-Advanced-Economies-A-Historical-Perspective-41899> accessed 30 September 2020.

harm domestic investors. This subsidisation of domestic holders is thought to provide an incentive for them to hold domestic sovereign debt since it mitigates their effective credit risk.

Broner, Didier, Erce and Schmukler[7] argue that the pattern of capital flows and, specifically, the retrenchment observed during crises (i.e. the collapse of gross capital flows) is consistent with the above idea of a differential credit risk between foreign and domestic investors in domestic sovereign debt. This pattern is also supported by previous research[8] according to which, during periods of heightened sovereign default risk, foreign investors will seek to sell their sovereign debt assets to domestic investors, who have an incentive to buy them in the expectation that their issuer will prioritise their repayment. In this line of research, the possibility of discrimination among foreign and domestic creditors is an exogenous assumption, which is posited to explain other patterns in the data, especially with regard to capital flows.

Erce and Mallucci[9] empirically examine *selective* sovereign defaults (defined as defaults with an element of discrimination between domestic and foreign investors in sovereign debt). A challenge in such empirical analyses is to distinguish in the dataset between domestic and foreign investors, as their residence is not, normally, determined. Erce and Mallucci choose to define investors based on the legal regime governing instruments in default, while Reinhart and Rogoff[10] choose to classify domestic and external defaults based on the currency of denomination of the instruments in default. Both approaches are expected to lead to relevant proxies for the origin of investors. In the assembled dataset, it is found that only 28 out of the 182 default episodes were *joint* defaults (defined as defaults where the sovereign defaulted without discriminating across instruments or their investors). What one could conclude from this empirical study is that selective defaults are, in practice, common. The same study also finds that the impact of a default on the domestic economy is felt via two different channels, depending on the type of selective default. If a country defaults on its 'domestic' bonds (as defined above) then a contraction in domestic credit represents the most active channel ('credit channel'), whilst where default is on its 'foreign' bonds then it is the loss of access to foreign intermediaries that has the strongest adverse effect on the domestic economy ('trade channel').

7 Fernando Broner, Tatiana Didier, Aitor Erce and Sergio Schmukler, 'Gross Capital Flows: Dynamics and Crises' (2013) 60 *Journal of Monetary Economics* 113.

8 Fernando Broner, Alberto Martin and Jaume Ventura, 'Sovereign Risk and Secondary Markets' (2010) 100 *American Economic Review* 1523.

9 Aitor Erce and Enrico Mallucci, 'Selective Sovereign Defaults' (2018) *Board of Governors of the Federal Reserve System, International Finance Discussion Paper* 1239 <https://www.federalreserve.gov/econres/ifdp/files/ifdp1239.pdf> accessed 30 September 2020.

10 Carmen M. Reinhart and Kenneth S. Rogoff, 'The Forgotten History of Domestic Debt' (2008) *National Bureau of Economic Research Working Paper 13946* <https://www.nber.org/papers/w13946> accessed 30 September 2020.

It is possible to question the relevance of selective default to advanced economies and, *a fortiori*, to the economies of EU countries. In the Erce and Mallucci dataset, the sample of countries in default includes only two advanced economies, with all remaining economies in the sample comprising emerging and developing countries. Specifically, the Greek default of 2011 is classified as a joint default, while the Cypriot default of 2013 is classified as a domestic default. In addition to the low representation of advanced countries in the sample, the case of Cyprus involves a *sui generis* case of 'discrimination' against domestic investors that runs against the grain of the literature surveyed above. The (temporary) default of Cyprus was due to a 'distressed exchange' of domestic sovereign bonds, used as a public debt liquidity management tool. Therefore, none of the two advanced economies in the sample of the Erce and Mallucci dataset actually discriminated against foreign investors.

In general, there are significant caveats in the classification of defaults as having actually affected domestic or foreign investors, given that sovereign bonds are actively traded in the secondary markets, and the identity of their holders, at the time of default, cannot readily be determined. In addition, in the context of the EU, foreign investors would (also) include those hailing from other countries of the Union: a selective default scenario against other EU Member States would not seem to be one that market participants could discount when making their portfolio choices (hence, not a persuasive explanation for the home bias of banks' sovereign debt holdings). Overall, even if discrimination among different classes of investors (or, more accurately, instruments) may be an empirical fact across many sovereign default cases, it does not seem to be the most relevant explanation for the decision of commercial banks in the EU to hold domestic sovereign debt.

1.3.2 Pro-cyclicality of sovereign debt

Another line of reasoning that seeks to explain why banks choose to hold domestic sovereign debt stresses the liquidity aspect of domestic sovereign bonds, which allows banks to use them to expand their credit portfolios when there are abundant investment opportunities, i.e. when the economy is growing. A complementary element of this explanation is the pro-cyclical nature of the domestic sovereign debt from the perspective of domestic macroeconomic developments: the credit risk of sovereign bonds is minimal when the demand for positive net present value investments is higher, and vice versa. As a result, the usefulness of domestic sovereign debt to secure liquidity is higher exactly when it is needed the most. This pro-cyclical profile argument is also combined with another element, namely the bank owners' limited liability: if the government defaults, potentially leading to the insolvency of a bank that holds sovereign debt, losses will be shifted to depositors instead of being absorbed by the bank's owners. This set of considerations provides an explanation for the attractiveness of domestic sovereign bonds as an investment option.

In the stylised model of Gennaioli, Martin and Rossi,[11] when the macroeconomy experiences an upswing, banks can use their domestic sovereign bond holdings to obtain liquidity and finance available projects with a rate of return above risk-free investments. In case of a sovereign default, the cost will be borne mainly by depositors. In this stylised representation, banks have an incentive to load their balance sheets with sovereign debt. In this sense, sovereign bonds exhibit pro-cyclical returns, as they represent a source for securing liquidity when investment opportunities abound (their *ex post* return co-moves with their *ex post* marginal utility), while their default risk materialises only when the economy is in decline, and there are no investment opportunities. Another way to formulate the rationale for holding domestic sovereign bonds offered by this study is that domestic sovereign bonds allow banks to implement a 'carry-trade' from the unproductive state of nature (in which their losses are bounded by limited liability) to the productive state of nature (in which their losses are shifted to banks' creditors).

Another variant of this explanation focuses on banks' behaviour during periods of elevated sovereign risk, and posits that due to the risk profile of sovereign debt, banks may have an incentive to increase their domestic sovereign debt holdings at times of elevated country risk. This is usually termed as the 'risk-shifting hypothesis' (or 'gamble for resurrection' if banks are themselves in a dire situation). The pro-cyclical risk profile of domestic sovereign debt incentivises banks to increase their holdings of domestic sovereign debt as follows: if sovereign credit risk were to materialise, banks would in any event become insolvent, whereas if the economy were to recover, banks would reap the extra yields. This behaviour is in contrast with the normal investment behaviour in securities, where it is risk–return considerations that determine the demand for securities: in the case of domestic sovereign debt instruments, demand becomes higher just as risk increases.

There is strong empirical evidence for this type of behaviour during the European sovereign debt crisis. Andreeva and Vlassopoulos[12] examine the determinants of the domestic sovereign debt purchases for a large sample of euro-area banks during the 2008Q1 to 2015Q2 period. What they find is that there is a statistically and economically strong link between the purchased amounts of domestic sovereign bonds and the level of sovereign risk, as well as the co-movement of each bank's market risk and that of the respective sovereign, but only during the 2011Q4 to 2012Q2 period. During this period, the European Central Bank ('ECB') announced and implemented two programmes, the aim

11 Nicola Gennaioli, Alberto Martin and Stefano Rossi, 'Sovereign Default, Domestic Banks and Financial Institutions' (2014) 69 *Journal of Finance* 819, 829–830 (Gennaioli et al. (2014)).

12 Desislava C. Andreeva and Thomas Vlassopoulos, 'Home Bias in Bank Sovereign Bond Purchases and the Bank-Sovereign Nexus' (2016) *European Central Bank Working Paper 1977* (Andreeva and Vlassopoulos (2016)) <https://www.ecb.europa.eu/pub/pdf/scpwps/ecbwp1977.en.pdf> accessed 30 September 2020.

of which was to offer inexpensive liquidity to banks ('the very long term refinancing operations' or 'VLTROs'). Their interpretation of these findings is that the normal negative relationship between sovereign risk and banks' purchases of sovereign bonds is observed when the co-dependence of sovereigns' and banks' risk is low (the same relationship that one would expect to find for foreign investors); however, when the sovereign risk increases, the home-bias behaviour effect kicks-in and banks purchase more sovereign bonds, reinforcing the sovereign–banks nexus. Therefore, it is inferred that due to the ample liquidity offered by the ECB via the VLTROs during a period of elevated sovereign stress and significant intertwining of the banks' and sovereigns' credit risk, banks resorted to domestic sovereign purchases undeterred by the high levels of sovereign risk. On the contrary, the level of sovereign risk and the banks' interdependence with sovereign risk provided stronger incentives to banks to purchase domestic sovereign bonds. The 'risk-shifting' behaviour of domestic credit institutions is not replicated by foreign credit institutions, for which domestic sovereign debt is assessed with the standard risk–return approach. For this class of investors, the dependence structure between sovereign risk and their solvency or the existence of investment opportunities is clearly much weaker compared to domestic banks.

Similar empirical results are provided by Acharya and Steffen,[13] who have used a large sample of European banks spanning the 2007–2013 period. In that study, sovereign holdings are not directly observed but are inferred via a statistical model that links the returns of sovereign debt instruments with the returns of banks' stocks.[14] Given this caveat, the study finds that during the period stretching from March 2010 to June 2012 – which includes the period of the first major ECB liquidity injections – banks in distressed countries[15] increased their domestic sovereign debt exposure, a result that is consistent with the findings of Andreeva and Vlassopoulos. In addition, it is found that less-well capitalised banks tend to purchase more domestic sovereign bonds, with the econometric analysis showing that this result is driven by banks in distressed countries.[16] The econometric analysis also infers that, for banks in distressed countries, the lower their capital the larger their holdings of distressed countries' bonds, a relationship that is consistent with the 'risk-shifting hypothesis.'

13 Viral V. Acharya and Sascha Steffen, 'The "Greatest" Carry Trade ever? Understanding Eurozone Bank Risks' (2015) 15 *Journal of Financial Economics* 215 (Acharya and Steffen (2015)).

14 The model is validated using the detailed European Banking Authority transparency exercise data published for five snapshots during the sample period.

15 Specifically, Greece, Italy, Ireland, Portugal and Spain.

16 In the Andreeva and Vlassopoulos study (2016), it is found that higher levels of sovereign risk may incentivise banks to purchase domestic sovereign bonds, while the Acharya and Steffen (2015) study finds a tendency to increase holdings of sovereign debt when the bank is weakly capitalised. In both cases, the explanation is found in limited liability and the ability of bank owners to shift risk to the bank's creditors.

It should be emphasised that the analysis here does not merely explain banks' incentives to hold highly liquid assets in general but, specifically, explains the home bias observed in banks' sovereign debt holdings. The procyclical dependence between the realisation of sovereign risk and the existence of investment opportunities (or banks' solvency) is the main feature that singles out sovereign debt compared to alternative liquid assets. The existence of limited liability and the ability of banks to shift risk to depositors in the bad states of nature (i.e. during crises) are necessary ingredients in the above incentive mechanism. The end result is that banks do not completely internalise the risk of holding domestic sovereign bonds.[17]

1.3.3 Moral suasion and financial repression

What lies at the heart of this hypothesis is the idea that governments will want to apply pressure on domestic banks to purchase domestic sovereign debt, especially during times of elevated sovereign risk, when there is no sufficient demand from other investors. Naturally, this hypothesis is mostly relevant for countries with either structurally high borrowing costs (e.g. developing countries) or with elevated borrowing costs due to the effects of a financial crisis.[18] An interesting aspect of the financial repression hypothesis is that forcing banks to purchase domestic sovereign debt may enhance the government's credibility towards foreign investors.

In the model of Perez,[19] moral suasion is practised by the government and also acts as a commitment device: forcing banks to load their balance sheets with domestic sovereign debt enables governments to credibly commit that there will be no default on sovereign debt and, consequently, renders feasible their continuing borrowing from the international capital markets. As no selective default is allowed in this analysis, a default on foreign investors will also have a spillover impact on the domestic economy, meaning that the government will face increasing costs depending on how tight the sovereign–banks

17 The explanation, above, is based on the limited liability of banks' shareholders. However, this explanation does not directly bring banks' creditors, including household depositors, into the picture. Specifically, if a bank loads risky domestic sovereign debt then one would expect that, in the face of its elevated riskiness, a deposit run would take place (in other words, one would expect that market discipline would deter banks from excessive risk-taking). Acharya and Steffen (2015) document the withdrawal of around 60% of funding by the United States Money Market Funds from the weakly capitalised European banks during the November 2010–December 2012 period. This is consistent with a withdrawal of funding from banks in distressed countries, which took advantage of ECB liquidity to load their balance sheets with domestic sovereign debt.

18 Another case in which financial repression has been historically observed is during wartime (Carmen M. Reinhart and Kenneth S. Rogoff, *This Time is Different: Eight Centuries of Financial Folly* (Princeton University Press 2009) (Reinhart and Rogoff (2009)).

19 Diego J. Perez, 'Sovereign Debt, Domestic Banks and the Provision of Public Liquidity' (2015) *Stanford Institute for Economic Policy Research Discussion Paper* 15-016 <https://siepr.stanford.edu/sites/default/files/publications/15-016_0.pdf> accessed 30 September 2020.

nexus is. Testable hypotheses originating from the theoretical analysis are then examined, using data on the sovereign debt holdings and corresponding yields for the case of Argentina. Some features of the data can be easily explained using standard credit risk–return arguments, e.g. the positive co-variance of sovereign spreads with the level of public debt. However, this theoretical model is apt to provide an explanation for an additional feature of the data, which, at first sight, may appear counter-intuitive, namely, the negative co-variance of sovereign spreads with the level of *domestically held* public debt. This latter phenomenon is attributable to the commitment effect of domestically held public debt, therefore demonstrating the credibility effect of the government's financial repression.

In a somewhat similar manner, Chari, Dovis and Kehoe[20] show that financial repression may be the optimal policy if a government cannot commit to repay its debt. If a government can credibly commit to repaying its debt, financial repression can never be an optimal policy due to the consequential crowding-out of more profitable investments. The *ex ante crowding-out cost* emphasised in this literature represents the main negative effect imposed on the economy by a financial repression policy: banks are forced to purchase sovereign debt at prices above-market prices while foregoing more favourable investment opportunities, e.g. in the private sector of the economy.

The Acharya and Steffen study referenced above[21] provides further evidence to support the moral suasion hypothesis. Specifically, it is found that banks from distressed countries that were bailed-out by their governments seem to hold, on average, higher amounts of domestic bonds, as is consistent with the moral suasion hypothesis.

More direct evidence of the moral suasion mechanism is provided by De Marco and Macchiavelli,[22] who investigate the relationship between the ownership structure of banks, their holdings of domestic sovereign debt and the need for a bail-out. In this study, the proxy for political influence is the participation of (local or central) government in banks' ownership or the presence of current or former political figures in their boards of directors.[23] The sample is based on the European Banking Authority ('EBA') set of banks that participated in the EU-wide stress tests and recapitalisation exercises between 2010 and 2013, jointly holding more than 60% of the total banking assets in

20 Varadarajan V. Chari, Alessandro Dovis and Patrick Kehoe, 'On the Optimality of Financial Repression' (2018) *Federal Reserve Bank of Minneapolis Research Department Staff Report* 1000 <https://pkehoe.people.stanford.edu/sites/g/files/sbiybj12736/f/financialrepression_0.pdf> accessed 30 September 2020.

21 Acharya and Steffen (2015).

22 De Marco and Macchiavelli (2016).

23 In the case of Italy, it is assumed that the ownership of a bank by a foundation is equivalent to being owned by the government, as these banks were formerly state-owned and the foundations are influenced by political groups. Proxying political influence with the number of politicians in the banks' boards is, admittedly, less than perfect, as additional channels of political influence may exist.

Europe. The econometric analysis concludes that politically influenced banks increased, above average, their holdings of sovereign debt when they received a bail-out from the state, especially in the distressed countries. This result offers persuasive empirical evidence for the existence of a moral suasion channel leading to increased holdings of domestic sovereign debt.

1.3.4 Sovereign debt's preferential regulatory treatment and use as collateral

The use of sovereign debt as collateral in repo transactions and in the interbank market provides yet another reason to explain why banks choose to hold sovereign debt as part of their liquidity management strategy. Although this feature of sovereign debt need not explain why banks favour their bonds issued by their *own* governments, it helps to explain (in conjunction with the regulatory treatment of sovereign bonds and the particulars of the risk framework of different central banks) why banks have an extra incentive to hold more sovereign debt in general, including more *domestic* sovereign debt. In the context of the EU, there are valid grounds on the basis of which to deduce that the overall regulatory and institutional context (both banking regulation and central bank collateral policy) was and remains conducive to the holding, by commercial banks, of substantial amounts of sovereign debt.

It is often the case that sovereign debt enjoys a favourable regulatory treatment, from the perspective of banks' capital requirements and associated capital costs, which is decoupled from the credit risk of the sovereign. In addition, sovereign debt usually enjoys a more favourable treatment compared to private debt with similar characteristics. In the particular case of the EU, the transposition of the Basel accords has translated into a more favourable treatment of the debt issued by EU sovereigns from the perspective of its risk weighting. Specifically, banks under the Basel III accord[24] can calculate the credit risk weights of their assets by either using the standardised approach ('SA'), which is based on rules of thumb linking the characteristics of an instrument with risk weights, or the internal ratings-based ('IRB') approach, which is based on internal models developed by the banks. The current transposition of the Basel accords in Europe allows banks to assign a zero risk-weight to the government bonds of all countries in the EU.[25] This approach represents a widely

24 For the historical evolution of the Basel accords and their transposition within the EU with respect to the treatment of sovereign debt, see European Systemic Risk Board, *Report on the Regulatory Treatment of Sovereign Exposures* (2015) (ESRB (2015)), 14–16 <https://www.esrb.europa.eu/pub/pdf/other/esrbreportregulatorytreatmentsovereignexposures032015.en.pdf> accessed 30 September 2020.

25 The Basel III determines risk weights of sovereign debt based on the ratings of the credit agencies, and according to the rule of thumb pertaining to the SA approach, sovereign debt of countries with a rating AA– or higher will carry zero risk-weight, while the weights increase up to 150% for countries rated below B–. However, these rules of thumb are overwritten in practice by the clause pertaining to the EU countries, thus decoupling the risk weights applied to their debt from their ratings.

inclusive version of a clause in the original Basel accord, according to which banks can assign a zero weight to debt issued by the government of their home jurisdiction where this is denominated in their domestic currency. This favourable treatment also extends to sovereign debt whose credit risk is evaluated based on the IRB approach. In that case, banks are allowed to make 'partial' use of SA to evaluate the credit risk of their sovereign debt portfolio, even if they use the IRB approach for credit risk.[26] Furthermore, even for banks that actually use the IRB approach to evaluate the risk of the sovereign debt they hold, the estimated probability of default seems to be quite low, being equal to a (weighted) average of 0.3% for a sample of 102 banks,[27] and reflecting the low probability incidence of sovereign defaults. The resulting minimisation of capital requirements creates strong incentives for banks to hold sovereign debt, in general, including domestic sovereign debt.

The regulatory framework is also favourable towards sovereign debt as regards its role in addressing liquidity risk. This is because the Basel framework (starting from Basel II) treats favourably the use of sovereign debt as collateral in secured lending or repos. Specifically, the standardised haircuts for mitigating liquidity risk prescribed by the framework are lower for sovereign debt as compared to corporate debt of the same maturity and rating. Therefore, the Basel framework treats sovereign debt as a more cost-effective way for banks to manage liquidity. Furthermore, the regulations pertaining to the two liquidity ratios that banks need to satisfy (i.e. the liquidity coverage ratio ('LCR') and the net stable funding ratio ('NSFR')) also privilege sovereign over private debt. In the case of the LCR, sovereign debt with zero risk-weight and sovereign debt denominated in the domestic currency are assigned the characterisation of 'Level 1' assets, meaning that they are classified under the most liquid asset class, i.e. the one that is the most effective in addressing liquidity stress scenarios. By comparison, high-quality private debt is categorised in the 'Level 2' asset class, being considered as less effective to secure liquidity under stress. The above inevitably shapes banks' incentives in favour of holding sovereign debt on their balance sheets. Similarly, the regulation introducing the NSFR in the EU[28] assigns a lower required amount of stable funding to sovereign debt

26 Yannik M. Schneider and Sascha Steffen, 'Feasibility Study: Transition to a New Regime for Bank Sovereign Exposure?' (Study provided at the request of the European Parliament's Committee on Economic and Monetary Affairs, November 2017) <https://www.europarl.europa.eu/RegData/etudes/STUD/2017/602112/IPOL_STU(2017)602112_EN.pdf> accessed 30 September 2020.

27 Bank for International Settlements, Basel Committee on Banking Supervision, 'Regulatory Consistency Assessment Programme (RCAP): Analysis of Risk-Weighted Assets for Credit Risk in the Banking Book' (July 2013) <https://www.bis.org/bcbs/publ/d363.htm> accessed 30 September 2020.

28 Regulation (EU) 575/2013 of the European Parliament and of the Council of 26 June 2013 on prudential requirements for credit institutions and investment firms and amending Regulation (EU) 648/2012 [2013] OJ L176/1.

on the liability side, thereby privileging domestic sovereign debt (and sovereign debt in general) over private debt.[29]

Central bank collateral frameworks may also have an impact on the incentives of commercial banks to hold sovereign bonds. Prior to 2007, the Eurosystem Collateral Framework ('ESCF') classified the sovereign debt of all euro-area countries under the 'Tier One, Category 1' assets. What this meant is that these instruments received the lowest possible haircut (0.5%) over their market value when used as collateral against central bank lending.[30] After 2007, the ESCF stipulated that the 'first best' of the available credit ratings issued by any of the accepted external credit assessment institutions ('ECAIs') would determine the eligibility and haircuts applicable to instruments for which external assessments are available.[31,32] This approach was criticised as prone to pro-cyclicality,[33] given that credit ratings are pro-cyclical.[34] The critics' argument was that the collateral framework tended to weaken the differentiation of sovereign bonds during booms,[35] while at the same time exacerbating that differentiation at times of stress or outright financial crises. The reservations of policymakers and academics *vis-à-vis* reliance on credit ratings as a risk metric, especially in the aftermath of the global financial crisis of 2007–2009, have been reflected in the policy recommendations of the FSB, which has stated that 'central banks should reach their own credit judgements on the financial instruments that they will accept in market operations.'[36]

There is also a strand of criticism focusing on the broadening of the eligible collateral that the ECB undertook around the time of the outbreak of the global financial crisis in 2007. The collateral rules pertaining to sovereign debt (e.g. the minimum credit rating or the composition of the rating agencies) were adjusted after 2007, mainly with a view to aligning credit standards with

29 ESRB (2015), 20–21.

30 Willem H. Buiter and Anne Sibert, 'How the Eurosystem's Treatment of Collateral in Its Open Market Operations Weakens Fiscal Discipline in the Eurozone (and What to Do about It)' (2005) *Centre for Economic Policy Research Discussion Paper* 5387 (Buiter and Sibert (2005)).

31 Corrado Macchiarelli and Mara Monti, 'The ECB Collateral Policy beyond Conventional Policy Stimulus' (In-depth analysis requested by the European Parliament's Committee on Economic and Monetary Affairs, Monetary Dialogue, July 2018) <https://www.europarl.europa.eu/cmsdata/150490/LSE%20final%20publication.pdf> accessed 30 September 2020.

32 Kjell G. Nyborg, 'Central Bank Collateral Frameworks' (2015) *Swiss Finance Institute Research Paper* 15–10, 23–34 <http://www.stat.uchicago.edu/~mykland/ecoll_art_Feb2015_11_complete.pdf> accessed 30 September 2020.

33 Grégory Clayes and Inês G. Raposo, 'Is the ECB Collateral Framework Compromising the Safe-Asset Status of Euro-Area Sovereign Bonds?' (*Bruegel*, 8 June 2018) (Clayes and Raposo (2018)) <https://www.bruegel.org/2018/06/is-the-ecb-collateral-framework-compromising-the-safe-asset-status-of-euro-area-sovereign-bonds/> accessed 30 September 2020.

34 Carmen Broto and Luis Molina, 'Sovereign Ratings and Their Asymmetric Response to Fundamentals' (2016) 130 *Journal of Economic Behaviour and Organization* 206.

35 Buiter and Sibert (2005).

36 Financial Stability Board, *Principles for Reducing Reliance on CRA Ratings* (2010), 3 <https://www.fsb.org/wp-content/uploads/r_101027.pdf> accessed 30 September 2020.

the overall market conditions.[37] For example, in 2008, the credit threshold for sovereign debt was lowered from A– to BBB–. Moreover, in February 2009, the Dominion Bond Rating Service agency was added to the group of accepted ECAIs.[38] Eberl and Weber[39] have argued that the ECB's adjustments to the collateral framework during the crisis were 'in contrast to Bagehot's call for good collateral,' while Sinn[40] has expressed the view that the collateral framework featured 'extremely low collateral requirements.'

Discussing these criticisms, Bindseil, Corsi, Sahel and Visser[41] argue that, for liquid assets such as sovereign bonds, the haircut framework focuses on *market* rather than *credit* risk. This approach is justified by referring to the Eurosystem's use of short-term credit operations for the conduct of monetary policy. In addition, the same authors note that, in contrast to the argument of Buiter and Sibert[42] about non-sufficient discrimination among sovereign bonds, markets discriminated significantly amongst the various instruments after the outbreak of the crisis. Furthermore, the ECB relied on the market prices of government bonds to value collateral also during the pre-crisis period. In other words, there *was* a market-based element of differentiation across government bonds, as argued by Issing.[43] It is, therefore, not easy to identify a causal link between the ESCF and the incentives of euro-area banks to hold government debt.[44] Finally, the pro-cyclicality argument drawn from a central bank's reliance on external ratings may well be relevant to discussions on how to improve the relevant central bank's collateral framework, but it is not directly relevant to the incentives of banks to hold sovereign debt. It is recalled that the rationale for the ESCF's reliance on external ratings is that it avoids burdening the ECB

37 Ulrich Bindseil, Marco Corsi, Benjamin Sahel and Ad Visser, 'The Eurosystem Collateral Framework Explained' (2017) *European Central Bank Occasional Paper* 187 (Bindseil et al. (2017)) <https://www.ecb.europa.eu/pub/pdf/scpops/ecb.op189.en.pdf> accessed 30 September 2020.

38 Karl Whelan, Guntram B. Wolff and Alvaro Belke, 'Eurosystem Collateral Policy and Framework' (Compilation of notes provided at the request of the European Parliament's Committee on Economic and Monetary Affairs, Monetary Dialogue, November 2014) <https://www.europarl.europa.eu/RegData/etudes/IDAN/2014/587299/IPOL_IDA(2014)587299_EN.pdf> accessed 30 September 2020.

39 Jakob Eberl and Christopher Weber, 'ECB Collateral Criteria: A Narrative Database 2001–2013' (2014) IFO Institute, *Leibniz Institute for Economic Research at the University of Munich Working Paper* 174, 45 <https://econpapers.repec.org/paper/cesifowps/_5f174.htm> accessed 30 September 2020.

40 Hans-Werner Sinn, *The Euro Trap. On Bursting Bubbles, Budgets, Beliefs* (Oxford University Press 2014), 164.

41 Bindseil et al. (2017), 37 and 51.

42 Buiter and Sibert (2005).

43 Otmar Issing, 'One Size Fits All! A Single Monetary Policy for the Euro Area' (Speech at the International Research Forum, Frankfurt am Main, 20 May 2005) <https://www.ecb.europa.eu/press/key/date/2005/html/sp050520.en.html> accessed 30 September 2020.

44 The counter-argument here would be that the market prices incorporate the information of the central bank's collateral policy, which in this case could be interpreted as sending a signal of risk similarity across sovereign bonds.

Governing Council with decisions that could be perceived as having political overtones.[45]

Overall, the ESCF does not strike the authors as extraordinarily accommodative *vis-à-vis* sovereign debt, when benchmarked against the collateral frameworks of other central banks.[46] This also applies to the crisis period when all central banks widened their eligible collateral pools, in a bid to adjust to the prevailing market conditions.[47] Concluding, while there are reasons to believe that the favourable regulatory treatment of sovereign debt strengthened banks' incentives to hold government bonds, a similar argument is harder to make when it comes to the effect of the ESCF on the incentives of banks to hold government bonds.

There is indeed empirical evidence to the effect that the regulatory framework, in general, and the abovementioned prudential regulatory framework, in particular, can play a role in shaping the incentives of banks to hold sovereign bonds. The study of Acharya and Steffen,[48] mentioned previously, provides empirical evidence that banks with higher risk-weighted assets ('RWAs')/assets ratio ('risk density') will also tend to hold more sovereign debt exposures in order to lower the risk density of their balance sheets. What this suggests is that the favourable regulatory treatment of sovereign bonds in Europe created incentives for banks to purchase more sovereign debt. Interestingly, it is found that this behaviour characterises banks in non-distressed countries holding risky sovereign debt, while for banks in distressed countries there is no statistically significant relationship between their risk density and their domestic sovereign debt holdings as, in their case, it is the 'risk-shifting' and 'moral suasion' mechanisms that provide the main sources of motivation for their sovereign debt holdings.

Andreeva and Vlassopoulos[49] also find that regulatory arbitrage, driven by the favourable treatment of sovereign debt in the EU, accounts for some of the motivation of banks in non-distressed countries to hold sovereign debt issued by distressed countries. Specifically, a positive relationship between foreign banks' risk density and their holdings of risky sovereign debt is observed in the data, as banks seek to decrease their risk density.

Whilst the regulatory perspective is, therefore, valid, it only answers in the most general form the question of why banks in Europe may choose to hold sovereign debt, in general, and domestic sovereign debt, in particular. Besides,

45 See, for instance, Clayes and Raposo (2018).

46 For a comparative analysis, see European Central Bank, *Collateral Eligibility Requirements: A Comparative Study across Specific Frameworks* (2013) <https://www.ecb.europa.eu/pub/pdf/other/collateralframeworksen.pdf> accessed 30 September 2020.

47 Tobias Adrian and Hyun S. Shin, 'Liquidity and Leverage' (2009) *Federal Reserve Bank of New York Staff Report* 328 <https://www.newyorkfed.org/medialibrary/media/research/staff_reports/sr328.pdf> accessed 30 September 2020.

48 Acharya and Steffen (2015), 228.

49 Andreeva and Vlassopoulos (2016).

this factor does not appear to constitute the main rationale for the decision of banks to hold sovereign debt during sovereign crisis periods. The discussion above, on the Acharya and Steffen analysis,[50] points to several other factors for the decision of banks in distressed countries to invest in sovereign debt. At the same time, one should not underestimate the importance of this factor, since the zero risk weights of sovereign debt can allow banks to exhibit 'risk-shifting' behaviour and governments to engage in 'moral suasion,' none of which is hindered by the current regulatory treatment of sovereign debt (different considerations would presumably apply if sovereign debt holdings were costly in terms of capital).

1.3.5 Concluding remarks

Without prejudice to the foregoing, the most general (and, in the authors' view, the most plausible) explanation why banks choose to hold domestic sovereign debt is the pro-cyclical risk profile of domestic sovereign debt, featuring high liquidity when the economy is in a good state and only bounded losses in cases of bank defaults, triggered by sovereign debt default, due to the limited liability of bank owners. There is empirical evidence that this explanation is, indeed, valid as regards the incentives of euro-area banks to hold sovereign debt on their balance sheets (especially debt issued by their own sovereign). At times of financial crisis, the 'gambling for resurrection' behaviour argument, which is a specific form of this explanation based on the pro-cyclical risk profile of domestic debt, and relevant when a bank faces a high risk of insolvency, also seems to take hold, explaining the decision of banks to hold (or to even increase their holdings of) sovereign debt. Another, this time political, reason that also seems to have steered the investing behaviour of certain banks towards domestic sovereign debt during the period of turbulence in Europe was moral suasion, as evidenced by the behaviour of bailed-out banks under state control.

Turning to EU-specific reasons, the regulatory treatment in the EU of sovereign debt, especially domestic sovereign debt, is a consequence of the transposition of the Basel accords, which privilege sovereign over private debt, thereby incentivising investments in sovereign debt securities. As regards the ESCF, and its direct link to credit rating agencies, this seems to have been set-up in a way that has led to a sharp deterioration in the capacity of sovereign debt to secure liquidity at times of stress. The set-up of the ESCF reflects the Eurosystem's aim of avoiding to 'politicise' its monetary policy operations. However, the result has been that, during periods of financial turbulence, banks' exposure to sovereign risk is amplified, leading to an increase in their liquidity risk.[51]

50 Acharya and Steffen (2015).

51 Higher liquidity risk was partly addressed by the widening, following the start of the crisis, of the scope of collateral eligible for Eurosystem credit operations.

On the other hand, the possibility of a selective sovereign default, of discriminating against the foreign holders of sovereign debt and of privileging domestic investors does not seem to represent a core motivation for the purchases of domestic sovereign debt by banks in the EU. The EU institutional setting, the constraints that the latter imposes on governments' behaviour but, also, historical experience are the main reasons why the possibility of a selective sovereign default can be considered a less significant factor behind banks' investment decisions.

Overall, political considerations seem to have determined to a significant degree the 'rules of the game' and the concomitant incentives for banks to hold domestic sovereign debt. The end result has been a further strengthening of the sovereign–banks nexus, which will be examined in the next section.

1.4 The sovereign–banks nexus

This section presents the implications of banks' investments in sovereign debt on the creation of a sovereign–banks feedback loop. In addition, this section analyses the various contagion mechanisms operating along the two directions ('upward' and 'downward') and how one direction amplifies the other.

The sovereign–banks nexus encompasses a number of different transmission channels. An own body of research has developed in respect of each of those channels. In a nutshell, the sovereign–banks nexus arises because stress in sovereign borrowing – understood as the reduced willingness of investors to purchase sovereign debt, and their expectation of higher rates of return if they are to do so – may lead to stress in the banking system. Stress may be amplified within the banking system due to the interconnectedness of financial institutions and then in turn affect the real economy by further weakening its fundamentals and, with them, the ability of the sovereign to borrow on the capital markets, further exacerbating the initial shock on sovereign debt. For its part, a risk scenario for the banking system will typically manifest itself in higher borrowing costs for the sovereign, giving rise to the same self-reinforcing loop. Figure 1.1. depicts the various propagation channels.

Two characteristics of the sovereign–banks nexus are noteworthy. First, it is self-reinforcing (i.e. there are no automatic stabilisers to support the economy after the loop has been set in motion), meaning that only policy intervention can halt a further deterioration in the overall economic conditions. Second, its various mechanisms operate irrespective of the initial source of the shock: once a shock has materialised and impinged on either the banking system or the sovereign, the same vicious circle will start operating both through the impact of that shock on the real economy (due to reduced lending) and through the mutual undermining of the creditworthiness of banks and the sovereign alike.

A corollary of the above is that once one of the two poles (either the banking system or the sovereign) has stabilised, following successful policy intervention, the feedback loop is weakened, and the recovery prospects of the

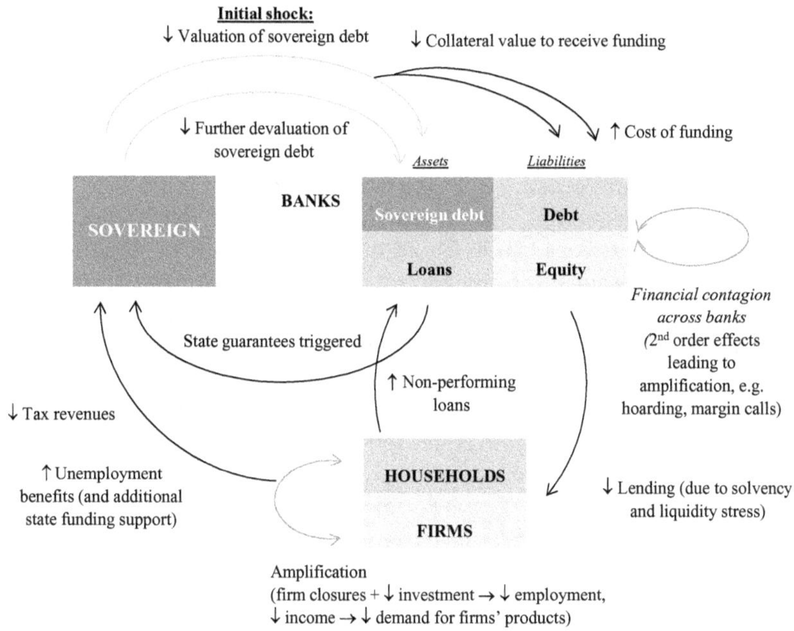

Figure 1.1 The sovereign–banks loop

other pole may increase substantially. For example, an intervention that leads to an upgrade of the creditworthiness of a sovereign is likely to also help with the funding of its banks and, as a result, allow the flow of credit to support economic growth, which, in turn, is likely to further enhance the sovereign's tax revenues, providing a further boost to the sovereign's creditworthiness. Consequently, with the appropriate policy measures in place, it is possible to transform a negative feedback loop into a positive one.

The remainder of this section analyses in greater detail the individual links that the sovereign–banks nexus comprises. The severity of the risk posed by the sovereign–banks nexus is due to the mutual reinforcement of these individual links. Therefore, these links should not be seen in isolation from one another but, rather, as operating synchronously, in a general equilibrium framework. Sections 1.4.1 and 1.4.2 elaborate on the direct transmission channels that lead from the sovereign to banks and vice versa. Section 1.4.3 covers the phenomenon of financial contagion, which reinforces endogenously external shocks that impinge on the financial system. Section 1.4.4 analyses the macro-financial linkages between banks and the real economy. Finally, Section 1.4.5 reviews the evidence for the link between the macroeconomic situation and sovereign creditworthiness.

1.4.1 From sovereigns to banks

Banks' holdings of sovereign debt are the most important 'direct' link between states and banks.[52] Once markets have begun to question the creditworthiness of a sovereign, a vicious, self-reinforcing feedback loop between banks' solvency (or liquidity) and the credit risk pricing of their sovereign is set in motion. The co-movement between market perceptions of the sovereign's credit risk and that of domestic banks is stronger in times of crisis.[53]

As explained in Section 1.2, banks may hold significant amounts of sovereign debt and demonstrate a bias in favour of domestic sovereign debt. In June 2020, the 111 significant institutions in the euro area were holding, in total, around €3.16 trillion of sovereign debt.[54] Out of this amount, €1.72 trillion (representing a 54% share) were held in domestic sovereign bonds. The total equity held by these institutions at the same time was €1.51 trillion, meaning that only their holdings of domestic sovereign debt were significantly higher than their total equity, i.e. their loss-absorption capacity. These numbers show vividly the risk potential of the sovereign–banks loop.[55]

It bears noting that sovereigns are subject to the same 'run' mechanism observed during bank runs.[56] The characteristic of this mechanism is the strategic complementarity between the actions of individual bank lenders (mostly bank depositors) who have the incentive to be the first to withdraw their deposits in the wake of negative news, thus leading to a self-fulfilling realisation of the bad scenario (that of a bank default). Similar to bank runs, investors in sovereign debt have the incentive to offload, as quickly as possible, their sovereign bond holdings, leading to a further increase in sovereign yields and precipitating the realisation of a sovereign default scenario.[57]

52 If one excludes the deposits by the treasury which in some countries are placed in the central bank, rather than commercial banks.

53 See Marcel Fratzscher and Malte Rieth, 'Monetary Policy, Bank Bailouts and the Sovereign-Bank Risk Nexus in the Euro Area' (2019) 23 (4) *Review of Finance* 745.

54 See European Central Bank, *Publication of Supervisory Data* <https://www.bankingsupervision.europa.eu/banking/statistics/html/index.en.html> accessed 30 September 2020. These data are well suited to assess banks' risk-taking as banks' consolidated balance sheets are used (specifically, the highest level of consolidation within the euro area), meaning that intragroup transactions are excluded.

55 Similar conclusions regarding the relative sizes of sovereign debt exposures to euro area countries and banks' capital buffers are reached by Mario Bellia et al. in 'The Sovereign-Bank Nexus in the Euro Area: Financial and Real Channels' (2019) *European Economy Discussion Paper* 122 <https://ec.europa.eu/info/publications/sovereign-bank-nexus-euro-area-financial-and-real-channels_en> accessed 17 December 2020, who use consolidated data for banking groups from the 2018 and 2015 EBA transparency exercises.

56 Douglas W. Diamond and Philip H. Dybvig, 'Bank Runs, Deposit Insurance, and Liquidity' (1983) 91 *Journal of Political Economy* 401 (Diamond and Dybvig (1983)).

57 See, for instance, Russell Cooper and Kalin Nikolov, 'Government Debt and Banking Fragility: The Spreading of Strategic Uncertainty' (2018) 59 International Economic Review 1905 (Cooper and Nikolov (2018)).

In the case of an increase in sovereign yields, there are four main channels that could lead to a deterioration of the domestic banks' credit risk. First, there is the direct valuation impact on the sovereign debt instruments held on the banks' balance sheets. Even if this debt is not marked-to-market and is held at the banking book (thus being immune, from an accounting perspective, to price fluctuations), valuation losses are visible to market participants who may revise their risk assessment of banks that hold large amounts of sovereign debt.

Second, banks will face an increased cost of funding and heightened rollover risk of their existing funding arrangements. In this situation, it may become challenging to secure liquidity, and they may need to revert to their central bank, as lender of last resort ('LOLR'), having to pay above-market rates. As a result of the higher funding cost, banks will tend to incur losses, further eroding their capital base.

A third, related channel of contagion could potentially operate via the credit ceilings used by credit rating agencies to assess the creditworthiness of corporate businesses operating within a jurisdiction. According to the credit ceiling policy, a firm's rating should remain below the sovereign rating of its home country. The argument for this practice is that a sovereign default will unavoidably have a substantial negative impact on all non-sovereign debt issuers operating within the defaulting sovereign's jurisdiction. Although there are exceptions to this policy,[58] it remains the case that this represents the dominant market practice, apt to lead to a situation where otherwise sound institutions can face a steep increase in their funding costs only because they operate out of a debt-ridden sovereign jurisdiction. Credit rating downgrades can lead to cliff-effects as investors may face credit rating thresholds in terms of the securities they are allowed to invest in. Hence, a rating ceiling-driven automatic downgrade can have an adverse discontinuous impact on the banking system as a whole.

Fourth, the liquidity risk of banks will also be elevated due to the decreased value of domestic sovereign bonds tendered as collateral in securities financing transactions (such as repos). Gabor and Ban[59] describe the cliff-effects that impacted the euro-area repo market during the unfolding of the financial crisis. In contrast to the United States ('US'), the fragility of sovereign debt in the euro area meant that during the crisis banks faced acute liquidity issues as the repo market – which is instrumental for their liquidity management – was significantly affected.

58 In 2015, Moody's revised upward the ceilings of non-sovereign issues operating in 11 euro area countries, above the sovereign ratings. The rationale for this decision was that the exit risk from the euro area had diminished as a result of the policy measures undertaken by the euro area authorities.

59 Daniela Gabor and Cornel Ban, 'Banking on Bonds: The New Links Between States and Markets' (2015) 54 *Journal of Common Market Studies* 617.

1.4.2 From banks to sovereigns

This, obverse, channel of contagion is well documented in the extant literature, and even if it is not always possible to deduce a cause and effect relationship between a banking sector and a sovereign crisis, there is potent evidence of a correlation between the two, which warrants (and has, in fact, provided the basis for) policy measures to avoid a spillover to the sovereign of the effects of banking crises.[60]

The main channel here is that of a sovereign bail-out of the banking sector through government funds, resulting in an over-stretching of public finances, especially if the failing bank is relatively large or if there is a common shock affecting a set of banks such as, for instance, the bust of a real estate boom, as in the case of Ireland during the European sovereign debt crisis. Cooper and Nikolov[61] consider the link between bank bail-outs and the valuation of sovereign debt: in their analysis, the sovereign's decision to bail-out banks has an impact on the pricing of sovereign debt. These authors argue that it is not easy to rationalise the government's commitment to bail-out its banks in the sense that this commitment is ultimately responsible for the feedback loop between the sovereign and the banks, while at the same time leading, endogenously, to a drop in the price of sovereign debt. However, this study does not encompass a productive sector relying on financial intermediation to increase economic output. In analyses such as that of Gennaioli et al.,[62] the incentive of the government to rescue banks hinges on the loss of output that the failure of the banking system would entail.

In their analysis of the fiscal costs of financial (and, in particular, banking sector) instability, Eschenbach and Schuknecht[63] have found that episodes of financial instability both increase the variability of fiscal balances and bring about very large fiscal costs, with public debt rising by as much as 50% of the Gross Domestic Product ('GDP') during such episodes.[64] State-sponsored bank bail-outs have been common in advanced economies. Stolz and Wedow[65] estimate that, during the first phase of the global financial crisis of 2007–2009,

60 The concrete measures taken in the EU with a view to addressing the first channel of contagion, as well as their legal shortcomings, will be explored in more detail in Chapter 4 of this work.

61 Cooper and Nikolov (2018).

62 Gennaioli et al. (2014).

63 Felix Eschenbach and Ludger Schuknecht, 'The Fiscal Costs of Financial Instability Revisited' (2002) *European Central Bank Working Paper* 191 <http://www.ecb.europa.eu/pub/pdf/scpwps/ecbwp191.pdf> accessed 30 September 2020.

64 These authors also suggest that the costs in question may also serve as a rationale for the deficit and debt targets in the Stability and Growth Pact.

65 Stéphanie M. Stolz and Michael Wedow, 'Extraordinary Measures in Extraordinary Times: Public Measures in Support of the Financial Sector in the EU and the United States' (2010) *European Central Bank Occasional Paper* 117 (Stolz and Wedow (2010)) <https://www.ecb.europa.eu/pub/pdf/scpops/ecbocp117.pdf?bed4406a139a0ef78e97945b06bfd7f1> accessed 30 September 2020.

both the US and the EU Member States committed around 26% of their GDP to support the financial sectors.

In their research into the history of financial crises, and in their assessment of the fiscal implications of the 2007 US banking crisis, Laeven and Valencia[66] and Reinhart and Rogoff[67] confirmed that banking crises will often be followed by sovereign crises, and that the 2007 US banking crisis was no exception to this empirical rule. Using data on the credit default swap rates on European sovereigns and banks, Acharya, Drechsler and Schnabl[68] documented how the announcement of government-funded bank bail-outs increases sovereign credit risk, shifting risk from banks to their sovereign. Mody and Sandri[69] had earlier shown how the presumption of euro-area sovereign intervention to rescue domestic banks, in conjunction with the projection of the relevant euro-area Member State's sovereign debt, resulted in a sharp rise in sovereign debt spreads. Similarly, Alter and Schüler[70] presented evidence to show how credit risk had spilt over from European banks to their sovereigns prior to government intervention, whereas it moved from sovereigns to banks post-intervention once a government contingent liability had crystallised. In the same vein, Singh, Gómez-Puig and Sosvilla-Riverob[71] documented an increase in the transmission risk from banks to their sovereigns after the latter announced guarantee programmes to prop up the solvency of their domestic lenders.

Finally, there is an indirect channel through which the stress that banks face is transmitted upwards to the sovereign. This channel passes through the link of the financial intermediation function of the banking sector, which then impacts real economic activity and output and, consequently, the debt repayment capacity of the sovereign. This indirect link will be elaborated on later in this chapter.

66 Luc Laeven and Fabian Valencia, 'Systemic Banking Crises: A New Database' (2008) International Monetary Fund Working Paper WP/08/224 <https://www.imf.org/external/pubs/ft/wp/2008/wp08224.pdf> accessed 30 September 2020.

67 Reinhart and Rogoff (2009).

68 Viral V. Acharya, Itamar Drechsler and Philipp Schnabl, 'A Pyrrhic Victory? Bank Bailouts and Sovereign Credit Risks' (2014) 69 (6) Journal of Finance 2689. For data on the correlation between credit default swaps on sovereigns and commercial banks at the height of the euro area sovereign debt crisis, see *also* Acharya and Steffen (2015); Paul De Grauwe, 'Governance of a Fragile Eurozone' (2011) *Centre for European Policy Studies Working Document* 346 (De Grauwe (2011)) <https://ssrn.com/abstract=1898618> accessed 30 September 2020; Adrian Alter and Yves S. Schüler, 'Credit Spread Interdependencies of European States and Banks during the Financial Crisis' (2012) 36 *Journal of Banking and Finance* 3444 (Alter and Schüler (2012)).

69 Ashoka Mody and Damiano Sandri, 'The Eurozone Crisis: How Banks and Sovereigns Came to Be Joined at the Hip' (2011) *International Monetary Fund Working Paper* WP/11/269 <https://www.imf.org/en/Publications/WP/Issues/2016/12/31/The-Eurozone-Crisis-How-Banks-and-Sovereigns-Came-to-Be-Joined-At-the-Hip-25363> accessed 30 September 2020.

70 Alter and Schüler (2012).

71 Manish K. Singh, Maria Gómez-Puig and Simón Sosvilla-Riverob, 'Sovereign-Bank Linkages: Quantifying Directional Intensity of Risk Transfers in EMU Countries' (2016) 63 *Journal of International Money and Finance* 137.

1.4.3 From banks to other banks and to other financial institutions

The interconnectedness between different segments of the financial system also serves as an amplification channel once an economic shock affecting any one of them has manifested itself. The concept of interconnectedness here refers, in the first place, to the direct links that exist between financial institutions (e.g. in the interbank market or via the lending and borrowing relationships that banks have with other financial institutions), such as insurance firms, pension funds or shadow banks. For example, investment funds and other financial institutions alone (excluding banks, insurance corporations, pension funds and central counterparties with a banking licence) had provided €2.31 trillion of funding to euro-area banks by the end of 2018,[72,73] confirming the strong interlinkages that exist between the various segments of the financial system.

In addition, interconnectedness refers to the indirect links between financial institutions, which can lead to the amplification of an initial trigger, even in the absence of mutual exposures between institutions. Such links exist, for example, due to exposures to common asset classes, as a result of which negative developments in those asset classes will lead to contagion affecting multiple institutions that may not be directly connected via bilateral exposures. The spread, in 2008, of negative news about a segment of the US mortgage market, and the resulting global financial crisis illustrate this phenomenon.[74] The practice of securitisation played a critical role in 'spreading' globally to different categories of investors through exposure to this market segment through repackaged securities. Securitised assets proved popular among investors as they received good credit ratings due to their (supposedly) diversified composition. Shin[75] argues that securitisation facilitated an expansion of lending, and was a necessary ingredient for it, with lowered credit standards spreading throughout asset-backed instruments.

Investor perceptions of the risk of institutions of the same type (e.g. money market funds) or institutions based in the same country (e.g. Spanish banks) or institutions based in countries considered to belong to the same group (e.g. southern European countries) further exacerbated financial contagion. There is an expanding literature in financial economics that dispenses with the market efficiency hypothesis according to which investors can only make random errors in the valuation of firms, and explores mechanisms that may lead to a systematic underestimation or overestimation of the risks posed by specific

72 European Systemic Risk Board, *Annual Report 2018* (2019), 46 <https://www.esrb.europa.eu/pub/pdf/ar/2019/esrb.ar2018~d69ff774ac.en.pdf?19dcfbedd2f1a4460b9e7dd2368da6de> accessed 30 September 2020.

73 For comparison, the total consolidated assets of euro area institutions at that point in time were around €24.42 trillion, according to the Consolidated Banking Data published by the ECB.

74 Frederic S. Mishkin, 'Over the Cliff: From the Subprime to the Global Financial Crisis' (2011) 25 *Journal of Economic Perspectives* 49.

75 Hyun S. Shin, 'Securitisation and Financial Stability' (2009) 119 *Economic Journal* 309.

sets of either firms or sovereigns. For example, Benzoni, Collin-Dufresne, Goldstein and Helwege[76] seek to explain the contagion-like behaviour exhibited by sovereign yields during the European sovereign debt crisis, and suggest that although investors form their valuations based on observable relevant variables, they also tend to update those valuations once new information has become available, leading to higher correlations in credit risk valuations over and above those justified by economic fundamentals alone.[77]

Another important form of indirect link is to do with the use of assets as collateral to secure funding: an impact on the valuation of an institution's debt will also decrease the ability of other institutions to secure funding if the latter hold (some of the) debt of the former. The practise of re-hypothecation of collateral would tend to exacerbate the total impact of an initial valuation shock, as multiple collateral chains would be affected.[78] Finally, market reliance on credit ratings represents another factor conducive to indirect contagion (as has been already analysed in Section 1.3.4).

A critical research question in the contagion analyses within financial networks is whether a higher degree of interconnectedness enhances the stability of the system[79] or leads to an amplification of initial shocks[80] or to a 'robust-yet-fragile' property, where, after the initial shock has exceeded a threshold value, a regime change occurs, with the density of the network leading to further amplification rather than to the absorption of the shock.[81] Overall, however, it is clear that, because of the interconnectedness and the financial contagion to which it may give rise, initial shocks can be propagated through the financial system and amplified. As a consequence, institutions that were not impacted by the first-round effects are, eventually, impacted and may face severe liquidity or solvency issues even if starting from an initial position of financial robustness. The impact of interconnectedness on the real economy is explored in the following section.

76 Luca Benzoni, Pierre Collin-Dufresne, Robert S. Goldstein and Jean Helwegem, 'Modeling Credit Contagion via the Updating of Fragile Beliefs' (2015) 28 *Review of Financial Studies* 1960 (Benzoni et al. (2015)).

77 In this framework, contagion is 'rational,' as investors optimise within their information set, the added element being that their information set takes into account the possibility of model misspecification, i.e. the agents are not assumed to know the 'correct' model of the markets.

78 Manmohan Singh, 'Velocity of Pledged Collateral' (2011) *International Monetary Fund Working Paper* WP/11/256 <https://www.imf.org/external/pubs/ft/wp/2011/wp11256.pdf> accessed 30 September 2020.

79 Franklin Allen and Douglas Gale, 'Financial Contagion' (2000) 108 *Journal of Political Economy*.

80 Fabio Caccioli, Thomas A. Catanach and J. Doyne Farmer, 'Heterogeneity, Correlations and Financial Contagion' (2012) 15 *Advances in Complex Systems*.

81 Daron Acemoglu, Asuman Ozdaglar and Alireza Tahbaz-Salehi, 'Systemic Risk and Stability in Financial Networks' (2015) 105 *American Economic Review* 564 (Acemoglu et al. (2015)).

1.4.4 From banks to the real economy (and vice versa)

An important aspect of the sovereign–banks loop is the transmission of a crisis from the financial sector to the real economy and vice versa. This is an area of economic theory that rose to prominence in the aftermath of the global financial crisis of 2007–2009. A consensus appears to have emerged that the main strands of research in macroeconomics pursued during the years of the so-called 'Great Moderation' (i.e. the period between 1984 and mid-2007)[82] did not pay sufficient attention to the linkages between the financial sector and the real sector. The implicit assumption seems to have been that the financial system acts simply as an intermediary, allocating savings to investors in an almost frictionless manner. However, following the global financial crisis, which originated in the financial system and subsequently spread to the 'real' economy, this approach no longer appears defensible.

There is a rich literature in macroeconomics describing the channels that could propagate a financial sector shock to the real economy and vice versa. The underlying economic mechanisms are based on market imperfections and, specifically, on agency and asymmetrical information issues that represent frictions in the process of financial intermediation. These mechanisms operate both on the supply and on the demand side of financial intermediation. The theoretical underpinning of the relevant analysis is that banks are institutions that specialise in monitoring the credit quality of borrowers, especially of those borrowers whose quality is less transparent, namely small enterprises and households.[83] When banks face solvency and liquidity constraints, their lending may be curtailed, precluding the extension of new loans.[84] According to the 'bank capital channel,'[85] a valuation shock to a bank's balance sheet (e.g. due to the holding of depreciated sovereign bonds) will be reflected in higher costs of funding or in a drop in the bank's capital position, which will then hinder its ability to extend new loans.[86] The ensuing shortage of credit may cause financ-

82 The main feature of the period of Great Moderation was the low volatility of economic growth rates (Charles Bean, 'The Great Moderation, the Great Panic and the Great Contraction' (Speech at the Annual Congress of the European Economic Association, Barcelona, 25 August 2009) <https://www.bis.org/review/r090902d.pdf> accessed 30 September 2020).

83 In contrast, large corporations usually can access capital markets as they are supposed to be less subject to informational asymmetries, for example due to detailed financial statements that they publish or their ability to approach investors.

84 This seems an innocuous line of argumentation, however there is a debate whether banks create 'money' (new means of payment) or they lend existing savings, constrained in the latter case by monetary policy. This discussion seems in fact to be misguided as both sentences seem to be true but at different levels, the former at the level of the individual institution and the latter at the level of the whole banking system (Michael McLeay, Amar Radia and Ryland Thomas, 'Money Creation in the Modern Economy' (2014) 54 *Bank of England Quarterly Bulletin* 14).

85 Bruce C. Greenwald and Joseph E. Stiglitz, 'Financial Market Imperfections and Business Cycles' (1993) 108 *Quarterly Journal of Economics* 77.

86 The so-called 'bank lending channel' is a similar mechanism (see, for example, Jeremy Stein, 'An Adverse-Selection Model of Bank Asset and Liability Management with Implications for the

ing issues for non-financial corporations and, especially, smaller firms, which may lack other, readily available sources of funding. Acharya and Mora[87] provide evidence that, at the outset of the financial crisis, US banks faced, on the aggregate, a shortage of funding, and had to reduce their lending activities.[88]

On the demand side, and given the informational asymmetry between non-financial corporations (as seekers of funding) and banks (as potential lenders), a weak balance sheet will decrease the chances of financial corporations to obtain external financing, as a drop in the net worth of a borrower will weaken the insurance of banks as providers of funds. High net worth functions as collateral that can be realised while, at the same time, 'signalling' to the investor the borrower's quality, helping to overcome informational asymmetry and agency problems. Therefore, irrespective of potentially binding constraints hindering the expansion of credit on the banks' side, borrowers will also find it harder to secure funding in the light of the standard credit scoring criteria applied by the lenders. The binding constraints that banks face to expand their lending, even for projects with economic value, and the weakening balance sheets of non-financial corporations, due to the drying up of lending and its effect on their investment plans, lead to a downward self-reinforcing spiral that can deepen recessions. Minetti[89] provides an argument why, in the context of a credit crunch, also the quality of funded projects deteriorates, as only smaller projects with less added value can be realised. The cancellation of investment projects may also have an impact on employment and wages due to lower demand for labour, therefore hitting consumer demand and multiplying the initial shock to the real economy.

The impact of a credit crunch will be heterogeneous across firms, households and consumers. Therefore, even if a large macroeconomic impact is bound to occur, the extent of the economic recession will also depend on the specificities of each economy. For example, larger firms with access to the capital market could substitute bank loans with the issuance of securities. However, for smaller firms, bank credit may be non-substitutable, meaning that, without it, they may forego lucrative investment opportunities. Furthermore, households

Transmission of Monetary Policy' (1998) 29 *RAND Journal of Economics* 466), which focuses on banks' liability management. However, as Disyatat notes, the emphasis that such models put on policy driven changes in banks' liabilities as a driver of credit developments is misplaced and the main factor driving credit expansion is the balance sheet strength (and the risk perception of it), which is consistent with the bank capital channel (Piti Disyatat, 'The Bank Lending Channel Revisited' (2010) *Bank for International Settlements Working Paper* 297 <https://www.bis.org/publ/work297.pdf> accessed 30 September 2020).

87 Viral V. Acharya and Nada Mora, 'A Crisis of Banks as Liquidity Providers' (2015) 70 *Journal of Finance*.

88 Empirical research that examines the channels operating on the supply or the demand side face econometric challenges as one cannot easily disentangle demand from supply effects. The use of natural experiments allowing the identification of treatment effects or the utilisation of techniques to address endogeneity like the use of instrumental variables are employed for this purpose.

89 Raoul Minetti, 'Bank Capital, Firm Liquidity, and Project Quality' (2007) 54 *Journal of Monetary Economics* 2584.

with savings may still be able to afford the purchase of durable goods, whilst households with fewer savings may postpone such purchases. Haltenhof, Lee and Stebunovs[90] examine the impact of the credit crunch during the global financial crisis of 2007–2009 for US firms and households. On their estimate, the credit crunch on firm loans and consumer instalment loans during the crisis was alone responsible for a 5.1% increase in unemployment.

The impact on employment, investment and consumption may subsequently lead to a reverse effect, from the real sector to the banking system, via the realisation of credit risk on existing loans. The realisation of credit risk in banks' loan portfolios represents a critical link in the amplification of financial crises. The line of research examining this link has developed significantly in the aftermath of the financial and sovereign debt crises, and it is of special relevance for the euro area, where the balance sheets of some banks in distressed countries are still burdened with a legacy of non-performing loans ('NPLs'). The view that emerges from empirical studies is that the amount of non-performing loans is primarily related to the overall macroeconomic conditions, but it also varies according to bank-level policies,[91] e.g. banks that have expanded quicker their loan portfolio during the boom years may end up with more NPLs on their balance sheet, whilst banks with better management and efficiency indicators would overall tend to face less realised credit risk. Louzis, Vouldis and Metaxas[92] investigate the heterogeneity across Greek banks in terms of their NPLs during the first phase of the financial crisis, up until 2009Q3. Their study finds that features of management quality (like efficiency and return on equity) and the size of banks are the main bank-specific variables explaining this heterogeneity. In particular, evidence is provided of a link between poor management and higher NPLs as well as of a 'too-big-to-fail' behaviour characterising larger banks. Despite the existence of bank-specific elements related to the quality of banks' portfolios, all studies on the topic find that macroeconomic conditions represent the backdrop for the realisation of credit risk and for an increase in NPLs. In a related paper, Vouldis and Louzis[93] find that market variables (such as the sales of cars, supermarket sales, confidence indices, etc.) represented the best predictors of NPLs for a sample

90 Samuel Haltenhof, Seung J. Lee and Viktors Stebunovs, 'The Credit Crunch and Fall in Employment during the Great Recession' (2014) 43 *Journal of Economic Dynamics and Control* 31.

91 There are econometric challenges in this strand of research. For example, as regards the impact of non-performing loans on banks' lending activity, the empirical investigations need to account also for credit demand (which is not directly observable) and other bank-specific features.

92 Dimitrios P. Louzis, Angelos T. Vouldis and Vasilios L. Metaxas, 'Macroeconomic and Bank-Specific Determinants of Non-Performing Loans in Greece: A Comparative Study of Mortgages, Business and Consumer Loan Portfolios' (2011) 36 *Journal of Banking and Finance* 1012.

93 Angelos T. Vouldis and Dimitrios P. Louzis, 'Leading Indicators of Non-Performing Loans in Greece: The Information Content of Macro-, Micro- and Bank-Specific Variables' (2018) 54 *Empirical Economics* 1187.

of Greek banks, pointing to the dominance of the economic environment on the evolution of realised credit risk.

Even if the above analysis has made clear that a significant body of economic theory has been developed to explain the links between the financial sector and the real economy, there is an ongoing debate within the economics profession as to whether the current paradigm of macroeconomic analysis (e.g. based on the Dynamic Stochastic General Equilibrium ('DSGE') model and its variants)[94] is satisfactory for studying macro-financial linkages, or whether a change of paradigm is required. This discussion sheds some light on the surprise with which most policymakers observed the protracted recessions that manifested themselves in advanced European economies over the past decade, triggered by the European sovereign debt crisis.

If downplaying the risk of recessions driven by financial factors was something of a trend in macroeconomic research produced during the period of the Great Moderation,[95] this was not the case for economists writing during earlier periods of turbulence, such as Keynes[96] or Schumpeter.[97,98] An expanding body of research conducted after the outbreak of the financial crisis elaborates on the mechanisms in motion when stress is transmitted from the financial to the real sector (and vice versa), and on the related empirical evidence. The main element of the dominant macroeconomic paradigm in need of re-examination seems to be the underestimation of the potential economic impact of financial disruptions. Even if macro-financial interactions were well studied before the global financial crisis of 2007–2009, the dominant macroeconomic paradigm prevailing during the last decades was that of self-correcting business fluctuations that could not have led to the deep recessions witnessed worldwide, especially over the last ten years. Specifically, the research strand using DSGE models for the analysis of macroeconomic dynamics does not appear to be well-suited for studying crises engulfing both the financial sector and the real economy. This is so for a number of reasons.

First, these models focus on business cycles and, more specifically, on relatively mild fluctuations around the trend, rather than on severe financial crises.

94 A recent survey on the literature for macro-financial linkages notes that, 'even when banks are included [in theoretical models such as DSGE], their treatment is highly stylised. For example, many models simply assume the presence of banks, but do attempt to justify their existence, e.g. whether banks arise to overcome information asymmetries or because they are "special" in other ways' (Stijn Claessens and M. Ayhan Kose, 'Frontiers of Macrofinancial Linkages' (2018) *Bank for International Settlements Paper* 95, 119 (Claessens and Kose (2018)) <https://www.bis.org/publ/bppdf/bispap95.pdf> accessed 30 September 2020).

95 See Peter M. Summers, 'What Caused the Great Moderation? Some Cross-Country Evidence' (2005) 90 *Federal Reserve of Kansas Economic Review* 5.

96 John M. Keynes, *A Treatise on Money* (MacMillan 1930).

97 Joseph A. Schumpeter, *Business Cycles* (McGraw-Hill 1939).

98 This is consistent with the interesting point made by Claessens and Kose (2018), 64, namely, that the field of macroeconomics has exhibited 'an oscillating pattern between integration and separation of financial and real economy issues.'

This is reflected, at a more technical level, on the models' assumption of a steady state to which the economy reverts after each shock. Second, these models do not take into account the discontinuous nature of financial crises: when financial contagion occurs, and the credit intermediation function is impaired, far-reaching effects may ensue for the real economy. This is in contrast to what happens when lower intensity shocks impinge on the economy, which may only have a short-term impact and which do not disrupt the ability of the financial system to contribute towards bringing the economy back to a path of growth.

This class of general equilibrium models does not seem to be the most relevant to study the 'tipping-point behaviour' exhibited when an economy hit by a strong external shock enters into a deep financial crisis. Hubrich and Tetlow[99] find that a single-regime model of the macroeconomy is inadequate to capture the dynamics that arise during financial crises. Their study concludes that strong financial shocks lead the economy into a high-stress state during which the macro-financial linkage is very strong.[100] In contrast, during normal times, stress is of negligible importance. An important distinction in their econometric framework is between variance switching and coefficient switching. The former mainly signifies elevated uncertainty pertaining to the economic system, while the latter points to changes in the behaviour of economic agents during different phases. Coefficient switching seemed to characterise the US economy during the period under examination in their study (1988–2011), with the effect of financial factors increasing substantially during crises. Their conclusion is that the available data are consistent with a highly non-linear interaction between the financial system and the real economy. This highly non-linear interaction, where a large macroeconomic impact would result from an initial shock to a small segment of the financial system, seems to have taken many economists by surprise.[101]

It follows that, when shocks are only relatively small, and the process of financial intermediation is not severely disrupted, a recession may ensue, but the economy will most likely return to a state of growth. However, when the

99 Kirstin Hubrich and Robert Tetlow, 'Financial Stress and Economic Dynamics: The Transmission of Crises' (2015) 70 *Journal of Monetary Economics* 100.

100 Olivier Blanchard (2018) argues that even if current DSGE models exhibit certain flaws, they nonetheless display the right foundations and should be improved rather than discarded. In particular, a general equilibrium approach is critical for analysing contagion and the appropriate regulation (Olivier Blanchard, 'On the future of macroeconomic models' (2018) 34 Oxford Review of Economic Policy 43). Charles Goodhart, Nikolaos Romanidis, Dimitrios P. Tsomocos, and Martin Shubik (2019) elaborate on the methodological challenges to accommodate the process of financial intermediation during crises in DSGE models (Charles Goodhart, Nikolaos Romanidis, Dimitrios P. Tsomocos, and Martin Shubik, 'Macromodeling, default and money' in David Mayes, Pierre Siklos and Jan-Egbert Sturm (eds), *The Oxford Handbook of the Economics of Central Banking* (2019)).

101 Geoff Kenny and Julian Morgan, 'Some Lessons from the Financial Crisis for the Economic Analysis' (2011) European Central Bank Occasional Paper 130 <https://www.ecb.europa.eu/pub/pdf/scpops/ecbocp130.pdf> accessed 30 September 2020.

disruption of the financial sector exceeds a certain tipping point, after which banks cannot continue channelling funds to real economy agents, the feedback loops between the financial system and the macroeconomy start operating, leading to deeper and protracted recessions. Jordà et al. (2015)[102] use a comprehensive macroeconomic dataset for 17 advanced economies over the 1870–2013 period to examine the determinants of the severity of asset bubbles. They find that bubbles preceded by excessive credit growth impose higher costs to the economy when they burst, and the ensuing recessions tend to last longer. This finding is also consistent with the idea that disruptions in the flow of funding could pose a higher economic risk compared to other macroeconomic shocks.

The next, and final, step in closing the sovereign–banks loop is the impact of a recession on public finances, further undermining the sovereign's creditworthiness. This final step will be considered in the next section.

1.4.5 From the real economy to the sovereign (and vice versa)

A deepening economic recession will most likely have an impact on public finances by reducing the tax base. In addition, it may force the sovereign to reduce public investment, resulting in yet another hit on aggregate demand. In practice, governments facing sovereign debt financing issues and a worsening budget deficit will most likely respond to such developments by raising taxes. In the euro-area context, this response took the (polarising) form of fiscal tightening on the basis of memoranda of understanding ('MoU') in exchange for lending below market rates. The shrinking of the tax base attendant on economic recession episodes will adversely affect different economic sectors and market segments. Households will receive decreased income streams, meaning that state revenue from income tax will also decrease. Firms may close while others make losses, with a knock-on effect on state revenue from corporate taxes. Finally, a crisis-hit housing market will affect public finances via lower property tax and transfer tax revenues. The measurement of these effects in real-world recessions is difficult as their impact is confounded by the endogenous policy response of governments and the discretionary measures they may implement to boost the state budget.

In the context of the EU, and focusing on the early stage of the global financial crisis, up to 2008, Barrios and Farngnoli[103] attempt to disentangle the impact of discretionary measures from the net effect of cyclical developments.

102 Oscar Jordà, Moritz Schularick and Alan M. Taylor, 'Leveraged Bubbles' (2015) 76 *Journal of Monetary Economics*.

103 Salvador Barrios and Raffaele Fargnoli, 'Discretionary Measures and Tax Revenues in the Run-Up to the Financial Crisis' (2010) *European Commission Economic Paper* 419 <https://ec.europa.eu/economy_finance/publications/economic_paper/2010/pdf/ecp419_en.pdf> accessed 30 September 2020.

What they find is that discretionary measures are in most cases pro-cyclical as governments implement tax increases during periods of economic slowdown. One may safely assume that this holds true, *a fortiori*, for the period of the sovereign debt crisis in Europe. Sarmento[104] focuses on the value-added tax ('VAT') determinants for a set of 27 EU countries spanning the period between 1998 and 2011. This study finds that governments have used VAT as a primary means of raising revenue and achieving fiscal consolidation during a recessionary phase. Finally, and as regards the housing market, Lutz, Molloy and Shan[105] find that during the global financial crisis of 2007–2009 in the US, the drop in tax revenues was mainly driven by the general economic recession, rather than by tax revenue channels specific to the housing market.

The policy responses to a deepening recession caused by a crisis originating in the financial sector, irrespective of whether the cause is to be traced back to sovereign debt or to realised risk in the banking sector, have been the object of extensive debate, especially in the context of the euro-area crisis. One could, here, distinguish between 'austerity,' defined as a policy option, and forced fiscal consolidation based on decreased government consumption or tax increases due to the unavailability of public funding. This distinction is not always straightforward, as the existence of state funding is, to some extent, also a political decision in the context of the EU and EMU. There is the view that 'expansionary fiscal austerity,' comprising fiscal consolidation to regain the trust of markets before initiating a new virtuous cycle by re-starting public investment, is the optimal policy, or at least the best policy feasible given the political constraints to fiscal transfers across the EU and EMU. But there is also a different viewpoint, which emphasises the self-defeating aspects of attempting an abrupt fiscal consolidation in the midst of a recession. Using quantitative macroeconomic models, such as DSGE, a number of studies have argued that austerity – defined in this research strand as 'government spending below the (pre-crisis) trend' – has had adverse consequences for economic growth. Other studies have argued that austerity is a necessary element of a recovery after a sovereign funding shock. However, the negative impact of austerity on economic growth is not contested.

The discussion among academic economists has especially focused on the magnitude of fiscal multipliers in measuring the GDP impact of a change in government spending and on whether such multipliers are significantly different during recessions. Blanchard and Leigh's study[106] has been influential on the magnitude of fiscal multipliers. They argue that fiscal multipliers are larger

104 Joaquim Sarmento, 'The Determinants of Value Added Tax Revenues in the European Union' (2016) 21 *European Journal of Management Studies* 79.

105 Byron Lutz, Raven Molloy and Hui Shan, 'The Housing Crisis and State and Local Government Tax Revenue: Five Channels' (2011) 41 *Regional Science and Urban Economics* 306.

106 Olivier J. Blanchard and Daniel Leigh, 'Effects of Fiscal Policy in Deep Recessions: Simple and Hopefully Credible Empirical Evidence' (2013) 103 *American Economic Review* 117.

during recessions, and that this may explain why an abrupt fiscal consolidation may be pro-cyclical and worsen a recession. In particular, they identify a statistically significant negative relationship between expected fiscal consolidation and GDP for the 2010–2011 period and for the EU 27 economies. In a similar vein, House, Proebsting and Tesar[107] conduct a DSGE model-based exercise to identify the impact of fiscal austerity on output growth in a cross-country framework. The degree of austerity is defined as a shortfall in government purchases compared to an extrapolation from the pre-crisis trend. In their model, the main mechanism through which a cut in government spending affects the economy is the suppression of employment and GDP as prices are assumed to be 'sticky' and not to adjust to the reduced demand. It is found that the degree of austerity is the main factor behind the heterogeneity in output growth across 28 advanced economies. However, it bears noting that this type of macroeconomic exercises abstracts from the functioning of financial markets and the stock of national debt. Therefore, the distinction between a fiscal consolidation, deemed necessary due to financing (and, also, political) constraints, and 'austerity,' as a policy choice, is not emphasised. For their part, Alesina, Azzalini, Favero, Giavazzi and Miano[108] focus on the composition of fiscal consolidation, arguing that this matters for its effects on economic growth more than the state of the cycle during which it is introduced. In other words, they argue that fiscal multipliers may indeed be different during recessions, but what matters most is the relative weight of expenditure cuts compared to tax increases. Their analysis points to a lower macroeconomic cost of expenditure-based adjustments compared to tax-based ones.

A more detailed investigation of the effects of fiscal tightening, irrespective of whether it is a domestic policy choice made free of binding external financial constraints or a policy dictated by the lack of access to funding, is beyond the scope of our analysis in the present work. The important point here is that the impact of the initial shock may result in a deterioration in public finances, leading to either a worsening deficit and an increase in public debt (thus undermining sovereign creditworthiness) or to fiscal tightening, which, at least in the short to medium term, is bound to have an effect on real economic growth, further activating the amplification channels to banks, e.g. via increases in their stock of NPLs.

Finally, it bears noting that there is also a direct spillover effect in the opposite direction, namely, from the sovereign to the real economy. One channel in this direction operates via the increased cost of funding for non-financial

107 Christopher L. House, Christian Proebsting and Linda L. Tesar, 'Austerity in the Aftermath of the Great Recession' (2019) *Research Seminar in International Economics, University of Michigan, Working Paper* 672 <https://www.nber.org/papers/w23147.pdf> accessed 30 September 2020.

108 Alberto Alesina, Gualtiero Azzalini, Carlo Favero, Francesco Giavazzi and Armando Miano, 'Is It the "How" or the "When" that Matters in Fiscal Adjustments?' (2018) 66 *International Monetary Fund Economic Review* 144.

corporations ('NFCs'). The impact of sovereign risk on the funding of NFCs, which, in turn, hits the real economy, has been examined by Augustin, Boustanifar, Breckenfelder and Schnitzler.[109] Almeida, Cunha, Ferreira and Restrero[110] also identify direct links between a sovereign downgrade and corporate credit ratings and a related impact on debt issuance costs. Households will also suffer a direct negative impact on their wealth as a percentage of their savings may be invested in sovereign bonds, resulting in adjustments to their consumption and investment decisions.

1.4.6 Particular relevance for countries in a monetary union

The channel of contagion from sovereign to banks may be even more critical within than it is outside a monetary union, as has been convincingly shown in a body of research triggered by the outbreak of the sovereign debt crisis in the euro area. This is because the institutional set-up of a monetary union may render the price of sovereign bonds for countries within a monetary union particularly information-sensitive and prone to overreaction.

To start with, the relationship between the economic fundamentals of national economies and their sovereign bond pricing by markets seems to be much more prone to pro-cyclicality in the case of countries participating in a monetary union[111] compared to other countries. Specifically, research has shown that, in the context of the euro area and during the sovereign debt crisis, the yield spreads of distressed countries (Greece, Ireland, Italy, Portugal and Spain) were higher when compared with countries with similar macroeconomic fundamentals (such as the debt to GDP ratio, 'fiscal space' – defined as the debt to tax revenues ratio – and other 'fundamental variables' including the current account position, real economic growth and the real effective exchange rate).[112] For example, De Grauwe and Ji[113] find that the relationship between the debt to GDP ratio and fiscal space is significantly stronger compared to that for a test group of other advanced economies (both European and non-European ones), confirming the 'fragility hypothesis' formulated in De Grauwe, according to which countries in monetary unions are especially

109 Patrick Augustin, Hamid Boustanifar, Johannes Breckenfelder and Jan Schnitzler, 'Sovereign to Corporate Spillovers' (2018) 50 *Journal of Money, Credit and Banking* 857.

110 Heitor Almeida, Igor Cunha, Miguel A. Ferreira and Felipe Restrero, 'The Real Effects of Credit Ratings: The Sovereign Ceiling Channel' (2017) 72 *Journal of Finance* 249.

111 Pro-cyclicality here is defined as price undershooting during normal time periods and price overshooting at crisis times.

112 Specifically, although a structural break is identified as having taken place in 2008 for all countries, the estimated coefficients for the fundamental variables during the post-2008 period are much higher for the euro area countries.

113 Paul De Grauwe and Yuemei Ji, 'Self-Fulfilling Crises in the Eurozone: An Empirical Test' (2013) 34 *Journal of International Money and Finance* 15.

vulnerable to market sentiments and self-fulfilling sovereign crises.[114] A study by Poghosyan[115] finds an 'underreaction' of markets to the fundamentals of the euro-area distressed countries during the 1999–2009 period, and an 'overreaction' after 2009. Beirne and Fratzscher[116] distinguish between 'wake-up call' contagion (reflecting higher sensitivity of sovereign yields to fundamentals during crisis periods) and 'pure contagion' (reflecting herd or panic behaviour among investors), the latter caused by changing market perceptions decoupled from fundamentals. These authors find evidence that both types of contagion explain the sovereign yields of euro area economies. Empirical evidence consistent with these findings has also been provided in D'Agostino and Ehrmann.[117] In a similar vein, Coeuré (2016)[118] has remarked that sovereign debt in the euro area had been 'too safe before the crisis' and 'too risky' after the outbreak of the crisis.

The reason for this excess volatility is that the members of a monetary union do not have control over their currency, as a result of which they cannot use exchange rate adjustments nor the liquidity provision facility of their central bank. Consequently, the probability of a shock on the creditworthiness of the sovereign is even more relevant within a monetary union than it is outside one. In addition, in a monetary union, sovereign debt suffers from a 'demotion'[119] due to the uncertainties regarding the liquidity assistance that central banks may (or may not) be in a position to provide when sovereign debt denominated in the sovereign's own currency comes under market pressure, exacerbated by the easy access of investors to sovereign debt issued by other, healthier members of the same monetary union. The latter phenomenon is conducive to 'flight-to-quality' effects, which were a hallmark of the European sovereign debt crisis.

Furthermore, the increased fragility of sovereign debt creditworthiness for the countries participating in a monetary union could lead to situations where

114 De Grauwe (2011).

115 Tigran Poghosyan, 'Long-Run and Short-Run Determinants of Sovereign Bond Yields in Advanced Economies' (2012) *International Monetary Fund Working Paper* WP/12/271 <https://www.imf.org/external/pubs/ft/wp/2012/wp12271.pdf> accessed 30 September 2020.

116 John Beirne and Marcel Fratzscher, 'The pricing of sovereign risk and contagion during the European sovereign debt crisis' (2013) 34 Journal of International Money and Finance 60.

117 Antonello D'Agostino and Michael Ehrmann, 'The Pricing of G7 Sovereign Bond Spreads: The Times They Are A-Changin' (2013) *European Central Bank Working Paper* 1520 <https://www.ecb.europa.eu/pub/pdf/scpwps/ecbwp1520.pdf> accessed 30 September 2020.

118 Benoît Coeuré, 'Sovereign debt in the euro area: too safe or too risky?' (2016) Keynote address at Harvard University's Minda de Gunzburg Center for European Studies in Cambridge MA, 3 November 2016 <https://www.ecb.europa.eu/press/key/date/2016/html/sp161103.en.html> accessed 19 September 2020.

119 Vítor Constâncio, 'European Financial Architecture and the European Safe Asset' (Speech at the Conference on European Financial Infrastructure in the face of new challenges, Florence, 25 April 2019) <https://macroviews.net/wp/wp-content/uploads/2019/05/VC-speech-in-Florence-on-Sovereign-debt-and-safe-assets-April-25-2019-complete-fv2.pdf > accessed 30 September 2020.

the risk of default is transmitted by market sentiment and is decoupled from national economic fundamentals. The strand of economic literature concerned with so-called 'multiple equilibria' explores situations where the same 'fundamentals,' such as sovereign debt sustainability, could give rise to multiple outcomes, i.e. sovereign default or its exact opposite. The seminal work of Calvo[120] showed that when creditors know that a government can repudiate its debt based on cost–benefit considerations, two outcomes could be possible assuming all other economic variables to be fixed: one in which the interest rate charged on sovereign debt is low and the debt is serviced, and another one in which the interest rate is too high, forcing the government to repudiate its debt.[121] In other words, it is not necessarily the case that the interest rate charged on sovereign debt reflects the creditworthiness of the sovereign: the reverse direction of causation could also be in operation, with a sovereign's creditworthiness being undermined by market expectations that impose a high(er) interest rate. The insights that this literature provides are especially important for countries within a monetary union, as the trade-offs facing governments that share a currency are more limited compared to those of the government of a country that can count on central bank liquidity support or exchange rate adjustment. Specifically, the government of a country participating in a monetary union has to weigh the costs of an internal devaluation (with the concomitant social cost) against the cost of a default. Therefore, self-fulfilling expectations can dominate, with the expectations of creditors about the final outcome also determining the final outcome itself.[122]

In the light of the amplification mechanisms presented above, which are specific to a monetary union, the need to undertake decisive policy action against the risk of a trigger in the sovereign–bank nexus acquires pressing urgency. Overall, these transmission channels are attributable to the lesser degree of policy flexibility which the participation in a monetary union entails, e.g. as regards exchange rate and monetary policy.[123] As will be further elaborated in the next chapters, the policy proposals put forward aim to utilise the heterogeneity of countries within a monetary union by either relying on diversification

120 Guillermo A. Calvo, 'Servicing the Public Debt: The Role of Expectations' (1988) 78 (4) *American Economic Review* 647.

121 Gros presents a simple model with multiple equilibria and frames the discussion in the context of the euro area crisis (Daniel Gros, 'A Simple Model of Multiple Equilibria and Default' (2012) *Centre for European Policy Studies Working Document* 366 <http://aei.pitt.edu/35886/> accessed 30 September 2020). For a recent addition to this literature, see also Joao Ayres, Gaston Navarro, Juan Pablo Nicolini and Pedro Teles, 'Sovereign Default: The Role of Expectations' (2018) 175 *Journal of Economic Theory* 803.

122 The potential for informational contagion across countries is another relevant mechanism that could lead to elevated sovereign debt risk without a change in economic fundamentals, merely on account of bad news for other 'similar' countries. See, for example, Benzoni et al. (2015).

123 On the trade-offs facing countries within a monetary union, see also Section 3.2.

benefits or pooling common resources so as to render the monetary union robust against the realisation of such risks.

1.4.7 Concluding remarks

The foregoing discussion elaborated on the various channels that operate to create the sovereign–banks feedback loop. The interdependence of banks' balance sheets and government finances, on the one hand, and the financial intermediation function that banks perform *vis-à-vis* the real economy, on the other hand, are the two main elements that give rise to the loop.

The self-reinforcing nature of the loop and the fact that the activation of the various channels is independent from the origin of the triggering economic shock have significant policy implications, which will be elaborated on in the following chapters of this book. The former feature means that policy instruments to effectively counter the vicious circle are required. The latter feature means that policy measures addressing either the 'upward' or the 'downward' direction of the loop could also be complementary in addressing the other direction of contagion.

The multiplicity of the contagion channels and their mutual amplification strongly militate in favour of *ex ante* measures to prevent the feedback loop from manifesting itself in the first place. However, the analysis presented here also provides arguments for *ex post* policy instruments: the multi-faceted nature of the loop renders reliance on pre-emptive measures only insufficient to prevent the occurrence of crises triggered by the bi-directional feedback loop.

2 Case studies from the European sovereign debt crisis

2.1 Effects of commercial bank crises on sovereigns

2.1.1 Introductory remarks

As explained in more detail in Chapter 1, sovereigns are exposed to domestic banking crises through a number of different avenues. These include, in particular, the direct (or implicit) guarantee that they extend (or are generally perceived to extend) in respect of the liabilities of troubled domestic credit institutions, the activation of which may entail their fiscal deterioration, as guarantors, once a domestic banking crisis has materialised, and the state aid they may provide, in a crisis situation, to their banks. State guarantees and state aid can trigger a sovereign debt crisis where the size of a domestic banking sector and/or of its funding needs are substantial, adversely affecting public deficit and impairing public debt sustainability. The near-collapse of the Irish and Cypriot banking sectors, and the dire effects of those episodes for the Irish and Cypriot sovereigns, are cases in point. Subsections 2.1.2 and 2.1.3 provide a brief account of the abovementioned two episodes, helping to illustrate how the risk of a bank failure (or failures) can lead to an increase in the credit risk of the sovereign and, in extremis, threaten the sovereign with default.

One preliminary remark is apposite. Although the choice of case studies in this – and the following section – is not random, this chapter makes no pretence of being exhaustive in its account of sovereign default (or near-default) episodes in the euro area in the aftermath of the global financial crisis. The case studies chosen here are, merely, eloquent illustrations of the two-way link between sovereign and banking sector default, however much they may be substitutable by the examples of other euro area programme countries (such as Portugal and Spain) or even non-programme countries (such as Italy and Slovenia), which came up against challenges similar to those faced by the programme countries, only to narrowly escape their grim fate.

2.1.2 The case of Ireland

In the run-up to the outbreak of its banking and sovereign debt crises, Ireland had seen a dramatic increase in domestic bank (mainly mortgage) lending, accompanied by a sharp rise in property prices: it is telling of the proportions of the domestic mortgage loan-sustained housing bubble that the aggregate of the property-related lending to residents by domestic banks stood at over 147% of GDP at the end of 2008, compared to less than 106% of GDP for the United Kingdom's ('UK') domestic banking industry.[1] As a result, in November 2008, the combined balance sheet of the Irish banking sector grew to €1.8 trillion, compared with a GDP of around €180 billion, or over nine times the size of the Irish economy. What is more, mortgage loans were largely concentrated in a small number of banks, some of which specialised in property development, with most of these loans being used for investments that could only have paid off if property prices continued to rise. Between 2003 and 2007, Anglo Irish Bank expanded its loan book at an annual rate of over 20%, with assets growing from €26 billion (2003) to €97 billion (2007). The Irish Nationwide Building Society grew over a short period of time from a small mortgage lender to a €14 billion property development specialist, half of the funding of which was drawn from the international bond markets. Allied Irish Bank, one of Ireland's two principal 'high street' retail banks, also invested heavily in property-related loans, with its portfolio of mortgage loans rising from €16 billion in 2004 to €47 billion in 2007.[2]

The crisis impinged on the Irish economy through some of the channels described in the previous chapter. The initial trigger of the crisis was the slowing-down of the property bubble as the housing market overheating started becoming clear to market participants already in 2007, i.e. earlier than the peak of the global financial crisis. External factors, including the economic slowdown in Ireland's trading partners, also contributed to the bursting of the property bubble.[3] The shock to the construction sector hit public finances, severely reducing both tax income and employment and squeezing the fiscal space available to the government.[4] The ensuing collapse of the Irish construction sector and the consequent unemployment shock led to an increase in the volume of NPLs, which caused disquiet among international investors in respect of the Irish banks' exposure to property investment loans. Thus, it started becoming increasingly difficult for Irish banks to raise funds in the bond

1 Commission of Investigation into the Banking Sector in Ireland, *Misjudging Risk: Causes of the Systemic Banking Crisis in Ireland* (2011) (Nyberg Report (2011)), 7 <https://www.nuigalway.ie/media/housinglawrightsandpolicy/nationalpolicy/Nyberg-Report-Misjuding-Risk---Causes-of-the-Systemic-Banking-Crisis-in-Ireland.pdf> accessed 30 September 2020.

2 Karl Whelan, 'Ireland's Economic Crisis – The Good, the Bad and the Ugly' (Paper presented at the Bank of Greece Conference on the Euro Crisis, Athens, 24 May 2013) <https://www.karlwhelan.com/Papers/Whelan-IrelandPaper-June2013.pdf> accessed 30 September 2020.

3 K.P.V. O'Sullivan and Tom Kennedy, 'What caused the Irish banking crisis?' (2010) 18 Journal of Financial Regulation and Compliance 224.

4 Karl Whelan, 'Ireland's Economic Crisis – The Good, the Bad and the Ugly' (Paper presented at the Bank of Greece Conference on the Euro Crisis, Athens, 24 May 2013) <https://www.karlwhelan.com/Papers/Whelan-IrelandPaper-June2013.pdf> accessed 19 September 2020.

market.[5] The simultaneous hit on Ireland's real economy and banks initiated the downward spiral described in Chapter 1.

Faced with the prospect of the collapse of its domestic banking sector on account of the recession, the Irish government issued, in September 2008, a blanket guarantee in respect of the deposits and bonds of its six largest banks, the scale of which reinforced the potential for risk transmission from the banks to the already fiscally strained sovereign.[6] The impaired solvency of Irish banks only became apparent over time, with the estimates of the cost for the Irish taxpayer of recapitalising domestic banks standing at over €62 billion. The impending meltdown of the Irish banking sector, in conjunction with the exorbitant cost of its rescue, which could not be financed through government resources, was to force the Irish government to apply for EU-International Monetary Fund ('IMF') financial assistance in November 2010, barely six months after the Greek government had done likewise (see below). The mutual reinforcement of the economic recession and the bailout costs for saving domestic banks caused Ireland's public debt to soar from around 25% of GDP in 2006 to 107% at the end of 2011, and to 118% in 2013.

In the aftermath of the sovereign debt crisis several reports were drafted – some of them commissioned by the Irish government – to identify the root causes of the Irish banking sector's meltdown.[7] These found evidence of multi-level failure, affecting banks and government agencies alike. For instance, the Nyberg Report found that bank customers had misjudged property values, banks had failed in the assessment of their customers' credit quality, investors in banks had no sound understanding of the nature of the risk that their investments came with, regulators only had a poor grasp of the actual mortgage market exposure of banks, while the government had failed in its management of the regulator.[8] Furthermore, the Nyberg Report found that bank managers had failed to protect bank depositors and investors, while the central bank had failed to guard against the emergence of a banking crisis, as the focus of its supervisory practice had been on 'verifying governance and risk management models rather than attempting an independent assessment of risk.'[9]

5 Irish banks entered the crisis with apparently strong capital ratios, which, however, did not prove sufficient to absorb the losses generated by the combined impact of losses on the asset side and increasing funding costs on the liabilities side (ibid).

6 Irish banks were finding it increasingly difficult to raise funds on bond markets, and on 29 September 2008, two weeks after the collapse of Lehman Brothers, the senior management of Anglo Irish, the largest Irish bank, turned up at government buildings looking for help. At the time, Anglo Irish was possibly days away from defaulting on its liabilities, and the other banks were extremely concerned about the impact on their operations if such a default were to occur.

7 See Patrick Honohan, Donal Donovan, Paul Gorecki, and Rafique Mottiar (2010), Klaus Regling and Max Watson (2010), Nyberg Report (2011), Patrizia Baudino, Diarmuid Murphy and Jean-Philippe Svforonos (2020).

8 Nyberg Report (2011), vii.

9 Honohan et al (2010), 8.

Whatever the allocation of responsibility for the Irish banking sector crisis, this was not attributable primarily to fiscal profligacy nor to the imprudent running of public finances in the run-up to the near-collapse of Irish banks: where the government had failed was in precluding a housing bubble, and in averting the resulting banking crisis, which came to threaten the state of Ireland with sovereign default.[10]

2.1.3 The case of Cyprus

Already in 2009, the size of Cyprus's banking sector was equivalent to nine times its GDP and, although it had declined somewhat by mid-2012, it remained among the highest both in the euro area and the EU.[11] The disproportionate size of the Cypriot banking sector relative to that of the domestic economy was the combined result of expansive lending, both domestically and abroad (especially in Greece), largely secured through real estate assets the value of which was in decline, weak risk management practices, gaps in the supervisory framework and ineffective banking supervision, which delayed the recognition of loan losses and allowed for under-provisioning.[12] By the time of their near-collapse, in March 2013, the Bank of Cyprus and the Cyprus Popular Bank (hereafter, 'Laiki Bank'), the two largest domestic lenders, were severely under-capitalised. An EBA capital exercise conducted in December 2011 revealed that the capital shortfall of the Bank of Cyprus stood at €1.56 billion; the bank remained under-capitalised even after the Cypriot government had subscribed to a substantial capital increase, at the end of March 2012.[13] The position of Laiki Bank was no less parlous: the second-largest lender in Cyprus was close to collapse in early 2012, and had to be bailed out, in mid-2012, with a €1.8 billion capital injection, funded through an un-funded government bond (it bears noting that Cyprus had lost access to international capital markets by May 2011).

In March 2012, the Bank of Cyprus and Laiki Bank suffered a €4.5 billion 'haircut' on their Greek Government Bond ('GGB') holdings as a result of the restructuring of GGBs held by the private sector (the so-called 'Private-Sector Involvement' or 'PSI'), generating losses that the two lenders were unable to

10 This conclusion is broadly common to all the reports consulted in this section e.g. see Klaus Regling and Max Watson (2010), Nyberg Report (2011), Patrizia Baudino, Diarmuid Murphy and Jean-Philippe Svforonos (2020).

11 Independent Commission on the Future of the Cyprus Banking Sector, *Final Report and Recommendations* (October 2013) (Independent Commission (2013)), chart 2 <https://www.centralbank.cy/images/media/pdf/LSE_ICFCBS_Final_Report_10_13.pdf> accessed 30 September 2020.

12 For a detailed account see, ex multi, Alexander Michaelides, 'Cyprus: from boom to bail-in' (2014) 29 Economic Policy 639.

13 European Commission, 'Economic Adjustment Programme for Cyprus' (2013) European Economy Occasional Paper 149, 34 <http://ec.europa.eu/economy_finance/publications/occasional_paper/2013/pdf/ocp149_en.pdf> accessed 30 September 2020.

make good in the capital markets. The position of Laiki Bank was the most critical, as it had lost the ability to fund itself through domestic resources (including deposits), turning to wholesale funding[14] and, ultimately, to Emergency Liquidity Assistance ('ELA').[15] Shortly after recapitalising Laiki Bank, and with the prospect of the entire domestic banking sector collapsing, Cyprus's government applied, on 25 June 2012, to the Eurogroup President for financial assistance from the European Stability Mechanism ('ESM'), in line with Article 13(1) of the ESM Treaty.[16,17]

2.1.4 Concluding remarks

As the reader will appreciate, the case of Cyprus differs from that of Ireland.

Similar to Ireland, Cyprus was confronted with the challenge of a disproportionately large, poorly managed and inadequately supervised domestic banking sector, the liabilities of which became those of the government after the banking sector had lost the ability to fund itself on the capital markets.

However, differently from Ireland where the decisive blow to the sustainability of public finances was given by the blanket guarantee provided by the state in respect of the banks' liabilities, the case of Cyprus also provides an example of a scenario where, by the time that the domestic banking sector's problems had surfaced, the sovereign was already unable – on account of its negative credit standing – to avert the collapse of the banking sector.[18] In that sense, although the case of Cyprus demonstrates better than most the bi-directional nature of the feedback loop between banks and sovereign distress, the case of Ireland is the most cautionary of the two, as it more readily shows how a large, highly-leveraged, imprudently managed and poorly supervised banking sector is capable of causing, in and of itself, a sovereign debt crisis, making of the banking sector a fatal source of vulnerability even for a fiscally sound sovereign.

14 Cypriot banks issued a relatively low amount of bonds, worth 10% of Cypriot GDP. Instead they relied on deposit financing, necessitating the imposition of losses on its depositors once their equity was wiped out.

15 The combined borrowings of the Bank of Cyprus and Laiki Bank exceeded €11 billion.

16 In its application, Cyprus cited spillover risks from the exposure of its oversized banking sector to the Greek economy, as well as budgetary needs.

17 Treaty establishing the European Stability Mechanism of 2 February 2012 <https://www.esm.europa.eu/sites/default/files/20150203_-_esm_treaty_-_en.pdf> accessed 30 September 2020.

18 The position has been aptly summarised in the final report of the Independent Commission (2013), where it is stated that, 'the government's failure to correct Cyprus' deteriorating financial position in the 2009–2012 period … precipitated a fiscal crisis which caused it to be excluded from the international capital markets, and which left it without the resources to support its banks when they entered their critical phase in 2012' (para. 3.4.4).

2.2 Effects of sovereign crises on commercial banks

2.2.1 Introductory remarks

Commercial banks stand to see their financial position suffer in the event of a fiscal deterioration of the sovereign in the territory of which they are established, both because they often hold sovereign debt instruments on the asset side of their balance sheet, whose value may dramatically deteriorate in a sovereign debt crisis situation, and because financial markets will tend to penalise credit institutions established in the territory of a sovereign whose rating and creditworthiness are in question, given the perceived limits to its ability to support and recapitalise them, in case of urgency. The near-collapse of the Greek banking sector is a case in point, with the case of Cyprus also being instructive, even if for rather different reasons. Before turning to a brief account of the relevant aspects of these two episodes, a few words are in order on the extant literature's findings regarding the impact of sovereign crises on commercial banks.

The transmission of sovereign risk to banks' riskiness and profitability and the correlation between sovereign risk and bank stress have been confirmed by both recent research and practical experience. It is only after reports of bad news on the sustainability of public debt in Greece, Italy and Portugal in 2009 that the funding of their domestic banking sectors came under pressure, precisely because banks in those jurisdictions (also) held sovereign debt. The Committee on the Global Financial System[19] identified four channels through which sovereign risks can spill over to banks: first, a fall in the value of the government bonds held by banks; second, an increase in the funding costs of banks resulting from a deterioration in a sovereign's creditworthiness, which reduces the value of the collateral that banks can use to obtain liquidity from the central bank or from the wholesale markets; third, sovereign downgrades, which tend to be accompanied by lower ratings for commercial banks (hence, also, by an increase in their funding costs); and fourth, the effects of sovereign downgrades on the ability of the sovereign to support its banks. And, as explained by the Bank of England,[20] when banks are creditors to their governments, the impact on the banking system of sovereign crises is accentuated by the amount of public debt that banks have taken on in the run-up to a sovereign debt crisis, which reduces the ability of sovereigns to contain a banking crisis.

A particular feature of EMU countries that exacerbated the effects of the sovereign crises of some of its members was the large amount of domestic

19 Bank for International Settlements, Committee on the Global Financial System, 'The Impact of Sovereign Credit Risk on Bank Funding Conditions' (2011) Committee on the Global Financial System Paper 43 <https://www.bis.org/publ/cgfs43.pdf> accessed 30 September 2020.

20 Bank of England, *Financial Stability Report, June 2010* (2010) <https://www.bankofengland.co.uk/financial-stability-report/2010/june-2010> accessed 30 September 2020.

bonds that commercial banks held in their portfolios. Merler and Pisani-Ferry[21] have documented that the proportion of total government debt held by domestic banks stood at 30% in Germany, and at around 10% in France, Greece, Portugal, the Netherlands and Italy (the share was negligible in the case of the UK and the US). According to DeMarco and Macchiavelli,[22] at the end of 2010, the average (median) home exposure of European banks to their sovereigns stood at 74% of total sovereign debt exposure. Although EMU triggered a significant increase in cross-border bond investment within the euro area (see Lane;[23] and Waysand, Ross and de Guzman[24]), the home bias persisted even after the introduction of the euro. As explained in Chapter 1, one potential factor explaining these exposures is that holding domestic sovereign bonds, including those issued by troubled sovereigns, enabled banks to hold higher-yield instruments without having to set aside regulatory capital, as the risk weight of soverign bonds was, at the material time, and still remained at the time of writing, zero (in addition to the sources cited in Chapter 1, also see Acharya and Steffen;[25] and Korte and Steffen[26]). While a reduction in the exposure of banks to domestic debt or a change in its regulatory treatment would reduce the strength of the negative feedback loop between a government and its financial sector, it will be argued later in this work that neither would be sufficient to close the second channel of contagion.

Besides, as explained in Chapter 1 and as shown by Uhlig,[27] fiscally vulnerable governments have an incentive to encourage domestic banks to hold risky domestic bonds so that they can continue to borrow from the market (or can do so more cheaply). Battistini, Pagano and Simonelli[28] have argued that sovereign stress increases this incentive, giving rise to a correlation between rising sovereign yields and banks' holdings of domestic debt (the 'moral suasion' hypothesis). Finally, as shown by Kischenmann, Korte and Steffen, although

21 Silvia Merler and Jean Pisani-Ferry, 'Hazardous Tango: Sovereign-Bank Interdependence and Financial Stability in the Euro Area' (2012) 16 Banque de France Financial Stability Review 201.

22 De Marco and Macchiavelli (2016).

23 Philip R.R. Lane, 'The Real Effects of EMU' (2006) 20 (4) Journal of Economic Perspectives 47.

24 Claire Waysand, Kevin Ross and John De Guzman, 'European Financial Linkages: A New Look at Imbalances' (2010) International Monetary Fund Working Paper WP/10/295 <https://www.imf.org/external/pubs/ft/wp/2010/wp10295.pdf> accessed 30 September 2020.

25 Viral V. Acharya and Sasha Steffen, 'Analyzing Systemic Risk of the European Banking Sector' in Jean-Pierre Fouque and Joseph Langsam, *Handbook on Systemic Risk* (Cambridge University Press 2013).

26 Josef Korte and Sascha Steffen, 'A "Sovereign Subsidy" – Zero Risk Weights and Sovereign Risk Spillovers' (*VoxEU*, 7 September 2014) <https://voxeu.org/article/sovereign-subsidy-zero-risk-weights-and-sovereign-risk-spillovers> accessed 30 September 2020.

27 Harald Uhlig, 'Sovereign Default Risk and Banks in a Monetary Union' (2014) 15 (1) German Economic Review Special Issue: Special Issue on Government Debt in Democracies: Causes, Effects and Limits 23.

28 Niccolò Battistini, Marco Pagano and Saverio Simonelli, 'Systemic Risk, Sovereign Yields and Bank Exposures in the Euro Crisis' (2014) 29 (78) Economic Policy 203, 205.

domestic sovereign-to-banks links are at their strongest in the case of sovereigns facing fiscal challenges, sovereign-to-banks loops can also affect the banks of safer countries because of their exposure to non-domestic sovereign debt,[29] suggesting that the second channel of contagion is more pervasive and more pernicious than one may have thought, adding to the urgency of addressing it, for the sake of financial stability.

The intensity of the transmission risk from sovereigns to their banks can be even greater in the case of countries belonging to political or monetary unions devoid of 'risk sharing' mechanisms through which to tackle localised, asymmetric shocks.[30] As explained in Section 1.4, in monetary unions where countries cannot count on the central bank to finance expiring debt obligations or to issue new debt to support their banking systems, specific amplification mechanisms may operate that could exacerbate the impact of an initial shock by inducing capital flights and self-fulfilling expectations of sovereign default.[31] The case of the EU and EMU is a case in point: Articles 123 and 125 of the Treaty on the Functioning of the European Union ('the Treaty' or 'TFEU')[32] prohibit central banks from establishing 'overdraft … or any other type of credit facility … in favour of … central governments … or other public authorities' (the 'monetary financing prohibition'), and render illegal the assumption, by the Union or any of its Member States, of 'the commitments of central governments of … any Member State …' (the 'no bail-out' clause). Given the particular legal set-up of the EU and EMU, there is a heightened risk of a serious impairment of a sovereign's ability to come to the aid of its banks (e.g. by honouring a guarantee it has extended for their benefit), with a knock-on effect on the solvency of its banks, which neither their central

29 Karolin Kirschemann, Josef Korte and Sacha Steffen, 'The Zero Risk Fallacy? Banks' Sovereign Exposure and Sovereign Risk Spillovers (2017) Leibniz-Zentrum für Europäische Wirtschaftsforschung Discussion Paper 17-069 (Kirschemann et al. (2017)) <https://www.econstor.eu/bitstream/10419/172521/1/1009649329.pdf> accessed 30 September 2020.

30 See Maria Abascal, Tatiana Alonso and Sergio Mayordomo, 'Fragmentation in European Financial Markets: Measures, Determinants and Policy Solutions' (2013) Banco Bilbao Vizcaya Argentaria Working Paper 13/22 <https://www.bbvaresearch.com/KETD/fbin/mult/WP_1322_tcm348-394976.pdf> accessed 30 September 2020.

31 See also Brunnermeier et al. (2017, pp. 222-224) who links the increased risk of capital flights within a monetary union with the asymmetrical distribution of safe assets across the member state countries. The prohibition of monetary financing is not a necessary element of a monetary union (see e.g. a historical overview provided in John Ryan and John Loughlin, 'Lessons from historical monetary unions – is the European monetary union making the same mistakes?' (2018) 15 International Economics and Economic Policy 709). Jonathan Yiangou, Mícheál O'keefe and Gabriel Glöckler (2013) argue that the monetary financing prohibition was a causal factor in fostering deeper integration in the EU by constraining the feasible path of institutional development and by encouraging EU members to demonstrate policy credibility (Jonathan Yiangou, Mícheál O'keefe and Gabriel Glöckler, ''Tough love': How the ECB's monetary financing prohibition pushes deeper euro area integration' (2013) 35 Journal of European Integration 223).

32 Consolidated version of the Treaty on the Functioning of the European Union [2016] OJ C202/47.

bank nor other sovereigns can rescue, whether directly or indirectly, without breaching the TFEU's monetary financing prohibition and 'no bail-out' clause.

We explore, in the remainder of this chapter, the effects of sovereign debt crises on domestic banks, drawing on the indicative examples of Greece and Cyprus during the sovereign debt stage of the global financial crisis.

2.2.2 The case of Greece

It has aptly been observed that the 'origins of the Greek crisis were not to be found in the banking sector.'[33] From 2000 to 2007, Greece had one of the fastest-growing economies in the euro area (with an annual rate of GDP growth of 4.2%), as foreign investments and capital entered the country, largely encouraged by a sense of safety inspired by Greece's accession to the euro area.[34] However, while growth was strong, this was largely led by domestic demand, fuelled through borrowing, both public and private. At the same time, the production base did not adjust, and competitiveness declined rapidly, resulting in a deterioration of the external trade deficit. Finally, although revenue lagged behind, public spending kept increasing, leading to large current account deficits and historically high levels of public debt.[35] Greece came under severe pressure by the end of 2009, after financial markets had become weary of the credit risk posed by countries with large structural imbalances (including euro area countries, which, crucially, lacked a fiscal coordination mechanism, despite the pooling of their sovereignties in matters of monetary policy).

Consecutive sovereign debt downgrades (from A+ in September 2004 to CCC in June 2011), rising sovereign spreads, and open talk of a default on its debt, made it next to impossible for Greece to maintain access to international capital and money markets. The sovereign crisis had a knock-on effect on the Greek banking sector which, until 2009, was fundamentally healthy and profitable. The pressures that built on the banking sector were unprecedented, as reflected in the deteriorating fundamentals and asset quality ratios of Greek banks: at the start of 2010 (shortly before the Greek government requested financial support from the euro area countries and the IMF, in April 2010, and before the signing of the first Memorandum of Economic and Financial Policies, in May 2010), the

33 Yannis Stournaras, 'The Impact of the Greek Sovereign Crisis on the Banking Sector – Challenges to Financial Stability and Policy Responses by the Bank of Greece' (Keynote Speech given at the London Business School Greek Alumni Association and Stanford Club of Greece Event entitled 'Breaking the Bottlenecks – Steps Towards Sustainable Growth,' American School of Classical Studies, Athens, 8 June 2016) <https://www.bis.org/review/r160628a.pdf> accessed 30 September 2020.

34 Rebecca M. Nelson, Paul Belkin and Derek E. Mix, 'Greece's Debt Crisis: Overview, Policy Responses, and Implications' (2011) Congressional Research Service R41167 <http://www.fas.org/sgp/crs/row/R41167.pdf> accessed 30 September 2020.

35 Bank of Greece, *The Chronicle of the Great Crisis: The Bank of Greece 2008–2013 – Public Interventions and Institutional Actions to Safeguard Financial Stability and Overcome the Crisis* (2014) <http://www.bankofgreece.gr/BogEkdoseis/Selections%20from%20The%20Chronicle%20of%20the%20great%20crisis%20-%20the%20Bank%20of%20Greece%202008-2013.pdf> accessed 30 September 2020.

Greek banking sector already required capital of €23 billion, while its exposure to GGBs stood at €61 billion. As a result of the March 2012 Greek PSI, Greek banks suffered losses of around €38 billion, or 170% of their total Common Equity Tier 1 ('CET1') capital at the material time. Due to the liquidity squeeze, banks were no longer able to perform their intermediation role, severely restricting the financing of the real economy. In addition, deposits declined by €117 billion between September 2009 and December 2015 (a drop of 44%). This decline can be mainly attributed to depositor uncertainty regarding the prospect of Greece remaining in the euro area, but it was also symptomatic of the negative loan growth throughout that period. The significant deleveraging that Greek banks undertook[36] was partly a response to tight funding conditions and partly a consequence of the need to set aside more capital since the potential for contingencies rose considerably. As a consequence, it became even more difficult for Greek banks to play their role in financing the real economy. The considerable decline in household disposable income, a consequence of wage and pension cuts, tax hikes and rising unemployment, resulted in a significant increase of NPLs and impairments, undermining bank profitability. Despite efforts to support profitability by reducing costs, the high level of loan loss provisions resulted in a series of loss-making results right up to the first quarter of 2016, following which they slowly started returning to profitability.

2.2.3 The case of Cyprus

The case of Cyprus is somewhat peculiar. Although the Cypriot banking sector was (also) heavily exposed to sovereign risk in the run-up to the outbreak of the Cypriot sovereign debt crisis, it is GGBs rather than Cypriot sovereign debt instruments that Cypriot banks mostly held on their balance sheets. At the time of its near implosion, the Cypriot banking sector's exposure to GGBs stood at €5.7 billion, or one-third of Cyprus's GDP, which the Independent Commission on the Future of the Cypriot Banking Sector deemed to have been 'inappropriate and ultimately fatal.'[37]

Although it was the marked deterioration of a foreign sovereign that was to seal the fate of Cypriot banks, the poor state of the Cypriot sovereign itself conspired to make the crisis within the Cypriot banking sector unmanageable. The available evidence pointed towards a progressive and significant deterioration in all leading economic performance indicators in the period since around the time of Cyprus's accession to the euro area in January 2008.[38] Cyprus's difficulties were, at least to an extent, linked to the excessive growth of its

36 It is telling that between end-2010 and end-2015, loans to the private sector fell by €54 billion.

37 See Independent Commission (2013).

38 Gikas A. Hardouvelis, 'Overcoming the Crisis in Cyprus' (2014) 9 (1) Eurobank Research 225; Central Bank of Cyprus, *Annual Report* (2013) <https://www.centralbank.cy/images/media/pdf_el/CBC_2013_AR_GR_interactive.pdf> accessed 30 September 2020.

banking sector (partly fuelled through foreign deposits) and the credit boom (and private-sector indebtedness) that this contributed to. The credit boom fed domestic demand, leading to a rapid increase in the current account deficit. The global economic and financial crisis was to abruptly put an end to the lending boom, but it was to also cause losses for Cypriot banks, as their private-sector lenders started falling behind with their debt servicing obligations. In the period between 2008 and 2013, GDP slowed and, finally, contracted,[39] while Cyprus's debt-to-GDP[40] and unemployment ratios[41] also grew constantly and considerably. A combination of fiscal mismanagement (reflected in a very substantial increase in public spending, from 35% of GDP in the 1990s to almost 50% in 2012), declining competitiveness (which precluded Cyprus from generating the growth and revenue necessary to meet its debt obligations), continuous downgrades of Cyprus's sovereign ratings (which, already in May 2011, made it impossible for it to raise funds through the issuance and sale of government bonds in the international capital markets) and the onset of the financial crisis (which exposed or aggravated the vulnerabilities of an oversized, poorly managed and inadequately supervised banking sector, generating new and substantial liabilities for Cyprus in its effort to prop-up its banks) were largely to blame for Cyprus's predicament in the run-up to its sovereign debt crisis.[42] The available evidence also suggests that lower borrowing rates (partly attributable to Cyprus's adoption of the single currency and the associated perception of Cyprus as a credit-worthy borrower) allowed Cyprus to run higher current account and budget deficits, which inflated its economy, leading to a substantial credit expansion and, notably, to a housing bubble. It is telling that Cyprus moved from a budget surplus of around 3.5% of GDP in 2007 (or €538 million) to a budget deficit of 5.4% of GDP in 2013 (or €897 million), while bank lending increased considerably over the 2008–2011 period, before decelerating sharply as of 2012.

By the time Cypriot banks came under pressure, Cyprus had lost access to international capital markets, and turned to Russia for a €2.5 billion emergency loan. When, by mid-2012 – following the Greek PSI and the €4.5

39 The contraction has been dramatic: from 0.8% in the first two quarters of 2008 to −7.7% in the last quarter of 2013.

40 The progression was from around 48% in December 2008 to 86.6% in December 2012 and 111.5% in December 2013.

41 The rise in unemployment has been substantial: from 4.9% in 2008 to 7.9% in 2011 and 15.7% in the first two quarters of 2013.

42 The reader is referred to the findings of the Independent Commission on the Future of the Cypriot Banking Sector, *Interim Report* (June 2013) <https://www.centralbank.cy/images/media/pdf/ICFCBSInterimReport_EN.pdf> accessed 30 September 2020; Triparty Committee, *Report of the Investigation Committee on the State of the Cypriot Banking System and the Cypriot Economy* (2013) <http://www.sigmalive.com/uploads/default/files/porisma_erevnitikis_epitropis_piki.pdf> accessed 30 September 2020; and Parliamentary Committee on Institutions and Commissioner for Administration, *The Operation of the Cypriot Financial Sector Institutions, Joint Report* (May 2014), available on the website of the Cypriot House of Representatives.

billion 'haircut' it entailed for the GGB holdings of the Bank of Cyprus and Laiki Bank – the Cypriot government had to bail-out Laiki Bank, the second-largest bank in Cyprus, it was only able to do so through a €1.8 billion capital injection funded through an un-funded government bond.[43] Shortly afterwards, Cyprus was to turn to its EU partners and the IMF for financial assistance, conditional on the prior restructuring and resolution of its domestic banking sector. In March 2013, Cyprus's two largest commercial banks were resolved and/or restructured by folding Laiki Bank into the Bank of Cyprus, and by using 47.5% of the Bank of Cyprus's uninsured deposits (i.e. those over €100,000) to rebuild the capital of the Bank of Cyprus. For the first time since the inception of the euro area, uninsured depositors were called upon to bear the burden of a bank recapitalisation.[44] The Hellenic Bank, Cyprus's third-largest commercial bank and Cyprus's entire co-operative banking sector, were recapitalised out of public funds, to the tune of approximately €2 billion, to cover bad loans.

2.2.4 Conclusions

Both the Greek and the Cypriot banking sector crises illustrate how banking sector exposure to sovereign risk (through sovereign debt holdings) is apt to amplify the transmission of sovereign stress to domestic lenders, increasing banks' risk of default and, correspondingly, their funding costs, and forcing those that are the most exposed to sovereign debt to deleverage.

43 In an opinion issued in the matter of the recapitalisation of Laiki Bank, the Governing Council of the ECB noted that, 'in the absence of any alternative market-based funding sources for recapitalisation bonds,..., the acceptance of the bonds used for the recapitalisation as collateral could amount to a circumvention of the prohibition on direct purchases of debt instruments from central governments by the central bank' (see European Central Bank, 'Opinion of the European Central Bank of 2 July 2012 on the Recapitalisation of the Cyprus Popular Bank' CON/2012/50 (ECB (2012)), para. 3.2.2).

44 On 15 March 2013, the Eurogroup had controversially agreed on an 'upfront one-off stability levy applicable to resident and non-resident depositors,' covering insured and uninsured deposits alike. On 25 March, following widespread opposition to the proposed bank levy and the Cypriot Parliament's unanimous rejection, on 19 March, of draft legislation implementing it, the Eurogroup revisited its earlier decision, declaring the inviolability of insured deposits, but making the granting of financial support to Cyprus dependent on the prior recapitalisation and resolution of the Bank of Cyprus and Laiki Bank without use of public funds. To implement the second Eurogroup decision, the Central Bank of Cyprus, in its capacity as bank resolution authority, issued a number of resolution decrees, on the basis of powers conferred upon it under Cyprus's Resolution of Credit and other Financial Institutions Law of 22 March 2013. The Central Bank of Cyprus decrees mandated inter alia deposit haircuts (for uninsured deposits in Laiki Bank), deposit freezes (for uninsured deposits in the Bank of Cyprus), as well as the sale of some of the two banks' business. As a result, Cyprus reached an agreement on a comprehensive adjustment programme with its European partners and the IMF in March 2013. The programme's three objectives included stabilising and downsizing the banking sector, consolidating public finances, and strengthening competitiveness and economic growth through structural reforms.

Where the case of Cyprus differs from that of Greece is that whereas the Greek banking sector's sovereign exposure was to domestic sovereign debt, that of the Cypriot banking sector was to foreign (i.e. Greek) rather than to own (i.e. Cypriot) sovereign debt instruments. This paradox – which is to be explained by reference to the higher yields of GGBs, which made them a more attractive investment for Cypriot banks, and to the fact that the amount of Greek sovereign debt greatly exceeded that of Cypriot debt, making it more readily available in the market than its Cypriot equivalent – does not detract from the main commonality of the Greek and Cypriot banking sector crises: both were by-products of the dire budgetary situation of a sovereign (Greece), and of the inability of another sovereign (Cyprus) to stand by its banks at their time of need, on account of its budgetary weakness.

3 An economic analysis of policy options

3.1 Introductory remarks

The aim of this chapter is to provide an analysis of the economic arguments underlying the various policy options so far proposed in the academic literature and in policy discussions that aim to break the sovereign–banks loop. By way of introduction, we explore why fiscal rules represent the first line of defence against the first channel of contagion (i.e. the one moving from sovereigns to banks) but also why fiscal rules alone are not sufficient to close this channel of contagion. The focus of the analysis then shifts towards the European Banking Union, the EU's main policy response against the second channel of contagion (i.e. the one moving from banks to sovereigns). The economic arguments behind the European Banking Union are analysed, and the missing blocks and complementarities with other policies are discussed. The last – and largest – part of this chapter investigates the main policy options so far considered to address the channel of contagion moving from sovereigns to banks and, specifically, the revision of the regulatory treatment of sovereign debt, the creation of safe assets and the issuance of Eurobonds.

3.2 Fiscal policy and why fiscal measures may not be sufficient

Fiscal policy represents the main stabilisation policy tool available to countries participating in a currency union, as neither monetary policy nor exchange rate adjustments are available to them. During boom periods, governments are expected to prioritise debt sustainability so that fiscal space is available, switching to 'fiscal activism' when the economy is hit by a shock leading to an elevated risk of a recession.[1] Until the outbreak of the financial crisis, a rules-based

1 On the counter-cyclicality of fiscal policies, see, for example, Wyplosz and the literature therein (Charles Wyplosz, 'Fiscal Policy: Institutions versus Rules' (2005) *191 National Institute Economic Review* 64).

framework for promoting sound fiscal policies had been the primary approach through which to address the sovereign-banks contagion channel.[2]

The limited degree of freedom available to national economic policy for stabilisation and for achieving adjustments in the face of shocks represents a cost of participation in a monetary union. This cost is, however, outweighed by the significant economic and political benefits of participation in a monetary union. The economic benefits relate specifically to avoiding exchange rate volatility,[3] price stability, free trade in a market far larger than the domestic one,[4] and easier access to capital, labour and knowledge.[5] Purely economic considerations aside, a monetary union was also viewed as a necessary step towards a long term vision of a political union[6] (even if the link between the

2 In the case of a sovereign debt crisis, the main policy available to countries within a monetary union is internal devaluation (i.e. a fall in wages and prices), as monetary policy and exchange rate adjustments are no longer available nationally. For a detailed analysis, see Markus Brunnermeier, Harold James, Jean-Pierre Landau, *The Euro and the Battle of Ideas* (Princeton University Press 2016) (Brunnermeier et al. (2016)).

3 A strand in the literature of international economics examines the dichotomy of flexible versus fixed exchange rates (for a recent contribution in this debate, see, for example, Dominik Groll and Tommaso Monacelli, 'The Inherent Benefit of Monetary Unions' (2020) 111 *Journal of Monetary Economics* 63). Although this literature is inconclusive, it could be noted that, in it, the various 'frictions' relating to regulation, trade and mobility of factors of production are not well accounted for, as usually frictionless economic transactions are assumed. In addition, diversification benefits from pooling resources or policy cooperation are not considered. Even within this analytical framework, which would inherently tend to underestimate significantly the benefits of the monetary union, it is not clear that flexible exchange regimes are optimal.

4 Mongelli reviews the arguments of the Optimum Currency Area theory and its further development. In particular, he argues that endogenous market-based forces (or other forces due to the commitment represented by monetary integration) could operate after the introduction of a common currency and lead to enhanced integration of a geographical area, which, before the common currency's introduction, did not fulfil the criteria of an Optimum Currency Area (Francesco Mongelli, 'European Economic and Monetary Integration and the Optimum Currency Area Theory' (2008) *European Commission Economic Paper* 302 <https://ec.europa.eu/economy_finance/publications/pages/publication12081_en.pdf> accessed 30 September 2020).

5 Thygesen places these considerations in a historical context that led to the decision to move towards a single currency (Niels Thygesen, 'Why Did Europe Decide to Move to a Single Currency 25 Years Ago?' (2016) 1 *Intereconomics* 11). For a political economy perspective, see also Miguel Otero-Iglesias, 'Explaining the Resilience of the Euro: What the Political Economy Says' in Ognian Hishow, Miguel Otero-Iglesias, Federico Steinberg and Paweł Tokarski (eds), 'The Euro Paradox: Explaining the Resilience of the Single Currency' (2018) *German Institute for International and Security Affairs Working Paper* 1 <https://www.swp-berlin.org/fileadmin/contents/products/arbeitspapiere/AP_012018_EuroParadox_Tokarski.pdf> accessed 30 September 2020.

6 French President Jacques Chirac is quoted to have stated in 1996 that '[B]ehind the single currency was the entire political project that France and Germany have together for Europe and which was at stake' (quoted in Francis Snyder, 'EMU Revisited: Are We Making a Constitution? What Constitution Are We Making?' (1998) *European University Institute Working Paper* 98/6 (Snyder (1998)), 33 <https://www.peacepalacelibrary.nl/ebooks/files/BS-EMUWOR-FS.pdf> accessed 30 September 2020). Snyder reviews the discussion on the political aims of the monetary union just before the introduction of the euro (Snyder (1998), 31 *ff.*).

two has been debated).[7] The Maastricht Treaty of 1993 linked intrinsically the common currency with the European integration project, the origins of which are to be traced back to the determination of Western Europe's nations to promote peace in the European continent in the aftermath of World War II. Despite the fact that the 2010s had been rife with crisis episodes, the protracted economic recession in certain EU countries, highly polarised mass media coverage of the crisis management responses and the emergence of Eurosceptic parties across the Union, the public acceptance of the euro remained, at the time of writing, at record-high levels.[8] In this overall context, it would be difficult to deny that the common currency also carries great political significance, apart from the purely economic benefits it brings.[9]

Early on in the process of European integration, even before the common currency was launched, it was recognised that a fiscal rules framework should

7 In this vein, Habermas starts from the joint reference in the Lisbon Treaty to both the 'citizens' and the 'states' of Europe as the constituting subjects of the EU, and argues that during the unification process, involving also monetary integration, the balance gradually shifts from the states to the citizens as the area of European public interest is enlarged (Jürgen Habermas, 'The Crisis of the European Union in the Light of the Constitutionalization of International Law' (2012) 23 *European Journal of International Law* 335, 342 *ff.*). In this line reasoning, monetary integration represents a step towards political integration. Issing formulates the opposing view, according to which monetary integration reaches its limit on fiscal sovereignty, which is legitimised politically only at the national level (Otmar Issing, 'On the Relation of Monetary and Political Union' (2016) 1 *Intereconomics* 16).

8 According to the Eurobarometer survey of November 2019 (the one closest to the completion of the manuscript), 76% of respondents considered the single currency as good for the EU. In addition, 65% thought the euro is good for their country (a record figure). Although these figures also show that a significant segment of the public opinion remains sceptical about the single currency, the notion of a 'top-down' imposition of the euro by the European elites does not appear to accurately depict reality.

9 Several studies have analysed Eurobarometer data to infer European public opinion trends regarding monetary integration, especially during the crisis period. There is empirical evidence to suggest that, during the euro area crisis, support for the euro became more tightly linked to the EU's perceived institutional effectiveness and to the public's assessment of the benefits of European integration, and less so to identity factors (Sarah B. Hobolt and Christopher Wratil, 'Public Opinion and the Crisis: The Dynamics of Support for the Euro' (2015) 22 *Journal of European Public Policy* 238). This study shows that, contrary to popular accounts, even if the crisis exposed weaknesses in the common currency's institutional framework, support for the euro did not decrease, and identity-based considerations diminished in importance. Armingeon, Guthmann and Weisstanner emphasise the risk to political legitimacy (at the national and European level alike) due to the loss of national policy space following the common currency's introduction (Klaus Armingeon, Kai Guthmann and David Weisstanner, 'How the Euro Divides the Union: The Effect of Economic Adjustment on Support for Democracy in Europe' (2016) 14 *Socio-Economic Review*). Even if this study is concerned with the effects of monetary integration, it is more concerned with public perceptions of the effectiveness of democracy, rather than with support for the euro. Gros and Roth explore the public support for the euro in Germany during the most intense phase of the crisis, concluding that, if *trust* in the euro has declined, *support* for the common currency has not (Daniel Gros and Felix Roth, 'Do Germans Support the Euro?' (Centre for European Policy Studies, 15 December 2011) <https://www.ceps.eu/ceps-publications/do-germans-support-euro/> accessed 30 September 2020). Overall, it seems fair to conclude that, despite the deteriorating economic conditions in several countries during the last decade, support for the euro has remained surprisingly resilient.

be established, to ensure that countries pursue sound fiscal policies. The aim of the fiscal policy framework was to ensure that countries within the monetary union do not find themselves in distress when refinancing their debt (an event that the institutional framework of the EU and EMU were unprepared for). In addition, the strong economic interdependencies of the European economies, which would lead to cross-border spillovers in case credit risk materialised in one country, and the aim of preserving the centralised conduct of monetary policy was also seen as a reason for the creation of a framework through which to ensure that the participating Member States would internalise the externalities of their fiscal stance.

Specifically, the risk was recognised of an excessively expansionary fiscal policy that would put pressure on other countries participating to the monetary union to provide financial assistance or would constrain the central bank's monetary policy.[10,11] A framework of fiscal rules could also be considered as a pre-emptive means to address the risk posed by the sovereign–banks nexus, aiming to prevent the occurrence of a crisis that would activate the feedback loop.[12]

Since 1998, the supranational fiscal rules framework in the EU has been based on the Stability and Growth Pact ('SGP'), which represents the main

10 For example, a tightening of monetary policy could amplify a difficult budgetary situation in a country, turning it into a crisis. The impact of the fiscal situation on monetary policy is termed 'fiscal dominance' (see Isabel Schnabel, 'The Shadow of Fiscal Dominance: Misconceptions, Perceptions and Perspectives' (Speech at the Centre for European Reform and the Eurofi Financial Forum on 'Is the Current ECB Monetary Policy Doing More Harm than Good and What Are the Alternatives?' 11 September 2020) <https://www.ecb.europa.eu/press/key/date/2020/html/ecb.sp200911~ea32bd8bb3.en.html> accessed 30 September 2020). There are, also, other forms of cross-border spillovers of fiscal policy, which, however, are considered to be less important, and which do not, currently, affect the Union's institutional framework. For example, the idea that increased fiscal expenditure in a large euro area country may increase demand for exports from other euro area members or vice versa was discussed during the crisis (see, for example, Luc Eyraud, Vitor Gaspar and Tigran Poghosyan, 'Fiscal Politics in the Euro Area' (2018) *International Monetary Fund Working Paper* 17/18 <https://www.imf.org/en/Publications/WP/Issues/2017/01/30/Fiscal-Politics-in-the-Euro-Area-44601> accessed 30 September 2020).

11 See European Commission, 'One Market, One Money – An Evaluation of the Potential Benefits and Costs of Forming an Economic and Monetary Union' (1990) 44 *European Economy* 9, 101 *ff.* <https://ec.europa.eu/economy_finance/publications/pages/publication7454_en.pdf> accessed 30 September 2020.

12 Market forces were not trusted to bring budgetary discipline, as clearly stated in the report of the Committee for the Study of Economic and Monetary Union (Committee for the Study of Economic and Monetary Union, *Report on Economic and Monetary Union in the European Community* (1989) (Delors Committee (1989)), 20 <https://ec.europa.eu/economy_finance/publications/pages/publication6161_en.pdf> accessed 30 September 2020): '[R]ather than leading to a gradual adaptation of borrowing costs, market views about the creditworthiness of official borrowers tend to change abruptly and result in the closure of access to market financing. The constraints imposed by market forces might either be too slow and weak or too sudden and disruptive.'

constraint on national fiscal policies.[13] Specifically, the 3% and 60% thresholds for the budget deficit and sovereign debt, respectively, represent, since then, the main quantitative limits enshrined in the preventive arm of the SGP. The SGP rules[14] target these 'headline' measures of a country's fiscal stance, representing the main determinants of its ability to access the markets. It can be argued that some components of the budget deficit (and consequently of overall debt) do not lead to spillovers in other countries, e.g. pension policy, employment insurance policy, etc. These components reflect 'social contract' elements within each country. The logic behind the SGP approach was that what matters at the Union level are only the headline figures affecting sovereign creditworthiness rather than the various components of deficit and debt.[15] The SGP was also complemented by the Macroeconomic Imbalances Procedure, which monitors a wider set of imbalances that can also ignite a crisis when combined with high debt levels.[16]

The year-long (mis)application of the fiscal framework and the ensuing sovereign debt crisis exposed the framework's limitations. To start with, early into the existence of the SGP framework, enforcing its rules proved problematic, with some critics having emphasised the pro-cyclical features of its design.[17]

13 The SGP was introduced just before the common currency, as envisaged by 'Stage 3' of the Delors Report (Delors Committee (1989)), which proposed the concrete steps for achieving a monetary union. The preventive arm of the SGP entered into force in 1998, while the corrective arm in the following year. The former focuses on monitoring fiscal policies and seeks to preventing the building of imbalances while the latter addresses excessive imbalances through the Excessive Deficit Procedure.

14 Given the non-binding nature of its rules, the SGP could more accurately be labelled as featuring 'rule-bound discretion' (for an overview summarising the discussion during the early years of the SGP, see Martin Heipertz, 'The Stability and Growth Pact – Not the Best but Better than Nothing. Reviewing the Debate on Fiscal Policy in Europe's Monetary Union' (2003) *Max Planck Institute for the Study of Societies Working Paper* 03/10 <https://www.mpifg.de/pu/workpap/wp03-10/wp03-10.html> accessed 30 September 2020).

15 A caveat here is that parts of fiscal policy (and especially tax policy, which is not coordinated) may have direct cross-border (spillover) effects to other countries of the monetary union, e.g. in the form of tax competition, leading to a loss of revenues.

16 As noted by Baldwin et al., the high level of sovereign debt proved to be a crisis predictor only for Greece while, for example, Belgium and Italy, which entered the crisis with debt-to-GDP ratios exceeding 100%, did not face a sovereign debt crisis (Richard Baldwin et al., 'Rebooting the Eurozone: Step 1 – Agreeing a Crisis Narrative' (*VoxEU*, 20 November 2015) <https://voxeu.org/article/ez-crisis-consensus-narrative> accessed 30 September 2020).

17 This negative consensus assessment has been informed by the cases of France and Germany during 2003 (where the SGP rules were not enforced) and by the subsequent inability of the framework to avert the fiscal derailing of Greece between 2001 and 2009. Larch and Santacrose provide empirical evidence that the deficit rule was to a large extent not binding during the pre-crisis period, even if the debt-to-GDP was at relatively high levels, as high nominal GDP growth prevailed during these years, and this was interpreted as confirming a path towards debt reduction (Martin Larch and Stefano Santacrose, 'Numerical Compliance with the EU Fiscal Rules: The Compliance Database of the Secretariat of the European Fiscal Board' (2020) <https://ec.europa.eu/info/sites/info/files/numerical_compliance_with_eu_fiscal_rules_en_3.pdf> accessed 30 September 2020). Econometric

A promising direction taken in various proposals for the SGP framework's reform was to focus on the components that fall under the direct control of the government (e.g. most of the expenditure side of the budget), rather than on the overall deficit, which can also be impacted by highly cyclical components, especially on the revenue side.[18]

Even if ensuring sound fiscal balances should be the first line of defence against the risk of financial instability, there are several reasons why, in the particular context of a currency union, to focus solely on fiscal rules is not sufficient to address the contagion risk arising from the sovereign-banks feedback loop. First, even if considerably improved compared to what it had been pre-crisis,[19] the fiscal framework cannot address all sources of systemic risk, especially those apt to put a large strain on public finances. Second, as explained in Section 1.4.6, there are structural reasons why sovereign debt risks may abruptly rise in countries participating in a monetary union due to external shocks. These reasons include uncertainty about any liquidity support that the central bank may provide[20] and the easy investor access to safer debt denominated in the same currency. Third, fiscal adjustment within a monetary union tends to be a more protracted process, as countries need to implement internal devaluation[21] and cannot be assisted in their efforts by monetary policy tools such as an exchange rate adjustment. What aggravates the predicament of troubled sovereigns especially within a currency union is

---

studies on enforcement use a large sample and do not confine themselves to the exceptional cases referred to above, nor do they always reach pessimistic conclusions. For instance, Jong and Gilbert provide evidence that the corrective arm has been effective in promoting fiscal consolidation (Jasper De Jong and Niels Gilbert, 'Fiscal Discipline in the EMU? Testing the Effectiveness of the Excessive Deficit Procedure' (2018) *De Nederlandsche Bank Working Paper* 607 <https://ideas.repec.org/p/dnb/dnbwpp/607.html> accessed 30 September 2020).

18 See, for example, German Council of Economic Experts, *Annual Report 2017–18* (2017) <https://www.sachverstaendigenrat-wirtschaft.de/en/publications/annual-reports/previous-annual-reports/annual-report-201718.html> accessed 30 September 2020; and Agnès Bénassy-Quéré et al., 'Reconciling Risk Sharing with Market Discipline: A Constructive Approach to Euro Area Reform' (*VoxEU*, 17 January 2018) (Bénassy-Quéré et al. (2018)) <https://voxeu.org/article/how-reconcile-risk-sharing-and-market-discipline-euro-area> accessed 30 September 2020.

19 The set of improvements include a redirection of the monitoring framework towards the debt-to-GDP ratio and long-term debt sustainability (as opposed to the emphasis on annual deficits featuring during the pre-crisis period), involving also the possibility of sanctions at an earlier stage of the fiscal surveillance process (the 'Six Pack' reform introduced in 2011, applicable to all EU countries). In addition, the 'Two Pack' regulations introduced in 2013 further specified a more stringent framework for the euro area countries, due to the increased interdependence of these economies compared to the other EU member states.

20 Uncertainty about central bank support is elevated in the presence of a monetary financing prohibition and of a supranational central bank that is independent of national governments.

21 Internal devaluation consists of a combination of expenditure (including wage) cuts and tax hikes. The aim is to generate financial resources for countries facing financing constraints e.g. to help refinance their sovereign debt and to increase external competitiveness.

the interplay between the second and the third factors, as the implementation of internal devaluation is bound to hit economic activity, stoking further uncertainty across financial markets with regard to the creditworthiness of the troubled sovereign.[22]

Besides, the SGP framework introduced in the euro area does not consider explicitly the linkage between banks and governments. This could be justified by arguing that fiscal discipline at the government level would ensure that the sovereign–banks nexus would not be triggered, as the sovereigns would always have sufficient fiscal policy space to withstand economic shocks. As it turned out, however, imbalances were built and contagion channels also operated through the banking system.[23]

The increased fragility of sovereign debt creditworthiness for the countries participating in a monetary union could lead to situations where the risk of soverign default is transmitted by market sentiment and is decoupled from national economic fundamentals. The strand of economic literature concerned with so-called 'multiple equilibria' explores situations where the same 'fundamentals,' such as sovereign–debt sustainability, could give rise to multiple outcomes, i.e. sovereign default or its exact opposite. The seminal work of Calvo[24] showed that market expectations may undermine debt sustainability.[25] The reference here and in Section 1.4 is to self-reinforcing mechanisms, whereby market perceptions, e.g. related to the crisis management capacity and political willingness within the EU, drive debt sustainability for a given fiscal position. Such mechanisms can either lead to the overshooting of sovereign risk compared to the impact that would correspond to the size of an initial trigger (e.g. a worsening of macroeconomic fundamentals in a country due to fiscal policy decisions) or, alternatively, generate an increase in sovereign risk without a change in the underlying macroeconomic policy. The insights that this literature provides are especially important for countries within a monetary union, as the trade-offs facing governments that share a currency are more limited compared to those of the government of a country that can count on central bank liquidity support or exchange rate adjustment. Specifically, the

22 As further elaborated in De Grauwe (2011) and Brunnermeier et al. (2016).

23 For an analysis of the capital flows (channelled, to a large extent, through the banking system) that lead to unsustainable booms in various euro area countries, see, for example, Philip R. Lane, 'Capital Flows in the Euro Area' (2013) *European Economy Economic Paper* 497 <https://ec.europa.eu/economy_finance/publications/economic_paper/2013/pdf/ecp497_en.pdf> accessed 30 September 2020. Gourinchas, Philippon and Vayanos document the capital flows fuelling the credit growth in the Greek economy prior to the crisis and the 'sudden stop' that ensued when the crisis hit (Pierre-Olivier Gourinchas, Thomas Philippon and Dimitri Vayanos, 'The Analytics of the Greek Crisis' (2016) *National Bureau of Economic Research Working Paper* 22370 <https://www.nber.org/papers/w22370> accessed 30 September 2020).

24 Guillermo A. Calvo, 'Servicing the Public Debt: The Role of Expectations' (1988) 78 (4) *American Economic Review* 647.

25 For additional literature on multiple equilibria please see Note 121 on p 40.

government of a country participating in a monetary union has to weigh the costs of an internal devaluation (with the concomitant social cost) against the cost of a default.[26] Therefore, self-fulfilling expectations can dominate, with the expectations of creditors about the final outcome also determining the final outcome itself.[27]

The foregoing discussion does not deny the critical role of fiscal policy in addressing the risk of contagion arising from the sovereign–banks nexus. Nor does it call into question the objective importance of implementing a rules-based fiscal discipline framework in the euro area, whether from a conceptual or from a political perspective. Similarly, it is acknowledged that sound fiscal policies may have a pre-emptive role to play in averting crises. At the same time, there are a number of reasons why focusing only on fiscal policy may not be sufficient to avert the fallout of the sovereign–banks nexus, especially in the context of a monetary union such as the EMU. The fact that, apart from Greece, no other euro-area country that required financial assistance entered the crisis with an amount of debt that could be considered excessive provides a stark warning of the importance of looking beyond fiscal policy to address the contagion arising from the sovereign–banks nexus.

3.3 Closing the first channel of contagion from banks to sovereigns: Is the European Banking Union an optimal policy response?

The setting up of a European Banking Union constitutes the primary institutional response of the EU to the crisis that hit various European countries in the aftermath of the global financial crisis that originated in the US in 2007. The European Banking Union aims to strengthen the banking system and break the first channel of contagion (from banks to sovereigns) while also rendering monetary policy more effective. Specifically, the Five Presidents' Report[28] states that 'in a monetary union, the financial system must be truly single' and

26 The widely acclaimed success of the "whatever it takes" speech by Mario Draghi in 2012 can be interpreted within this analytical framework of multiple equilibria and shifting market expectations, as it was soon followed by a de-escalation in the sovereign yield spreads of Italy and Spain that could not be explained by a corresponding change in their fundamentals. Roberto de Santis estimates a measure of redenomination risk and finds that it reached a peak just before Draghi's speech while decreasing significantly after the technical details of the OMT programme were announced by the ECB (Roberto de Santis, 'Redenomination risk' (2018) 51 Journal of Money, Credit and Banking 2173).

27 The potential for informational contagion across countries is another relevant mechanism that could lead to elevated sovereign debt risk without a change in economic fundamentals, merely on account of bad news for other 'similar' countries. See, for example, Benzoni et al. (2015).

28 European Commission, The President, Jean-Claude Juncker, in close cooperation with Donald Tusk, Jeroen Dijsselbloem, Mario Draghi and Martin Schulz, *Completing Europe's Economic and Monetary Union* (2015) (Juncker et al. (2015)) <https://ec.europa.eu/commission/sites/beta-political/files/5-presidents-report_en.pdf> accessed 30 September 2020.

that 'a single banking system is the mirror image of single money.' The report proposes the completion of the European Banking Union in order to ensure the uniform transmission of monetary policy across Member States, instil the same level of confidence in money (in particular deposits) held throughout the monetary union and also break the negative feedback loop between banks and sovereigns. The official documents on the setting-up of the European Banking Union constantly point to the aim of disentangling the materialisation of banks' risks from sovereign distress,[29] testifying to the intrinsic link between the creation of the European Banking Union and the policy aim of breaking the sovereign–banks nexus. Indeed, the background to the setting-up of the European Banking Union is the coupling between the realisation of risks in the banking system and sovereign distress, and the contagion across Member States that this may lead to.[30]

As elaborated in Section 4.1, the European Banking Union consists of three pillars. The first pillar is the SSM, which seeks to ensure the application of common supervisory policies and practices to all systemically important banks and the further harmonisation of the regulatory practices applied to the smaller banks. The second pillar is the Single Resolution Mechanism ('SRM'), managing a Single Resolution Fund ('SRF'), the aim of which is to ensure an orderly resolution of failing banks. The third pillar is a common deposit insurance, which would significantly de-link the public guarantees on banks' deposits from the fiscal position of the guarantor state.[31] The fact that these three

29 See Council Regulation (EU) 1024/2013 of 15 October 2013 conferring specific tasks on the European Central Bank concerning policies relating to the prudential supervision of credit institutions [2013] OJ L287/63; and Regulation (EU) 1022/2013 of the European Parliament and of the Council of 22 October 2013 amending Regulation (EU) 1093/2010 establishing a European Supervisory Authority (European Banking Authority) as regards the conferral of specific tasks on the European Central Bank pursuant to Council Regulation (EU) 1024/2013 [2013] OJ L287/5. For example, Council Regulation (EU) 1024/2013 starts by stating that '[T]oday, the solidity of the banking sector is in many instances still closely linked to the Member State in which they are established' and that, 'developments in one Member State can create risks for economic development and the stability of the euro area as a whole.' See also Benoît Cœuré, 'Why the Euro Needs a Banking Union' (Speech at the Conference 'Bank Funding – Markets, Instruments and Implications for Corporate Lending and the Real Economy,' Frankfurt am Main, 8 October 2012) (Cœuré (2012)) <https://www.ecb.europa.eu/press/key/date/2012/html/sp121008_1.en.html> accessed 30 September 2020, representing a policy maker's perspective on the rationale for establishing a European Banking Union during the peak of the crisis.

30 A complementary policy initiative is the strengthening of a Capital Markets Union with the aim of enhancing private risk sharing and diversification in the financial system (see, for example, German Council of Economic Experts, *Annual Report 2018–19* (2018) (GCEE (2018)), Ch. 5 <https://www.sachverstaendigenrat-wirtschaft.de/en/media/annual-report-201819.html> accessed 30 September 2020).

31 Two early formulations of the three-pronged structure for the European Banking Union are José Manuel Barroso, 'State of the Union 2012 Address' (Speech at the Plenary session of the European Parliament, Strasbourg, 12 September 2012) <https://ec.europa.eu/commission/presscorner/detail/en/SPEECH_12_596> accessed 30 September 2020; and Cœuré (2012).

elements are currently in different stages of completion means that the full benefits of the European Banking Union have yet to be reaped.

The study by Farhi and Tirole[32] represents a critical tool for structuring the discussion about the European Banking Union and for linking the rationale for a banking union with the risk of spillovers across the euro area. For the purpose of our discussion of the Farhi and Tirole study, the focus of our attention will be on the first and the second pillars of the European Banking Union, i.e. the centralisation of banking supervision, under the SSM, and the orderly resolution of ailing banks, including potential support for them via a centralised fund, under the SRM/SRF.[33] The Farhi and Tirole study shows that, under certain conditions, the centralisation of banking supervision combined with commitments for banking support can be viewed as an optimal policy response within a monetary union, as it sets aligned and welfare-enhancing incentives for supervisors, sovereigns and banks alike. These authors present a theoretical model to illustrate two mechanisms that are at work when supervision within a monetary union is national, and how these mechanisms could lead to lax national supervision and excessive risk-taking by banks. The model considers the banking system of a country ('domestic' and 'foreign' are henceforth used with respect to that country) that issues debt held partially by foreign creditors and partially by domestic banks. The model considers the incentives of the sovereign, of domestic banks, of real economy agents in the country (consumers and firms) and of the foreign creditors of the sovereign. The underlying assumption is that the sovereign has an incentive to bail out its banks in order to avoid a shrinking of credit in the domestic economy (it is assumed that a bank failure would substantially disrupt the economy and, as a result, governments would favour a bank bail-out, however much it may place more weight on the welfare of real economy agents compared to that of bankers).[34] Knowing that politicians will offer them a bail-out if risks materialise, bankers have an incentive to take as much risk as their supervisors will allow. In turn, the foreign creditors of the government have an incentive to support the sovereign in case of debt repayment difficulties, as they do not want to risk spillovers in the case of a sovereign default towards their countries. Consequently, national supervisors (who are assumed to have the same incentives as the sovereign government) will tend to exercise lax supervision vis-à-vis domestic banks, as they count on foreign support if risks materialise, i.e. if the sovereign has to bail out domestic banks leading to a sovereign default as a consequence.

32 A first draft of that paper had already appeared in 12 March 2014 (as mentioned in Emmanuel Farhi and Jean Tirole, 'Deadly Embrace: Sovereign and Financial Balance Sheets Doom Loops' (2018) 85 *Review of Economic Studies* 1781, fn. 15).

33 Additional institutional elements and the deposit insurance will be taken up later.

34 This is an important point: banks' bail-outs do not happen necessarily because of connections between bankers and politicians but also because of political incentives related to the citizens' welfare.

The above mechanism is based on two overall welfare-reducing elements. The first is the impossibility for national supervisors to commit to 'tough' supervision (so-called 'time inconsistency'). Time inconsistency arises because national supervisors cannot commit to exercising their tasks with the maximum intensity possible so as to minimise the risks that banks undertake, as they strategically count on the possibility of sovereign debt forgiveness or on financial transfers by foreign creditors. The second is the existence of spillovers (externalities) from a sovereign default affecting foreign creditors, which could also arise because of lax domestic supervision.[35] On their side, foreign creditors are concerned about the externalities of a sovereign default to their economies. As a result, national supervisors would be incentivised to turn a blind eye when domestic banks load excessive amounts of domestic sovereign debt (or, in general, increase their risk exposures to the domestic economy). Domestic banks have the incentive to load as much sovereign debt as their national supervisors will allow, as domestic debt is more profitable than safe foreign assets if the good scenario materialises (due to its higher yield compared to safe foreign debt). If the bad scenario were to materialise, banks would expect to receive a bail-out from the sovereign, whilst, for their part, bank owners will be protected by limited liability. The result of these two mechanisms is excessive risk-taking by banks, lax national supervision, more frequent than needed bank bail-outs and the need for foreign creditors' support.

The delegation of supervision to a supranational supervisor (as in the case of the European Banking Union) in conjunction with a commitment to provide funds to the domestic economy when a shock impinges that could trigger banks' default, represents a Pareto optimal institutional change, as it improves the welfare of both domestic citizens and foreign creditors. The time-inconsistency channel is deactivated and the need for foreign support is minimised. Concretely, the need for a foreign transfer due to a strategically lax domestic supervision is avoided and funds are transferred only when an exogenous shock materialises that could not have been addressed by stricter domestic regulation. To sum it up, the European Banking Union aligns incentives, commits banking supervisors to optimal standards of supervision, averts foreign transfers in favour of domestic banks and limits solidarity only to the amount that is absolutely necessary and is caused solely by strong exogenous shocks. This analysis is illustrated graphically in Figure 3.1.

The domestic sovereign debt held by banks is the instrument that can trigger the sovereign–banks doom loop in the Farhi and Tirole framework. The authors acknowledge that allowing banks to increase the domestic bias of their

35 A sovereign default could always occur in the Farhi and Tirole model if a substantial external shock occurs. However, the emphasis here is on sovereign defaults that could have been avoided if national supervision had not been lax and if strategic foreign aid could not be counted on.

sovereign debt holdings is not the only reflection of lax supervision, and that manifestations of lax supervision may also be visible in other parts of banks' balance sheet, e.g. risky mortgage loans. In addition, as explained in Chapter 1, banks and the domestic economy are also linked through other parts of the balance sheet of banks, which also play a role in the amplification of the sovereign-banks nexus (such as loans to domestic firms and households, state guarantees on assets, etc.). Therefore, the model should not be taken as referring exclusively to the supervisory requirements imposed on sovereign debt holdings, but as referring more broadly to the supervisory requirements for prudent risk taking and diversification. Even if the government–banks nexus is, in reality,

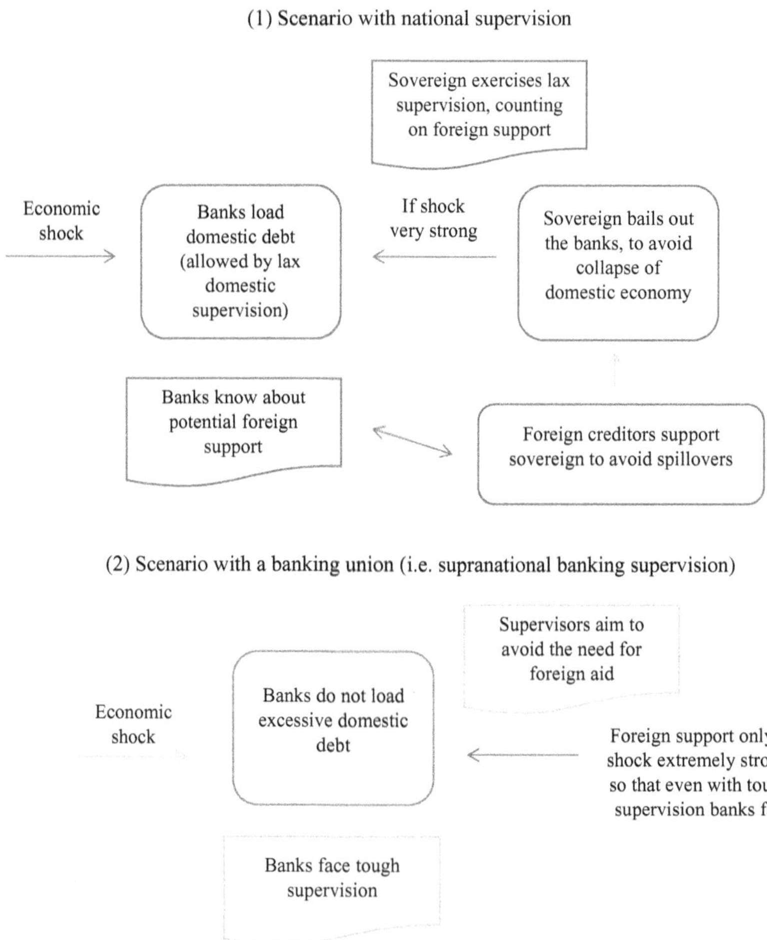

Figure 3.1 The mechanism that the European Banking Union seeks to address, based on the Farhi and Tirole analysis. Scenario (1) is relevant where a national supervisor is in charge, while (2) is relevant where a supranational supervisor is in charge.

not only attributable to the sovereign debt holdings of banks, the model points to the existence of a clear connection between weakening the sovereign–banks nexus via centralised supervision and the reduction in the home bias of banks' sovereign debt, an element that has not been addressed by the current EU institutional and regulatory settings. The regulatory context within which the SSM currently exercises its supervision does not prevent banks from demonstrating domestic bias in their sovereign debt portfolios. At the same time, there is no union-wide safe asset that would allow banks to rebalance their portfolios away from domestic sovereign debt without side-effects on sovereign funding or contagion potential (see Sections 3.4.1 and 3.4.2).

According to the annual risk assessment of the SSM for 2020, sovereign debt sustainability concerns represented one component of the most important risk driver for the euro area banking system, labelled as the 'economic, political and debt sustainability challenges in the euro area.'[36] However, the regulatory framework does not place restrictions on the amount or composition of banks' sovereign portfolio (as will be explained in more detail under Section 3.4.1). In the authors' view, this represents a critical limitation to the effectiveness of bank supervision and to reaping the full benefits of the European Banking Union by decoupling the risk nexus between banks and their sovereigns.

The second pillar of the European Banking Union is the SRM. 'Resolution' is a general term referring to the restructuring of a bank in distress while simultaneously prioritising the public interest in the continuation of a bank's critical functions, in the preservation of financial stability and in a minimisation of public costs. Consequently, the SRM's stated mission is to 'ensure an orderly resolution of failing banks with minimal costs to the taxpayers and the real economy.'[37] The primacy of the financial stability objective is mostly connected to the bail-out approach,[38] while the aim of avoiding moral hazard implies the use of bail-in.[39] In general, there is an inherent tension between the two

36 European Central Bank, Banking Supervision, *Risk Assessment for 2020* (2019) <https://www.bankingsupervision.europa.eu/ecb/pub/ra/html/ssm.ra2020~a9164196cc.en.html#toc2> accessed 30 September 2020.

37 From the SRM mission statement available at <https://ec.europa.eu/info/business-economy-euro/banking-and-finance/banking-union/single-resolution-mechanism_en> accessed 30 September 2020.

38 The term 'bail-out' refers to the use of public funds (either domestic or foreign) for resolving a bank, and it can take various forms including recapitalisation, provision of guarantees, bridge funding, purchase of assets, etc.

39 The term 'bail-in' refers to the imposition of losses on private stakeholders, especially banks' owners and creditors, in order to recapitalise a bank in distress, and is contrasted to bail-outs whereby public funds are used for the recapitalisation. A bail-in can be accomplished in a number of ways. Both statutory and contractual bail-in tools can be used to write down, convert into bank's shares or cancel financial instruments to recapitalise a bank. Bail-in could also include tools such as transfer of shares into a bridge institution or an asset management vehicle, which would most probably lead to a decrease in the value of the shares held by the bank owners.

objectives. The use of public funds to recapitalise or resolve banks can be justified on grounds of public interest (financial stability and real economy implications) while avoiding the use of public funds to support banks and resorting to bail-ins is thought to reduce moral hazard and excessive risk-taking on the part of banks. This is a typical time-inconsistency problem, as public authorities cannot credibly commit to always avoid using public funds due to the serious repercussions that an eventual bank failure may have for the economy.[40] The problem is confounded by the difficulty of reliably quantifying the impact of a bank failure on financial stability and the real economy. The consensus view is that although a bail-in will, in general, be the optimal option,[41] a resolution framework should allow a degree of flexibility so that bail-outs are also possible where contagion and financial stability risks threaten to materialise.[42]

Resolution in the Farhi and Tirole framework follows, implicitly, a pecking order when bail-ins in the form of capital depletion are the first mechanism of loss absorption, followed by public support from the home government and, only where this is not possible, complemented by funds from foreign creditors. The EU resolution framework, which is based on the BRRD (as its legal framework), the SRM (as its resolution authority) and the SRF (as the available fund), envisages a priority of the bail-in option, followed by public backstops that are either domestic or provided by the EU institutions (the SRF, the ECB in the form of ELA, the ESM) depending on the situation of the bank in distress (temporary illiquidity, 'failing or likely to fail,' insolvent) and the support instrument considered, e.g. provision of guarantees, liquidity or capital, purchase of assets.

Overall, there are strict constraints on the use of public funds to resolve banks. First, at least 8% of total liabilities (including equity and debt creditors of the bank) should have absorbed losses using bail-in instruments, while the funding provided by the SRF is limited to a maximum of 5% of total

40 See, for example, Varadarajan V. Chari and Patrick J. Kehoe, 'Bailouts, Time Inconsistency, and Optimal Regulation: A Macreconomic View' (2016) 106 *American Economic Review* 2458.

41 This view has been expressed clearly in the FSB (2011), which has guided the development of the BRRD in the EU.

42 A reference paper on the shortcomings of bailouts is Emmanuel Farhi and Jean Tirole, 'Collective moral hazard, maturity mismatch, and systemic bailouts' (2012) 102 American Economic Review, where it is argued that banks have an incentive to increase their leverage and risk-taking if they anticipate policy support interventions that are untargeted (e.g. due to the uncertainty during a crisis). The reason is banks' incentive to keep up with competitors and the fact that prudent risk-taking would lower their net worth. For an overview of the discussion regarding the trade-offs involved when using a bail-out or a bail-in approach to resolve banks, see Giovanni Dell'Ariccia, Maria Soledad Martinez Peria, Deniz O. Igan, Elsie Addo Awadzi, Marc C. Dobler, Damiano Sandri, 'Trade-Offs in Bank Resolution' (2018) *International Monetary Fund Discussion Note* 18/02 <https://www.imf.org/en/Publications/Staff-Discussion-Notes/Issues/2018/02/09/Trade-offs-in-Bank-Resolution-45127> accessed 30 September 2020.

liabilities.[43] As a general proposition, the new framework attaches higher relative weight to the aim of avoiding the use of public funds and prioritises the option of loss-absorption by private bank creditors. However, the use of public funds is not excluded where the public interest is at stake. Thus, the new framework represents a shift from the dominant approach followed in Europe during the global financial crisis (and, to a large extent, in other countries, such as the US), where the most common approach to resolving banks involved the use of public funds.[44] The aim of prioritising bail-in over bail-out is, in addition, supported by the Total Loss Absorption Capacity ('TLAC') and the Minimum Requirements for own funds and Eligible Liabilities ('MREL') standards,[45] which require banks to hold liabilities that can be bailed-in when the bank faces negative shocks to its capital position.

The possibility offered by the new European resolution framework of using public (national) funds to perform a so-called 'precautionary recapitalisation' has been criticised as a 'loophole'[46] on the grounds that this option circumvents

43 The minimum 8% limit of bail-in should not be understood as an upper bound of private sector involvement that should be topped-up by public funds (GCEE (2018)), rather the private losses can well exceed this limit. For further details on the conditions for the use of public funds, see also Section 5.2.2.3.

44 For a comprehensive comparative overview of the interventions to save financial institutions in EU and the US, see Stolz and Wedow (2010). It is concluded that the crisis response in the US has been similar to that in the EU and involved mainly public interventions such as government guarantees, capital and liquidity injections and asset protection. Véron reviews the gradual shift of the EU approach to resolution, from a pro-bail-out stance during the global crisis phase to a pro-bail-in stance afterwards (Nicolas Véron, 'Bank Crisis Management and Resolution: What Is Missing?' (2018) in Jochen Andritzky and Jörg Rocholl (eds), *Ideas from the 'Future Europe' Forum* (Centre for European Policy Studies (Brussels), European School of Management and Technology (Berlin), German Council of Economic Experts (Wiesbaden) 2018) (Véron (2018)). This author points out that a joint statement of EU leaders in the early phase of the crisis on 16 October 2008 which stated that, '[T]he European Council reaffirms its commitment that in all circumstances the necessary measures will be taken to preserve the stability of the financial system, to support major financial institutions, to avoid bankruptcies and to protect savers' deposits,' was interpreted as a clear sign that public interventions would be the norm for ailing banks. As a result of this approach, the impact of the financial assistance measures towards the banking sector contributed by 5.9% to the debt-to-GDP ratio in the euro area over the 2008–2012 period (João Domingues Semeano and Marien Ferdinandusse, 'The Fiscal Impact of Financial Sector Support Measures: Where Do We Stand a Decade on From the Financial Crisis?' (2018) *European Central Bank Economic Bulletin* 6 <https://www.ecb.europa.eu/pub/economic-bulletin/focus/2018/html/ecb.ebbox201806_04.en.html> accessed 30 September 2020).

45 Both TLAC and MREL were introduced in the European Banking Union through the BRRD.

46 See, for example, Thomas Philippon and Aude Salord, 'Bail-Ins and Bank Resolution in Europe: A Progress Report' (*VoxEU*, 22 March 2017) <https://voxeu.org/content/bail-ins-and-bank-resolution-europe-progress-report> accessed 30 September. There seems to be a perception that only bail-in can be considered a sign of a well-functioning resolution process, even if there are circumstances where bail-out is optimal from a social welfare perspective. For example, Garicano, in a pessimistic assessment of the European Banking Union, identifies as a worrying sign the number of cases whereby banks were bailed out using public funds (e.g. Veneto Banca and Banca Popolare di Vicenza in 2017, Norddeutsche Landesbank in 2019), rather than bailing in investors (Luis Gari-

the restrictive framework applicable where a bank is declared 'failed or likely to fail' (see Figure 3.2 for a depiction of the possible approaches under the BRRD/SRM framework). It seems, however, that there exist valid reasons for keeping the precautionary recapitalisation possibility within the framework.

First, the precautionary capitalisation option also entails the bail-in of creditors[47] and, as a result, market discipline is still imposed on banks' creditors. Therefore, precautionary recapitalisation differs in this crucial respect from the approach followed in the early stages of the global financial crisis when European governments purchased for a positive price a number of financial institutions in distress, as in the cases of Fortis, Dexia and the Royal Bank of Scotland.[48] Second, there are grounds to grant sufficient flexibility for this type of intervention as it could be required in the case of a systemic event when bail-in and resolution procedures risk aggravating the macroeconomic conditions and triggering a protracted recession.[49]

On the other hand, as will be analysed in more detail in Chapter 5, there are a number of challenges to be addressed before the new resolution regime can be considered to be effective. In this chapter, only the size of the SRF will be commented upon, while the remaining legal and institutional challenges being discussed in more detail in Chapter 5.

The question of whether the size of the SRF is sufficient is a critical element when considering the ability of the second pillar of the European Banking Union to effectively fulfil its role. The BRRD sets a target of at least 1% of total covered deposits to be built by national collections of fees from the banks

cano, 'Two Proposals to Resurrect the Banking Union: The Safe Portfolio Approach and SRB+' (Paper prepared for European Central Bank Conference on 'Fiscal Policy and EMU Governance,' Frankfurt, 19 December 2019) (Garicano (2019)) <https://www.bruegel.org/wp-content/uploads/2020/02/Two-proposals-to-resurrect-the-Banking-Union-by-Luis-Garicano.pdf> accessed 30 September). Clemens Fuest, the Director of the München-based Ifo institute is even reported to have stated that, '[D]ie Rettung der italienischen Krisenbank Bank Monte dei Paschi sei ein weiteres Beispiel für die europäische Krankheit des Regelbrechens' (see <https://www.welt.de/finanzen/article160741700/Ifo-Chef-prognostiziert-schwieriges-Jahr-fuer-deutsche-Sparer.html> accessed 30 September 2020).

47 Specifically, shareholders and subordinate creditors (see Marco Bodellini, 'Greek and Italian "Lessons" on Bank Restructuring: Is Precautionary Recapitalisation the Way Forward' (2017) 19 *Cambridge Yearbook of European Legal Studies* 144).

48 See, for example, Véron (2018).

49 Véron argues that precautionary capitalisation is useful during systemic events following the line of argumentation elaborated in Avgouleas and Goodhart which posits that the risk of contagion and an ensuing systemic crisis may mean that bail-in is not the optimal approach in all situations (Nicolas Véron, 'Precautionary Recapitalisations: Time for a Review' (In-depth analysis provided in advance of the European Parliament's Committee on Economic and Monetary Affairs, Public Hearing with the Chair of the Single Resolution Board, July 2017) <https://www.europarl.europa.eu/RegData/etudes/IDAN/2017/602090/IPOL_IDA(2017)602090_EN.pdf> accessed 30 September 2020; Emilios Avgouleas and Charles Goodhart, 'Critical Reflections on Bail-Ins' (2015) 1 *Journal of Financial Regulation* 3 (Avgouleas and Goodhart (2015)).

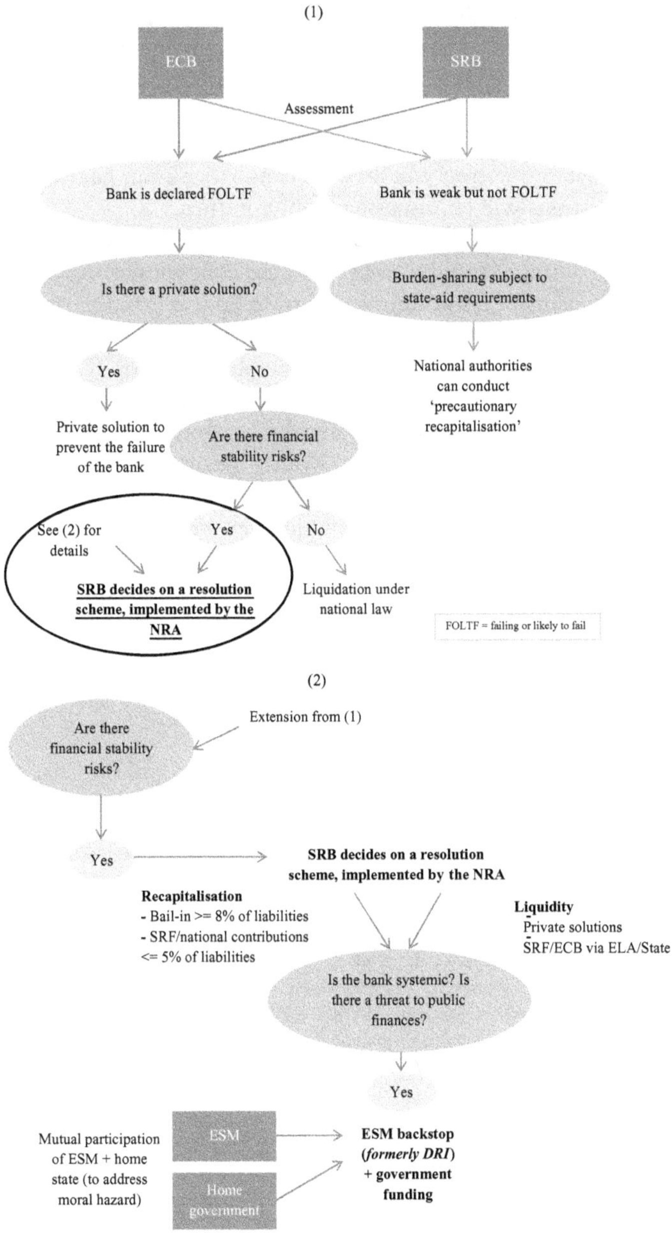

Figure 3.2 The recovery and resolution options of the current resolution framework for the systemically important banks supervised under the SSM.

for the resolution fund until 2024.[50] The SRF stood at €33 billion in 2019, while its target size by the end of 2023 stands at around €55 billion.[51] The size of the SRF fund has been assessed as potentially insufficient for two reasons, first with respect to its capacity to support liquidity provision in resolution, and second, as regards its overall sufficiency to implement the resolution in the case of large banks or systemic events.[52,53] With respect to liquidity provision in resolution there is a broader question whether the central bank can have a role to play in it. These questions will be discussed below, in turn.

Starting with the SRF's size and how sufficient this is to support the liquidity provision necessary during a resolution process, the following remarks are apposite. Liquidity provision in resolution is critical to address funding shortfalls due to the expiration of liabilities or liquidity shocks attributable to depositor runs (a self-reinforcing process that requires a credible backstop to bolster market confidence). In many bank resolution instances, the nominal amount of liquidity funding will be substantial for a number of reasons, namely, (a) the maturity transformation function of banks (which means that, in general, the maturity of a bank's liabilities will be shorter than its assets, giving rise to constant refinancing needs, the fulfilment of which can be challenging in a resolution and low market confidence environment);[54] (b) the highly leveraged business model of banks (which means that it is debt, rather than equity, that dominates their liability side); and (c) the incentives of banks' creditors to 'run'

50 According to the SRF Intergovernmental Agreement among the participating Member States, the national contributions will be mutualised fully by 2024, while until then they will be allocated to different compartments of the fund (see below, Section 4.3.2).

51 Single Resolution Board, *SRF Grows to €33 Billion after Latest Round of Transfers* (Press Release, 17 July 2019) <https://srb.europa.eu/en/node/804> accessed 30 September 2020.

52 De Groen and Gros estimate, based on historical data, that the SRF size would be sufficient for most bank failures especially if the possibility of utilising additional funds (e.g. from national deposit guarantee funds) is considered. However, the estimations have certain caveats, most significantly the assumption that banks will need to be resolved only once (in contrast to the historical experience) and the assumption that no contagion and systemic risk will materialise. In addition, these authors conclude that the SRF would not be able to cover the liquidity required during resolutions. Finally, they note that the ECB would also be constrained to fill the liquidity provision function as the ECB can only provide liquidity to credit institutions while resolution may lead to the formation of a non-banking entity in need of funding (Willem Pieter De Groen and Daniel Gros, 'Estimating the Bridge Financing Needs of the Single Resolution Fund: How Expensive Is It to Resolve a Bank?' (2015) *Centre for European Policy Studies Special Report* 122 <https://www.ceps.eu/ceps-publications/estimating-bridge-financing-needs-single-resolution-fund-how-expensive-it-resolve-bank/> accessed 30 September 2020).

53 There is also the issue of the low SRF transitional size until it reaches its intended size. The Member States have agreed that if the SRF funds prove to be insufficient during the period until the SRF is fully built-up (i.e. until 2024), a Loan Facility Agreement could be utilised, in which each Member State would provide an individual credit line to back its national compartment of the SRF.

54 For example, the part of liabilities covered by the overnight market would have to be rolled over on a daily basis.

when a bank is placed under resolution.[55] Therefore, it is conceivable that the liquidity provision needed for the resolution of a large bank could exceed the total size of the SRF (and, even, of the SRF and the ESM earmarked backstop amount *combined*, which is around €120 billion).[56] A critical point here, further emphasising the importance of liquidity support, is that official liquidity support may be needed to also implement resolution based on private sector involvement (like 'sale of business' or 'bail-in' tools of the BRRD), which suggests that the need for liquidity support will not only be restricted to situations where public resolution measures are implemented.[57]

The need for liquidity provision may, to some extent, be covered through the provision of ELA. However, ELA is aimed to address *temporary* illiquidity shocks of *solvent* banks, hence the non-optimal alignment of the aims of ELA with those of resolution liquidity funding.[58] Assuming that the size of the SRF is not optimal to manage liquidity needs for banks under resolution and given that ELA is not designed for this purpose, the requirement emerges for a larger and targeted backstop to support the funding of entities under resolution. The alternative funding support from the state, via the provision of guarantees, risks triggering the sovereign–banks loop, especially given the potentially large relative size of the funding needs of banks compared to the domestic economy. The liquidity provision gap of the resolution toolkit is directly linked to the adequacy of the SRF, to which a revamped ESM could, potentially, provide an answer, as discussed in more detail below.

Another pressing issue is that of the creation of a 'fiscal backstop' (or 'common backstop' as per the Five Presidents' Report[59]) for cases where a systemic shock would deplete the SRF's resources. The credibility of this backstop is a critical element in weakening the sovereign–banks loop as, in the presence of

55 Diamond and Dybvig (1983).

56 During 2015, the combined ECB and Bank of Greece lending to the Greek banks reached 71% of the country's GDP, and most of this was provided via the ELA facility (Peter Praet, 'The ECB and Its Role as Lender of Last Resort During the Crisis' (Speech at the Committee on Capital Markets Regulation Conference on the Lender of Last Resort – An International Perspective, Washington DC, 10 February 2016) <https://www.ecb.europa.eu/press/key/date/2016/html/sp160210.en.html> accessed 30 September 2020). This provides an illustration of the size of funding support that could be reached during an unfolding liquidity crisis that would trigger resolution of banks.

57 Following the 2014 FSB *Key Attributes of Effective Resolution Regimes for Financial Institutions*, moral hazard concerns should be minimised by resorting to public means of funding only when there is no private sector alternative and the provision of funding addresses financial stability risks. In addition, losses due to the provision of funding should be recovered *ex post*. Moral hazard could occur if the bank's owners have an incentive to resort to public funding during a resolution in case this is less costly for them (Financial Stability Board, *Key Attributes of Effective Resolution Regimes for Financial Institutions* (2014) <https://www.fsb.org/2014/10/key-attributes-of-effective-resolution-regimes-for-financial-institutions-2/> accessed 30 September 2020).

58 For example, one could raise doubts whether a national central bank when asked to provide ELA to a cross-border bank in its jurisdiction, which is under a resolution process, would factor in the decision's externalities to other countries.

59 Juncker et al. (2015).

a credible backstop, the market would no longer question sovereign solvency by factoring in the support that sovereigns may be required to provide to their ailing banks. The 2018–2019 Report of the German Council of Economic Experts assesses the issue of a fiscal backstop to the SRF as one of the main missing pieces in weakening the sovereign–banks nexus.[60] Given the centralisation of supervision brought about by the SSM, this backstop is not bedevilled by moral hazard concerns, as the scenario of a strategic relaxation of national supervisors counting on foreign support via the fiscal backstop has already been addressed by centralised supervision.[61]

Under the amended ESM Treaty, agreed by the December 2019 Eurogroup, a revolving credit line by the ESM is to provide the requisite fiscal backstop, replacing the 'Direct Recapitalisation Instrument' ('DRI') of the ESM.[62] The new instrument will have a different focus: rather than being a recapitalisation tool, it is intended to support liquidity and loss absorption.[63] The nominal cap for the revolving credit line is intended to be aligned with the SRF size, thereby doubling the total capacity of the single resolution pillar. Finally, the new instrument is expected to lower the credit risk undertaken by the ESM, as the exposure arising from the possible use of this new tool will be towards the SRM (and, ultimately, towards the banks that contribute with fees to the fund) rather than to a specific bank.[64,65]

Despite these improvements, the new facility does not allay fully the concerns with the ability of the new resolution scheme to effectively address cases of ailing large banks or generalised banking crises such as those that began around 2009–2010. As regards the provision of liquidity during resolution, both ELA and national guarantees look set to remain an essential part of the toolkit, despite their shortcomings. With respect to the funding needed for resolution

60 The other two elements mentioned in this report are a change in the regulatory privilege for sovereign debt and the tackling of obstacles to further financial integration within the EU.

61 Tordoir, Carmassi, Hauptmeier and Jahning note that national solutions in resolution 'do not reflect the reality that large euro area banks are now supervised at European level, creating a mismatch between liability and control' (Sander Tordoir, Jacopo Carmassi, Sebastian Hauptmeier and Malte Jahning, 'The State of Play Regarding the Deepening Agenda for Economic and Monetary Union' (2020) *European Central Bank Economic Bulletin* 2 <https://www.ecb.europa.eu/pub/economic-bulletin/articles/2020/html/ecb.ebart202002_03~13fd3ff790.en.html> accessed 30 September 2020).

62 For a detailed account of the DRI, see Section 5.2.

63 See also Section 5.2.1.

64 Fitch Wire, 'Proposed Reforms Could Boost ESM's Intrinsic Risk Profile' (*Fitch Ratings*, 5 July 2018).

65 Another reason why this is important is because the higher creditworthiness of the ESM enables this institution to pass these lower costs to the recipients of its funding, which is critical for the effectiveness of ESM interventions (see also Jasper Aerts and Pedro Bizarro, 'The Reform of the European Stability Mechanism' (2020) 15 (2) *Capital Markets Law Journal* 159 (Aerts and Bizarro (2020)).

measures, the doubling of the public backstop represents an improvement, which, however, need not suffice for systemic events.[66]

The third pillar of the European Banking Union, namely EDIS, is a necessary complement to the other two pillars[67] while at the same time representing a thorny issue given the mutualisation of risks across countries that it entails. The aim of EDIS is to instil the same level of confidence in money, which in modern economies mainly takes the form of bank deposits (irrespective of the country in which the bank operates). Insuring retail deposits of up to a certain amount (€100,000 according to the European Commission's (hereafter, 'the Commission') EDIS proposal[68]) would further weaken the sovereign-banks loop as the ensuing boost to confidence in the safety of money could have significant *ex ante* preventive effects on the occurrence of banking crises.

Bank runs caused by the lack of credible deposit insurance is an amplification channel that precipitated financial crises as demonstrated by the widespread bank runs taking place in the Greek banking system in different waves during the 2010s, reaching their peak in 2015, and in Spain during 2012. In these cases, bank runs were driven by a shock on the depositors' confidence for the safety of their claims towards banks, which was caused by the lack of confidence in the fiscal capacity of the sovereigns to insure depositors for the losses they could incur in the event of a bank failure. Restrictions in the set of covered deposits would not impair the market discipline that could constrain the degree of risk-taking by banks, as sophisticated wholesale depositors would still have an incentive to reallocate their deposits in the case of a bank engaging in excessive risk-taking.[69] As it is the case with insurance mechanisms, a payee (in this case, the national deposit guarantee schemes ('DGSs')) is entitled to a loss coverage in case a risk materialises (in this case, the failure of a domestic bank that would lead to depositor losses). In the context of the monetary union, the fear is that such a scheme would not lead to a relatively uniform distribution of benefits per country, with certain countries being consistently receivers of support and certain other countries being consistently net contributors (despite the

66 The scepticism on the adequacy of the resolution framework is in line with the empirical evidence, based on market data, that the BRRD does not seem to have affected market perceptions on the sovereign-banks nexus (Livia Pancotto, Owaip ap Gwilym and Jonathan Williams, 'The European Bank Recovery and Resolution Directive: A Market Assessment' (2019) 44 *Journal of Financial Stability*).

67 The instrumental role of the Federal Deposit Insurance Corporation in safeguarding financial stability in the US can be cited as a real-world example of the benefits from a credible deposit insurance scheme.

68 The Commission published a proposal for a European Deposit Insurance Scheme on 24 November 2015 (Proposal for a Regulation of the European Parliament and of the Council amending Regulation (EU) 806/2014 in order to establish a European Deposit Insurance Scheme COM(2015) 586).

69 Anginer, Demirgut-Kunt and Zhu provide empirical evidence that increased depositors' insurance may lead to moral hazard, leading to increased risk-taking on the part of the banks (Denis Anginer, Asli Demirgut-Kunt and Min Zhu, 'How Does Deposit Insurance Affect Bank Risk? Evidence from the Recent Crisis' (2014) 48 *Journal of Banking and Finance* 312).

fact that contributions would be collected by banks rather than by states, and would be based on banks' risk[70]). This fear has, so far, stalled progress towards the adoption of EDIS.

A number of quantitative studies have sought to analyse the effects of the introduction of EDIS. The analysis of the effects of EDIS produced by the Commission[71] concluded that, because of pooling, the same level of EDIS funding could offer more deposit protection compared to the individual DGSs. Carmassi, Dobkowitz, Evrard, Parisi, Silva and Wedow[72] explore the existence of cross-border subsidies in different EDIS schemes (i.e. the structural net contribution of some banking systems towards others), which seems to be a deterrent factor in the adoption of EDIS. They argue that cross-subsidisation would be avoided if the risk (and, consequently, also the fees) attributed to each bank were to be calculated based on the complete sample of participating banks, rather than only the banks of each country. Their results show that, even for loss rates higher than those observed during the global financial crisis of 2007–2009, no cross-subsidisation would take place.

Jokivuolle and Pennacchi[73] are more sceptical regarding the potential for cross-subsidisation and stress that deposit insurance is a non-diversifiable insurance contract as banking crises occur in clusters. As a result, calculating risk-based fees on the basis of expected losses may lead to a subtle form of cross-subsidisation due to the fact that riskier banks pay a lower insurance fee than their actual contribution to risk once the undiversifiable component of risk is taken into account. Therefore, these authors identify the risk of moral hazard for banks in the form of, for example, preferring insured deposits or investing in loans with excessive risk. The proposed solution is that riskier banks should pay a larger insurance fee than their expected loss would imply so as to compensate for the systematic risk component.[74]

70 For the methodology underpinning the risk-based contributions of banks into a deposit guarantee scheme, see European Banking Authority, *Guidelines on Methods for Calculating Contributions to Deposit Guarantee Schemes* (2015) <https://eba.europa.eu/regulation-and-policy/recovery-and-resolution/guidelines-on-methods-for-calculating-contributions-to-deposit-guarantee-schemes-dgss-> accessed 30 September 2020.

71 See the non-paper entitled 'Effects Analysis on the European Deposit Insurance Scheme' that was published on 11 October 2016, available at <https://ec.europa.eu/info/sites/info/files/161011-edis-effect-analysis_en.pdf> accessed 30 September 2020.

72 Jacopo Carmassi, Sonja Dobkowitz, JohanneEvrard, Laura Parisi, André Silva and Michael Wedow, 'Completing the Banking Union with a European Deposit Insurance Scheme: Who is Afraid of Cross-Subsidisation?' (2018) *European Central Bank Occasional Paper* 208 <https://www.ecb.europa.eu/pub/pdf/scpops/ecb.op208.en.pdf> accessed 30 September 2020.

73 Esa Jokivuolle and George Pennacchi, 'Designing a Multinational Deposit Insurance System: Implications for the European Deposit Insurance Scheme' (2019) 17 (1) *IFO Institute, Leibniz Institute for Economic Research at the University of Munich* 21 <https://www.ifo.de/en/publikationen/2019/article-journal/designing-multinational-deposit-insurance-system-implications> accessed 30 September 2020.

74 Another proposal in a similar vein has been made by Bénassy-Quéré et al., (2018) and Isabel Schnabel and Nicolas Véron (2018), who propose country risk premiums based on policy parameters

A few more arguments are apposite on the quantitative analyses just reviewed. First, these analyses do not consider the endogenous market response to the setting-up of a credible deposit guarantee scheme, which would tend to lower the risk of bank failures (and, consequently, of the probability that the deposit scheme would need to actually be tapped), weakening the sovereign-banks loop. Second, concerns about excessive risk-taking by banks in specific countries due to moral hazard seem to underestimate the fact that, with the advent of the SSM, supervision is no longer national, hence the 'regulatory capture' mechanism described in the Farhi and Tirole framework has been de-activated. Finally, as the Five Presidents Report notes,[75] EDIS would spread risks to a wider pool of financial institutions compared to national schemes, thus minimising any cross-border contributions across banking systems.

Overall, the discussion in this section provides some first evidence on the complementarity among the various policy proposals, which seems to have been somewhat neglected in the public debate. On the first pillar of the European Banking Union, which is often considered 'complete,' it has been highlighted above that centralised supervision will not bring the envisaged benefits in breaking the sovereign–banks loop when banks exhibit a strong domestic bias in their sovereign debt holdings. Therefore, the domestic bias of sovereign debt needs to be addressed, an issue that is analysed later in this chapter. Furthermore, the current resolution framework may not be optimal or sufficient to address systemic events. In addition, it falls short of being a 'single' framework, as each country retains its national insolvency framework, which it could apply to its banks. These shortcomings have to be weighed against the objective difficulties of creating a genuinely single resolution framework, also considering the improvements made in the course of the last several years, e.g. with respect to the improved range of instruments available to the ESM as a backstop. Finally, regarding EDIS, the general sense is that there seem to be ways to minimise the risk of cross-border subsidisation which, especially if the overall benefits for crisis-prevention at the Union level are factored in, could weigh more than the concern with (largely non-systematic) transfers across national banking systems.

---

such as weak creditor rights, lengthy insolvency procedures and other factors that would increase the risk of a bank failure (Bénassy-Quéré et al. (2018)). Importantly, these country-specific factors focus on legal and institutional factors, providing sound incentives for improvement at the national levels, and do not include sovereign yields, which would risk reinforcing the sovereign-bank loop. See also Schoenmaker D., 'How Should the Euro Area Build a Stable Deposit Insurance System?' (2018) in Jochen Andritzky and Jörg Rocholl (eds), *Ideas from the 'Future Europe' Forum* (Centre for European Policy Studies (Brussels), European School of Management and Technology (Berlin), German Council of Economic Experts (Wiesbaden) 2018).

75 Juncker et al. (2015).

3.4 Closing the second channel of contagion from sovereigns to banks

3.4.1 Revision of the regulatory treatment of sovereign debt holdings and its challenges

Banks' holdings of sovereign bonds represent the most direct link between sovereigns and banks. As elaborated in Chapter 1, a home bias in sovereign bond holdings ensues due to structural factors related to banks' risk management incentives and the sovereigns' incentives to default. However, the favourable regulatory treatment of sovereign bonds within the EU allows banks to hold sovereign bonds without requiring a corresponding shock-absorbing capital buffer, thereby reinforcing the structural tendency of banks to hold sovereign debt. Bonner[76] documents that the current, favourable treatment of sovereign bonds directly affects banks' demand for this type of instrument, irrespective of the structural reasons referred to in Chapter 1. Therefore, changing the regulatory approach to the holding of sovereign bonds seems to be the most obvious way to weaken the sovereign–banks loop as it would prompt banks to either hold more capital against potential losses in their sovereign bond portfolio or, alternatively, to decrease the amount of sovereign bonds that they hold on their balance sheet.

Various proposals have been advanced on how to modify the regulatory treatment of sovereign bonds, and these will be discussed in the paragraphs that follow. These proposals place the emphasis on reducing banks' holdings of domestic sovereign debt, so as to counteract the home bias of banks' sovereign debt holdings discussed in Chapter 1. A secondary aim of some of these proposals is to reduce the overall holdings of sovereign debt, both domestic and non-domestic. This secondary aim is prompted by the experience of recent crises such as, for instance, in the case of Dexia Bank, in Belgium, and Laiki Bank and the Bank of Cyprus, in Cyprus, during 2012–2014 (see Chapter 2), since, in both these cases the abovementioned credit institutions faced solvency issues due to their exposure to non-domestic sovereign debt.

The main counterarguments to those proposals primarily focus on the implications of such changes for the funding of sovereigns in the context of a monetary union, such as the EMU. In the particular context of the EU, an important aspect of any change of the regulatory treatment of sovereign bonds is whether this would affect differently those of the EU countries that retain their own national currency compared to the euro-area countries. At times of crisis, euro-area countries face the so-called 'sovereign debt demotion' effect and the 'risk overshooting' effect (see above, Section 1.4.6), which elevate their sovereign risk compared to non-euro area countries and emphasize the need for a revision of the regulatory treatment of sovereign debt. For their part,

76 Clemens Bonner, 'Preferential Regulatory Treatment and Banks' Demand for Government Debt' (2016) 48 *Journal of Money, Credit and Banking* 1195.

non-euro area Member States may be facing exchange rate risks if their banks are required to diversify their sovereign debt portfolio away from domestic sovereign bonds. The discussion that follows considers changes affecting only countries using the common currency.

As a general proposition, banking regulation seeks to either increase the loss-absorbing capacity of banks or to disincentivise banks from undertaking risky activities. In the case of sovereign debt, the latter is the main option under discussion. The former option, which may involve the imposition of increased capital requirements but without placing restrictions on the amount of banks' sovereign holdings, is not considered to be an efficient approach. This is due to the nature of the risk inherent in sovereign debt holdings: because sovereign exposures are concentrated and because sovereign defaults can be considered as tail (i.e. rare) events, to commit an additional, large amount of capital to cater for them could be disruptive to the operations of most banks. The former feature (i.e. the concentrated nature of sovereign debt) means that there is bound to be a substantial hit on banks' capital buffers in case of a default, except if the capital requirements for banks are increased to levels that are much higher than at the time of writing. The fact that sovereign defaults are occurring much less frequently than, for example, corporate or household defaults also renders less efficient the option of trying to address sovereign debt risk via a requirement for across-the-board increased capital. A permanent increase in banks' capital levels could hit banks' profitability and their ability to perform their credit intermediation function as leverage constraints would be binding.[77] Therefore, the latter option (i.e. trying to disincentivise banks from holding sovereign debt) is the most widely discussed option. This can be accomplished either through a price channel or through a volume constraint, or through a combination of the two. The price-based option consists of increasing the 'cost' to banks for engaging in the activity of holding sovereign debt, whereby 'cost' refers to the corresponding capital requirements for each euro of sovereign debt held. The volume-based option aims to place restrictions directly on the overall amount of banks' holdings of sovereign debt or its composition, for example, constraining the 'domestic bias.'

Even if limiting banks' sovereign debt holdings would, *ceteris paribus*, create the expectation of weakening the contagion channel from sovereigns to banks, this expectation would rest on two assumptions: (a) the sovereign's funding would not be endangered if domestic banks held lower amounts of debt in the steady state; and (b) the transition phase during which banks offload part of their domestic sovereign debt holdings so as to reach a lower prescribed level of sovereign exposure would not lead to turbulence in the sovereign debt markets and, more concretely, to higher sovereign yields due to the sell-off of sovereign

77 For a different view, see Anat Admati and Martin Hellwig, 'Bank Leverage, Welfare, and Regulation' (2018) *Rock Center for Corporate Governance at Stanford University Working Paper* 235 <https://papers.ssrn.com/sol3/papers.cfm?abstract_id=3257957> accessed 16 December 2020.

debt. The former assumption has been disputed as there is a fear that if banks are disincentivised from holding sovereign debt, then governments may themselves face funding difficulties. This risk is stressed in the relevant European Systemic Risk Board ('ESRB') report:

> [A] key question will … be to what extent a diversification mandate, in particular in the euro area, would give rise to financial institutions from other euro area countries substituting for domestic banks in funding sovereigns. The question is most critical for the ability of sovereigns to engage in anti-cyclical policies at times when the downturn of the economy itself puts a strain on their finances.[78]

The latter assumption amounts to the requirement that regulatory adjustment on the part of banks will not itself induce excessive sovereign bond yield increases.

The assessment of either of these assumptions is far from straightforward. Any informed assessment would need to rely on scenarios that, themselves, are subject to uncertainty. Therefore, although the various proposed regulatory changes share the common objective of decreasing the level of domestic sovereign bond holdings, they differ with respect to their implications and transition effects.

In addition, there is the view that banking regulation is not an appropriate tool through which to address the issue of sovereign risk, which is a systemic risk linked to domestic fiscal policy. Therefore, according to this view, no change in the regulatory treatment of sovereign risk is needed: instead, sovereign risk should be addressed through an improved governance mechanism of fiscal policies at the level of the EU.[79] However, for the reasons explained in Section 3.2, sound fiscal policies represent a necessary but not sufficient condition for addressing sovereign risk in the context of a monetary union, which is why policy measures in addition to enhanced fiscal surveillance should be considered and discussed, however helpful fiscal surveillance may be. The remainder of this section will elaborate on the price- and volume-based options for reducing banks' sovereign holdings, their potential combinations, the main criteria for deciding between the two approaches and the potential for their combination.

The price-based option raises the challenging question of reliably measuring sovereign default risk. One option would be for banks to assess the sovereign risk they undertake and to assign the corresponding risk weights based on their internal models, consistently with the risk-based capital approach introduced in banking regulation since Basel II. Even if the measurement of credit risk is

78 ESRB (2015), 128.

79 See ESRB (2015), 111–112 for this view, expressed by a minority of EU countries in the context of an Expert Group discussing this topic under the auspices of the ESRB.

one of the main specialities of a banking institution, measuring the credit risk of a sovereign is fundamentally different compared to the measurement of the credit risk of a firm or a household. To start with, whilst a credit risk measurement methodology for households will be applied to potentially thousands of bank clients, the corresponding methodology for sovereign risk will only be applied to the few sovereigns towards whom a bank has exposure. This means that while the former model simply needs to be 'correct' in a statistical sense (i.e. its overall success rate in predicting defaults when applied thousands of times should be satisfactory), the credit risk model for a sovereign will only be tested very few times, hence the challenge of assessing its suitability from a risk management perspective. The historical observations that can be used to measure sovereign risk will be scarce, while one needs to factor in that an error in such a credit risk model may threaten the viability of the bank as the total exposure amount will typically be large compared to its capital. For example, using end-2013 data, the Bank for International Settlements' Basel Committee on Banking Supervision finds that EU sovereign debt comprises 9% of twenty large EU banks' assets, an amount that is bound to be significant for the capital level of any bank.[80] In addition, the Bank of England measures the exposures of UK banks to vulnerable EU countries during the first phase of the European crisis as being equal to 30% of UK banks' Tier 1 capital.[81]

The uncertainty inherent in any modelling approach, combined with the severe consequences of an erroneous estimate, undermine the possibility of addressing sovereign credit risk based on the standard risk management toolkit.[82] Haldane[83] argues that if the model risk (i.e. the uncertainty associated with risk estimations based on statistical or econometric modelling) is sufficiently large, a risk-based capital buffer may be worse-performing compared to a rule-based capital level.[84]

Moreover, the assessment of the credit risk of sovereigns, and especially of the home country of a credit institution, may trigger self-fulfilling expectations (as also analysed in detail in Chapter 1), which, confounded by the inherent uncertainty surrounding the measurement of credit risk, would place a bank

80 Bank for International Settlements, Basel Committee on Banking Supervision, *Regulatory Consistency Assessment Programme (RCAP) – Assessment of Basel III Regulations – European Union* (Implementation Report, December 2014) <https://www.bis.org/bcbs/publ/d300.htm> accessed 30 September 2020.

81 Bank of England, *Financial Stability Report* (December 2011) <https://www.bankofengland.co.uk/financial-stability-report/2011/december-2011> accessed 30 September 2020.

82 Nassim Taleb, 'Errors, Robustness, and the Fourth Quadrant' (2009) 25 *International Journal of Forecasting* 744.

83 Haldane A., 'Constraining Discretion in Bank Regulation' (Paper given at the Federal Reserve Bank of Atlanta Conference on 'Maintaining Financial Stability: Holding a Tiger by the Tail(s),' Federal Reserve Bank of Atlanta, Atlanta, 9 April 2013) <https://www.bis.org/review/r130606e.pdf> accessed 30 September 2020.

84 For a further discussion on the potential use of banks' models to measure sovereign credit risk, also see ESRB (2015), 123–126.

in an awkward situation of conflicting incentives. Even if, according to the textbooks, the main function of banks is credit risk assessment,[85] a bank would always have an incentive to downplay the credit risk of its home sovereign to the knowledge of market participants. In addition, the disincentive of banks to recognise elevated credit risk would be higher for its exposure to sovereigns compared to individual firms or households. Overall, aiming to reflect more accurately sovereign debt risk by relying on banks' own assessment of credit risk can be less than straightforward.

Consequently, the use of a rule-based assignment of risk-weights seems to be a more promising path to take on the road to regulatory change. The responsibility for the assessment of sovereign risk would then be transferred, for instance, to credit rating agencies. Even if this is not a perfect solution, as their credit ratings are prone to pro-cyclicality (see Chapter 1), credit rating agencies do not face the same incentive issues as banks do when they perform this assessment themselves. Therefore, both Lenarčič, Mevis and Siklós[86] and the ESRB[87] view the use of the standardised approach for defining the risk-weights of sovereign debt more favourably compared to the internal models-based approach.

Volume-based approaches for regulatory reform usually take the form of a limit on sovereign exposures. In contrast to the price-based approach, the idea is not to directly link the amount of each sovereign debt security held to the required capital, based on the credit risk of the security but, rather, to decrease risk by inducing a more diversified portfolio of sovereign debt securities. Ideally, after the introduction of concentration limits for each specific sovereign, the corresponding sovereign paper should be re-distributed away from domestic credit institutions and towards foreign entities, thus weakening the sovereign-banks loop.

Lenarčič et al. conducted a detailed analysis of the transition effects of both price- and volume-based changes in the regulatory treatment of sovereign bonds. According to their analysis, both grandfathering and phasing-in could be options to allow for the smoother implementation of concentration limits by providing more time for the sovereign debt portfolio re-adjustment. The former option would only involve the implementation of concentration limits on new purchases (not on the total stock of sovereign debt holdings), while phasing-in would only gradually decrease the concentration limits. Similarly, risk-weights could only increase gradually. The slower re-adjustment of banks'

85 See, for example, Jean Rochet, 'Solvency Regulations and the Management of Banking Risks' (1999) 43 *European Economic Review* 981.

86 Andreja Lenarčič, Dirk Mevis and Dóra Siklós, 'Tackling Sovereign Risks in European Banks' (2016) *European Stability Mechanism Discussion Paper* 9 (Lenarčič et al. (2016)) <https://www.esm.europa.eu/sites/default/files/21032016_esm_discussionpaper1_final.pdf> accessed 30 September 2020.

87 ESRB (2015).

portfolios due to the use of grandfathering, phasing-in and gradual risk-weight increase would eliminate the risk of market disruption.[88]

It is also possible to combine the price- and volume-based approaches. An interesting proposal in this direction was circulated in the form of a position paper of the *Bundesministerium der Finanzen* (hereafter, 'the BMF proposal),[89] which combines price- and volume-based constraints for the one part of banks' sovereign debt holdings, while the risk-free current assumption is applied to a 'base' level of sovereign holdings in order to facilitate the funding of sovereigns. Specifically, according to the BMF proposal, the current favourable treatment of sovereign debt would still continue, but only up to a certain 'base' level, which would be defined as a percentage of a bank's capital (specifically, the indicative calibration of 33% of Tier 1 capital was proposed). Above that level, risk-weights would increase proportionally to the excess amount of sovereign debt held above the 'base' amount. The steepness of the increase would also be affected by the credit risk of the country. The tentative implementation of the risk assessment in this proposal is through recourse to credit rating agencies. Finally, the proposal foresees a comfortable transition period of five to seven years so as to avoid causing market turbulence.

Another way to combine the price- with the volume-based approach is to define stepwise concentration limits that would depend on the rating of the sovereign bonds.[90] For example, banks could be allowed to hold an amount equal to 100% of their Tier 1 capital in sovereign bonds rated between AAA and AA– while they would be allowed to hold bonds with lower ratings (e.g. lower than CCC+) only up to a lower percentage of their Tier 1 capital (e.g. 25%). This proposal still allows banks to retain an exposure towards their domestic sovereigns, which would, however, shrink as the credit rating of the sovereign would deteriorate.

The Euro Zone Basket proposal (hereafter, 'the EZB proposal') of Matthes and Rocholl[91,92] also defines a part of banks' sovereign debt holdings that

88 The authors note the important role that the ECB could play during the transition process, as sovereign bond purchases by the ECB could smoothen the impact of the regulatory change. It is nevertheless acknowledged that disruptions in the sovereign debt markets cannot be excluded.

89 *Bundesministerium der Finanzen*'s proposal 'Position Paper on the Goals of the Banking Union' (2019) is available at <http://prod-upp-image-read.ft.com/b750c7e4-ffba-11e9-b7bc-f3fa4e77dd47> accessed 30 September 2020.

90 Jochen Andritzky, Niklas Gadatsch, Tobias Körner, Alexander Schäfer and Isabel Schnabel, 'Removing Privileges for Banks' Sovereign Exposures – A Proposal' (2016) 2016.1 *European Economy* 139.

91 Dietrich Matthes and Jörg Rocholl, 'Breaking the Doom Loop' (2017) *European School of Management and Technology White Paper* 17-01 (Matthes and Rocholl (2017)) <http://financial-stability.org/wp-content/uploads/2017/12/2017-10_ESMT-WP_breaking-the-doom-loop.pdf> accessed 30 September 2020.

92 Dietrich Matthes and Jörg Rocholl, 'Breaking the Doom Loop' (2018) in Jochen Andritzky and Jörg Rocholl (eds), *Ideas from the 'Future Europe' Forum* (Centre for European Policy Studies (Brussels), European School of Management and Technology (Berlin), German Council of Economic Experts (Wiesbaden) 2018) (Matthes and Rocholl (2018)).

would still be considered as risk-free for the purposes of banking regulation and an excess part to which a credit rating-driven risk-weight would attach. The difference with the BMF proposal is that the favourably treated part (i.e. the one to which a zero risk-weight would attach) is defined separately for the sovereign debt of each EU country and tallies with the fraction of the banks' total sovereign debt holdings corresponding to that country's ECB capital key, i.e. it reflects the size of the economy and the population of that country. Therefore, a bank's sovereign debt holdings would still be treated as risk-free if their composition reflects the ECB capital key whilst, the more it deviates from this composition, a larger part of it would be risk-weighted. As a result, deviations from a diversified portfolio that reflects the size of each country would warrant more capital. The end result is that home bias would be reduced, and more sovereign debt would be held by banks from other EU countries. Such a proposal would also require a phase-in horizon to allow the reallocation of banks' sovereign debt portfolio without disrupting the market.

The proposals above seem to offer ways forward towards the much-needed revision of the regulatory treatment of sovereign bonds. In particular, these proposals still allow banks to fund their home sovereigns up to a certain degree while still enjoying the benefits of the current, favourable treatment of sovereign debt. Therefore, the risk that sovereign funding would be disrupted in the medium and long run is minimised. The BMF and the stepwise concentration limits proposals do not prescribe the composition of this favourably treated pool of sovereign debt (it merely limits the amount to be treated as risk-free to a percentage of banks' capital), whilst the EZB proposal does not limit the amount of sovereign debt that receives a favourable zero risk-weight as long as its composition is diversified according to the EU countries' ECB capital keys. Therefore, the EZB proposal 'subsidises' (i.e. attaches a zero risk-weight to) a specifically diversified composition of a bank's sovereign debt portfolio, which is the same for all countries and, as a result, it tends to prompt banks in 'safer' countries to load more 'risky' debt on their balance sheets and vice versa. One could easily imagine a situation in which an additional amount of a 'risky' sovereign bond would receive a zero risk-weight while the same amount of a home country's sovereign debt would be potentially 'penalised' with non-zero risk-weight as it would lead to a deviation from the prescribed portfolio diversification.

It can be argued that the abovementioned substitution would neither impact negatively the sovereign funding of the 'safer' countries nor have a significant effect on the risk of domestic banks. On the one hand, the excess part of domestic sovereign debt held by banks in 'safe' countries that would receive a non-zero risk-weight would, in any case, receive a very low weight, while the sovereign debt of such countries would, in any event, function as a safe asset, being highly sought after also by non-domestic entities. Furthermore, banks operating in 'safer' sovereigns in any case purchase risky foreign debt based primarily on risk–return considerations and as part of their normal investment strategy,[93] meaning that concerns with pushing banks into more risky portfolios may be overstated. In addition, a more diversified portfolio would also have a risk-reducing element since no sovereign debt is completely safe. Finally, the lower probability of crises in other parts of the EU – which would also have negative repercussions for the 'safer' economies – would lower the risk for banks operating in 'safer' countries. The strength of these various effects would also depend on the elasticity of demand for sovereign debt with respect to capital charges, which is highly uncertain. However, it appears difficult to argue that the riskiness of some banks would increase if all these factors are taken into consideration. Consequently, the strength of the EZB proposal would be that the overall benefit from all EU banks holding such a diversified portfolio would represent a Pareto improvement for all EU countries, i.e. all countries would be at least better-off with the new regulation. The 'weaker' countries would benefit because the sovereign–banks loop that poses a risk for their economies would be substantially reduced. This would also apply to the 'safer' economies, both directly (as their own risk of contagion would be lowered) and indirectly (as the lower risk of a sovereign crisis in the other EU countries would also benefit their economies).

There is, however, one respect in which the EZB approach could be potentially problematic (from a financial stability and political perspective), namely, that banks in 'safer' countries would be incentivised by decree (rather than by normal market forces) to take on more risk from other countries, with less strong fiscal fundamentals. The BMF proposal is, in this respect, less intrusive, as it allows banks to determine themselves their sovereign debt portfolio, as long as this does not exceed a given percentage of their capital base. As a result, the BMF proposal still allows – but only to a moderate degree – some home bias in the banks' composition of their sovereign debt portfolios. In the context of a still incomplete banking union, in which national governments could still be required to contribute to the costs of a bank failure (as the SRF may not be sufficient), the BMF proposal would represent a pragmatic option politically, as it would avoid incentivising banks in 'safer' countries from holding riskier debt.

What both proposals have in common is the requirement for a year-long transition period (explicitly mentioned in those proposals): banks would need to adapt their sovereign debt portfolios to the new regime, and sufficient time should be allowed for this transition in order to avoid causing turbulence in the sovereign debt markets. Their impact on the sovereign debt market segment and on sovereign funding would be a combination of the effects analysed

93 As documented, for example, by Frey and Weth for Germany (Rainer Frey and Mark Weth, 'Banks' Holdings of Risky Sovereign Bonds in the Absence of the Nexus –Yield Seeking with Central Bank Funding or De-Risking?' (2019) *Deutsche Bundesbank Discussion Paper* 19/2019 <https://www.bundesbank.de/en/publications/research/discussion-papers/banks-holdings-of-risky-sovereign-bonds-in-the-absence-of-the-nexus-yield-seeking-with-central-bank-funding-or-de-risking--798138> accessed 30 September 2020).

by Lenarčič et al.[94] separately for price- and volume-based methods, alleviated by the favourable treatment still pertaining to a part of banks' sovereign debt holdings. In addition, the politically tricky trade-off between concentration and credit risk presents a limitation of the regulatory proposals discussed above: either banks are incentivised to diversify, which, however, may increase the risk of banks in 'safe' countries, or non-negligible concentration risk in banks' balance sheets due to the domestic bias is to be tolerated, in which case there may still be scope for the emergence of a sovereign–banks doom loop.[95] Even if regulatory proposals may represent an improvement at the monetary union level, incentivising banks operating in 'safe' countries to hold riskier sovereign debt portfolios could be problematic for the countries concerned.

Given the existence of transition risks, and the tension between concentration and credit risk, a complementary policy option to the proposed change in the regulatory treatment of sovereign debt would be the creation of European safe assets or the issuance of Eurobonds, to support and facilitate such change. The additional element of safety that could be achieved either via tranching or via joint debt issuance would assist in resolving the limitations of the regulatory revision proposals. These complementary policy options are discussed in the following two sections.

3.4.2 Safe assets

At the time of writing, the EU was lacking a safe asset, defined as one that is not tied or linked to a specific sovereign. In general, sovereigns are the main producers of safe assets within their jurisdiction via the issuance of public debt. Given the domestic bias of banks in respect of their sovereign debt holdings (the reasons for which have been analysed in Chapter 1), the scarcity of safe assets in the domestic banks' balance sheets will encourage a capital flight away from sovereigns that face elevated credit risks, especially in the context of a monetary union (as analysed above in Section 1.4.6). This section will elaborate on the importance of safe assets in breaking the sovereign–banks nexus and present the main policy proposals for the creation of a safe asset not tied to a specific sovereign.

The economic literature defines safe assets in a number of slightly different ways. For example, a safe asset has been defined as an asset that 'yields the same pay-off at any point in time and state of the world'[96] or as an asset that does not

94 Lenarčič et al. (2016).

95 See also Spyros Alogoskoufis and Sam Langfield, 'Regulating the Doom Loop' (2018) *European Systemic Risk Board Working Paper* 74 (Alogoskoufis and Langfield (2018)) <https://www.esrb.europa.eu/pub/pdf/wp/esrb.wp74.en.pdf> accessed 30 September 2020.

96 Markus Brunnermeier, Sam Langfield, Marco Pagano, Ricardo Reis, Stijn Van Nieuwerburgh and Dimitri Vayanos, 'ESBies: Safety in the Tranches' (2017) 32 (90) *Economic Policy* 175 (Brunnermeier et al. (2017)).

lose its value in times of crisis.[97] At the risk of a tautology, a safe asset is any asset that market participants perceive to be safe across time.

The safe asset concept features prominently in the literature that emphasises information frictions. For the purposes of this literature, the above tautological definition of a safe asset is underpinned by the acknowledgement that information on each different security is not a public good that is equally distributed but, instead, requires effort and involves costs. More concretely, Dang, Gorton and Holmström introduce the concept of 'information sensitivity' as an attribute of securities, which is related to the distribution of payoffs that a security offers across different scenarios ('states of nature'), such as booms and distress periods. An insight offered by their analysis is that securities, which, due to their information sensitivity, require from economic agents to privately collect information on them, may be traded less during distress periods. By contrast, a safe asset would remain information insensitive even during crises, as market participants would not be incentivised to engage in information-acquisition during times of uncertainty and, consequently, their willingness to trade this asset would not decrease.

The safe asset concept features prominently in literature that emphasises information frictions. For the purposes of this literature, the above tautological definition of a safe asset is underpinned by the acknowledgment that information on each different security is not a public good equally distributed among market participants but, instead, requires effort and involves costs. In particular, this literature refers to situations where understanding the state of the macroeconomic fundamentals (fiscal or others, for instance related to the impact of the COVID-19 pandemic) represents something of a challenge, as it involves a 'costly state verification'.

More concretely, Dang, Gorton, and Holmström[98] introduce the concept of 'information sensitivity' as an attribute of securities, which is related to the distribution of payoffs that a security offers across different scenarios ('states of nature'), such as booms and distress periods. An insight offered by their analysis is that securities, which, due to their information sensitivity, require that economic agents privately collect information on them, may be traded less during distress periods. By contrast, a safe asset would remain information insensitive even during crises, as market participants would not be incentivised to engage in information-acquisition during times of uncertainty and, consequently, their willingness to trade this asset would not decrease. Information sensitivity could potentially lead to the freezing of the market for some assets because the collection of the information necessary to understand the true state of their fundamentals is not feasible or prohibitively 'costly' in terms of resources. 'Information insensitive' assets in contrast are less prone to this effect

97 Brunnermeier et al. (2016).

98 Tri Vi Dang, Gary Gorton and Bengt Holmström, *The Information Sensitivity of a Security* (*unpublished manuscript* – 2015).

because low-payoff states are less probable to materialise in their case due to the use, in their context, of diversification and tranching, as discussed later in this chapter.

Related to the above, there is empirical work pointing to a link between increased scrutiny of financial securities and the amplification of financial contagion. For example, Brancati and Macchiavelli[99] provide empirical evidence according to which, during crisis periods, there is increased 'production of information,' reflected in the lower dispersion of forecasts by market analysts, which is linked to the higher cost of default risk and lower trading volumes, i.e. market freezes. Similar phenomena have been documented by Prati and Sbracia (2010),[100] who provide empirical evidence of a link between uncertainty and intensifying pressure on exchange rates. Based on the insights offered by this strand of the literature, safe assets would be information-insensitive securities, the price of which would withstand increased scrutiny by market participants even during periods of crisis. The discussion in Section 1.4.5 highlights that the sovereign debt of distressed countries proved to possess a degree of information sensitivity that went beyond what would be justified by the underlying fundamentals of the respective countries.

A practical working definition, suitable for the analysis that follows, would be that safe assets are immune to non-negligible price decreases during periods of higher risk aversion amongst market participants, i.e. periods of crises and financial volatility. Consequently, they are assets, which, first, will not suffer substantial valuation decreases when held on the balance sheet of banks; second, they can be used as stable collateral to secure liquidity without substantial haircuts and, finally, they can be sold without suffering fire sale-related price decreases when the institution that holds them wishes to realise them in order to obtain liquidity. At the time of writing, due to its size and credit quality features, the German *Bund* was the primary example of a *de facto* safe asset within the monetary union.

Caballero, Farhi and Gourinchas studied the macroeconomic implications of the scarcity of safe assets.[101,102] The main message of their work is that safe asset scarcity can have macroeconomic consequences and lead to a decrease in output, especially when interest rates are low. The mechanism works through the positive relationship of safe asset demand with output and safe interest rates. The intuition is that demand for safe assets increases with output, due to the liquidity services they offer, and also increases with the return on safe assets,

99 Emanuele Brancati and Marco Macchiavelli, 'The Information Sensitivity of Debt in Good and Bad Times' (2019) 133 *Journal of Financial Economics* 99.

100 Alessandro Prati and Massimo Sbracia, 'Uncertainty and Currency Crises: Evidence from Survey Data' (2010) 57 *Journal of Monetary Economics* 668 (Prati and Sbracia (2010)).

101 Ricardo Caballero, Emmanuel Farhi and Pierre-Olivier Gourinchas, 'Safe Asset Scarcity and Aggregate Demand' (2016) 106 *American Economic Review: Papers and Proceedings* 513.

102 Ricardo Caballero and Emmanuel Farhi, 'The Safety Trap' (2017) 85 *Review of Economic Studies* 223 (Caballero and Farhi (2017)).

due to the incentives thus offered for investments into them. When a lower bound in interest rates does not allow the downward adjustment of safe asset demand to reduced supply through a reduction in interest rates, adjustment of demand will operate through a contraction in output to restore a new equilibrium. Intuitively, economic agents may find that, when risk materialises, there are no sufficient assets through which to sustain their economic activity, e.g. safe assets used by banks as collateral to satisfy liquidity demand, and, as a consequence, output will contract.

The absence of a euro-area-wide safe asset also has direct implications for financial stability and, in particular, for the risk posed by the sovereign–banks nexus.[103] Currently, the inherent home bias of sovereign holdings (as explained in Chapter 1) and the constraints to national policy for adjusting imbalances (as explained in Section 3.2) reinforce the sovereign-to-banks contagion channel and represent an ever-present vulnerability, especially in the case of countries with weaker economic fundamentals.

There are at least four effects through which the creation of a euro-area-wide safe asset could help to address the vulnerability posed by the sovereign-banks contagion channel.

First, the creation of safe assets would assist with the implementation of an eventual revision to the regulatory treatment of sovereign debt, without endangering the funding of sovereigns. From this perspective, the creation of a safe asset could be seen as complementary to the revision of the regulatory treatment of sovereign bonds. The aim behind the introduction of a euro-area-wide safe asset would be to facilitate a reduction in the sovereign debt home bias of banks so that the latter are not exposed, to the same degree, to the materialisation of sovereign risk in their home countries, while at the same time ensuring that national governments are not exposed to the risk of a shortage in demand for their sovereign debt issuance. To put it simply, the creation of a safe asset would provide an answer to the question, 'if (say) Italian banks held fewer Italian bonds, could you get other countries' banks to hold more?'[104] whereby Italy is used as a proxy for any country that is vulnerable to external shocks. The ultimate aim of the creation of a safe asset would be to encourage banks in the euro area to hold more bonds of *all* governments while at the same time discouraging each country's banks from holding too much sovereign debt of *their own* government. In this way, the existence of a euro area-wide safe asset would facilitate the smooth rebalancing of banks' portfolios, which is a process fraught with transition risks, as was explained in the previous section. Bénassy-Quéré et al.[105] explicitly link the introduction of a euro-area-wide safe

103 Gourinchas and Jeanne link the shortage of safe assets to financial instability (Pierre-Olivier Gourinchas and Olivier Jeanne, 'Global Safe Assets' (2012) *Bank for International Settlements Working Paper* 399 <https://www.bis.org/publ/work399.pdf> accessed 30 September 2020).

104 Martin Sandbu, 'The Landing Zone for Europe's Banking Union' (*Financial Times*, 16 January 2020).

105 Bénassy-Quéré et al. (2018).

asset to the revision of the regulatory treatment of sovereign debt, treating it as complementary thereto. Specifically, these authors consider the revision of the regulatory treatment of sovereign debt as a prerequisite for the introduction of safe assets,[106] via limits on concentrated exposures of sovereign debt, as the former policy measure would incentivise banks to hold the safe asset in the quantities required. This complementarity between the two policy instruments is the most straightforward answer to why safe assets could contribute to breaking the sovereign–banks loop: it is by not putting at risk the ability of states to fund themselves that safe assets would enable the implementation of changes in the regulatory treatment of sovereign bonds, since the sovereign debt funding currently undertaken by domestic banks would be more equally spread out and shared with non-domestic banks.[107]

Second, a euro-area-wide safe asset would enable banks to post collateral and obtain funding when needed the most, i.e. during a sovereign debt crisis. A banking system that remains largely unscathed by market pressures on sovereign debt refinancing, both because it holds fewer domestic sovereign bonds and because it possesses safe assets that can be posted as collateral, would provide a protective buffer against several of the sovereign-to-banks transmission channels of contagion (examined in detail in Chapter 1). Specifically, as liquidity problems become especially prevalent during crisis periods for many economic agents, such as firms and households, banks would be able to secure liquidity themselves and, in turn, provide funding to the rest of the economy. Thus, banks could continue posting safe assets as collateral in repo transactions, to address their liquidity needs. Furthermore, banks would also be able to provide funding in the interbank market, indirectly supporting other economic agents. The freezing of the interbank market is a highly multiplicative process (as most contagion phenomena), whereby problems in a handful of banks are transmitted to other banks, which, in turn, transmit them further within the interbank network, leading to their amplification. Therefore, a structural, across-the-board change in the capacity of banks to withstand shocks in sovereign creditworthiness, even if it may not appear so substantial at the individual bank level, could make the difference between a generalised protracted

106 Similar to the path to safe assets proposed by Garicano (2019), which is discussed below. In general, the timing for the introduction of the two policy proposals (i.e. whether the introduction of the safe assets should precede the change in the regulatory treatment of sovereign debt, or vice versa) would need further reflection.

107 The complementarity between the introduction of a European safe asset and the revision of the regulatory treatment of banks' sovereign exposures is also stressed in Spyridon Alogoskoufis, Margherita Giuzio, Thomas Kostka, Anouk Levels, Luis Molestina and Michael Wedow, 'How Could a Common Safe Asset Contribute to Financial Stability and Financial Integration in the Banking Union?' in European Central Bank, *Financial Integration and Structure in the Euro Area* (March 2020) <https://www.ecb.europa.eu/pub/fie/article/html/ecb.fieart202003_02~2b34819f75.en.html> accessed 16 December 2020.

economic depression and a temporary turbulence from which the economy can recover quickly.

Third, and related to both of the previous points, a safe asset would deactivate the amplification impact of the flight-to-quality channel, which is inherent in a monetary union setting and is caused by the asymmetry in the provision of safe assets across that union (as explained in Section 1.4.6). As explained previously, the solvency and liquidity situation of banks would be de-linked, to a large extent, from the creditworthiness of their home sovereign, as valuation losses and collateral degradation would be avoided. In the current institutional situation, where there is a clear sovereign debt bias in the banks' portfolio, valuation losses and collateral degradation do not occur solely due to the direct effect of the home sovereign facing elevated market pressure, but are further amplified by the flight-to-quality phenomenon to which monetary unions are prone. This phenomenon is caused exactly because of the asymmetrical distribution of safe assets within the monetary union, leading to self-fulfilling crises.[108]

A related argument is that a safe asset would offer protection to countries against movements in market sentiment that are not justified by their fundamentals. The introduction of a class of investors (the intermediaries issuing safe assets) that would purchase sovereign bonds based on a fixed set of portfolio weights would represent a stable demand source for the sovereign debt of each Member State, which would be less volatile in the face of shifts in market sentiment. The smoothing of demand for sovereign debt would be an additional positive consequence of the introduction of a euro area-wide safe asset.

Finally, the de-linking between the credit risk of banks and that of the sovereign would also weaken market expectations that an ailing sovereign would have to ultimately assist its banks (an expectation that can further undermine market perceptions of sovereign creditworthiness), improving the prospects of the sovereign managing to tackle temporary credit repayment pressures. Brunnermeier et al.[109] argued in a similar vein that the introduction of safe assets could endogenously reduce the number of cases where the contagion channel from sovereigns to banks operates.[110]

Establishing symmetry in the provision of safe assets across the Union could be seen as undesirable from the perspective of the countries whose sovereign

108 Marco Pagano, 'The Sovereign-Bank Nexus and the Case for European Safe Bonds' (*European Economy, Banks, Regulation and the Real Sector*, 4 July 2016) <https://european-economy.eu/2016-1/the-sovereign-bank-nexus-and-the-case-for-european-safe-bonds/> accessed 30 September 2020.

109 Brunnermeier et al. (2017).

110 Endogenous effects on market perceptions render even more challenging the task of accurately evaluating policy proposals regarding the creation of safe assets. This issue will be elaborated on later in this work. Suffice it to note here that it is generally accepted that such endogenous effects would predominantly tend towards breaking the sovereign-banks loop, rather than reinforcing it.

debt enjoys a safe haven status. Krishnamurthy and Vissing-Jorgensen[111] estimate that the global safe asset status of the US Treasuries has saved 73 basis points yields on average for the US government during the 1926–2008 period thanks to the liquidity and safety of US Treasuries, which market participants value. This premium is referred to in the literature as 'convenience yield.' Paret and Weber[112] estimate the convenience yield of the German *Bund*, and find that it has increased in the post-crisis period. Consequently, an argument could be put forward that the creation of a Union-wide safe asset would dissipate the premium earned by countries with stronger fundamentals on their funding cost, thereby working against their national interest. Referring specifically to Germany, Brunnermeier et al.[113] argue that there are at least two opposing effects that could compensate such countries. First, a safe haven would decrease the probability of crises, something that would be beneficial also for the German economy, not least on account of its export orientation. Second, the proliferation of crises within the monetary union due to sources of instability in its financial architecture could de facto increase demand for national contributions to address the consequences of financial contagion, in which case countries with stronger fundamentals would be asked to contribute disproportionally more compared to countries with weaker fundamentals. The instability of the current financial architecture is illustrated by the 'safety trilemma,' elaborated on by Van Riet,[114] namely that keeping a national safe asset is incompatible with simultaneously allowing free capital mobility and safeguarding financial stability in the EMU.

Another line of criticism of safe assets is that their introduction may undermine incentives for fiscal prudence. This criticism will be discussed in more detail in the following paragraphs. Suffice it to make two points here. The first is that the design of a safe asset is critical to the validity (or otherwise) of this criticism. The second is that the safe asset proposals discussed below are neither intended as crisis management tools nor as funding instruments for sovereigns who have lost market access, hence they cannot be misused as tools to derail public finances. Rather, the aim of their introduction is to avert the amplification of financial stress from the banking system to the sovereign.

The various policy proposals for creating a safe asset in the monetary union utilise two elements: pooling and tranching. Pooling allows to reap diversification

111 Arvind Krishnamurthy and Annette Vissing-Jorgensen, 'The Aggregate Demand for Treasury Bills' (2012) 120 *Journal of Political Economy* 233.

112 Anne-Charlotte Paret and Anke Weber, 'German Bond Yields and Debt Supply: Is There a "Bund Premium"?' (2019) *International Monetary Fund Working Paper* WP/19/235 <https://www.imf.org/en/Publications/WP/Issues/2019/11/01/German-Bond-Yields-and-Debt-Supply-Is-There-a-Bund-Premium-48730> accessed 30 September 2020.

113 Brunnermeier et al. (2017).

114 Ad Van Riet, 'Addressing the Safety Trilemma: A Safe Sovereign Asset for the Eurozone' (2017) *European Systemic Risk Board Working Paper* 35 <https://www.esrb.europa.eu/pub/pdf/wp/esrbwp35.en.pdf> accessed 30 September 2020.

benefits. Tranching enhances credit quality by establishing a seniority of claims in case of default. The two elements of pooling and tranching are also important in order to address the risk redistribution side-effect that could occur if banks hold regulation-induced diversified portfolios of sovereign bonds instead of their current domestically biased portfolio. Risk redistribution could occur because of the trade-off between concentration risk and credit risk when it comes to different sovereign bond portfolios. For example, a proposal to incentivise diversification would lead banks in home countries exhibiting strong fundamentals to load their portfolios with sovereign bonds of other countries with weaker fundamentals. Therefore, the credit risk of these banks will tend to increase even if their portfolios were to now be more diversified. The essential added element that would enable a simultaneous reduction of credit and concentration risk is tranching, i.e. the subordination of part of a diversified portfolio to the remaining part, providing a credit risk enhancement for the benefit of the holders of the senior part. Then, the senior part of the portfolio would feature, simultaneously, higher diversification and lower credit risk compared to the current domestically biased sovereign debt portfolios. In what follows, the different pooling and tranching configurations will be discussed alongside the pros and cons of each option (see Table 3.1 for an overview).

Table 3.1 Overview of the various proposals for the creation of a safe asset

	Only Pooling	*Tranching and Then Pooling*	*Pooling and Then Tranching*
Reference	Matthes and Rocholl[a]	Wendorff and Mahle[b]	Brunnermeier et al.,[c] ESRB HLTF[d]
Advantages	Reduces home bias. Simplicity.	Creates safe assets.	Creates safe assets. In addition: (1) Safe asset proportional to all countries; (2) Good safe asset multiplier.
Shortcomings	(1) First-order effect: risk redistribution across countries; (2) Not sufficient to create a safe asset.	(1) Safe asset backed disproportionally by highly rated countries; (2) Small safe asset multiplier.	(1) Concerns about the demand for the junior tranche; (2) Operational complexity, need for parameterisation.

[a] Matthes and Rocholl (2017) and Matthes and Rocholl (2018).

[b] Karsten Wendorff and Alexander Mahle, 'Staatsanleihen neu ausgestalten: Für eine stabilitätsorientierte Währungsunion' (2015) 95 *Wirtschaftsdienst* 604.

[c] Markus Brunnermeier et al., 'European Safe Bonds (ESBies)' (2012) (Brunnermeier et al. (2012)) <https://personal.lse.ac.uk/vayanos/Euronomics/ESBies.pdf> accessed 30 September 2020.

[d] European Systemic Risk Board, High Level Task Force on Safe Assets (HLTF), *Sovereign Bond-Backed Securities: A Feasibility Study* (2018) (ESRB HLTF (2018)) <https://www.esrb.europa.eu/pub/task_force_safe_assets/html/index.en.html> accessed 30 September 2020.

The option of using only the pooling component was also discussed in the previous Section 3.4.1, under the EZB proposal of Matthes and Rocholl.[115] The aim of that proposal is to reduce the home bias of banks' sovereign debt holdings rather than to create a safe asset. In fact, it is generally accepted that only using pooling does not create a portfolio that can be considered to represent a safe asset. For example, Brunnermeier et al.[116] estimate that a portfolio of sovereign debt comprising all euro-area countries in proportion to their GDP would exhibit a five-year expected loss rate of 2.79% while the corresponding rate for the AAA-rated euro area states is less than 0.5%.[117] Therefore, the diversification benefits of pooling do not suffice to create a safe asset. Furthermore, Brunnermeier, James and Landau[118] show that contagion across countries could be the consequence of banks holding a diversified portfolio of euro area government debt. Therefore, the effectiveness of pure pooling in breaking the contagion loop within a country may come at the cost of creating a new transmission channel across countries. It follows that what is necessary to create a safe asset is a combination of pooling and tranching. The order of the two elements is crucial. One option is to create safe assets by starting with tranching at the national level, i.e. separating each national issuance of sovereign debt into a senior and a junior tranche. As a second step, the senior tranches would be pooled together at the euro area level to create a safe asset. The other option is to first pool sovereign debt from different countries and to then create two tranches of the pooled portfolio. The latter sequence seems to be more efficient when assessed by the total amount of safe assets that is being created per unit of safe assets in the underlying portfolio (i.e. the total amount of sovereign debt of the AAA countries), the so-called 'safe asset multiplier.' Maximising the amount of safe assets created is important as the liquidity of a safe asset increases with its amount, as does its utility for market participants, as mentioned above, in our discussion of the 'convenience premium.'

The size of the junior tranche ('subordination level') is a critical design parameter in the above schemes for the creation of a safe asset. A relatively large subordination level (e.g. 50%) would further enhance the credit quality of the safe asset but it would decrease its supply (equivalently, it would decrease the safe asset multiplier). A relatively low subordination level (e.g. 10%), which means that only 10% of the total pooled portfolio would be subordinated to the remaining senior tranche, would create more assets, but their 'safety' status could then become questionable as the protective buffer of the junior tranche is not sufficiently deep to absorb losses.

115 Matthes and Rocholl (2017) and Matthes and Rocholl (2018).

116 Brunnermeier et al. (2017), 190.

117 These estimations use 2015 data for the main underlying parameters, so they are subject to change, however they are used here to indicate the insufficiency of pure pooling to create a safe asset.

118 Brunnermeier et al. (2016).

Considering the two options for the safe asset creation involving a different sequence of tranching and pooling, we consider first the option of tranching at the national level and, then, pooling the national senior tranches to create a safe asset. Two distinct variants of this proposal have been discussed, depending on whether the subordination level would be country-specific or uniform. Overall, this option does not seem to be an efficient way to create a safe asset due to the safe asset 'destruction' that takes place when the tranching at the national level precedes the pooling of the portfolio, as explained in more detail below.

A country-specific subordination level (e.g. based on the level that would render the senior tranche of each individual country an AAA bond) would lead to a safe asset that would be disproportionally backed by the sovereign debt of the AAA countries (e.g. the subordination level could be larger than 75% for Italy, while it would be 0% for Germany or for other countries, which already have a AAA rating).[119] Therefore, even if in that case the safe asset would comprise sovereign debt from all monetary union countries, its composition would be highly skewed towards the countries with higher credit ratings rather than reflecting the size of each country. This scheme would therefore leave a large part of the sovereign debt from the most vulnerable countries in the junior tranche, as a result of which flight-to-safety phenomena would still be likely to occur. Consequently, this scheme would only to an extent help to break the link between banks' balance sheets and the creditworthiness of their home country.

A uniform subordination level, on the other hand, would lead to another undesirable effect: the 'destruction' of safe assets already existing due to the application of tranching above the 'efficient' level for high credit quality countries. For example, the 'efficient' subordination level for the AAA countries would be 0% as their sovereign debt is already safe, while a much higher, positive level would be required for countries below the investment grade. Even a 50% subordination level, the senior debt of no more than seven euro-area countries, would qualify for an AAA rating. Due to the safe asset 'destruction' effect, the credit enhancement for the securitised portfolio that is achieved with the increase of the subordination level is very low, compared to where pooling precedes tranching (a scenario examined below).

In contrast, the option of first pooling the sovereign debt of the different countries and then tranching the pooled portfolio is a promising one for the creation of safe assets. The ensuing senior securities are named in the literature European Safe Bonds ('ESBies')[120] or senior sovereign bond-backed securi-

119 Álvaro Leandro and Jeromin Zettelmeyer, 'The Search for a Euro Area Safe Asset' (2019) *Peterson Institute for International Economics Working Paper* 18–3 (Leandro and Zettelmeyer (2019)) <https://www.piie.com/publications/working-papers/search-euro-area-safe-asset> accessed 30 September 2020.

120 ESRB HLTF (2018) uses the terms senior/junior sovereign bond-backed securities for the ESBies/EJBies.

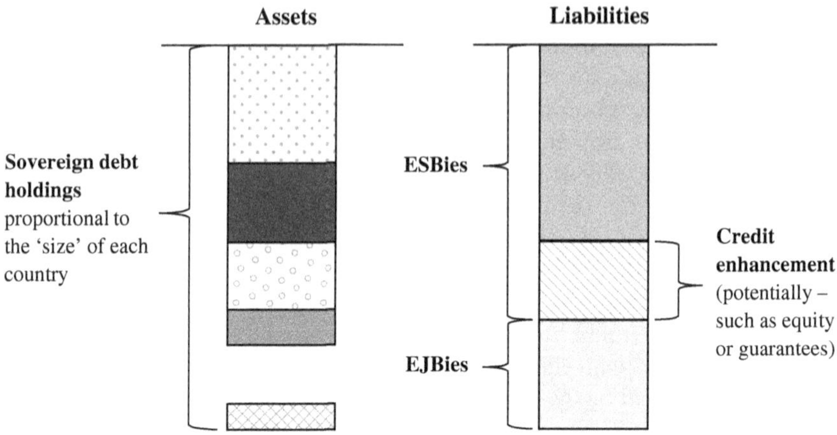

Figure 3.3 Balance sheet of a special purpose entity issuing ESBies (adapted from Brunnermeier et al. (2012)).

ties ('SBBSs') (Figure 3.3). The broader concept has been elaborated on in a sequence of papers.[121] The proposal has been investigated in detail by the ESRB and the Commission.[122] An already expanding secondary literature has developed around this concept, analysing different aspects of its implementation.[123] An important advantage of this scheme is that it enables the creation of a significant amount of safe assets, which could potentially be even safer than the German *Bund*.

The proposal in Brunnermeier et al.[124] is that a European Debt Agency ('EDA')[125] would purchase a diversified portfolio of European sovereign debt and issue two types of instruments to fund the purchases: a *senior* synthetic security backed by the proceeds of the diversified portfolio (ESBies) and a *junior* security, which would take the first hit in case of a default or haircut in

121 Brunnermeier et al. (2012) and Brunnermeier et al. (2017).

122 See ESRB HLTF (2018); and European Commission, 'Proposal for a Regulation of the European Parliament and of the Council on sovereign bond-backed securities' COM/2018/339.

123 For example, Alogoskoufis and Langfield (2018); David Cronin and Peter G. Dunne, 'How Effective are Sovereign Bond-Backed Securities as a Spillover Prevention Device' (2019) 96 *Journal of International Money and Finance* 49 (Cronin and Dunne (2019)); Markus Demary and Jürgen Matthes, 'Can a Reliable Framework for Sovereign-Backed Securities Be Established?' (2017) 5 *Intereconomics* 308; Jean Dermine, "Banks" Home Bias in Government Bond Holdings: Will Banks in Low-Rated Countries Invest in European Safe Bonds (ESBies)?' (2020) *European Financial Management*; Markus Pasche, 'ESBies as a Basis for a TARGET2 Settlement Mechanism' (2017) *Munich Personal RePEc Archive Paper* 83012 <https://mpra.ub.uni-muenchen.de/83012/> accessed 30 September 2020.

124 Brunnermeier et al. (2012).

125 On the question of the agent for the issuance of ESBies, see later in this section and, also, in Section 5.3.1.1.

any of the underlying securities (EJBies). Equity or joint guarantees could offer additional credit enhancement to the ESBies. As a result, the credit quality of ESBies would benefit from both diversification and tranching.[126]

The subordination level is a critical parameter for ESBies, due to the trade-off between safety and the amount of assets created. Brunnermeier et al.[127] propose a subordination level equal to 30%, and estimate that ESBies benefiting from this level of tranching would exhibit desirable features both as regards their level of safety and the amount of safe assets created. Specifically, the five-year expected loss rate of ESBies could be as low as 0.09%, while the corresponding value for a German *Bund* is 0.13%. In addition, even after subjecting ESBies to an adverse calibration, specifically assuming excess contagion among the large euro area countries, the five-year expected loss rate increases to 0.42%, which is still safer than German *Bunds* (in the adverse scenario, the latter would feature a loss rate equal to 0.5%).[128] In addition, ESBies would then have a safe asset multiplier of 1.74, which could lead to the generation of approximately €3.3 trillion of safe assets.[129]

Besides the subordination level, additional design elements of ESBies could be critical in order to set the right incentives for the national policies of the participating Member States and to cater for investor demand. One of them is the definition of the country's weights in the securitised portfolio, and it seems widely accepted that these weights should reflect the economic importance of each country rather than the amount of national debt. The aim would be to avoid creating perverse incentives for excessive debt issuance, as could be the case if the latter approach were to be adopted instead. Kraemer's paper[130] is, to our knowledge, the only paper that assumes that ESBies would be issued in proportion to the national debt, and finds a negative impact on the credit quality of ESBies. On the contrary, Brunnermeier et al.[131] analyse the credit risk of ESBies using relative GDP as the weighting parameter. ESRB HLTF[132] proposes that the weights of the sovereign portfolio backing the ESBies should be based on the ECB capital key, on the grounds that the latter represents a well-established measure of economic importance, linked to GDP and population, and it is slowly changing as it is regularly updated every five years. Leandro and

126 This is in addition to other credit enhancements that are also related to the institutional framework underpinning their issuance, e.g. capital injected into the EDA.

127 Brunnermeier et al. (2012), 191.

128 These results were corroborated in ESRB HLTF (2018), where other risk measures besides the expected loss are used, while more adverse scenarios are examined. Overall, it is found that the senior SBBS tranche has similar risk properties to the euro area sovereign bonds with the lowest risk.

129 The total amount of sovereign debt issued by AAA countries, according to 2015 data, was equal to €1.9 trillion.

130 Moritz Kraemer, 'How S&P Global Ratings Would Assess European "Safe" Bonds (ESBies)' (*Standard & Poor's Ratings Direct*, 25 April 2017) (Kraemer (2017)) <https://www.politico.eu/wp-content/uploads/2017/05/2017_04-How-we-would-rate-ESBies.pdf> accessed 30 September 2020.

131 Brunnermeier et al. (2017).

132 ESRB HLTF (2018).

Zettelmeyer[133] follow a different approach, capping the amount of debt that can be securitised from each country to a percentage of its GDP (60%). The general conclusion that ESBies would feature a credit risk assessment consistent with their safe asset status does not seem to depend on the choice of the weighting scheme when a measure of economic importance, rather than the issued amount of debt, is used to define the weights.

Another important design feature is the target amount of safe assets. The main consideration behind the amount of issued ESBies is the aim to ensure a liquid ESBies market while also retaining a liquid secondary market for national sovereign debt (the latter is critical to ensure price formation in the sovereign market and to avoid interference with other policies, such as monetary and fiscal policy). In addition, a substantial reduction in the size of the sovereign bond markets could drive up government financing costs.[134] In fact, a liquid sovereign market could be a precondition for including the sovereign debt of each country into the securitisation pool, and this would represent an additional safeguard against moral hazard concerns. The rationale is that, apart from their role as funding instruments, ESBies would also have a preventive role to play against the emergence of the sovereign–banks loop and, therefore, the market access condition for each participating country would ensure that the purchases of sovereign debt to be securitised would always be conducted at market prices. The market access condition could be decided based on the amounts and maturity of issuances. Based on these considerations, ESRB HLTF[135] sets an initial target of €1.5 trillion for the total pool of sovereign debt to be securitised, which could be potentially increased later after ensuring that both markets (ESBies and national sovereign bond markets) function smoothly.

Concerns have been raised on investor appetite for the junior tranche, which, according to the baseline proposal, would represent 30% of the total securitised portfolio. Responding to this concern, the ESRB HLTF[136] explored another variant of the ESBies idea: this would consist in splitting the EJBies securities pool (which represents 30% according to the most widely discussed 'optimal' calibration by Brunnermeier et al.[137]) into a 20% mezzanine tranche and a 10% junior tranche. The rationale for this additional layer is to cater for market demand for investment-grade securities and limit the non-investment grade part to a smaller, 10% share, which could be easily absorbed by investors

133 Leandro and Zettelmeyer (2019).
134 Therefore, it is not desirable to securitise all the outstanding amount of a country's sovereign debt.
135 ESRB HLTF (2018).
136 Ibid.
137 Brunnermeier et al. (2017).

with a higher risk appetite.[138] The analysis presented by ESRB HLTF[139] concludes that all three tranches feature tail risk properties, which render them competitive investment choices, in addition to their hedging properties against generalised risk.

The question whether ESBies should be issued by a public authority or by private agents has also been debated. As previously mentioned, Brunnermeier et al.[140] suggest that an EDA would issue ESBies (and EJBies). Brunnermeier et al.,[141] ESRB HLTF[142] and Garicano[143] all mention the possibility of a private special purpose entity (or entities) to issue ESBies. In the case of a public entity, ESRB HLTF notes the requirement for a limited amount of paid-in capital, which would require political agreement. The envisaged principle is that the public entity should operate on the basis of a binding order book from investors so that there is an uninterrupted pass-through of the sovereign bonds' proceeds to the investors of the issued assets, avoiding the need to introduce additional sources of funding into the balance sheet of the issuing entity.

Garicano also proposes a step-wise path towards ESBies, which begins with a reform of the regulatory approach to sovereign debt.[144] This initial step towards regulatory reform follows the EZB proposal of Matthes and Rocholl, which penalises departures from a diversified sovereign debt portfolio (as discussed in Section 3.4.1), and would culminate in the private issuance of ESBies. The idea is that incentivising banks to hold a diversified portfolio of sovereign bonds would pave the way for a privately issued safe asset, which would be backed by the diversified portfolio of sovereign debt. After the introduction of the distance-based charges, the endogenous market response would be to create a securitised diversified asset consisting of a sovereign bond mix in order to satisfy the banks' demand. The final step would involve tranching, following a pre-defined calendar. According to the proposal, already from the beginning of the process (i.e. once the change in the regulatory treatment of sovereign debt has been enacted), the tranching step should be agreed and planned for. This will avert the risk of a situation where governments abandon this step once their banks have offloaded their domestic sovereign bond portfolio and foreign banks have bought some part of it. When tranching is introduced, only the senior tranche will be eligible for a zero risk-weight.

138 According to Brunnermeier et al. (2017), a junior tranche corresponding to the 30% of the total portfolio would have a loss rate which would be higher than a weighted portfolio of the four lowest rated euro area countries (Italy, Portugal, Cyprus, Greece). Furthermore, it is argued that EJBies would be a preferable way for investors (e.g. hedge funds) to get exposure to sovereign risk compared to the option of buying via a prime broker a diversified pool of sovereign bonds.

139 ESRB HLTF (2018), Vol. II, 53 *ff.*

140 Brunnermeier et al. (2012).

141 Brunnermeier et al. (2017).

142 ESRB HLTF (2018).

143 Garicano (2019).

144 Ibid.

The complexity of the SBBSs' proposal has led to criticisms from different perspectives. In contrast to the objections raised against the Eurobonds idea (which will be examined in the next section), the focus of the concerns raised seems to be more on the operationalisation of the proposal rather than representing principled rejections thereof. This is due to the absence from the various safe asset proposals considered here of debt mutualisation, a feature that *is* present in the Eurobonds proposal. These criticisms will be examined in the paragraphs that follow.

There is a line of criticism that disputes the safety features of ESBies. Kraemer[145] represents a tentative credit rating of ESBies by one of the major credit rating agencies, namely Standard & Poor's. His assessment assumes that the weights of countries in the portfolio underpinning the safe assets would be proportional to the issued debt. As a result, it is assumed that Italian sovereign debt would represent 27.6% of the total portfolio, while in Brunnermeier et al.[146] this percentage is only 16.5%. As mentioned earlier, weighting the securitised portfolio by issued debt per country is an option that does not appear satisfactory due to the incentives it could create for excessive debt issuance. Therefore, the pessimistic BBB-tentative rating of ESBies proposed in Kraemer's analysis does not seem to be relevant to safe asset proposals relying on weighting schemes based on either the ECB capital key or relative GDP.[147]

Another line of criticism focuses on the market reaction to the introduction of SBBSs, especially as regards a potential re-assessment of sovereign risk. In this direction, the question has been posed whether endogenous changes in market perceptions would significantly impact the history-based credit risk analysis underpinning the SBBS idea. De Grauwe and Ji[148] refer to the potential for negative correlations across sovereign bond yields while investors crave safety during a crisis. However, this possibility does not seem to us to necessarily represent a threat to the viability of a safe asset: on the contrary, a tranched diversified pool backing ESBies would be well hedged against the occurrence of negative correlations in the underlying sovereign bond portfolio.[149] Cronin

145 Kraemer (2017).

146 Brunnermeier et al. (2017).

147 See also Kan Ji, 'A Review on ESBies: The Senior Tranche of Sovereign Bond-Backed Securities' (CPB Netherlands Bureau for Economic Policy Analysis Background Document, June 2018) <https://www.cpb.nl/sites/default/files/omnidownload/CPB-Background-Document-June 2018-A-review-on-ESBies.pdf> accessed 30 September 2020. As has been already explained, the credit risk of senior SBBS is found to be close to the safest euro area sovereign bonds according to the simulation exercises conducted in Brunnermeier et al. (2017) and ESRB (2018).

148 Paul De Grauwe and Yuemei Ji, 'Financial Engineering Will Not Stabilise an Unstable Euro Area' (*VoxEU*, 19 March 2018) (De Grauwe and Ji (2018)) <https://voxeu.org/article/financial-engineering-will-not-stabilise-unstable-euro-area> accessed 30 September 2020.

149 In general, ESBies would be endangered more by highly correlated shocks impinging simultaneously on more than one country, rather than by the negative correlations which reflect flight-to-safety behaviour during crises.

and Dunne[150] provide econometric evidence that the senior tranche would be protected during times of crisis, and that the spillover impact from the junior to the senior tranche would be lower during crisis periods. This reflects the intuition that a safe asset earns a premium during a crisis due to flight-to-safety effects, consistent, for example, with the theoretical predictions of Caballero and Farhi,[151] referred to previously.

It has also been argued that schemes such as ESBies (or, indeed, any measure that reduces the exposure of banks to their own government) could increase the marginal costs of debt issuance when this is combined with unsustainable fiscal policies.[152] This effect would materialise by rendering debt default or debt restructuring a more credible possibility (or, equivalently, by rendering a no government bail-out commitment more credible), as the implications of a sovereign default for the domestic banking sector would be significantly reduced. On the other hand, a default would always entail costs, which would disincentivise governments from defaulting, while the weakening of the link between sovereign and domestic banks' credit risk would have a positive impact on governments' funding costs.[153]

Furthermore, De Grauwe and Ji dispute the effectiveness of ESBies in preventing a capital flight from the countries of the periphery to the countries of the euro-area core, which would destabilise the former set of countries. The reason they cite is that since a sizeable national sovereign debt market would still be in place, the potential for a destabilising capital flight still exists. However, this criticism is valid only if the introduction of ESBies is not simultaneously accompanied by a change in the regulatory treatment of sovereign debt and a subsequent rebalancing of the banks' portfolios towards the newly created safe asset. Where banks have significantly reduced their home bias by substituting domestic sovereign bonds with ESBies, a flight of investors away from periphery bonds will have a limited impact on the balance sheets of periphery banks and on their ability to post collateral for funding, as banks are expected to directly hold a smaller amount of domestic bonds, while ESBies could withstand market pressures due to their built-in diversification and

150 Cronin and Dunne (2019).

151 Caballero and Farhi (2017).

152 Álvaro Leandro and Jeromin Zettelmeyer, 'A Safe Asset for the Euro Area? Evaluating Alternative Proposals' in Jochen Andritzky and Jörg Rocholl (eds), *Ideas from the 'Future Europe' Forum* (Centre for European Policy Studies (Brussels), European School of Management and Technology (Berlin), German Council of Economic Experts (Wiesbaden) 2018).

153 In a similar vein, Garicano (2019) argues that fears that the yields on the non-securitised part of the sovereign debt would be prohibitively high are unfounded as the weakening of the sovereign-banks nexus would also diminish fears of contagion and would improve the market cost of sovereign financing. On the other hand, invoking the Modigliani-Miller theorem, the same author argues that the overall cost of sovereign debt would not change. This argument is also discussed in the next Section 3.4.3, where it is argued that when contingent pay-offs are changed, as happens with the introduction of securitisation, then the Modigliani-Miller theorem does not necessarily hold.

tranching features. Alogoskoufis and Langfield[154] provide quantitative calculations showing that a reinvestment of an increasing percentage of banks' current sovereign debt holdings into ESBies would lead to a monotonic decrease of both concentration and credit risk. Therefore, the risk of a destabilising capital flight would be lower under a regime where safe assets have been introduced in conjunction with a corresponding change in the regulatory treatment of sovereign bonds.

The ESRB report[155] refers to a number of concerns expressed by national debt management offices ('DMOs') on the impact of the issuance of SBBS on national markets. The most critical argument concerns the risks inherent in the excessive shrinking of national markets, such as higher government costs. As explained previously, this concern can be addressed by balancing the relative sizes of SBBS and national markets to allow sufficient liquidity in both. In addition, the assessment of the rising cost risk due to the thinning of the sovereign bonds market could draw upon the historical experience in the euro area with large scale purchases of sovereign bonds by the ECB in the context of the quantitative easing programmes. Such purchases have not shown evidence that sovereign funding could be endangered. In addition, unlike quantitative easing, SBBS would substitute the sovereign bonds taken out of the market with new securities, meaning that their impact on sovereign bond markets can only be even less pronounced.[156,157]

Thus, it seems indisputable that the version involving pooling sovereign bonds and then tranching, as proposed by Brunnermeier et al., is the most promising avenue to create a Union-wide safe asset. The analysis presented above shows that it would be crucial to complement the introduction of ESBies with a change in the regulatory treatment of sovereign debt, so as to reduce the home bias in banks' sovereign bond holdings. In other words, these two policy proposals should not be considered in isolation: instead, they are complementary to one another, with the effective implementation of the one being conditional on the implementation of the other. ESBies would help address the transitory effects of the regulatory impact by facilitating a smoother euro-area-wide portfolio rebalancing by banks, following the path described by Garicano. The reduction in home bias brought about by a change in the regulatory treatment of sovereign bonds would eliminate the risk of contagion across countries, which could materialise if ESBies were to be implemented

154 Alogoskoufis and Langfield (2018).

155 ESRB HLTF (2018).

156 This argument is made by Cronin and Dunne (2019).

157 Other concerns from DMOs that are reported in ESRB HLTF (2018) focus on operational aspects, e.g. whether the purchases of sovereign bonds to assemble SBBS should take place in primary or secondary markets. Overall, it seems that such operational issues while critical can always be addressed via relevant political agreements or institutional design that would not compromise the principles behind the safe asset creation idea and, most importantly, the aim to avoid debt mutualisation.

without a change in the regulatory treatment of sovereign debt, as described by De Grauwe and Ji. On the other hand, there are operational issues with the implementation of ESBies, especially as regards the interplay between the operation of national DMOs and the SBBS issuers. The ESRB HLTF[158] represents a substantial contribution in clarifying how these issues could be tackled.

Overall, the issuance of European safe assets would present several advantages. Starting with the advantages of safe assets for banks, their issuance would help mitigate, *ex ante*, the risks to which these are exposed when holding domestic debt, as regards the valuation of their assets but also since the creation of good collateral – other than government bonds – would weaken the feedback loops between banks and their respective national sovereign, helping banks to become less dependent on the fiscal situation of the national sovereign of the seat of their establishment. Thus, if banks were to hold the senior tranches of ESBies, instead of the government bonds of their home sovereign, their funding position in the money markets would be more resilient after their home sovereign has come under fiscal pressure or found itself in a financial distress situation. It follows that one of the main advantages of European safe assets for euro area credit institutions (and, in the authors' view, the main policy justification for their introduction, rather than a mere positive side-effect thereof)[159] is that their introduction would result in the creation of a large volume of assets, which commercial banks can pledge to their national central bank ('NCB')[160] in return for Eurosystem liquidity in good times as in bad.[161] Besides, establishing a euro-area-wide, integrated market for safe assets would generate a larger volume of safe assets in the euro area (similar in size and liquidity to the market for US Treasury bonds),[162] reducing the risk of a 'flight to quality' (or safety), helping to avert a situation where even small shocks, such as changes in ratings, can lead to large cross-border capital flows, and, indirectly, contributing to greater stability *and* convergence within the

158 ESRB HLTF (2018).

159 The literature has so far treated the creation of good collateral as no more than a mere positive side-effect of the issuance of a common, euro area safe asset. For a reflection of this trend, close to the time of publication of this work, see Matthias Goldmann et al.,'The Case for Corona Bonds – A Proposal by a Group of European Lawyers' (*Verfassungsblog*, 5 April 2020) <https://verfassungsblog.de/the-case-for-corona-bonds/> accessed 30 September 2020, where 'the creation of a safe asset for institutional and retail investors alike' is viewed positively but, mostly, as a 'collateral benefit.'

160 In the remainder of this book, the term 'NCB' shall refer, unless otherwise indicated, to the national central bank of a Member State that has adopted the euro, and whose Governor is a member of the Governing Council of the ECB.

161 In this constellation, the implementation and transmission of the single monetary policy would also be smoother and more efficient.

162 This point was aptly made by former Commission President Jacques Delors in an interview published in November 2011 by Germany's *Frankfurter Allgemeine Zeitung* ('Vergessen Sie nicht das Interesse Europas an einem großen Markt von Staatsanleihen in Euro. Das wäre hilfreich für den Wettbewerb mit dem Dollar und würde Kapital anziehen') (Im Gespräch: Jacques Delors, 'Wir stehen am Abgrund' (*Frankfurter Allgemeine Zeitung*, 26 September 2011)).

euro area.[163] Last but not least, European safe assets could serve as part of a political compromise to de-privilege sovereign bonds in bank capital regulation and, potentially, be used to cushion the effect that such de-privileging would have on sovereign bond markets. In conjunction with a deeper Capital Markets Union, and a stronger banking system, European safe assets could also have an indirect role to play in making the single currency more relevant as a global reserve currency.[164]

The next section digs deeper into the Eurobonds proposal, which, on the one hand, inherits all the positive features of the euro-area-wide safe asset proposal, as elaborated in this section, but also raises justifiable concerns over moral hazard, having led to a heated debate among academics, policymakers and other opinion leaders.

3.4.3 Eurobonds

Proposed by several commentators as a means of breaking the sovereign–banks contagion link, the issuance of Eurobonds has also met strong resistance due to the fact that its issuance would entail some form of joint liability amongst Member States, which critics perceive as fraught with moral hazard risks. The discussion around Eurobonds re-emerged with some intensity after the outbreak of the COVID-19 pandemic, with the issuance of Eurobonds being considered, by some, as deserving to be part of the European response to the pandemic's impact on the economy. Given the symmetrical nature of the crisis caused by the COVID-19 pandemic (i.e. the fact that this latest crisis was not caused by specific policy choices in individual Members States but, rather, impinged upon all Member States as an exogenous economic shock), the recent discussion around Eurobonds has unfolded in a very different context compared to that of the earlier European sovereign debt crisis, when

163 Stijn Claessens, Ashoka Mody and Shahin Vallée, 'Paths to Eurobonds' (2012) *International Monetary Fund Working Paper* WP/12/172 <https://www.imf.org/en/Publications/WP/Issues/2016/12/31/Paths-to-Eurobonds-26034> accessed 30 September 2020.

164 This last point was raised by Christine Lagarde, in her exchange of views with the Parliament's Committee on Economic and Monetary Affairs on 28 August 2019, on the occasion of her confirmation as President of the ECB (see European Parliament, Committee on Economic and Monetary Affairs, 'Draft Report on the Council Recommendation on the Appointment of the President of the European Central Bank' C9-0048/2019 – 2019/0810(NLE)). There, Lagarde also stressed that, '[A] safe asset that is not sensitive to idiosyncratic sovereign risk and appreciates in times of crisis could help mitigate the negative feedback loops between sovereigns and domestic banks – as well as flights to safety – which were observed during the last crisis. A common sovereign safe asset of sufficient volume would also facilitate efficient capital allocation within the monetary union and facilitate financial integration.' Lagarde nevertheless acknowledged that, '[F]or all its possible benefits, it has to be acknowledged though that by having implications for sovereign risks and fiscal incentives, a common safe asset is inherently a politically sensitive topic. Nor is it strictly necessary for undertaking important further steps in deepening EMU.'

Eurobonds were proposed to address a crisis perceived to have been caused, to a large extent, by the flawed policies of individual Member States.

In a nutshell, the premise of Eurobonds is the idea that mutualised European debt would pave the way for stable, low funding rates for all Member States. The cost of sovereign borrowing would no longer be influenced by market fluctuations due to changing market sentiments, and the pooling together of several Member States would smooth out the impact of asymmetrical shocks affecting individual Member States, depressing Eurobond funding rates. In addition, Eurobonds would represent a safe asset that can serve as collateral, thereby protecting banks from liquidity shocks caused by domestic macroeconomic shocks. Both of these two functions of Eurobonds would effectively break the sovereign-banks nexus, as both the funding of sovereigns and that of their domestic banks would become less costly and less volatile.

Broadly speaking, and abstracting from the various different Eurobond and safe asset proposals, a Eurobond-based policy response could potentially go further in addressing the funding issues faced by some sovereigns and in eliminating the downward channel of contagion compared to safe asset proposals, at the expense, however, of more pronounced concerns over inducing moral hazard. Furthermore, the various Eurobond proposals are simpler and easier to operationalise compared to the various safe asset proposals discussed in the previous section, where issues of relevance to their exact calibration and financial engineering seem to be critical in ensuring that safe assets achieve their stated aims. On the other hand, the legal complexities surrounding the implementation of (most) Eurobond proposals are more severe, due to the debt mutualisation element they entail and the constraints that the currently applicable European legal framework places on such mutualisation.[165] This last point deserves some further explanation.

Most Eurobond proposals, to date, are based on some form of joint guarantee for their repayment. Consequently, even if a particular Member State were to face budgetary difficulties on account of a serious economic depression, other Member States would collectively guarantee the repayment of the pooled debt, making it difficult to imagine a plausible scenario in which a Eurobond would face actual default risks (unless, that is, substantial shocks were to materialise which would impinge simultaneously on more than one euro area Member States, impairing their ability to service their joint debt). Therefore, Eurobonds can be considered to be safe debt by construction, offering all of the positive effects analysed in the previous section from the perspective of addressing the sovereign–banks contagion channel. More specifically, the revision of the regulatory treatment of sovereign bonds, discussed earlier in this chapter, would also be possible in the case of Eurobonds, and the same is true of the enhanced stability brought about by their use of safe collateral. The added-value of Eurobonds compared to the safe asset solution would be that

165 For a discussion of the legal parameters of the issuance of Eurobonds – and, especially, those involving debt mutualisation – the reader is referred to the discussion in Chapter 5.

even if the two previous positive effects were to prove insufficient to diminish the sovereign default risk of a euro area country, the joint guarantees embedded in the Eurobond scheme would dispel any remaining doubts about the credit risk that investors in Eurobonds would face.

At the same time, the presence, in the case of Eurobonds, of joint guarantees creates the additional complication of moral hazard risks. The security offered by the guarantee of other Member States could prompt irresponsible fiscal behaviour by individual Member States, the consequences of which would be paid for by taxpayers in other Member States. Given the less-than-ideal experience with fiscal surveillance in the euro area and the constraints faced by European institutions in enforcing rules of fiscal prudence at the national level, the risk emerges of beggar-thy-neighbour policies on the part of individual Member States, free-riding on the back of the fiscal support of other Member States.

Moral hazard risks are well documented in the literature. For instance, Kopf[166] argues that, under a Eurobond scheme, individual Member States would be incentivised to default on their Eurobond obligations so as to provoke their repayment by other Member States. Relevant to this argument is the uncertainty that surrounds identifying a critical point of economic stress beyond which a government would be genuinely unable to fulfil its obligations towards repaying foreign investors. Obviously, the 'ability' of a country to repay its debt also depends on domestic political economy factors, which, in a Eurobond scheme, would be externalised. In other words, there are two factors at work here, whose interplay adds to the complex relationship between the economic and political considerations that underpin a normal (domestic) insolvency scenario: first, the difficulty of establishing the fulfilment of the conditions for an insolvency; and second, the impact on other Member States of an individual country's decision to default on its Eurobond obligations. As a result, in a Eurobond scenario, a Member State's decision whether to repay its pooled debt becomes an issue with far-reaching and, potentially, polarising implications, giving rise to distributional conflicts across states.

It could be argued that the safeguard to the risk of beggar-thy-neighbour behaviour would be the disciplining effect of a shoot-up of yields in the non-mutualised part of the joint debt that the default of a country participating in the issuance of a mutualised Eurobond would entail. All Eurobond proposals build on this mechanism to address their inherent moral hazard risks. There are, for instance, proposals to mutualise national debt up to a level of GDP (e.g. 60%, labelled as 'blue' debt in the Eurobond proposal of Delpla and Von

166 Christian Kopf, 'Restoring Financial Stability in the Eurozone' (2011) *Centre for European Policy Studies Policy Brief* 237 (Kopf (2011)) <https://www.ceps.eu/wp-content/uploads/2011/03/Policy%20Brief%20No%20237%20Kopf%20on%20Restoring%20Financial%20Stability%20rev.pdf> accessed 30 September 2020.

Weizsäcker,[167] with debt above that level being issued nationally and labelled as 'red' debt) or to mutualise short-term debt only.[168] In these Eurobond variants, the 'red' part of the debt or the long-term sovereign debt, respectively, remain a national responsibility (i.e. no solidarity is expected from other countries), with the resulting market discipline exerting pressure on governments to pursue fiscally prudent policies. The transition to the 'blue' mutually guaranteed sovereign debt could be facilitated by a no-restructuring guarantee attached to a progressively lower part of each national debt and provided by the ESM (labelled the 'purple' debt by Bini-Smaghi and Marcussen). This guaranteed part of debt would decrease every year by 1/20 of the excess government debt over 60% of GDP, therefore smoothing the debt-reduction efforts of euro area countries, preserving fiscal discipline and paving the way for the mutualisation of sovereign debt equal to 60% of GDP in a 20-year horizon.[169]

At least some of the Eurobond proposals aimed to address the COVID-19 pandemic also seem to follow the same logic: moral hazard is to be addressed by ensuring the mutualisation of only part of the debt that their issuance would entail (specifically, the part aimed at addressing the effects of the pandemic). The remaining part of the debt would still be a national responsibility and, thus, subject to market disciplining effects.

Another Eurobond variant involves differentiating the price at which individual countries would participate in a given Eurobond scheme. For example, De Grauwe and Moesen[170] propose different interest rates for each country participating in a Eurobond issuance, based on the national yields at the date of issuance, while Muellbauer[171] proposes the annual re-setting of national interest rates, based on pre-specified economic performance targets. This would lead to higher costs for countries with weaker economic fundamentals. Delpla and Von Weizsäcker criticise such price differentiation across countries suggesting that this type of 'explicit redistribution' from fiscally weaker to stronger countries may not be politically desirable, even if the net effect from the issuance of Eurobonds would probably be positive for the weaker countries (see Table 3.2 for an overview of the proposals and how they address the moral hazard concern).

167 Jacques Delpla and Jakob Von Weizsäcker, 'The Blue Bond Proposal' (*Bruegel*, 5 May 2010) (Delpla and Von Weizsäcker (2010)) <http://bruegel.org/wp-content/uploads/imported/publications/1005-PB-Blue_Bonds.pdf> accessed 30 September 2020.

168 Thomas Philippon and Christian Hellwig (2011), 'Eurobills, not Eurobonds' (*VoxEU*, 2 December 2011) (Philippon and Hellwig (2011)) <https://voxeu.org/article/eurobills-not-euro-bonds> accessed 30 September 2020.

169 Lorenzo Bini-Smaghi and Michala Marcussen, 'Strengthening the Euro Area Architecture: A Proposal for Purple Bonds' (2018) *SUERF Policy Note* 35 <https://www.suerf.org/policynotes/2733/strengtheningthe-euro-area-architecture-a-proposal-for-purple-bonds> accessed 30 September 2020.

170 Paul De Grauwe and Wim Moesen, 'Gains for All: A Proposal for a Common Euro Bond' (2009) 44 (3) *Intereconomics: Review of European Economic Policy* 132 (De Grauwe and Moesen (2009)).

171 John Muellbauer, 'Resolving the Eurozone Crisis: Time for Conditional Eurobonds' (2011) *Centre for Economic Policy Research Policy Insight* 59 (Muellbauer (2011)) <https://cepr.org/sites/default/files/policy_insights/PolicyInsight59.pdf> accessed 30 September 2020.

Table 3.2 Overview of the various Eurobond proposals. The main features of each proposal are summarised, i.e. the Eurobond issuer, the mechanism embedded to address moral hazard, the main aims as expressed by the authors and the intended size of the Eurobond issuance. The proposals are presented in chronological order

Reference	*Eurobond Proposal (Using the Proposed Name)*	*Issuer*	*How Moral Hazard Is Addressed*	*Aimed to Address Shocks On*	*Amount of Pooled Debt*
De Grauwe and Moesen (2009)	**Eurobonds** guaranteed collectively by the euro area governments.	A European institution such as the EIB.	Different interest rates per country (based on initial conditions of Eurobond issuance).	1) Liquidity (due to flight-to-quality); 2) Negative externalities of rising spreads (e.g. on banks).	Of 'sufficient size to make these bonds liquid instruments.'
Delpla and Von Weizsäcker (2010)	**Blue and Red bonds.** Mutualise only the national debt up to 60% of each country's GDP, subject to the assessment of an independent fiscal board.	Not specified.	1) Only debt up to 60% of GDP is joint (and senior); 2) Junior debt above will be financed at market rates (also: prudent treatment as collateral by the ECB); 3) An independent Board to examine fiscal policies and Blue Bond allocations.	1) Liquidity (due to flight-to-quality); 2) Rising spreads (due to flight-to-safety).	C. €5,6 trillion = 60% of euro area GDP, i.e. around five times the German *Bund* market (calculations with 2010 data).

Table 3.2 Continued

Reference	*Eurobond Proposal (Using the Proposed Name)*	*Issuer*	*How Moral Hazard Is Addressed*	*Aimed to Address Shocks On*	*Amount of Pooled Debt*
Juncker and Tremonti (2010)	**E-bonds** issued by a European agency (follows the Delpla and Weiszäcker proposal).	An EDA, as a successor to the EFSF.	1) Similar to Delpla and Von Weizsäcker; 2) Governments would pay market rates on the part of debt not mutualised; 3) Conversion rate between E-bonds and existing sovereign debt discounted on market prices; 4) Complementary debt restructuring.	1) Address sovereign market stress; 2) Create a liquid safe asset; 3) Enable debt restructuring.	Up to 40% of EU GDP. In exceptional circumstances up to 100% of a country's issuances.
Muellbauer (2011)	**Conditional Eurobonds** guaranteed collectively by the euro area governments.	Not specified.	Annual setting of time-varying interest rates different per country and based upon a set of clear performance targets (determined by a new European monetary and fiscal authority).		

(*Continued*)

Table 3.2 Continued

Reference	*Eurobond Proposal (Using the Proposed Name)*	*Issuer*	*How Moral Hazard Is Addressed*	*Aimed to Address Shocks On*	*Amount of Pooled Debt*
Philippon and Hellwig (2011)	**Eurobills** issued only in the short-maturity range, i.e. <1 year.	Joint DMO of euro area countries.	1) Eurobonds pertain only to <1-year maturities; 2) Countries give up their right to issue short-term debt (<1 year); 3) Frequent rollovers give more bargaining power to fiscal surveillance.	1) Self-fulfilling liquidity runs; 2) In addition, it strengthens existing fiscal surveillance framework.	10% of euro area GDP.
Sachverständigenrat (2011)[a]	**European Redemption Fund,** which would fund above 60% of national GDP under strict conditionality of debt-reducing fiscal policy.	Existing debt above 60% of GDP would be transferred (roll-in phase of five years) to the common redemption fund. Refinancing via fund bonds.	Fiscal discipline safeguards, e.g. national debt brakes in the constitutions, mark-up national tax injected into the fund.	1) Bring national debt down to the 60% Maastricht limit, over a period of c. 25 years; 2) Participating states can fund part of their debt at low rates.	C. €2,3 trillion = government debt exceeding 60% of debt-to-GDP ratio (calculations with 2011 data).

[a] Sachverständigenrat zur Begutachtung der gesamtwirtschaftlichen Entwicklung, 'Verantwortung für Europa wahrnehmen' (2011) *Statistisches Bundesamt, Wiesbaden Jahresgutachten* 2011/12 <https://www.sachverstaendigenrat-wirtschaft.de/fileadmin/dateiablage/an2011/ga11_ges.pdf> accessed 30 September 2020.

A prerequisite for the issuance of Eurobonds would be to prevent the hypothetical situation in which a country could default on its mutualised part of the debt and continue servicing the national part, on the strategic expectation that the remaining countries would continue servicing the mutualised debt. Although such behaviour would no doubt constitute a breach of trust amongst the Members of a monetary union, it cannot be excluded, especially by anti-European or populist governments, willing to prioritise domestic policy considerations over their international obligations. Appropriate safeguards are, therefore, desirable to avert a strategic default scenario from ever materialising, which is why the design features of some of the hitherto Eurobond proposals include safeguards to address the related concerns. For instance, in the Eurobond proposal of Delpla and Von Weizsäcker, it is stated explicitly that the repayment of the mutualised debt takes priority over the repayment of the non-mutualised part ('any government funds used to service and repay government debt will always first be used to satisfy the claims of the Blue Bonds holders').[172]

A useful way to think of the potential benefits of Eurobonds on the sovereigns' funding costs is to decompose the total interest rate paid by a country on its sovereign debt[173] into three parts: (a) a base 'safe rate' component; (b) a credit risk premium; and (c) a liquidity risk premium.[174] Although this decomposition is conceptual and not directly observable, it is possible, using (in a combined way) proxies from relevant market prices and suitable statistical techniques, to infer how these three components comprise the total yield of a sovereign bond. It is, therefore, stressed upfront that this is a conceptual framework to structure our understanding of sovereign yields and a useful first-order approximation tool rather than an exactly observable decomposition.[175] A few caveats on this approach can be directly mentioned, and they are also relevant for the discussion that follows.

First, the definition of a risk-free component is relative, as there is always an amount of risk inherent in any contract. In the context of the monetary union to which the euro area Member States participate, one could use the yield of the German *Bund* as a risk-free benchmark rate and focus on the premia of sovereign debt cost that other issuing countries incur over the German

172 Delpla and Von Weizsäcker (2010), 3.

173 The reference, here, is to a specific sovereign bond issuance.

174 Although exchange risk is also important in explaining cross-country differences of sovereign yields, it is not relevant for the euro area countries.

175 Lawrence Fischer, 'Determinants of the Risk Premiums on Corporate Bonds' (1959) 67 *Journal of Political Economy* 217.

sovereign debt.[176,177] This is a satisfactory approach as the two remaining add-on components – those of credit and liquidity risk – represent risk premia through which the sovereign-banks contagion channel could operate for each individual country.

Second, the two risk components are not independent as there are interactions and feedback loops between them. For example, Ericsson and Renault[178] examine both theoretically and empirically the interaction between credit and liquidity risk for corporate bonds. What they argue in favour of is decomposing the risk premium into *three* components: the credit risk spread, the 'pure' liquidity spread and a third (positive) component, to countenance the interaction between the two types of risk. The reason for the existence of a mutually reinforcing feedback loop between the two risks is that when the bond issuer enters into financial difficulties, the ability of the bond holder to sell the security without an additional discount component due to the illiquidity of the market is crucial, as there will in any case be a discount due to the emergence of heightened credit risk. The possibility of an additional discount during a forced sale gives rise to the interaction term between default and liquidity risk. This mechanism is generic, and it applies to sovereign and to corporate debt alike.

Similar conclusions are also derived by He and Xiong,[179] who focus on the rollover risk as the channel leading to increased credit risk when liquidity dries up. This channel operates via the weakened incentives of equity holders to issue debt to refinance expiring debt due to the increased cost engendered by the low liquidity. The mechanisms and incentives analysed in this line of research also have their counterparts in the sovereign debt market. The shorter the maturity of debt, the stronger this mechanism is, leading to a maturity risk element that can be seen as being incorporated into the interaction component between credit and liquidity risk. The important point is that the credit risk premium and the liquidity risk premium are not two independent components of the risk premium over the risk-free rate but two mutually reinforcing risk components. Pagano and Von Thadden[180] have also demonstrated that the interaction between 'fundamental' risk (i.e. credit risk) and liquidity risk was important for the pricing of euro area bonds during

176 The German *Bund* yield was following the general downward trend in interest rates that began in the early 1980s. In contrast to the countries that faced market distress during the financial crisis of the early 2010s, this trend has not been reversed and has continued up to the time of writing (subject to temporary fluctuations) reinforced by the flight-to-quality phenomenon.

177 For a discussion on how to define a risk-free rate in the context of the euro area, see Alain Monfort and Jean Renne, 'Decomposing Euro-Area Sovereign Spreads: Credit and Liquidity Risks' (2014) 18 *Review of Finance* 2103.

178 Jan Ericsson and Olivier Renault, 'Liquidity and Credit Risk' (2006) 61 *Journal of Finance* 2219.

179 Zhiguo He and Wei Xiong, 'Rollover Risk and Credit Risk' (2012) 67 *Journal of Finance* 391.

180 Marco Pagano and Ernst-Ludwig Von Thadden, 'The European Bond Markets under EMU' (2004) 20 *Oxford Review of Economic Policy* 531.

the early period of the monetary union and, specifically, during the period stretching from 2001 to 2004.

The different Eurobond proposals place varying degrees of emphasis on the reduction of either the credit risk or the liquidity risk premium. For example, Juncker and Tremonti[181] emphasise the liquidity premium reduction that would be achieved by their proposed Eurobonds as they refer to the 'absence of well-functioning secondary markets.' Kopf[182] seems to imply that Juncker and Tremonti pin their hopes solely on the liquidity premium reduction, although there *are* references in their proposal to the confidence-restoring effect of the issuance of Eurobonds, and to their use as collateral for central bank liquidity. Delpla and Von Weiszäcker[183] argue that there is an interaction between the two risk components due to the self-fulfilling dynamics that can turn a liquidity crisis into a solvency crisis.

An argument put forward against Eurobonds is that instead of helping weaker countries pay affordable rates on their sovereign debt, their issuance would merely redistribute the cost from the mutualised part of the debt to the national part. Taking the example of a country paying a high interest rate on its sovereign debt – say, 5% – then, in the case of a mutualised issuance of 50% of its debt, the interest rate on the mutualised part would be lowered to, say, 2.5%, but the rate on the part that remains a national responsibility could shoot up to, say, 7.5%. This prediction could be justified by invoking the Modigliani-Miller theorem,[184] as Kopf does. According to this theorem, originally formulated in the context of corporate finance, the weighted average of equity and debt cost for an economic entity would remain the same, independently of the chosen mix of financing source, as long as the firm's fundamentals have not changed (in the situation under examination here, the economic entity in question would coincide with each individual sovereign issuer participating in a Eurobond issuing scheme). It is, however, submitted that predictions based on the Modigliani-Miller theorem would seem to disregard the change of the 'fundamentals' backing each national sovereign debt stock occurring in the case of the mutualisation of part of their debt, affecting both the mutualised and the non-mutualised component thereof. In other words, the existence of joint guarantees represents a change in the 'fundamentals' of a sovereign issuer of debt, and in the overall pricing of its funding. It seems to take no advanced analytical argumentation to convincingly illustrate that as each sovereign's debt would be mutually guaranteed by other sovereigns (18 to be precise, assuming the current number of euro area countries), the default risk on each sovereign's debt would be lower as, even in a case of distress, there would be another

181 Jean-Claude Juncker and Giulio Tremonti, 'E-Bonds Would End the Crisis' (*Financial Times*, 5 December 2010) (Juncker and Tremonti (2010)).

182 Kopf (2011).

183 Delpla and Von Weiszäcker (2010).

184 Franco Modigliani and Merton H. Miller, 'The Cost of Capital, Corporation Finance and the Theory of Investment' (1958) 48 *American Economic Review* 261.

18 countries that would step-in to honour the debt payments of the sovereign in distress.

It is acknowledged that the above seemingly simplistic argument regarding the expected decrease in credit risk due to the existence of joint guarantees needs to be qualified. The two elements that render the Eurobond financing arrangement more complex than it appears at first sight are, first, an implicit assumption about the co-movement[185] of default risk between the participating countries, which is critical for the financial viability of the scheme, and second, the introduction of the so-called 'step-in risk' due to the obligation of countries to assist other countries facing financial difficulties. These two critical elements will be elaborated on in the following paragraphs.

We first focus on the mutualised part of sovereign debt and examine the assumptions that are necessary to ensure an actual enhancement in the credit quality of the mutualised stock of sovereign debt.

The first assumption is that of non-perfect co-movement across the economic shocks impinging on the various national economies backing the joint Eurobond guarantees. This is what ensures that the risk diversification benefits accrue to all countries participating in the scheme.[186] In fact, it is well-known that, under certain conditions, a diversified portfolio of assets represents a lower overall risk compared to the holding of individual securities (suffice it to refer, here, to the seminal work of Markowitz[187]). Due to this, diversification has been described as the only 'free lunch' that exists in economics. Diversification benefits are at their highest when the dependence of default risk among the participating sovereigns is relatively low and the fluctuations of default risk are minimised.

This first assumption is, therefore, capable of turning one of the economic weaknesses of the monetary union, namely, the asymmetrical impact of shocks on different members of the monetary union, due to the underlying differences

185 Although it is sometimes used in this context, the term 'correlation' properly speaking denotes the degree to which two variables co-move in a linear way. On the other hand, sovereign defaults can be characterised as 'tail' events, i.e. they only happen rarely. In addition, it can be reasonably assumed that the dependence structure between default risk across countries is asymmetrical as signified by the convergence of yields during the pre-crisis period and their subsequent divergence afterwards. Given these departures from a linear relationship, the term 'co-movement' seems more pertinent.

186 The quantification of net gains for each country when comparing the funding costs with and without mutualisation is an exercise that is quite complex, and which has not, to our knowledge, been undertaken, not least because it would be fraught with a very high degree of uncertainty if it were to adopt the requisite intertemporal perspective. However, qualitative arguments can still be formulated and will inform the discussion presented here. Our view is that due to the high degree of uncertainty involved, adopting or rejecting such schemes is not primarily a financial engineering exercise – however crucial the finance arrangements may be – but is practically bound to be informed by heuristics, proof-of-concepts (e.g. like the relevant measures taken to address the COVID-19 pandemic, which represent a prototype experience of mutualised debt) and political preferences.

187 Harry Markowitz, 'Portfolio Selection' (1952) 7 *Journal of Finance* 77.

in their competitiveness, export orientation, sectoral specialisation etc., into an advantage as regards the potential effectiveness of a Eurobond scheme. Specifically, the EMU has been described as not satisfying the conditions for being an 'optimum currency area,'[188] i.e. an area where fixed exchange rates could work, a result that would require high labour and capital mobility and convergence in the economic fundamentals of the participating countries. In a pessimistic description, Krugman[189] identifies the existence of 'asymmetric shocks' (i.e. shocks that are country or region-specific) as the main threat to currency unions given that the participation of countries in a union has deprived them of adjustment tools, such as exchange rate depreciation or the use of the central bank to finance sovereign debt (see Section 3.2 for more details). However, in the context of a potential Eurobond issuance, the existence of such asymmetrical shocks could actually prove to be an advantage as it implies a low level of co-movement in the shocks impinging on the individual countries participating in the monetary union. Such a low level of co-movement increases the so-called diversifiable component of the overall risk, i.e. the part of the risk that is not common to all economies of the monetary union. The pooling of resources underpinning a Eurobond issuance would minimise specifically the diversifiable component of risk, i.e. would provide a hedge against shocks that impinge with different intensity on the individual countries.

The second assumption for lowering the risk fluctuations (as regards the upward movements of each country's individual risk) boils down to the quality of economic governance for each individual country. The important point is that the various national economic policies would be to some extent endogenous to a Eurobond issuance, i.e. they would not be exogenously given but could be impacted, both in the positive and in the negative, from the mutualisation of part of the sovereign debt. This is so for a number of reasons. First, the issuance of a mutualised asset could potentially help to alleviate the increases in risk that are due to the mechanisms analysed in Section 3.2, and which are linked to the loss of adjustment tools that participation in a monetary union entails. On the other hand, there is the risk that the issuance of a Eurobond could increase moral hazard risks and lower the quality of national economic policies, which could then potentially increase the upward fluctuations of credit risk, undermining in turn the viability of the mutualised debt. Therefore, addressing moral hazard risks is a critical element of any Eurobond issuance proposal, and this is reflected in the emphasis that the different Eurobond proposals have placed on embedded mechanisms to address the potential for rent-seeking policies (as examined earlier).

Furthermore, another precondition for the success of a Eurobond issuance is that the large majority of the participating countries (also when weighted by

188 Robert Mundell, 'A Theory of Optimum Currency Areas' (1961) 51 *American Economic Review* 657.

189 Paul Krugman, 'Revenge of the Optimum Currency Area' in Daron Acemoglu, Jonathan Parker and Michael Woodford (eds), *NBER Macroeconomic Annual* (University of Chicago Press 2012).

their size) are solvent and financially robust. This condition, which, although important, has not been stressed in previous works, echoes the shift in the economic understanding of the benefits of diversification that has taken place in the aftermath of the 2007–2008 global financial crisis. Specifically, the positive view of diversification has been displaced by a more nuanced view that acknowledges the potential for contagion arising in an interconnected system. Recent versions of this revised assessment of the risk-reducing properties of diversification state that up to a certain threshold in the size of an initial shock, diversification enhances the possibility of an economic system to absorb the impact; however, when the initial shock exceeds that threshold, interconnectedness (i.e. diversification) could increase the vulnerability of the system as it would imply that the impact would be felt by more entities within that system.[190]

In the case of a Eurobond issuance, such potential for contagion could be created by the step-in risk arising from the obligation of the participating Member States to assist an ailing member. This possibility of contagion via the step-in risk is mitigated by ensuring that the mutualised issuance takes place in a situation when most of the countries are robust financially since, in that case, they are better able to withstand even larger-sized economic shocks without further negative consequences. In addition, in the case of the euro area, debt mutualisation would not replace a set of relatively independent national economies with an *ex nihilo* interconnected system of national economies: hence, it cannot be argued that a new channel of contagion would be created where none existed before. On the contrary, as the euro area sovereign debt and, more recently, the COVID-19 pandemic crisis has shown, the euro-area economies are already highly interlinked, leading to the very real possibility of financial contagion across them. In this context, the mutualisation of some part of the sovereign debt would probably increase the shock-absorbing capacity of the monetary union as a whole more than it would increase the vulnerability of individual countries due to the step-in risk.

Regarding the non-mutualised part of the sovereign debt, also there one would expect a positive impact from the mutualisation scheme. Even if this part of debt could feature a higher cost compared to the mutualised part, this higher cost would be compensated by a lowering in the overall cost of funding due to the existence of joint guarantees. The increased safety of the mutualised part of sovereign debt means that the 'higher-risk' stock of debt would shrink significantly and, as a result, the non-mutualised part of the national sovereign debt could also be impacted positively by a Eurobond issuance.

As regards the liquidity risk premium reduction, Delpla and Von Weiszäcker[191] assume a 30 basis points liquidity risk premium over the US government bond market and calculate that out of the debt below the 60% of

190 Acemoglu et al. (2015).

191 Delpla and Von Weiszäcker (2010).

GDP threshold, a reduction of this liquidity risk premium (due to the creation of a 'safe asset' of the scale similar to the US sovereign bond market) would decrease by 10% the net present value of the legacy debt up to the 60% of GDP. In other words, the argument is that an important positive effect is possible solely due to the liquidity risk premium reduction.

Another effect of a Eurobond issuance – especially relevant for significant size Eurobond issuances – would be that they would facilitate the planning of an orderly sovereign debt restructuring mechanism. This argument is emphasised both by Juncker and Tremonti and by Delpla and Von Weizsäcker. In both cases, the argument is that the mutualised part of the debt would represent a large amount of the total sovereign debt; therefore, the systemic consequences of a restructuring would be avoided, and restructuring could take place on the ringfenced part of the debt that remains as a national responsibility. Debt restructuring is a policy fraught with risks, including the risk of triggering self-fulfilling crises (see Section 1.4.6), especially in the context of banks with sovereign bond portfolios featuring a strong home bias. As a result, debt restructuring could have adverse economic and social consequences, e.g. to pension funds, insurance companies, i.e. institutional investors who fulfil a critical social role. In addition, a policy of debt restructuring would raise issues of consistency with the regulatory treatment of sovereign debt (see also Chapter 5), which is why its consequences for government funding and investor incentives should be carefully considered. However, irrespective of the policy stance towards sovereign debt restructuring, the issuance of Eurobonds would objectively alleviate, to some extent, the consequences of a debt restructuring where the latter is unavoidable.

Last but not least, Eurobonds would confer to European banks the collateral buffer they need to enhance their resilience in the face of shocks to their sovereign. As analysed in Section 3.4.2 on safe assets, the collateral enhancement held by commercial banks would be a crucial tool through which to address the contagion transmission mechanism from the sovereign to the banking system. In this respect, the size of the Eurobond issuance is a critical parameter: larger Eurobond issuances would also be more conducive to breaking the transmission of financial stress to banks as the availability of collateral would increase.

At the time of writing, a debate was ongoing on the European response to the economic crisis borne out of the COVID-19 pandemic. This debate was also relevant for the Eurobonds discussion, both because the issuance of Eurobonds (more accurately, 'Coronabonds,' as the declared aim of their proposed issuance was to fund actions to alleviate the crisis induced by the pandemic) was amongst the policy actions proposed at the height of the pandemic but, also, because the COVID-19 pandemic exemplifies a situation in which the moral hazard argument loses most of its validity. The reason is that the economic crisis triggered by the pandemic did not result from any specific national policies; hence European support would not find itself under the risk of 'rewarding' any beggar-thy-neighbour behaviour. There is a critical distinction to be made between the issuance of Eurobonds for symmetrical shocks, on the one hand, and asymmetrical shocks, on the other, and it is fair to say that debt mutualisation of the type proposed to address the symmetrical shock of the COVID-19 pandemic was already taking place, but in a more indirect and more complex way. In a commentary to a Greek newspaper, ESM Managing Director Klaus Regling explained the mechanism as follows:

> The EIB – and to a smaller extent the European Commission – issue such debt for all twenty-seven EU member-states, and the ESM for the nineteen euro area countries. These three institutions have issued mutualised debt, i.e. European debt, for many years already. Today, these institutions have around €800 billion in outstanding European debt. All three provide financing at interest rates well below the funding costs of most EU Member States.[192,193]

The main alternative proposed to Coronabonds came in the form of ESM credit lines, either without or only subject to 'light' conditionality, in conjunction with a temporary and targeted 'European Recovery Fund,' as a top-up to the Union's budget, funded by debt issued by the Commission on the capital markets under guarantees of the Member States. The ESM alternative was criticised on the grounds that it would entail a 'stigma' for countries resorting to the ESM for support, affecting market perceptions of their sovereign solvency and, as a result, leading to higher spreads.

To conclude, the Eurobond policy option seems to be effective in breaking the sovereign–banks contagion channel: as explained above, the issuance of Eurobonds would allow for a reduction in both the credit and the liquidity risk premiums paid by countries facing financial distress, while at the same time weakening the negative impact of the interaction between these two types of risk. Furthermore, and related to these positive effects, the issuance of Eurobonds is apt to support banks' funding both by reducing its costs and by creating high-quality collateral. The foregoing benefits of Eurobonds are to be balanced against the concerns raised by the thorny issue of moral hazard. In contrast to the perceptions created by some of the participants in the public

192 The similarity between a mutualised Eurobond (here, a Coronabond) with the ESM credit line has been explained in similar terms by the Handelsblatt: 'Bei Corona-Bonds haften die Euro-Länder gemeinschaftlich für die begebenen Anleihen. Wenn also Italien in Zahlungsschwierigkeiten gerät, müssten die anderen Euro-Staaten dafür geradestehen. Auch bei Hilfen des ESM oder Anleihekäufen der EZB ist dies aber nicht wesentlich anders. Zwar kaufen die nationalen Notenbanken des Euro-Systems die Anleihen formell auf eigene Rechnung. Wenn sie aber ausfallen, müssten wohl doch alle Euro-Länder einspringen. Letztendlich unterscheiden sich die Varianten also nicht so sehr' (Jan Mallien, 'Die Bundesbank sollte bei Corona-Bonds nicht rumeiern' (*Handelsblatt*, 2 April 2020)).

193 Klaus Regling, 'The Time for European Solidarity is Now' (*Kathimerini*, 2 April 2020) <http://www.ekathimerini.com/251284/opinion/ekathimerini/comment/regling-the-time-for-european-solidarity-is-now> accessed 30 September 2020.

discourse on the subject, the Eurobond proposals put forward so far have not neglected this issue. On the contrary, they have placed significant emphasis on addressing the moral hazard side-effects of Eurobonds, so much so that, however valid, moral hazard concerns do not appear to pose insurmountable obstacles in considering seriously the splitting of debt into a mutualised and a residual part, which would still be a national responsibility, hence exposed to the effects of market discipline. This split can be accomplished by either focusing on a specific amount of debt (e.g. 60% of GDP) or on different parts of the maturity spectrum (e.g. by mutualising only short-term debt). In contrast, suggestions for addressing moral hazards through interest rate differentials seem to be politically risky as they conflate debt mutualisation and market discipline. Where Eurobonds appear more problematic is in respect of the compatibility of their issuance with primary EU law, an issue examined in greater detail in Chapter 5.

4 Closing the first channel of contagion from banks to sovereigns

Hitherto European actions and their critique

4.1 Introductory remarks

As suggested in the introduction to this work, it was primarily through the creation of the European Banking Union that Europe and the euro area sought to close the first channel of contagion.

According to the Statement of the Euro Area Summit of 29 June 2012,[1] the rationale for the establishment of the European Banking Union was to 'break the vicious circle between banks and sovereigns.' The creation of the European Banking Union was tabled at the Euro Area Summit, at the height of the euro-area fiscal crisis, where it was decided to invite the President of the European Council

> to develop, in close collaboration with the President of the European Commission, the President of the Eurogroup and the President of the European Central Bank, a specific and time-bound road map for the achievement of a genuine Economic and Monetary Union.

as in accordance with a report by the President of the European Council dated 26 June 2012.[2] One of the four elements of this report was the creation of the European Banking Union. The latter was to result in the establishment of a 'Europeanised bank safety net,' consisting of:

(1) An SSM, exclusively for the banking sector (excluding the insurance and securities sectors) and mainly for credit institutions legally incorporated in euro-area Member States (the first pillar of the European Banking Union);
(2) An SRM for unviable credit institutions (mostly for those legally incorporated in the euro area), and an SRF to cover any resulting funding gaps (the second pillar of the European Banking Union); and

1 Euro Area Summit, *Statement* (29 June 2012) <https://www.consilium.europa.eu/media/21400/20120629-euro-area-summit-statement-en.pdf> accessed 30 September 2020.

2 European Council, The President, Herman Van Rompuy, 'Towards a Genuine Economic and Monetary Union' EUCO 120/12.

(3) An EDIS, which, coupled with the SRB (part of the SRM), could form a 'European Deposit Insurance and Resolution Authority' (the third pillar of the European Banking Union).

The institutional architecture of the European Banking Union, which is, first and foremost, an *organisational and governance* (as opposed to a *regulatory*)[3] type of solution to the banking sector shortcomings brought to light by the sovereign financial crisis, bears both similarities to, and significant differences from, institutional structure models used in other areas of EU law. In some respects, it makes sense to compare the SSM (and, to a lesser extent, the SRM) to the European System of Central Banks ('ESCB'), not least because both EMU and the European Banking Union have one key component in common, namely the ECB. Moreover, both the SRM/SSM and the ESCB centralise executive functions through supranational structures (the Governing/General Council, in the case of the ESCB, the SRB, in the case of the SRM, and the ECB Supervisory Board, in the case of the SSM). However, the SRM/SSM's decentralisation features are stronger compared to those of the ESCB since, without prejudice to the pivotal role of the SRB within the SRM, and of the ECB Supervisory Board within the SSM, national authorities retain certain operational powers both in the case of the SSM and, in particular, in the case of the SRM. Another point of difference between the ESCB and the SRB is this: because the latter relies on the agency model, it cannot adopt rules (instead, it is to operate within the confines of the SRM). The ECB, by contrast, is a fully-fledged EU institution, possessed of own-regulatory powers and operating independently of other EU institutions, Member State governments or (other) third parties. It follows that, in its capacity as supervisor, the ECB disposes of far wider, own powers, including the power to adopt final acts (irrespective of whether it may rely on preparatory acts issued by the national competent authorities ('NCAs')). The SRB, in contrast, is bound to act at the behest of the Commission and, mostly, through the national resolution authorities ('NRAs'). This is despite the fact that, as supervisor, the ECB is to act subject to the legal parameters established by Regulation (EU) 1024/2013[4] ('the SSM Regulation' or 'SSMR'), exercising its powers on the basis of Regulation (EU) 575/2013[5] ('Capital Requirements Regulation' or 'CRR') and of the national

3 The legal acts on the basis of which the European Banking Union is to operate were not adopted with the banking union project in mind, and apply to all EU Member States, whether or not they participate in the European Banking Union.

4 Council Regulation (EU) 1024/2013 of 15 October 2013 conferring specific tasks on the European Central Bank concerning policies relating to the prudential supervision of credit institutions [2013] OJ L287/63.

5 Regulation (EU) 575/2013 of the European Parliament and of the Council of 26 June 2013 on prudential requirements for credit institutions and investment firms and amending Regulation (EU) 648/2012 [2013] OJ L176/1.

implementation of Directive 2013/36/EU[6] ('CRD IV'), meaning that the ECB's discretionary decision-making powers are considerably more restrained when it acts as supervisor, compared to what they are when it acts as a monetary policy authority.[7]

With the foregoing remarks in mind, we examine, below, each of the three pillars of the European Banking Union, exploring their main operational, legal and other shortcomings, and the impact of those shortcomings on the delivery by the European Banking Union of its main end-objective, namely, the closure of the first channel of contagion.

4.2 The single supervisory mechanism: Overview of legal and operational shortcomings and concerns

4.2.1 Operational set-up and related concerns

The aim of the SSM, the first of the three pillars of the European Banking Union, was to foster financial stability by centralising, at the level of the ECB, the supervision of significant financial institutions, thereby doing away with the home bias of national supervisors thought to account for the bulk of the pre-crisis supervisory failures.[8]

The SSMR, a Council Regulation complemented by an ECB Regulation (Regulation (EU) 468/2014[9] ('the SSM Framework Regulation')), was the

6 Directive 2013/36/EU of the European Parliament and of the Council of 26 June 2013 on access to the activity of credit institutions and the prudential supervision of credit institutions and investment firms, amending Directive 2002/87/EC and repealing Directives 2006/48/EC and 2006/49/EC [2013] OJ L176/338.

7 The SSM is not dissimilar to the European Competition Network, which also rests on the existence of parallel competences, those of the European Commission and the competent Member State authorities, all of which maintain their institutional independence as part of a decentralised system, where the European Commission plays the leading role, to ensure the consistent functioning of the Network. For a comparison between the European Competition Network and the SSM, see Agnese Pizzolla, 'The Role of the European Central Bank in the Single Supervisory Mechanism: A New Paradigm for EU Governance' (2018) 43 (1) *European Law Review* 3, 10–14.

8 For a thorough overview of the three pillars of the European Banking Union, with an emphasis on SSM, see, *ex multi*, Klaus Lackhoff, *Single Supervisory Mechanism, A Practitioner's Guide* (Beck – Hart – Nomos 2017); Christos V. Gortsos, *The Single Supervisory Mechanism (SSM), Legal Aspects of the First Pillar of the European Banking Union* (Nomiki Bibliothiki 2015); and Eddy O. Wymeersch, 'The Single Supervisory Mechanism for Banking Supervision: Institutional Aspects' in Danny Busch and Guido Ferrarini (eds), *European Banking Union* (2nd edn, Oxford University Press 2019). For works that also cover other aspects of the European Banking Union, see, for instance, Gianni Lo Schiavo (ed.), *The European Banking Union and the Role of Law* (Elgar Financial Law 2019).

9 Regulation (EU) 468/2014 of the European Central Bank of 16 April 2014 establishing the framework for cooperation within the Single Supervisory Mechanism between the European Central Bank and national competent authorities and with national designated authorities (SSM Framework Regulation) [2014] OJ L141/1. The legal basis for the SSM Framework Regulation is Article 6(7) of the SSMR, which also lays down its minimum content ('[T]he framework shall include, at least, the following …').

secondary law basis for the conferral of supervisory powers to the ECB. Article 127(6) TFEU, which provided the primary law basis for the SSMR, imposed constraints on the SSM's design by stating that the ECB may assume *specific* prudential supervisory *tasks* over banks and other financial institutions (except insurance firms). This was intended to limit the ECB's scope of action in matters of bank supervision to those tasks considered indispensable to guarantee financial stability and to ensure the coherent and effective application of the EU's prudential supervisory rules.[10]

Because the ECB does not have the institutional capacity to single-handedly exercise supervision over the 130 significant institutions ('SIs')[11] subject to its direct supervision, Joint Supervisory Teams ('JSTs'), composed of staff drawn from the ECB and the NCAs, have been established, one for each SI, with every JST headed by a coordinator drawn from the staff of the ECB.[12] When exercising their tasks in a JST, NCA staff members are to follow the instructions of the ECB coordinator.[13] Where an NCA is represented in the JST with more than one member, it is to designate a sub-coordinator.[14] If, in a given jurisdiction, an NCB that is not an NCA is to participate in a JST (because national law provides for its involvement in prudential supervision), it is to appoint a sub-coordinator.[15]

JSTs are the functional units through which the day-to-day supervision of SIs is to be conducted. Their tasks include the preparation and organisation, respectively, of the annual supervisory examination programme and the operational supervision of all banks subject to direct ECB supervision on a consolidated, sub-consolidated and single entity level,[16] the commission and coordination of on-site inspections of SIs, the preparation of draft decisions, in close coordination with the ECB's competent Directorates General and horizontal services[17] and the exercise of a number of accessory tasks (including the approval of internal models, the participation in crisis management meetings and integration into colleges of supervisors). The existence of JSTs means

10 The assessment, in this section, of the implications of the transfer to the ECB of certain micro-prudential supervisory tasks draws on Phoebus Athanassiou, 'The Institutional Architecture and Tasks of the ECB' in Federico Fabbrini and Marco Ventoruzzo (eds), *Research Handbook on EU Economic Law* (Edward Elgar 2019).

11 The number of SIs mentioned here includes those of Bulgaria and Croatia, which have acceded to the close cooperation mechanism.

12 SSM Framework Regulation, Art. 3(1).

13 Ibid., Art. 6(1). This functional subordination may well give rise to legal issues under national civil service law.

14 Ibid., Art. 6(2).

15 Ibid., Art. 5(3).

16 This task involves procuring information, assessing risk, preparing the supervisory review and evaluation process, performing ad hoc analyses, assisting in policy work and regulatory projects, evaluating recovery plans and processing formal authorisation requests.

17 The ECB's Supervisory Board subsequently reviews those draft decisions and decides on the proposals to be passed on to the ECB's Governing Council for a final decision.

that the NCAs continue to play a major role in the supervision of SIs, both in terms of local expertise and experience (e.g. on national laws implementing EU directives), and in the daily communication with the directly supervised SIs (where the presence of native speakers is necessary).

The exact allocation, between the ECB and the NCAs, of supervisory competences over SIs and less significant institutions ('LSIs') has been the source of controversy,[18] fuelled by litigation before national and EU courts alike. Although Article 6(4) of the SSMR confers upon the ECB *exclusive* competence for certain supervisory tasks in respect of credit institutions and groups falling within the scope *rationae personae* of the SSM, only those credit institutions classified as 'significant' are supervised *directly* by the ECB. Moreover, the text of Article 6(6) of the SSMR[19] could be read to suggest that certain supervisory powers over so-called LSIs[20] remain vested in the NCAs. The conclusion to which the combined reading of the foregoing provisions could lead is that the SSMR does not confer on the ECB the *exclusive* competence over banking supervision in the euro area, and that although the ECB is to have exclusive competence over (all) credit institutions in the SSM with regard to the performance of the tasks enumerated in Article 4(1) of the SSMR (such as, for instance, the issuance and withdrawal of banking licences), the ECB is to only be competent, in addition, for the supervision of SIs. This was the interpretation that the *Bundesverfassungsgericht* (Germany's Federal Constitutional Court) sided with in its July 2019 ruling in the *Banking Union* case.[21] There, in its assessment of whether the EU had exceeded the competences conferred upon it by the Treaties in adopting the European Banking Union legislative framework, the *Bundesverfassungsgericht* ruled that the SSMR did not confer full banking supervision on the ECB: instead, the NCAs essentially retained their supervisory powers over LSIs, which they exercised on the basis of their own primary competences in all areas of banking supervision that are not subject to the SSMR. This interpretation cannot be right as the ruling of the *Bundesverfassungsgericht* contradicts the earlier (May 2019) decision of the Court of Justice of the European Union ('the Court' or 'CJEU') in the *Landeskreditbank* (or *L-bank*) case (it is recalled that the exclusive competence

18 On the allocation of competences between the ECB and the NCAs, see, generally, Christos V. Gortsos, 'Competence Sharing Between the ECB and the National Competent Supervisory Authorities within the Single Supervisory Mechanism (SSM)' (2015) 16 European Business Organization Law Review 401; Takis P. Tridimas, 'The Constitutional Dimension of Banking Union' in Stefan Grundmann and Hans-W. Micklitz (eds), *The European Banking Union and Constitution* (Hart Publishing 2019) (Tridimas (2019)), 43–44.

19 The division of tasks between the ECB and the NCAs, which is primarily based on their relative size, economic importance and the scale of their cross-border activities, does not apply to certain tasks (those appearing in Articles 4(1)(a) and (c), 14 and 15 of the SSMR), which the ECB has *sole* competence to carry out for *all* credit institutions established in the participating Member States.

20 SSMR, Art. 6(4).

21 Order of 30 July 2019 (Europäische Bankenunion) 2 *BVerfGE* 1685/14, 2 *BVerfGE* 2631/14.

to interpret EU law rests with the CJEU).[22] There, in the context of litigation over whether a bank that satisfied the requirements for qualifying as an SI could exceptionally be classified as an LSI, in order to continue being subject to national supervision, the Court upheld the interpretation of the General Court[23] that the ECB had exclusive competence for the supervision of SIs and LSIs alike, and that the NCAs were merely tasked with *implementing* certain *derivative* supervisory tasks, in support of the ECB's supervisory competences, with the SSMR catering for the 'decentralised implementation' of those competences.[24] The necessary implication of the Court's ruling is that the premise of the NCAs' supervisory powers (such as they are) over LSIs is not national but EU law, in the form of the SSMR, and that those powers are not domestic but EU law powers.

Despite being next to unavoidable, given the limited capacity of the ECB relative to the scale of the challenge of single-handedly supervising all banks operating in the euro area, the division of SSM tasks between the ECB and the NCAs is apt to give rise to a number of legal complications. In particular, the Eurosystem NCAs are 'responsible for assisting the ECB' in the exercise of its supervisory tasks,[25] while performing certain tasks under the SSMR: it follows that the NCAs are closely involved in the exercise, by the ECB, of its direct supervisory powers under the SSMR, while the ECB has an 'oversight' role in connection with the exercise, by the NCAs, of their tasks under the SSMR.[26] The involvement of the NCAs in the ECB's work, as direct supervisor (with the NCAs cooperating with and supporting the ECB in most supervisory procedures, e.g. by engaging in certain preparatory acts), and the ECB's monitoring role over NCAs inevitably complicate the task of deciding on the allocation of responsibility for the day-to-day supervision of banks in the SSM. Besides, following a consultation with the relevant NCA, the ECB may decide to take over direct supervisory responsibility over institutions or groups classified as LSIs,[27] including responsibility for the conclusion of pending supervisory action.[28] What is more, the ECB has the power to require the NCAs to

22 *Landeskreditbank Baden-Württemberg – Förderbank v. ECB* [2019] ECLI:EU:C:2019:372.

23 *Landeskreditbank Baden-Württemberg – Förderbank v. ECB* [2017] ECLI:EU:T:2017:337, para. 22.

24 *L-bank* [2019], paras 38 and 41.

25 SSMR, Art. 6(3).

26 Article 6(5)(c) of the SSMR, read in conjunction with Article 6(1), final sentence, thereof. While the ECB will not exercise direct supervision over LSIs, SSMR grants the ECB several powers through which to monitor how NCAs supervise LSIs; these include (a) addressing regulations, guidelines and general instructions to NCAs (Art. 6(5)(a)); (b) requesting ad hoc/continuous information from the NCAs (Art. 6(5)(e)); and (c) carrying out general investigations and on-site inspections, led by on-site inspections teams whose leader would be chosen by the ECB (Arts 10–13).

27 SSMR, Art. 6(5)(b). The criteria and procedure for the taking up, by the ECB, of direct supervision over an LSI are fleshed out in Articles 67–69 of the SSM Framework Regulation. These include the fact that the institution or group may be *close* to meeting any one of the significance criteria set out in Article 6(4) of the SSRM or that the NCA has failed to comply with the instructions of the ECB.

28 *SSM Framework Regulation*, Art. 48.

make use of their own supervisory powers where the SSMR does not confer such powers on the ECB.[29] To the extent that the ECB can 'pull the strings,' even in connection with LSIs, it is legitimate to wonder how exactly to apportion supervisory responsibility between the ECB and the NCAs.[30] A related question is that of the jurisdictional competence to adjudicate over disputes in connection with 'composite supervisory procedures' (defined as those involving both the ECB, as supervisor, and the NCAs). In the *Berlusconi* case, the Grand Chamber of the CJEU ruled that, in order to reflect the unitary design of composite supervisory procedures and to ensure effective judicial protection, the review of the legality of discretionary supervisory decisions taken by the ECB under the SSM legal framework is subject to judicial review *exclusively* by the EU courts, with the exclusive competence of the latter extending over the review of NCA preparatory acts taken under national law on which the ECB may have based its discretionary supervisory decisions; and that it is only where a national preliminary act 'is a necessary stage of a procedure for adopting an EU act in which the EU institutions have only a limited or no discretion, so that the national act is binding on the EU institution,' that the national courts are themselves competent to rule on any irregularities that may vitiate such a national preparatory act.[31]

Finally, it is recalled that it is only through the NCAs of the non-euro-area Member States that the ECB can act in the case of supervised entities established outside the euro area, where a 'close cooperation' agreement, within the meaning of Article 7 of the SSMR, has been established.[32] It bears noting that the legal effect of the conclusion of a close cooperation agreement is that the signatory Member State is equated to a 'participating Member State,' as

29 SSMR, recital (35) and Art. 9(1). This power is, presumably, limited to SIs.

30 On the issue of the allocation of supervisory responsibility under the SSM, see Phoebus Athanassiou, 'Non-Contractual Liability under the Single Supervisory Mechanism: Key Features and Grey Areas' (2015) 30 (7) *Journal of International Banking Law and Regulation* 382.

31 *Berlusconi and Finanziaria d'investimento SpA (Fininvest) v. Banca d'Italia et al.* [2018] ECLI:EU:C:2018:1023, paras 42 to 47. For an assessment the ruling of the Court see, *ex multi*, Paul Dermine and Mariolina Eliantonio, 'Case Note: CJEU (Grand Chamber), Judgment of 19 December 2018, C-219/17, Silvio Berlusconi and Finanziaria D'investimento Fininvest SpA (Fininvest) v. Banca D'Italia and Istituto per La Vigilanza Sulle Assicurazioni (IVASS)' (2019) 12 (2) *Review of European Administrative Law* 237; Herwig C.H. Hofmann, 'Multi-Jurisdictional Composite Procedures – The Backbone to the EU's Single Regulatory Space,' *University of Luxembourg Law Working Paper* 003-2019 <https://ssrn.com/abstract=3399042> accessed 30 September 2020; Märt Maarand, 'The Impact of the Judgment in Case C-219/17, Berlusconi and Fininvest, on Court Jurisdiction regarding Legality of Acts by Institutions of Single Resolution Mechanism' (2019) 5 (2) *International Comparative Jurisprudence* 149.

32 SSMR, Art. 7(1), 2nd para. Article 7 of the SSMR provides that non-euro area Member States may enter into a 'close cooperation agreement' with the ECB, the effect of which is to bring credit institutions and groups incorporated in their territory within the remit of the ECB's supervisory authority. At the time of writing, Bulgaria had requested the establishment of close cooperation between the ECB and the Bulgarian National Bank, while several other countries had expressed interest in the close cooperation model, but had yet to commit either way.

defined in the SSMR, and that all of its banks become part of the SSM. One significant difference between supervision in a euro area and a non-euro-area country is that the ECB is *not* allowed to take legally binding decisions directly applicable to (significant) banks in the relevant non-euro area country:[33] the Supervisory Board of the ECB is to take and address its draft decisions to the NCA, which is to then ensure, through national-level action, that the supervised bank applies those decisions. The pivotal role of the NCAs, as the ECB's interface with supervised entities established outside the euro area, is also apt to blur the boundaries between their responsibility and that of the ECB in the context of the operation of a 'close cooperation' agreement.

What can be deduced from the foregoing is that the ECB's success as a banking sector supervisor will greatly depend on how smoothly the JSTs operate and on how efficiently the ECB and the NCBs will cooperate, going forward, in the context of the SSM. As much as it may be among the main strengths of the SSM,[34] the involvement of national supervisors in the day-to-day activities of the SSM could also develop into one of its weaknesses.

4.2.2 Other legal concerns and open questions

The conferral to the ECB of micro-prudential powers and tasks, in conjunction with the continuing involvement of the NCAs in the ECB's exercise of its supervisory tasks inevitably give rise to a number of other, mostly legal concerns, of which the most relevant for the purposes of this work are touched on below.[35]

The first of these concerns arises from the ECB's application of *national law* in the exercise of its supervisory powers and in the performance of its supervisory tasks. Where relevant, the ECB is to rely on the national implementation of EU directives in the field of banking supervision rather than directly on the rules set out in those directives,[36] and this despite the fact that the ECB is a fully-fledged EU institution.[37] The unprecedented application by the ECB, in the exercise of its supervisory tasks, of national law (in the form of the domestic transposition of certain EU directives, including CRD IV and the CRR, which, significantly, encompass a number of options and discretions for the

33 As implicit from the combined reading of Articles 139(e) and 132 TFEU.

34 This is on account of the long-standing expertise of banking supervisors in domestic banking supervision, also acknowledged in recital (37) to the SSMR.

35 For a more extensive overview of those concerns, see Giovanni Bassani, *The Legal Framework Applicable to the Single Supervisory Mechanism* (Wolters Kluwer 2019) (Bassani (2019)), Ch. 3: The National Powers' Debate.

36 The point is made in Asen Lefterov, 'The Single Rulebook: Legal Issues and Relevance in the SSM Context' (2015) *European Central Bank Legal Working Paper* 15, 36 <https://www.ecb.europa.eu/pub/pdf/scplps/ecblwp15.en.pdf> accessed 30 September 2020, with reference to Article 4(3) of the SSMR.

37 TEU, Art. 13(1) (ex Art. 9).

national authorities)[38] represents a novelty, the implications of which, inter alia on the balance of powers between the EU and its Member States, and on the practicalities of the judicial review of the ECB's exercise of its supervisory powers, have yet to be tested.[39] Of the range of legal issues that this particular feature of the SSM could give rise to, three stand out the most. The first is to do with the boundaries of the jurisdiction of national courts over the ECB when acting as supervisor, and with the extent to which the General Court may have to, at least, take cognisance of national law when adjudicating over a claim in damages against the ECB, for unlawful supervisory acts or omissions (in this regard, the reader is referred to our brief account of the *Berlusconi* case, earlier in this chapter). The second is to do with the ECB's predicament if faced with a situation where it has to apply national rules that may be in conflict with Union law, within the meaning of the landmark ruling of the CJEU in *Simmenthal*:[40] is the ECB to 'set aside' those rules, so as to preserve the effectiveness of Union law or is it, alternatively, to abstain from taking supervisory measures on their basis, with the same aim but with an impact on the effectiveness of its supervisory action? The third is to do with situations where the ECB would choose to interpret and apply national rules differently to an NCA, generating legal uncertainty or breaching the principle of legitimate expectations.[41] Even in those cases where the above concerns would not affect the overall effectiveness of the ECB's supervision (and with it, the SSM's effectiveness in closing the first channel of contagion), they could create scope for different supervisory outcomes, both across the different SSM jurisdictions and within the same jurisdictions, as between SIs and LSIs, with an impact on the achievement of a level playing field for banks within the SSM.

A second concern regards the administrative law aspect of supervisory decisions under the SSM, and the EU due process principles applicable to them. Where it is the NCAs that perform preparatory supervisory acts and issue prudential supervisory decisions (as the case is with regard to LSIs), it is national administrative rules and procedures – based on national administrative law – that will apply.[42] Conversely, where it is the ECB that performs prudential supervisory functions and issues prudential supervisory decisions (as the case

38 For an extensive account of the options and discretions available under EU law, and their impact on the ECB's exercise of its micro-prudential supervisory tasks, see Bassani (2019), Ch. 4: Options and Discretions Available in Union Law.

39 This is, in particular, true of the application by an EU institution, such as the ECB, of national law for the purposes of the exercise of its supervisory tasks, and of the attribution to the ECB of significant new powers, in a field where the EU had no direct role until the establishment of the SSM. For a thoughtful account of the constitutional aspects of the European Banking Union, see Tridimas (2019).

40 *Amministrazione delle Finanze dello Stato v. Simmenthal SpA* [1978] ECLI:EU:C:1978:49.

41 This point is aptly made in Laura Wissink, 'Challenges to an Efficient European Centralised Banking Supervision (SSM): Single Rulebook, Joint Supervisory Teams and Split Supervisory Tasks' (2017) 18 (3) *European Business Organization Law Review* 431 (Wissink (2017)), 440.

42 Articles 6(3) and 6(7) of the SSMR are not crystal clear on this point.

is with SIs), it is EU administrative law and due process principles that will apply. Although the latter are only partially codified,[43] they can be inferred from the general principles of law common to the constitutional traditions of the Member States, identified by the Court in its relevant jurisprudence since its landmark ruling in *Algera*.[44] It is recalled that the EU law due process principles applicable under the SSM are set out in Article 22 of the SSMR, read in conjunction with Articles 31–33 of the SSM Framework Regulation. A related concern regards the due process guarantees applicable to the ECB in the exercise of its investigatory powers pursuant to Articles 10–13 of the SSMR, and the bifurcation of the competence for judicial review between Member State courts and the CJEU in connection with those powers.[45] However undesirable, the resulting legal uncertainty does not appear apt to impair the effectiveness of the SSM in closing the first channel of contagion.

A third concern, already hinted at earlier in this chapter, regards the *apportionment of liability* between the ECB and the NCAs for supervisory acts or omissions. The SSM is an integrated *system* of European supervision, not a legal entity possessed of legal personality. Since only the ECB and the NCAs are possessed of legal personality, only they can be held legally liable for the acts or omissions of the SSM, which are imputable to them. The SSM legal framework is not always clear with respect to the allocation of liability between the ECB and the NCAs. Suffice it nevertheless to note that in those cases where the ECB issues binding instructions to the NCAs, which the latter are under a legal duty to comply with, it is, *a priori*, the ECB that would be liable for the NCAs' acts or omissions, in line with the *Krohn*[46] jurisprudence of the

43 For details, see Klaus Lackhoff, 'The SSM Framework Regulation as a Source of ECB Administrative Procedural Law' (European System of Central Banks Legal Conference, 2016) <https://www.ecb.europa.eu/pub/pdf/other/escblegalconference2016_201702.en.pdf> accessed 30 September 2019.

44 *Dineke Algera, Giacomo Cicconardi, Simone Couturaud, Ignazio Genuardi, Félicie Steichen v. Common Assembly of the European Coal and Steel Community* [1957] ECLI:EU:C:1957:7. Notable examples of those principles are: (a) the right to be heard; (b) the right of access to files; and (c) the duty of decision-makers to provide reasons for their decisions. The guidance provided by the Court in its case-law with regard to the contours of the EU due process principles at stake has since been complemented by the due process provisions of the Charter of Fundamental Rights of the European Union, declared legally binding by Article 6(1) TEU.

45 Due process guarantees do not apply to the exercise by the ECB of its investigatory powers (SSM Framework Regulation, Art. 25(1)) nor to the procedures before the Administrative Board of Review (SSM Framework Regulation, Art. 25(2)). However, Article 20 of Decision ECB/2014/16 concerning the establishment of an Administrative Board of Review and its Operating Rules [2014] OJ L175/47 enshrines the right of access to the ECB's files, as a necessary safeguard of the applicant's rights of defence.

46 *Krohn & Co. Import-Export GmbH & Co. KG v. Commission of the European Communities* [1986] ECLI:EU:C:1986:85. If a subject were to be affected by an act of an NCA adopted in accordance with a mandatory ECB instruction, it would have locus standi to appeal before the ECJ. That said, the jurisdiction of Union courts (or national judicial instances) over national acts adopted in accordance with ECB instructions cannot be established *in abstracto* (the decisive element is how much discretion an ECB instruction allows to the relevant NCA).

Court (this establishes the principle of liability of EU institutions for mandatory instructions which they issue to national authorities).[47] Where liability for damage rests with the ECB, recital (61) to the SSMR provides that, in line with Article 340 TFEU, the ECB is to make good any damage caused by it or its servants in the performance of their duties, in accordance with the general principles common to the laws of the Member States. This is consistent with Article 41(3) of the Charter of Fundamental Rights of the European Union.[48] The criteria for liability have been laid down in *Bergaderm*,[49] and they closely follow the pattern for Member State liability developed in *Francovich*[50] and in *Brasserie du Pêcheur*.[51] Where liability is with the NCAs, e.g. because they have acted independently or because they had a margin of appreciation (even where they acted under instructions from the ECB), their liability for damage is to be judged in accordance with their national law.[52] The standard of liability imposed by the SSMR on the ECB is equivalent to that of the European supervisory authorities ('ESAs') (despite the fact that these are not, by and large, vested with direct supervisory responsibilities), but it is stricter compared to that of most national supervisory authorities, which, in many cases, enjoy immunities as a matter of national law (in particular, most national supervisors are only liable for bad faith or gross negligence).[53]

An interesting question is whether a limitation of the ECB's liability may be inferred first from the general principles common to the laws of the Member States in matters of supervisory liability, and second, from the case law of the Court and, in particular, from (a) *Bergaderm*, which lays down the 'sufficiently serious violation' criterion, and provides that the rule of law breached should

47 *Krohn* was inter alia followed in *L'Étoile commerciale and Societé Comptoir National Technique Agricole (CNTA) SA v. Commission of the European Communities* [1987] ECLI:EU:C:1987:337; *Asia Motor France v. Commission of the European Communities* [1990] ECLI:EU:C:1990:230; *Oleifici Italiani SpA and Fratelli Rubino Industrie Olearie SpA v. Commission of the European Communities* [1998] ECLI:EU:T:1998:204.

48 Charter of Fundamental Rights of the European Union [2016] OJ C202/389. Article 41(3) provides that '[E]very person has the right to have the Union make good any damage caused by its Institutions or by its servants in the performance of their duties, in accordance with the general principle common to the laws of the Member States.'

49 *Laboratoires pharmaceutiques Bergaderm SA and Jean-Jacques Goupil v. Commission of the European Communities* [2000] ECLI:EU:C:2000:361.

50 *Andrea Francovich and Danila Bonifaci and others v. Italian Republic* [1991] ECLI:EU:C:1991:428.

51 *Brasserie du Pêcheur SA v. Bundesrepublik Deutschland and The Queen v. Secretary of State for Transport, ex parte: Factortame Ltd and others* [1996] ECLI:EU:C:1996:79.

52 Recital (61) states as much. The same recital implicitly acknowledges that there may be cases of *joint* liability, which are bound to raise concerns in terms of the apportionment of liability but, also, procedurally, as the ECB is only amenable to the jurisdiction of the General Court, whereas the NCAs are, at least at first instance, amenable to the jurisdiction of the national courts.

53 For a more detailed account, see, *ex multi*, Martina Almhofer, *Die Haftung der Europäischen Zentralbank für rechtswidrige Bankenaufsicht* (Mohr Siebeck 2018) 206–209.

have been intended to confer rights to individuals; and (b) *Peter Paul*,[54] where, in its interpretation of the (now repealed) Second Council Directive 89/646/EEC,[55] the Court ruled that the *Schutznormtheorie*-based limitation of supervisory liability in German law was compatible with the above directive, which did not contain any express rule granting rights to depositors. However, it bears noting that CRD IV identifies depositor protection as one of the rationales of banking supervision; that recital (30) to the SSMR refers to depositor protection;[56] and that there is a body of case law of the Court that refers to consumer and depositor protection as being among the key rationales of banking supervision.[57] Would the above provide a basis for the drawing of inferences with regard to potential limitations of liability also for the benefit of the ECB when acting as a supervisor? Confronted with this question, the Court should be expected to draw on the case law of the High Court, the *Conseil d'Etat*, the *Bundesgerichtshof* and the *Corte di Cassazione*. The supervisor's *reckless indifference* as to the *lawfulness* of its acts and their *consequences*, identified by the High Court as the mental requirement for the Bank of England to be held liable in litigation arising from the collapse of Bank of Credit and Commerce International[58] is not without parallels to the requirement of *faute lourde* (effectively, gross negligence) traditionally applied by the French *Conseil d'Etat* with regard to the non-contractual liability of the *Commission Bancaire*.[59] A similar standard of liability is implicit in the jurisprudence of the German *Bundesgerichtshof* relative to the liability of Germany's *Bundesaufsichtsamt* (as it then was)[60] as well as of the Italian *Corte di Cassazione* in the matter of the third-party liability of

54 *Peter Paul, Cornelia Sonnen-Lütte and Christel Mörkens v. Bundesrepublik Deutschland* [2004] ECLI:EU:C:2004:606.

55 Second Council Directive 89/646/EEC of 15 December 1989 on the coordination of laws, regulations and administrative provisions relating to the taking up and pursuit of the business of credit institutions and amending Directive 77/780/EEC [1989] OJ L386/1.

56 This is despite the fact that Article 1 of the SSMR suggests that the purpose of the ECB's supervision is to ensure the stability of the financial system, not to protect individual interests as such.

57 See *Panagis Pafitis and others v. Trapeza Kentrikis Ellados A.E. and others* [1996] ECLI:EU:C:1996:92, para. 49; *Société civile immobilière Parodi v. Banque H.Albert de Bary et Cie* [1997] ECLI:EU:C:1997:345, para. 22; and *Criminal proceedings against Massimo Romanelli and Paolo Romanelli* [1999] ECLI:EU:C:1999:71, para. 12.

58 *Three Rivers DC v. Bank of England (No.3) [2003] 2 A.C. 1; [2000] 2 W.L.R. 1220; Three Rivers DC v. Bank of England (No.3)(Summary Judgment) [2001] UKHL 16.* For an account of the House of Lords Ruling, see Mads Andenas and Duncan Fairgrieve, 'Misfeasance in Public Office, Governmental Liability and European Influences' (2002) 51 *International and Comparative Law Quarterly* 757 (Andenas and Fairgrieve (2002)).

59 See, for instance, *Conseil d'Etat, Assemblée du 30 novembre 2001, 219562, Ministre de l'économie et des finances c/ M. Kechichian et autres (recueil Lebon); Conseil d'Etat, Assemblée, du 29 décembre 1978, 96004 (recueil Lebon).* For an account of the jurisprudence of the French *Conseil d'Etat*, see Duncan Fairgrieve, *State Liability in Tort: A Comparative Law Study* (Oxford University Press 2003).

60 See *Wetterstein (Urteil vom 15.02.1979), BGHZ 74, 144*; and *Herstatt (Urteil vom 12.07.1979), BGHZ 75, 120.*

the Banca d'Italia and the Consob.[61] Notwithstanding the clear stipulations in the Treaty and the SSMR, it may not be illegitimate, judging by the hitherto national jurisprudence, to also countenance limitations to the ECB's liability (when applying Article 340 TFEU) in the not-so-fanciful guise of what appears to be a general principle common to the laws of the Member States. Does the complexity of allocating liability for supervisory acts and omissions under the SSM, and the uncertainty regarding the standard of the ECB's liability as banking supervisor, have an impact on the SSM's ability to achieve its key aim of closing the first channel of contagion? It would seem not, although a certain impact on depositors and consumers of banking services seems likely.

Related to the above, a fourth concern regards the requirements of *standing* for private (so-called 'non-privileged') applicants in annulment proceedings against supervisory actions of the ECB. It is recalled that the (somewhat restrictive) legal basis for annulment proceedings is to be found in Article 263(4) TFEU[62] (read in conjunction with Article 263(1) thereof),[63] the application of which depends on the interpretation of the key notions of 'implementing measures,' 'direct concern' and 'regulatory act.' Despite the existence of a long line of relevant jurisprudence (mostly on the interpretation of Article 230 of the Treaty Establishing the European Community ('TEC'),[64] the precursor to Article 263(4) TFEU), the issue of standing remains a treacherous one, and it is neither the remit nor the ambition of this work to resolve it. Suffice it to note that, in recent years, the Union courts have repeatedly explored the question of the standing of private applicants in actions for annulment brought against the ECB, acting in the exercise of its monetary policy competences (rather than in its supervisory role), and that, although those actions were scuppered on admissibility grounds, useful inferences can nevertheless be drawn from them with regard to the admissibility of actions for annulment brought against the ECB, acting in its supervisory capacity.[65] In *Von Storch*,[66] the CJEU stated that the applicants in an action for annulment brought against the decision of the ECB to launch the Outright Monetary Transactions ('OMT') programme

61 *Banca Popolare di Fabrizia (Cass 22, Luglio 1993, n. 8191)*; *Cassa di Risparmio di Prato (Cass 27 Ottobre 1994, n. 8836)*; and *HVST (Cass 3 Marzo 2001, n. 3132)*.

62 'Any natural or legal person may, under the conditions laid down in the first and second paragraphs, institute proceedings against an act addressed to that person or which is of direct and individual concern to them, and against a regulatory act which is of direct concern to them and does not entail implementing measures.'

63 'The Court of Justice of the European Union shall review the legality of legislative acts, of acts of the Council, of the Commission and of the European Central Bank, other than recommendations and opinions, and of acts of the European Parliament and of the European Council intended to produce legal effects *vis-à-vis* third parties.'

64 Consolidated version of the Treaty establishing the European Community [2002] OJ C325/33.

65 Indeed, one would expect locus standi to be easier to establish in litigation arising in a supervisory context, as direct concern on the applicant should be less difficult to demonstrate.

66 *European Central Bank v. Sven A. von Storch* [2016] ECLI:EU:C:2016:846.

lacked standing, because the act concerned did not directly affect their legal situation, as it required certain acts of implementation.[67]

Similarly, in *Accorinti*,[68] with reference to an action for annulment brought against Decision ECB/2012/3,[69] the General Court ruled that, since the decision in question left a margin of discretion to the NCAs, the claim did not comply with the requirements on standing and was, therefore, to be dismissed as inadmissible. Without prejudice to the foregoing, Union courts have not closed the door to the possibility for private applicants to obtain a judgement on the validity of acts of the ECB. For instance, in its ruling in *Von Storch*,[70] the CJEU invoked the case of *Uniòn de Pequenos Agricultores*,[71] where it was established that, if natural or legal persons cannot directly challenge Community measures of general application because they do not fulfil the admissibility requirements laid down in the precursor to Article 230 TEC, they could, depending on the circumstances of the case, either indirectly plead the invalidity of such acts before the Union courts under Article 277 TFEU, or challenge those acts before their national courts, requesting that, absent any own competence to declare those acts inadmissible, national courts make a reference to the Union courts for a preliminary ruling on their validity.[72] Despite impairing the admissibility of actions against ECB supervisory decisions, the exacting standing requirements applicable to the ECB do not seem apt to affect

67 The Court reasoned that,'[J]edoch liegt die in Art. 263 Abs. 4 AEUV vorgesehene Voraussetzung, dass eine natürliche oder juristische Person von der angefochtenen Entscheidung unmittelbar betroffen sein muss, nur dann vor, wenn zwei Kriterien kumulativ erfüllt sind, nämlich zum einen, dass die beanstandete Maßnahme sich auf die Rechtsstellung der betreffenden Person unmittelbar auswirkt, und zum anderen, dass sie ihren Adressaten, die mit ihrer Durchführung betraut sind, keinerlei Ermessensspielraum lässt, ihre Umsetzung vielmehr rein automatisch erfolgt und sich allein aus der Unionsregelung ohne Anwendung anderer Durchführungsvorschriften ergibt ... Daher hat das Gericht ... rechtsfehlerfrei entschieden, dass u. a. der OMT Beschluss, selbst wenn er verbindliche Rechtswirkungen entfaltete, keinesfalls als eine Handlung angesehen werden könne, die sich auf die Rechtsstellung der Rechtsmittelführer unmittelbar auswirke, weil er in jedem Fall Durchführungsmaßnahmen bedürfe, damit er sich möglicherweise auf die Stellung der Rechtsmittelführer auswirken könne' (ibid., paras 40–41).

68 *Alessandro Accorinti and others v. European Central Bank* [2014] ECLI:EU:T:2014:611.

69 Decision ECB/2012/3 of the European Central Bank of 5 March 2012 on the eligibility of marketable debt instruments issued or fully guaranteed by the Hellenic Republic in the context of the Hellenic Republic's debt exchange offer [2012] OJ L77/19.

70 See *Von Storch*, para. 50.

71 *Uniòn de Pequeños Agricultores v. Council of the European Union* [2002] ECLI:EU:C:2002:462.

72 Ibid., para. 40, where the CJEU stated that, '[W]here natural or legal persons cannot, by reason of the conditions for admissibility laid down in the fourth paragraph of Article 173 of the Treaty, directly challenge Community measures of general application, they are able, depending on the case, either indirectly to plead the invalidity of such acts before the Community Courts under Article 184 of the Treaty or to do so before the national courts and ask them, since they have no jurisdiction themselves to declare those measures invalid (see *Foto-Frost v. Hauptzollamt Lübeck-Ost* [1987] ECLI:EU:C:1987:452, para. 20), to make a reference to the Court of Justice for a preliminary ruling on validity.'

the effectiveness of the SSM in achieving its core objective of closing the first channel of contagion.

Most of the foregoing concerns have yet to play out before the Union courts. This is less on account of their invalidity and rather more so because precious few opportunities had yet presented themselves at the time of writing.[73] The authors' prediction is that it is only a matter of time before such opportunities present themselves. However, even if it may shed light on the delimitation of competences between the ECB and the NCAs and, more broadly, between the EU and the Member States, the outcome of future litigation is, in the authors' view, unlikely to be equally eloquent on the overall aptitude of the SSM to contribute towards closing the first channel of contagion.

4.3 Bank recovery and resolution directive and the single resolution mechanism: Overview and shortcomings

4.3.1 From the bank recovery and resolution directive to the single resolution mechanism

The BRRD establishes a comprehensive set of domestic and cross-border recovery and resolution powers and articulates a process through which effective recovery and resolution planning is to take place to ensure the 'resolvability' of those of the EU credit institutions that are subject to its scope of application.

Broadly speaking, the BRRD's contents reflect the G-20 too-big-to-fail agenda and correspond to the 2011 FSB *Key Attributes of Effective Resolution Regimes for Financial Institutions*. This is reflected in the BRRD's key objective, which is to ensure the continuity of a failing credit institution's critical economic functions, and of the BRRD's loss and cost allocation mechanisms, which, notably through the bail-in tool of Article 43 of the BRRD, seek to avoid recourse to public funds, by shifting those losses and costs to a credit institution's shareholders and creditors (including its depositors). The BRRD relies on a network of national authorities and national resolution funds to resolve failing banks. While its enactment signalled a major step forward in overcoming fragmented national practices with a potential impact on European financial stability, the enactment of the BRRD alone would not suffice to overcome fragmentation in the euro area, where, despite the existence of a

73 One notable exception is that of the *Trasta* cases (in reverse chronological order: Joined cases C-663/17 P, C-665/17 P and C-669/17 P *European Central Bank v. Trasta Komercbanka and others* [2019] ECLI:EU:C:2019:923; *Trasta Komercbanka v. European Central Bank* [2017] ECLI:EU:T:2017:623) and *L-bank* [2017], where the Court explored the question of the standing of private parties (in particular, bank shareholders) in actions for annulment (in particular, the annulment of an ECB supervisory act addressed to Trasta Komercbanka). For an account of the *Trasta* cases, see Giorgia Marafioti, 'The Trasta Komercbanka Cases: Withdrawals of Banking Licenses and Locus Standi' in Chiara Zilioli and Karl-Philipp Wojcik (eds), *Judicial Review in the European Banking Union* (Edward Elgar 2021).

common currency, no single authority responsible for the resolution of its larger banks was, until recently, in place.

In December 2012, the Council acknowledged that, in the context of the European Banking Union, bank resolution had to be exercised at the same, pan-European level (and, possibly, by the same authority), given the adverse effect on the effectiveness of recovery and resolution action caused by the tension between centralised bank supervision, exercised at the level of the ECB, and decentralised bank resolution, exercised at the national level.[74] Another argument in favour of centralising bank resolution decisions had to do with market perceptions of the Member States' (in)ability to successfully deal with bank failures nationally, reinforcing negative feedback loops between sovereigns and banks and maintaining fragmentation and competitive distortions across the Single Market. The perception that a network of national authorities, even if coordinated at the intergovernmental level, was not operationally adequate to curb uncertainty and prevent bank runs or contagion to other parts of the euro area and the Single Market, provided the decisive impetus for the establishment of the SRM, the second pillar of the European Banking Union.

4.3.2 Single resolution mechanism and single resolution fund

The legal basis for the SRM, which has aptly been described as being 'nested within the BRRD framework,'[75] is Regulation (EU) 806/2014[76] ('the SRM Regulation' or 'SRMR'), adopted on the basis of Article 114 TFEU.[77] For the purposes of the SRM, resolution decisions are to be prepared and monitored centrally by the SRB, an EU agency, whose task is to ensure coherence in the taking of resolution decisions and in the application of the common resolution rules. The SRB, which became operational on 1 January 2015, applies to the banks in the SSM-participating Member States, the Single Rulebook on bank resolution provided for in the BRRD, with the NRAs retaining responsibility for its application in the remaining Member States. As the SRB is an EU agency, the scope for it to exercise discretion in deciding whether to take

74 European Council, 'Conclusions' EUCO 205/12. <https://www.consilium.europa.eu/uedocs/cms_data/docs/pressdata/en/ec/134353.pdf> accessed 30 September 2020.

75 Simon Gleeson, 'The Single Resolution Mechanism and the EU Crisis Management Tools' in Gianni Lo Schiavo (ed.), *The European Banking Union and the Role of Law* (Elgar Financial Law 2019), 218.

76 Regulation (EU) 806/2014 of the European Parliament and of the Council of 15 July 2014 establishing uniform rules and a uniform procedure for the resolution of credit institutions and certain investment firms in the framework of a Single Resolution Mechanism and a Single Resolution Fund and amending Regulation (EU) 1093/2010 [2014] OJ L225/1.

77 This Treaty provision aims to allow the adoption of measures for the approximation of national provisions aiming at the establishment and functioning of the Single Market.

resolution measures is limited by the *Meroni*[78] doctrine, as elaborated on by the Court in the *ENISA*[79] and the *ESMA-short selling*[80] cases. However, it is the SRB, rather than the Commission, that is to *de facto* take resolution decisions under the SRM, with the Commission having 24 hours within which to object to a resolution scheme proposed by the SRB (the Commission's eventual silence is tantamount to an endorsement of the scheme proposed by the SRB).

Although considerable, the powers of the SRB within the SRM are mostly *de facto* powers. This is both on account of the fact that the Commission and the Council retain the power to intervene, given the constraints that the *Meroni* doctrine places on the SRB, and because the BRRD makes no reference to the SRM.[81] The SRB's powers, although somewhat difficult to delimit, are not, in some respects, dissimilar to those of the ECB under the SSM. Despite the similarities, there are also significant differences between the SSM and the SRM, including in terms of their respective legal basis, and the division of competences between their 'core' and the NCAs, with the ECB yielding wide-ranging own-discretionary powers, which the SRB lacks.[82] Be that as it may, the SRB's powers constitute a *sine qua non* condition for the efficient exercise of the resolution powers vested in the SRM, which the SRB is to exercise subject to the SRMR's legal and operational environment, and the constraints that this imposes on its scope for discretion in the exercise of resolution action (the SRB can only opt for one of the resolution measures laid down in the SRMR).

Crucially, the SRMR also establishes an SRF, which is to replace national resolution funds for participating Member States. The SRMR lays down rules on the SRF's governance, as well as the criteria for determining bank contributions. In the initial phase, the SRF is to be composed of national compartments, to be merged after an eight-year transitional period. To avoid the

78 See *Meroni & Co., Industrie Metallurgiche, società in accomandita semplice v. High Authority of the European Coal and Steel Community* [1958] ECLI:EU:C:1958:7. The essence of the *Meroni* doctrine, as restated by the Court in the *ESMA-short selling* case, is that EU law prohibits the sub-delegation of discretionary powers vested in an EU institution. For a critical account of the *Meroni* doctrine, see Merijn Chamon, 'EU Agencies: Does the Meroni Doctrine Make Sense?' (2010) 17 (3) *Maastricht Journal of European and Comparative Law* 281.

79 *United Kingdom of Great Britain and Northern Ireland v. European Parliament and Council of the European Union United Kingdom of Great Britain and Northern Ireland v. European Parliament and Council of the European Union (ENISA)* [2006] ECLI:EU:C:2006:279.

80 *United Kingdom of Great Britain and Northern Ireland v. European Parliament and Council of the European Union* [2014] ECLI:EU:C:2014:18.

81 It is recalled that the adoption of the BRRD predated the establishment of the SRM, with the BRRD being couched in terms of the competent national authorities retaining their powers in each of the Member States.

82 For an account of those differences, see Agnieszka Smolenska, 'Single Resolution Board – Lost and Found in the Thicket of EU Bank Regulation' in Stefan Grundmann and Hans-W. Micklitz (eds), *The European Banking Union and Constitution* (Hart Publishing 2019), 176.

risk of legal challenges, and to help overcome Germany's opposition to the mutualisation of resolution funds on the basis of Article 114 TFEU, certain elements related to the functioning of the SRF, namely, the transfer of the contributions collected by the NRAs to the SRF and the mutualisation of the financial resources available in the national compartments, were still regulated, at the time of writing, in an SRF intergovernmental agreement ('IGA') among the participating Member States, which complemented the SRMR.

With the establishment of the SRM, the EU legislator devised a new approach for addressing bank failures in respect of banks that meet the public interest threshold.[83] In broad terms, the aim of this new approach was to shift the costs of bank failures from taxpayers to creditors and investors.[84] The key strength of the SRM, as a complement to the SSM, is that, if successful, it will enable the controlled resolution of failing banks, while at the same time establishing a central bail-out fund apt to cover a bank's losses, should bank shareholders and creditors be unable to do so themselves.

4.3.3 Remaining challenges in the field of resolution

Of the many challenges lying ahead in the field of resolution, it is submitted that six stand out. The first is linked to the overall efficiency of the newly introduced bank resolution set-up, the second to the adequacy of the funds necessary to finance bank resolution measures, the third to the interaction between the BRRD and the IGA, the fourth to the relationship between the BRRD and the SRMR, the fifth to the geographical scope of application of the SRM and the sixth to a number of legal challenges and open questions.

Starting with the first challenge, only one authority (the competent NRA) was, prior to the activation of the SRB, required to resolve a bank. Since the start of the operational life of the SRB, several authorities are required to resolve an SI or a cross-border group: the SRB (which is to determine whether the conditions for resolution are met, and propose a resolution scheme, i.e. identify the resolution tools to be deployed); the Commission (which, given the constraints on the SRB arising from the *Meroni* doctrine, has either to endorse, within 24 hours, the SRB's resolution scheme or make a reasoned objection to it, acting both as state aid and resolution authority); the ECB/SSM (which is to determine whether an institution is failing or likely to fail, after consulting

83 In considering whether to take resolution action, the SRB is to perform a public interest assessment, the aim of which is to ascertain whether resolution is to be considered as the preferred option, instead of normal insolvency proceedings under national law (SRMR, Arts 14 and 18(5)). For an outline of the SRB's approach in conducting public interest assessments, see Single Resolution Board, *Public Interest Assessment: SRB Approach* (2019) <https://srb.europa.eu/sites/srbsite/files/2019-06-28_draft_pia_paper_v12.pdf> accessed 30 September 2020.

84 It has aptly been observed that, 'bail-in replaces the public subsidy with private penalty' (Avgouleas and Goodhart (2015), 4). The argument is that, in a system that renders bail-in mandatory, creditors are incentivised to resume a monitoring function, thereby helping to restore market discipline.

the SRB, and may also withdraw the affected institution's licence, depending on the resolution tool opted for by the SRB); and the NRAs (which are to take 'all necessary measures' to implement the resolution scheme proposed by the SRB, making use of their national law powers under the domestic transposition of BRRD). Although the division of resolution competences among the SRB, the Council of the European Union (hereafter, 'the Council'), the Commission, the ECB and the national authorities does not lack in clarity, the new resolution set-up appears unwieldy. The need for the decisions taken by the SRB to be submitted, for approval, to the Commission (and, ultimately, the Council) adds further layers to the decision-making process, and these are likely to lead not only to a duplication of know-how at the level of each of these actors but, also, to bottlenecks and delays with an inevitable impact on the efficiency of the resolution process. The resolution of cross-border banking groups is even more complicated, as it requires the involvement of multiple NRAs. It remains to be seen whether the new set-up will cater for speed in the context of bank resolution or will instead prove too unwieldy, adversely affecting the effectiveness of bank resolution.[85]

Moving to the second challenge, it is recalled that the SRM establishes an SRF. Contributions to the SRF are to be raised nationally and transferred to the SRF pursuant to IGA. The SRF's target is set at 1% of the covered deposits of all credit institutions authorised in the participating Member States. The target amount of €55 billion is to be reached within eight years from 1 January 2016 (the date when the SRF is to come into effect). Herein lie two of the key potential weaknesses of the SRM, namely, in the likelihood that this may prove unable to deal promptly with a failed bank, and in the likelihood that its financial resources may prove inadequate to handle a genuine crisis. The lack of a sufficiently well-capitalised SRF for several years to come gives cause for concern. Besides, it remains to be seen whether, even when it does achieve its target amount, the SRF will be an adequate backstop in the event of the failure of one or more major financial institutions (see also the relevant discussion in Chapter 3). If it is not, then the sense of security that its establishment would create risks proving illusory. With these considerations in mind, the urgency of using the ESM as a backstop for the SRF becomes clear (see below, Chapter 5).

A third challenge is to do with the relationship between the BRRD and the SRMR: far from merely setting out procedural rules relevant to the handling of the resolution process, the SRMR also includes substantive ones, similar but not identical to (and, to that extent, overlapping with) those of the BRRD. This overlap could, potentially, generate difficulties, where the BRRD's national implementation diverges from the substantive resolution

85 On the experience, so far, with bank resolutions under the SRM framework, see below; and Jens-Hinrich Binder, 'Cross-Border Coordination of Bank Resolution in the EU: All Problems Resolved?' in Matthias Haentjens and Bob Wessels (eds), *Research Handbook in Cross-Border Bank Resolution* (Edward Elgar 2019), 42.

rules of the SRMR, potentially rendering the former inoperative and/or obsolete. Consistency between the BRRD and the SRMR could be achieved by fully aligning their text or by ensuring that the SRB consistently applies the BRRD's provisions instead of their national implementation (or any conflicting provisions in the SRMR).

A fourth challenge is linked to the interaction between the BRRD and the IGA, which, unlike BRRD, was adopted outside the EU framework, and which posits that the essentials of the SRM regime will remain constant. As mentioned earlier, it was in order to avoid possible legal challenges, and political opposition, that the transfer of the NRAs' contributions to the SRF was taken outside the perimeter of the SRMR and is, instead, regulated through the IGA. It follows that recourse to the IGA represented something of a sub-optimal compromise.[86] Leaving aside the legal format opted for, the rules themselves appear both reasonable and apt to lead to the level of funding matters-related certainty necessary for the ultimate success of the European Banking Union.

A fifth challenge relates to the geographical scope of application of the SRM. This is limited to banks in the SSM-participating Member States, and it is bound to pose difficulties in the case of EU banking groups with subsidiaries within and outside the remit of the SRM, unless the SRB and the relevant NRAs (which retain their BRRD competences in respect of non-SSM-banks) can manage to interact seamlessly, for the purposes of bank resolutions with a cross-border element.

We have left for last a number of legal challenges, not because these are the least significant but, rather, because they replicate some of those relevant to the SSM. Three of the most significant are as follows: first, the question of the apportionment of liability between the SRB and the NRAs, second, the question of the scope that the SSMR (in conjunction with the BRRD) may leave for purely national resolution powers and tools in competition with those that they jointly introduce, and third the question of the choice of forum before which to challenge resolution decisions. Of these three questions, the only one to which a relatively clear answer appears to have emerged since the activation of the SRM is the third one, and this is thanks to the jurisprudence of the CJEU. The reference is to the Grand Chamber's ruling in the *Iccrea Banca* case, a preliminary ruling request from the Regional Administrative Court of Lazio, Italy.[87] Following the logic of its earlier ruling in the *Berlusconi* case, the Grand Chamber came to the conclusion that, because in the case before it (determination of the supervised entities' annual *ex ante* contributions to the SRF), the

86 The March 2013 financial crisis in Cyprus has demonstrated the urgency of swift and decisive action, preferably backed by EU-level funding arrangements, to avoid scenarios where bank resolutions conducted nationally could undermine entire national economies, to check uncertainty and to prevent bank runs with cross-border contagion effects.

87 *Iccrea Banca SpA Istituto Centrale del Credito Cooperativo v. Banca d'Italia* [2019] ECLI:EU:C:2019:1036.

SRB was the *de facto* decision-maker, legal challenges could only be brought against the SRB before the General Court, despite the NRAs' parallel (but mostly administrative) involvement in those decisions. It is only in the case of extraordinary contributions – where the decision-making power rests with the NRAs – that judicial review is within the remit of the competent national courts. It follows that the choice of forum for judicial review will be a function of the degree of discretion and autonomy that the NRAs enjoy: where the NRAs lack such discretion and autonomy, because a particular decision falls within the scope of the SRB's decision-making powers, then the judicial review will be the preserve of the General Court.[88]

To what extent the above challenges adversely affect the effectiveness of the SRM in helping to close the first channel of contagion is difficult to assess. However, considering that the purpose of the SRM is to ensure the orderly resolution of failing banks by avoiding recourse to public funds, and with minimal costs for the real economy, any obstacle that may stand in the way of fulfilling that purpose is unlikely to bring the SRM any closer to helping to break the first channel of contagion.

4.4 European deposit guarantee scheme: Overview and state of play

Directive 2014/49/EU[89] ('the Deposit Guarantee Directive' or 'DGD') significantly strengthened the harmonisation of national DGSs inter alia through rules on *ex ante* funding requirements and the administration of national DGSs. DGD protects all deposits of up to €100,000, throughout the EU. It does not, however, mutualise deposit protection (it only goes as far as to provide for voluntary mutual borrowing between different schemes), nor does it signal the creation of a common deposit guarantee scheme, as a precondition for the completion of the European Banking Union. One of the unintended victims of the Cypriot banking crisis was public trust in the credibility of the legally enshrined €100,000 deposit guarantee threshold. It is recalled that, in response to the banking crisis, and in the context of its emergency financial support negotiations with the Commission and the IMF, the Cypriot government had, at one point, proposed the imposition of a 'one-off stability levy' on *all* insured

88 As a commentator has aptly observed, '[T]he criterion makes sense, but it might need further refinement in specific cases, particularly when there are discretional and non-discretional decisions bundled together in a complex single act made by the SRB and/or the national resolution authority' (Daniel Sarmiento, 'Resolution Litigation, Standing of Credit Institutions and the Iccrea Banca Judgment of the Court of Justice' (*Banking and Finance, Institutional Law, Justice and EU Litigation*, 5 December 2019) <https://eulawlive.com/blog/2019/12/05/resolution-litigation-standing-of-credit-institutions-and-the-iccrea-banca-judgment-of-the-court-of-justice/> accessed 30 September 2020.

89 Directive 2014/49/EU of the European Parliament and of the Council of 16 April 2014 on deposit guarantee schemes [2014] OJ L173/149.

demand deposits, including those below the insurance threshold. Although the idea of a levy was abandoned, following its emphatic rejection by the Cypriot Parliament on 19 March 2013, neither the Commission nor the Eurogroup had opposed it,[90] sparking criticism from various quarters.

In November 2015, the Commission proposed the establishment of an EDIS for bank deposits in the euro area, as the third pillar of the European Banking Union.[91] The establishment of a European deposit guarantee scheme had earlier been proposed in the Five Presidents' Report.[92] The Commission's EDIS proposal (the legal basis of which is the 'internal market clause' of Article 114 TFEU) builds on the system of national DGSs established under DGD and, in common with DGD, it would apply to deposits below €100,000 held with all banks in the European Banking Union. EDIS and the national DGS would intervene once any of those banks have become insolvent or is placed under resolution, triggering the pay-out of deposits or the financing of their transfer to another bank. EDIS was intended to develop in stages, with contributions to EDIS increasing over time. At its final stage, EDIS would fully finance the protection of bank deposits.

Progress towards the achievement of common deposit guarantee protection, a *sine qua non* condition for the completion of the European Banking Union, has for several years been arrested by opposition from some of the more influential Member States.[93] A common deposit guarantee regime would inevitably require a common fiscal backstop, similar to the one already agreed for the SRF in 2013,[94] independent of the fiscal capacity of individual Member States. In designing this fiscal backstop, one would need to factor in the constraints imposed by the 'no bail-out' clause of Article 125 TFEU, which, according to the ruling of the CJEU in *Pringle*,[95] would preclude Member States from assuming the financial obligations of other Member States by way of a 'joint and several guarantee,' but which would not be inconsistent with a 'multiple and several guarantee' of the Member States, along the lines of the ESM Treaty.

90 The Eurogroup statement on Cyprus, dated 16 March 2013, states that, '[T]he Eurogroup further welcomes the Cypriot authorities' commitment to take further measures mobilising internal resources, in order to limit the size of the financial assistance linked to the adjustment programme. These measures include the introduction of an upfront one-off stability levy applicable to resident and non-resident depositors.'

91 The Commission proposal was in the form of a regulation amending Regulation (EU) 806/2014, in order to establish an EDIS.

92 Jean-Claude Juncker, 'Completing Europe's Economic and Monetary Union', Report in close cooperation with Donald Tusk, Jeroen Dijsselbloem, Mario Draghi and Martin Schulz, 22 June 2015.

93 The reference is mostly to Germany but, also, to a number of other EU Member States.

94 See Council of the European Union, Economic and Financial Affairs, 'Outcome of the Council Meeting' 16603/14; Council of the European Union, Economic and Financial Affairs, 'Outcome of the Council Meeting' 15068/15; and Council of the European Union, Economic and Financial Affairs, 'Outcome of the Council Meeting' 10324/16.

95 *Thomas Pringle v. Government of Ireland, Ireland and the Attorney General* [2012] ECLI:EU:C:2012:756.

However challenging, the creation of common deposit guarantee protection is essential to 'underpin stability in the banking sector by providing strong and uniform insurance coverage for all such depositors, independent of their geographical location in the European Banking Union.'[96] Hence, ways in which to overcome Member State opposition to the creation of EDIS are well worth considering,[97] if only to obviate the need to explore more elaborate substitutes.[98] Besides, it has aptly been observed that EDIS

> is key to foster cross-border consolidation among banks because it will create mutual trust among participating Member States, thereby reducing their perceived need to ring-fence capital and liquidity … Therefore, progress on this pillar is also critical for banking competition and performance in an integrated system where banks can provide services on an equal footing across the entire market.[99]

By removing one of the major contributors to the bank–sovereign nexus, the creation of EDIS is bound to bring the EU several steps closer to the attainment of the declared objectives of the European Banking Union.

At the time of writing, there were signs that one of the EU Member States that had previously been at the forefront of opposition to the creation of a common European deposit insurance scheme was eager to see discussions over the completion of the European Banking Union being revived,[100] subject, nevertheless, to the fulfilment of a number of conditions.[101] Although some have

96 European Commission, 'Communication to the European Parliament, the Council, the European Central Bank, the European Economic and Social Committee and the Committee of the Regions on completing the Banking Union' COM(2017) 592.

97 EDIS could, for instance, be made conditional on risk-based contributions by banks, as a function of the amount of their sovereign holdings, and their sovereign's rating.

98 The harmonisation of insolvency rules for European banks or, alternatively, the complementing of national insolvency rules with an add-on layer of common, 'European' insolvency rules (a so-called '29th regime'), would be examples of possible substitutes to EDIS (see Martin Sandbu, 'How a Pan-EU Insolvency Regime Could Advance Banking Union' (*Financial Times*, 19 November 2019)). The implementation of either of these alternatives would likely prove even more demanding, from a technical and a political point of view, compared to the creation of EDIS.

99 Kerstin af Jochnick, 'Banking Performance, Competition and Financial Stability: A Supervisory View' (Speech at the 7th Frankfurt Conference on Financial Market Policy entitled 'European Banking – Too Much Competition?' organised by the Research Centre SAFE, Frankfurt am Main, 15 November 2019) (Jochnick 2019) <https://www.bankingsupervision.europa.eu/press/speeches/date/2019/html/ssm.sp191115_1~1274db139d.en.html> accessed 30 September 2020.

100 Olaf Scholz, 'Germany will Consider EU-wide Bank Deposit Reinsurance' (*Financial Times*, 5 November 2019) (Scholz (2019)).

101 '…such a scheme would be subject to certain conditions, one of which is that national responsibility must continue to be a central element. In the case of a bank failure, a three-tier mechanism would apply. First, the resources of the national deposit guarantee scheme would be used. Second, where national capacities have been exhausted, a European deposit insurance fund, administered by the SRB, would provide limited additional liquidity through repayable loans. Third, where additional financing may be necessary, the relevant member state would step in' (ibid.).

questioned the motivation behind this apparent change of heart,[102] others have seen in it a precondition for progress on Europe's most ambitious integration project since the creation of the single currency.[103]

Interestingly, one of the main arguments against EDIS was the concern that, for as long as banks hold in their books government bonds issued by their Member States, a common deposit insurance would, *de facto*, lead to a mutualisation of sovereign debt risks (see also the related discussion in Chapter 3).[104] Although the solution to overcome Member State opposition to EDIS need not be to drastically reduce or, a fortiori, ban commercial bank holdings of government bonds, this particular feature of the balance sheet of euro-area commercial banks draws attention to the collateral damage that the interdependence of sovereigns and banks can cause by slowing down the reforms necessary to complete the European Banking Union.

4.5 Other institutional and legal concerns thrown up by the European Banking Union

As already suggested earlier in this chapter, the rules governing the European Banking Union are apt to affect the constitutional principles of the EU, the division of powers between the EU and the Member States, and the institutional balance at the EU level. These rules also create scope for litigation, first on account of the complications thrown up by the ECB's reliance on a combination of Union and national substantive law for the exercise of its SSM competences, and second, because of the impact of the SRM's introduction on the ability of aggrieved stakeholders to avail themselves of their national constitutional rights and judicial remedies to challenge resolution measures adversely affecting their acquired property rights.

On the first of these two issues, we would refer the reader to our analysis earlier in this chapter, adding that, so far, only a handful of court cases relating to the SSM, and to the ECB's exercise of its powers thereunder, had been brought before the EU courts.[105] On the second issue, suffice it to note that the right to effective judicial protection (enshrined in Article 47 of the Charter of Fundamental Rights of the European Union), is one of the essential ele-

102 Patrick Jenkins, 'Scholz's Secret Motive: Why Germany Needs Full Banking Union' (*Financial Times*, 11 November 2019).

103 Andrea Enria – Chair of the ECB's Supervisory Board – has, for instance, stated that '[D]epositors must be sure that their money is well protected no matter whether it is deposited with a bank in France, Italy, Greece or Germany' (Sam Fleming, Jim Brunsden, Martin Arnold and Guy Chazan, 'German Eurozone Banking Plan Wins Cautious Backing' (*Financial Times*, 6 November 2019)).

104 The other main argument against common deposit guarantee is that in a system of common deposit insurance, the consequences of poor policy decisions in one Member State would be passed-off to depositors in all other Member States.

105 At the time of writing, the most recent of these cases included *Caisse Régionale de Crédit Agricole Mutuel Alpes Provence and others v. European Central Bank* [2018] ECLI:EU:T:2018:219; and *Crédit Mutuel Arkéa v. European Central Bank* [2017] ECLI:EU:T:2017:902.

ments of the 'rule of law' within the EU. It could be argued that some of the more intrusive resolution tools are bound to interfere with the freedom of contract, the right to property and the principles of non-discrimination/equal treatment, giving rise to litigation risks. As both the SSMR and the SRMR are EU regulations, they are directly applicable and binding on the EU Member States, meaning that arguments drawn from the supremacy of EU over national law could, in theory, be invoked as a shield against constitutional law-type complaints arising from supervisory or resolution decisions. The argument could therefore be made that if the SRB or the NRAs were to successfully invoke the supremacy of EU law argument, there could be a risk of potential claimants/applicants being left with no effective remedies.[106] The better view is that this risk is not particularly acute: as the CJEU has time and again stressed, the EU institutions and bodies are under a legal obligation to respect the rights enshrined in the EU Charted of Fundamental Rights (which is itself part and parcel of primary EU law) to observe its principles and to promote its application.[107]

Similarly, the European Banking Union is likely to affect the internal market, including the rules of competition law and state aid. Competition and state aid issues would mainly arise in the context of the implementation of BRRD, one of the key substantive law components of the European Banking Union. Starting with state aid rules,[108] and their interplay with the European Banking Union (in particular, the BRRD), we recall that the foundation of the EU state aid rules currently in place is that banks faced with capital shortfalls will have to bail-in equity and subordinated debt before they can be lawfully recapitalised with public funds.[109] The BRRD's bail-in rules go *beyond* the state aid rules' burden-sharing requirements, as they require a bail-in of equity and junior debt *as well as* a partial bail-in of senior debt, setting a minimum of 8% of liabilities to be bailed-in.[110] The BRRD's full bail-in rules only took effect in early 2016. What could give rise to legal concerns is the mismatch between the scope of the EU state aid framework, on the one hand, and the (narrower) scope of the European Banking Union bail-in framework under the SSM/

106 Also for that reason, it is essential to ensure that the BRRD's national transposition is fully in line with national constitutional law guarantees of property rights and the principle of equal treatment.

107 In this regard, see, in particular, the CJEU's rulings in *Steinhoff v. European Central Bank* [2019] ECLI:EU:T:2019:353; and *Ledra Advertising Ltd and others v. European Commission and European Central Bank* [2016] ECLI:EU:C:2016:701.

108 The state aid rules applicable at the time of writing were set out in the Communication from the Commission on the application, from 1 August 2013, of State aid rules to support measures in favour of banks in the context of the financial crisis ('Banking Communication') [2013] OJ C216/1.

109 The so-called 'Banking Communication' (see above) states that, 'before granting any kind of restructuring aid, including a recapitalisation, to a bank, all capital generating measures including the conversion of junior debt should be exhausted, provided that fundamental rights are respected and financial stability is not put at risk.'

110 BRRD, Art. 44(5)(a).

SRM, on the other. Had the two overlapped fully, there would be no case for the Commission to apply state aid rules to the banking sector. For as long as this is not the case, the Commission retains a legitimate interest to ensure that the provision of state aid to the banking sector does not undermine the level playing field between those financial institutions that hail from EU Member States participating in European Banking Union, and those that do not.

4.6 Centralisation of emergency liquidity assistance provision as a means of closing the first channel of contagion?

The recent banking and sovereign crises in the EU have seen renewed calls for a European LOLR, responsible for the provision of ELA to solvent but illiquid banks, so as to avert the risk of their collapse, and to absorb the impact of such an eventuality on their sovereigns, thereby contributing to closing the first channel of contagion.[111]

Under the pre-SSM set-up, both the granting of ELA and the assessment of the solvency of banks were national tasks. The establishment of the European Banking Union and the activation of the SSM could support a rethinking of the allocation of competences within the Eurosystem, as between the ECB and the NCBs, as far as ELA operations are concerned. In particular, it could be argued that, in the euro area, ELA is part of the Eurosystem's contribution to financial stability, within the meaning of Article 127(5) TFEU and Article 3(3) of the Statute of the European System of Central Banks and of the European Central Bank (hereinafter, 'the Statute').[112] This would mean that the provision of ELA may no longer be as detached from the NCBs' ESCB tasks as previously considered, and that there is, as a consequence, some scope to centralise the provision of ELA at the level of the ECB, at least for those of the euro-area banks that are directly supervised by the ECB.[113] This is also because, since the activation of the SSM, solvency assessments, which are a necessary condition

111 For a detailed assessment of some of the core questions arising in this context, see Basil Scouteris and Phoebus Athanassiou, 'National Central Bank Tasks and the Boundaries of the ECB Governing Council's Powers under Article 14.4 of the Statute: State of Play and Future Prospects' in Dimitrios Tzouganatos, Vassileios Kotsovilis, Theodoros Kontovazainitis and Eleftherios Voglis (eds), *Commemorative Volume in Memory of Professor Dr. Leonidas Georgakopoulos* (Bank of Greece, Centre for Culture, Research and Documentation, August 2016).

112 With the SSM in place, the ECB could have superior information on bank solvency and collateral quality. Moreover, as bank supervisor, the ECB could engage in early intervention measures and trigger the bank recovery and resolution process. Moreover, the BRRD provides a harmonised EU framework for bank recovery and resolution procedures and measures while, for its part, the ESM's direct and indirect bank recapitalisation tools provide for a fiscal backstop if bank resolution (and the related recapitalisation by the public sector) will endanger the fiscal sustainability of a Member State.

113 Such centralisation would also preserve incentives for prudence on the side of the ECB in its dual capacity as a supervisor and as an LOLR, and be incentive-compatible in the sense that, if an ELA

for the granting of ELA to illiquid (but solvent) credit institutions are, in the case of SIs, within the remit of the ECB. Since the activation of the SSM, to separate the provision of ELA from the assessment of solvency would signal, as far as SIs are concerned, a departure from the *status quo ante.* What is more, such separation could place the ECB in the awkward position of declaring, as supervisor, a bank solvent, only to then object to the granting to it, by its home NCB, of ELA, on account of its assessment that such provision would interfere with the objectives and tasks of the ESCB. Such an apparent contradiction in the ECB's stance could be avoided by centralising the provision of ELA at the level of the ECB, at least for SIs. Besides, whilst the objective and procedures of ELA are different from monetary policy credit operations, the types of risk are in principle similar (there is, for instance, counterparty risk associated with the credit institution, which is mitigated through the provision of collateral). If the risks of ELA are the same as in the case of the provision of credit through regular monetary policy operations, it would make sense that their provision be centralised at the level of the Eurosystem.

Whilst the activation of the SSM could lend support to a (partial) centralisation of the provision of ELA, with the ECB acting as LOLR for SIs, the attribution of an LOLR function to the ECB, as a means of helping to close the first channel of contagion, would come up against the same monetary financing prohibition challenges as those applicable to each of the NCBs, when acting as an LOLR.[114] The said prohibition, which, in recent years, has been extensively invoked in an ever-increasing variety of contexts,[115] is meant to serve a three-pronged objective, namely, to ensure that the ESCB can attain its primary price-stability objective, to preserve central bank independence and third, to contribute towards public sector fiscal discipline.[116] The unrestrained provision of ELA could be comparable, in terms of its effects, to the monetary financing, by an NCB, of government deficits. For, through the provision of ELA, the NCB would, potentially, either be assuming a state task (i.e. the provision of solvency support to an insolvent credit institution) or be engaging in indirect state financing via other means (e.g. by enabling the receiving banks

decision is taken on the basis of an inadequate solvency assessment, the decision maker would also bear the consequences.

114 This inter alia provides that, '[O]verdraft facilities or any other type of credit facility with the European Central Bank or with the central banks of the Member States in favour of Union institutions, bodies, offices or agencies, central governments, regional, local or other public authorities, other bodies governed by public law, or public undertakings of Member States shall be prohibited, as shall the purchase directly from them by the European Central Bank or national central banks of debt instruments.'

115 See, for instance, ECB (2012), para. 3.2.

116 See Committee of Central Bank of Governors, *Monetary Financing of Budget Deficits in Stage Three* (1991) <https://www.ecb.europa.eu/ecb/access_to_documents/document/cog_pubaccess/shared/data/ecb.dr.parcg2009_0018monetaryfinancing19910619.en.pdf?52698871f7aea5ab0bc875560fcf4a67> accessed 30 September 2020.

to purchase short-term treasury bills from a government that otherwise has no market access),[117] thus circumventing the objectives of Article 123 TFEU.[118]

4.7 Intermediate assessment: Does the European Banking Union break the first channel of contagion?

The euro-area sovereign debt crisis provided the impetus for the radical overhaul (in truth, for the wholesale replacement) of the pre-crisis national model for micro-prudential banking supervision, through the European Banking Union. Underlying the establishment of the European Banking Union was the realisation that banks conducting their business across borders and operating as cross-border channels of risk-transmission, could not be adequately supervised or resolved nationally. There is evidence to suggest that, in the first five years since the operational start of the European Banking Union, the resilience of the European banking sector has improved considerably. The average CET1 ratio of SSM-supervised banks rose from 11.3% at the end of 2014 to 14.3% at the end of 2018, thanks to an increase in CET1 capital and a reduction in their RWAs, while the level of NPLs on their balance sheets fell from €1 trillion in early 2015 to approximately €560 billion in November 2019,[119] making of banks less of a threat to their sovereigns than these had been before the launch of the European Banking Union. What is the impact of the shortcomings identified earlier in this chapter, of each of the three pillars of the European Banking Union, on their ability to close the first channel of contagion?

Starting with the SSM, its main strength lies in its promise to deliver coherence, consistency and equal treatment in terms of the practical implementation of EU prudential supervisory rules, as well as a higher standard of banking

117 The three main criteria endorsed by the ECB Governing Council in its opinions and convergence reports on the basis of which to determine whether the ELA operations of NCBs could breach the monetary financing prohibition are: (a) the *solvency* of the ELA recipient; (b) the *independence* of the NCB when providing ELA funding to its counterparty; and (c) its *temporary nature*. See, for instance, European Central Bank, *Convergence Report* (2012), 29 <https://www.ecb.europa.eu/pub/pdf/conrep/cr201205en.pdf?af1f4ecc8ca30834e2c70bb04af692fa> accessed 30 September 2020; European Central Bank, 'Opinion of the European Central Bank of 8 October 2008 at the request of the Belgian Ministry of Finance on a Preliminary Draft Law on Measures Promoting Financial Stability and in particular Establishing a State Guarantee for the Provision of Credit in the context of Financial Stability' CON/2008/46; and European Central Bank, 'Opinion of the European Central Bank of 10 September 2008 at the request of the Banque centrale du Luxembourg on Amendments to the Draft Law Improving the Legislative Framework for Luxembourg as a Financial Centre and Amending the Law of 23 December 1998 on Monetary Status and on the Banque centrale du Luxembourg' CON/2008/42.

118 In this regard, also see European Central Bank, *Annual Report* (2014) <http://www.ecb.europa.eu/pub/pdf/annrep/ar2014en.pdf> accessed 30 September 2020.

119 See Pentti Hakkarainen, 'The Future of European and Global Banking' (Panel intervention to Panel 1 at the 25th Dubrovnik Economic Conference, Dubrovnik, 15 June 2019) <https://www.bankingsupervision.europa.eu/press/speeches/date/2019/html/ssm.sp190615~cb32fd0e51.en.html> accessed 30 September 2020; and Jochnick (2019).

supervision, free of the distractions of national, non-prudential agendas. At the same time, both the ECB and the NCAs have a role to play in banking supervision: the interaction between the ECB and the NCAs, how well they will coordinate on a day-to-day basis, whether the ECB can rely, as supervisor, on cooperation with, and delegation to, national authorities for the exercise of its supervisory tasks and whether equivalent standards of supervision for SIs and LSIs can be achieved over time, across the SSM, will largely determine its success.[120] The foregoing observations have only lost some of their relevance in the aftermath of the rulings of the General Court and the CJEU in the landmark *L-bank* case, not least on account of the contradiction between them and the subsequent ruling of the *Bundesverfassungsgericht* in the *Banking Union* case. Even if it is unlikely to prove fatal to the achievement of their shared objectives, the in-built potential of the SSM for information asymmetries between the ECB and the NCAs (as well as between them and other competent authorities) should not be underestimated: in the peculiar, hub and spokes set-up of the SSM, the fact that the ultimate supervisory competence rests with the ECB need not suffice to fully absorb the effects of potential conflicts between it and the NCAs. Besides, irrespective of how clear the allocation of tasks between the ECB and the NCAs may be, legal fragmentation remains, in terms of the legal framework for single supervision: significantly, this is a three-tiered system consisting of rules directly applicable to supervised banks (such as the CRR), rules derived from non-directly applicable EU directives (such as the BRRD, as implemented in the different Member States), and rules that are purely national in nature. The resulting fragmentation creates scope for national discrepancies in several areas of prudential relevance (such as the granting and withdrawal of banking licences, and the fit and proper assessment of bank managers and administrators), whose impact on the efficiency of the SSM, and on its ability to break the channel of contagion moving from ailing banks to sovereigns may be hard to evaluate but could, in the long run, prove significant.[121] Finally, a few words are apposite on the, *a priori*, euro-area-only scope of the SSM. Unless its 'close cooperation mechanism' flourishes (also beyond the cases of Bulgaria and Croatia), the SSM will remain largely limited to the euro area, in which case cross-border banking groups with a presence both within and outside the SSM will continue to be

120 For an assessment of the effectiveness of cooperation between the ECB, as central supervisor, and the NCAs, in the context of the JSTs, see Wissink (2017), 444–447.

121 One indication of the impact of regulatory fragmentation is the very slow pace of cross-border consolidation in the banking sector. At the time of writing, Member States still had access to national options and discretions that prevented liquidity from being allocated freely within banking groups across different countries. This, in conjunction with the different national insolvency regimes, prevented banks from becoming more resilient by diversifying their portfolios across borders, which would also help weaken the sovereign–banks nexus.

subject to supervisory fragmentation.[122] Ultimately, the success of the SSM will also depend on whether the incentives for non-euro-area countries to accede to the close cooperation model despite their lack of voting rights in the ECB's Governing Council (the SSM's ultimate decision-making body) will prevail over their incentives to exploit their voting power within the EBA's Board of Supervisors, to thwart the SSM.[123] Gaps in regulatory integration between those of the EU Member States that participate in the SSM, on account of their participation in the euro area, and those that do not can be a source of vulnerability for the European banking system as a whole.[124]

Turning to the SRM, its establishment and the creation of the SRB were no doubt essential, both as a means of operationalising the novel BRRD framework for dealing with failing banks,[125] and as a means of removing the incentives of sovereigns to step-in and rescue non-viable banks, for lack of a structured alternative. At the time of writing, of the handful of banks declared 'failing or likely to fail' since the operational start of the SSM, only one had been resolved by the SRB.[126] The rest had been dealt with under the national bank insolvency regimes,[127] with the resulting fragmentation impairing the emergence of coherent, SSM-wide outcomes in the field of bank resolution and liquidation, and standing in the way of banking sector consolidation. One can only speculate on the reasons accounting for the sparse recourse, so far, to the SRB, which, unless reversed, could make of SRB-sponsored resolution the exception instead of the rule. What could begin to explain this phenomenon is, on the one hand, the somewhat capricious nature of the public interest assessment

122 For an account of the arguments for and against opting into the close cooperation mechanism, see Dalvinder Singh, 'Should Member States Join the Banking Union?' in Stefan Grundmann and Hans-W. Micklitz (eds), *The European Banking Union and Constitution* (Hart Publishing 2019).

123 An issue not touched on in this work, notwithstanding its importance, is that of the relationship between the EBA and the ECB. The danger of overlaps and institutional competition between them is ever present, not least on account of the interplay between the SSM, on the one hand, where the ECB holds the central role, and the single market, on the other hand, where the EBA has a key role to play as standard setter. Any such overlaps and competition are bound to adversely affect the efficiency of the SSM, and, by necessary implication, also its ability to contribute towards closing the first channel of contagion.

124 There is anecdotal evidence to suggest that one of the main reasons why the SSM's scope was restricted to the euro area only is because of the UK's opposition to treating single supervision as a single market issue. It remains to be seen whether or not the UK's scheduled exit from the EU will strengthen the incentives for some of the non-participating Member States to accede to the close cooperation mechanism.

125 Several instances of pre-BRRD bank resolutions in the EU had proved traumatic, with the resolutions of Banco Espírito Santo in Portugal, and Laiki Bank, in Cyprus being the most prominent.

126 The reference is to the resolution, in June 2017, of the Banco Popular Español, for the purposes of which the sale of business tool was deployed, resulting in the transfer of Banco Popular Español's shares to the Santander Group. For an account of what remained, at the time of writing, the only example of a resolution decision implemented in accordance with the legal framework that underpins the second pillar of the European Banking Union, see Bassani (2019), 25–28.

127 The reference is to the cases of the Banca Popolare di Vicenza (23 June 2017), Veneto Banca (23 June 2017) and ABLV Bank (24 February 2018).

('PIA'), which involves a delicate assessment of complex and competing interests, and, on the other hand, the division of resolution competences among the SRB, the Council, the Commission, the ECB and the NCAs, and its impact on the perceived efficiency of the new resolution set-up.[128] The involvement of many different actors in resolution decisions is, understandably, attributable to the constraints imposed by the *Meroni* doctrine.[129] However paradoxically, the complexity of the new resolution set-up, which, legally speaking, appears counterintuitive,[130] could have one positive (even if unintended) consequence: the mutualisation of responsibility for resolution decisions, which, given their sensitivity, can only benefit from being the fruit of collective reflection and decision-making, especially in the early stages of the SRM's institutional existence.[131] Without prejudice to the foregoing, it is fair to conclude that 'many of the challenges the SRM could face, and the SRB's ability to address them satisfactorily, remain untested.'[132]

Regarding EDIS, the third (elusive) pillar of the European Banking Union, the authors refer the reader to the discussion of its merits, earlier in this work. Suffice it to note here that, although its establishment no doubt represents a massive political and legal challenge, the creation of common deposit guarantee protection is essential for the stability of the banking sector, and for the efficient protection of the rights of unsecured depositors, wherever in the EU they may hold deposits. Without EDIS, neither risk reduction in the banking sector (an essential requirement for a stronger European Banking Union) nor depositor confidence and a level playing field for all SSM banks are likely to be fostered, in which case the European Banking Union is also likely to fall somewhat short of its objective to break the channel of contagion moving from ailing banks to sovereigns.

A few words are also apposite on one aspect of banking regulation that had yet to be brought within the fold of the European Banking Union, namely, the fight against money laundering. At the time of writing, EU law left the

128 That said, the resolution of the Banco Popular Español has demonstrated the SRB's ability to make and publish a complex decision under great time and market pressure.

129 The SRB's discretion covers only its preparatory powers in drafting a resolution plan and in recommending the use of resolution tools, which must be approved ultimately by the Commission and the Council.

130 Legally speaking, the need for the (tacit) endorsement by the Commission (and the Council) of SRB-proposed resolution schemes, and for them to provide reasons to justify their opposition to SRB-proposed resolution schemes, are somewhat counterintuitive, considering that the SRB is an agency, devoid of the institutional and legal status of the Commission and the Council (EU institutions subject to accountability requirements and enjoying a great measure of political legitimacy).

131 Besides, as recital (10) to the SRMR recognises, the BRRD 'does not completely avoid the taking of separate and potentially inconsistent decisions by Member States regarding the resolution of cross-border groups which may affect the overall costs of resolution.'

132 Nicolas Véron, 'Taking Stock of the Single Resolution Board' (Document requested by the Parliament's Committee on Economic and Monetary Affairs, March 2019), 14 <https://bruegel.org/wp-content/uploads/2019/04/IPOL_IDA2019634393_EN.pdf> accessed 30 September 2020.

enforcement of Europe's shared anti-money laundering ('AML') rules to the competent national authorities, despite differences in the national transposition of Directive 2015/849[133] ('the Fourth Anti-Money Laundering Directive' or 'AMLD4'). Moreover, the mechanism in place at the time of writing for information-sharing between supervisory and other competent financial sector authorities presented serious weaknesses, brought to light by the spectacular Danske Bank saga, and the lacklustre performance of the Danish and Estonian supervisory authorities,[134] and, before that, by the case of ABLV Bank.[135] The absence of efficient channels of communication and coordination between the national AML authorities, and between them and the ECB, the SSM-wide banking sector supervisor, in conjunction with the apparent inability of smaller EU Member States to rise up to the task of detecting suspicious transactions and deterring serious rule violations, are clear sources of vulnerability, apt to undermine both financial and systemic stability, at the expense of sovereign actors and, ultimately, national taxpayers. To enhance cooperation, the ESAs drafted guidelines on supervisory cooperation and were in the process of organising and facilitating various knowledge sharing activities. However, as the EBA acknowledged in 2019,

> there is a limit to how much convergence can be achieved through such actions and Level 1 changes would be required to further harmonise the

133 Directive 2015/849 of the European Parliament and of the Council of 20 May 2015 on the prevention of the use of the financial system for the purposes of money laundering or terrorist financing, amending Regulation (EU) 648/2012 of the European Parliament and of the Council, and repealing Directive 2005/60/EC of the European Parliament and of the Council and Commission Directive 2006/70/EC [2015] OJ L141/73.

134 The reference is to investigations in several countries, including the US and the UK, on suspicious payments of an estimated €200 billion ($220 billion), processed between 2007 and 2015 through the Estonian branch of Danske Bank, Denmark's largest bank. The money-laundering scandal in question, uncovered in September 2018 and thought to be amongst the largest in recorded history, highlighted the need for better cross-border monitoring and cooperation amongst the various national authorities responsible for the enforcement of AML rules.

135 The importance of closer cooperation between supervisory and other financial sector authorities is illustrated by the circumstances surrounding the temporary closure by the ECB of ABLV Bank, Latvia's third largest commercial bank, in February 2018, following public allegations against it of 'institutionalised money laundering as a pillar of the bank's business activities' (see <https://home.treasury.gov/news/press-release/sm0286> accessed 30 September 2020). In a statement released on 22 February 2018, the Chair of the Supervisory Board of the ECB stated that, '[W]hen creating the SSM framework, EU Member States chose to keep the responsibility for combatting money laundering at the national level. Breaches of anti-money laundering can be symptomatic of more deeply rooted governance deficiencies within a bank but the ECB does not have the investigative powers to uncover such deficiencies. This is the task of national anti-money laundering authorities. Only when such breaches have been established by the relevant national authority can the ECB take these facts into consideration for the purposes of its own tasks' (see Danièle Nouy, *Statement of 22 February* (Press Release, 22 February 2018) <https://www.bankingsupervision.europa.eu/press/pr/date/2018/html/ssm.pr180222.en.html> accessed 30 September 2020).

> legal framework with a view to minimising the potential for regulatory divergence in the anti-money laundering/counterfeiting pace.[136]

The possible transfer to the ECB of (some) AML-related competences (which, however, is not possible without an amendment to the Treaties)[137] or, alternatively, the establishment of an independent, dedicated EU agency, responsible for the policing of Europe's shared AML rules,[138] appear advisable as a means to overcome the lack of coordination and expertise that several national authorities seem to be beset with if one is to judge by recent, large scale money laundering episodes.

Finally, to the extent that one of the objectives of the European Banking Union was to promote financial integration, the limited measure of cross-border banking sector consolidation – one of the most eloquent metrics of integration – in conjunction with the remaining impediments to the cross-border provision of banking (including payment) services, suggests that common supervision and resolution may have yet to help counter the EU banking sector's traditional fragmentation along national borders. Whether it is shortcomings in EU banking supervision and resolution that are mostly to blame for the deficit in cross-border merger activity and in the cross-border provision of banking services, or whether these are mostly attributable to other, unrelated considerations, are not questions that lend themselves to a straightforward answer. In an October 2019 report, the EBA expressed the opinion that '[I]n the area of authorisations and licensing … changes to Level 1 legislation would be desirable to strengthen requirements for institutions to report on a more uniform and timely basis their cross-border activities,' adding that, '[T]his more accurate and timely information would better equip home and host competent authorities to respond, for instance through enhanced supervision or the exercise of supervisory powers, to address any additional risks identified.'[139] A subsequent EBA Staff Paper has, for its part, come to the conclusion that there are three main obstacles to the cross-border operation of banking groups in the EU: first, the territorial approach of the current regulatory framework, second, ring-fencing and limits to the circulation of funds across borders, and third, the incomplete nature of the European Banking Union, which stands in the way

136 European Banking Authority, *Potential Impediments to the Cross-Border Provision of Banking and Payment Services* (2019) (EBA (2019)), 6 <https://eba.europa.eu/file/178124/down> accessed 30 September 2020.

137 Attention is drawn to recital (28) to the SSMR, which, although recognising the close linkage between AML and the sphere of criminal law, which is a national competence under the Treaties, re-affirms that AML-related supervisory tasks, and the enforcement of the relevant rules, are not among the competences transferred to the ECB.

138 For an articulated proposal on the creation of a 'European AML Authority,' see Joshua Kirschenbaum and Nicolas Véron, 'A Better European Union Architecture to Fight Money Laundering' (*Bruegel*, 25 October 2018) <https://bruegel.org/2018/10/a-better-european-union-architecture-to-fight-money-laundering/> accessed 30 September 2020.

139 EBA (2019), 5.

of its transformation into a single jurisdiction.[140] What seems, in any event, clear is that cross-border banking sector fragmentation can be a factor of EU banking sector-wide instability, apt to counteract the benefits of the creation of a European Banking Union, and to undermine its overarching banking sector stabilisation agenda.

While the above remarks do not point to fatal design flaws in the construction of the European Banking Union, they do reflect the boundaries of the compromises of which it was the product. They also have something to say about the overall efficiency of the post-crisis set-up, and the likelihood that this will achieve its objective of breaking the first channel of contagion. It remains the case that, following the traumatic experience of the euro-area sovereign debt crisis, the EU has gone to great lengths to arm itself with a sophisticated institutional and legal set-up, the vocation of which is to forestall the threat of a future, bank-born crisis for sovereigns in EMU, and to address its fall-out, should such a crisis materialise, notwithstanding the elaborate precautions taken against it. To accuse the EU of complacency or inaction in closing the first channel of contagion would be to grossly misrepresent the facts, and to trivialise the fruit of its concerted efforts and labour, which, even if imperfect, is, overall, fit for purpose. Alas, for the reasons explained in the following chapter, charges of inaction and complacency would not be entirely out of place as regards Europe's progress in combatting the second channel of contagion, the one moving from sovereigns to their banks. It is this second channel of contagion that will be the focus of the remainder of this work.

140 Anna Gardella, Massimiliano Rimarchi and Davide Stroppa, 'Potential Regulatory Obstacles to Cross-Border Mergers and Acquisitions in the EU Banking Sector' (2020) *European Banking Authority Staff Paper* 7 <https://eba.europa.eu/about-us/staff-papers> accessed 30 September 2020.

5 Closing the second channel of contagion from sovereigns to banks

Legal assessment of policy options

5.1 Introductory remarks

As mentioned earlier in this work, commercial banks in the euro area held substantial amounts of government bonds in the run-up to the outbreak of the euro-area sovereign debt crisis. What is more, they often invested multiples of their equity in the bonds of a single sovereign issuer (more often than not their own sovereign). The value of the euro-area banks' holdings of domestic sovereign debt as a share of the total assets of monetary financial institutions remained high at the time of writing,[1] exposing euro-area banks to the spillover effects of an eventual fiscal crisis affecting the issuer of the sovereign bonds held in their portfolios.

Are commercial banks alone to blame for this? As already explained earlier in this work, and as further elaborated on below, the applicable EU regulatory framework at the time of the crisis (and still in force, at the time of writing, both in the EU and in the Organisation for Economic Co-operation and Development countries) encouraged banks to hold government debt, in the form of domestic sovereign bonds. At the time of writing, the CRR exempted sovereign bonds denominated in a bank's domestic currency from the applicable restrictions and limits on large exposures, and assigned to them, for regulatory purposes, a zero risk-weight against capital, with this exemption applying to all banks and to all their domestic and non-domestic euro-denominated sovereign debt holdings issued by EMU countries (also see below). By effectively encouraging banks to hold sovereign debt, the applicable regulatory framework has contributed to a reduction in the funding cost of governments, helping create a market for sovereign debt and, at the same time, reinforcing the relationship of dependence between commercial banks and sovereign issuers. Even after the outbreak of the sovereign debt stage of the financial crisis not only governments but also banks, especially in the periphery of the euro area, have been reluctant to subscribe to a tightening of the regulatory framework,

1 On the ratio of the holdings of domestic sovereign debt and total assets by monetary financial institutions, see European Central Bank, *Report on Financial Structures* (2017), 68 <https://www.ecb.europa.eu/pub/pdf/other/reportonfinancialstructures201710.en.pdf> accessed 30 September 2020.

which would see an increase in capital requirements and an introduction of restrictions to the size of sovereign exposures. This is despite the fact that limits on the holding of sovereign bonds and other, equivalent effect measures could be seen as essential to enhance financial stability and close the second channel of contagion.[2,3]

We examine, in the remainder of this work, the options, both *ex ante* and *ex post*, through which to close the second channel of contagion, their legal shortcomings, and the likelihood of their implementation in the short to medium term. The reader will, hopefully, forgive the authors a certain degree of overlap with Chapter 3, where some of the issues to be addressed, below, from a legal viewpoint, were examined from their economic perspective.

5.1.1 **Ex Ante** *measures: Limits on sovereign bond holdings and/or change in their favourable regulatory treatment*

According to Article 114(4) of the CRR, which implemented into EU law the Basel III framework, 'exposures to Member States' central governments and central banks denominated and funded in the domestic currency of that central government and central bank shall be assigned a risk-weight of 0%.' It follows that '[I]n the EMU, [Article 114(4) of the CRR] is, thus, immediately applicable to all banks and all their holdings of domestic and non-domestic sovereign debt issued by EMU countries and in euros, leading to a preferential treatment of sovereign bonds, irrespective of sovereign risk.'[4]

The rationale of attaching a zero risk-weight to sovereign debt issued in the issuer's own currency was that its central bank will invariably fulfil the sovereign's obligations, whatever their amount, by printing money.[5] The euro-area sovereign debt crises of 2009–2015 were to destroy the illusion that sovereign debt is risk-free, whatever the sovereign's rating, and irrespective of the market perception of their ability to meet their debt obligations.[6] Despite the euro-

2 The absence of action on this front could explain some of the reluctance of the less risk-prone economies of the North to complete the European Banking Union with the implementation of EDIS, unless the issue of the asymmetric risk of sovereign exposures has been addressed.

3 Interestingly, one of the German Finance Minister's preconditions for Germany's support to a common deposit guarantee scheme for bank deposits in the euro area is amending EU capital rules to remove incentives for banks to buy up large quantities of their home country's sovereign debt (see Scholz (2019)).

4 Kirschemann et al. (2017), 10. Besides, the same authors rightly observe by reference to Article 150 of the CRR, which permits banks using the IRB approach to apply the SA of Article 114(4) of the CRR to sovereign exposures only, and irrespective of their size, as long as these have a zero risk-weight under the SA, that '[T]he CRR is thus much more comprehensive in exempting sovereign bonds from applying risk-adjusted risk weights compared to the Basel accord.'

5 Lenarčič et al. (2016).

6 In this regard, also see Mario Draghi, 'The Interdependence of Research and Policymaking' (Speech given at the Lindau Nobel Laureate Meeting, Lindau, 23 August 2017) <https://www.ecb.europa.eu/press/key/date/2017/html/ecb.sp170823.en.html> accessed 30 September 2020.

area sovereign debt crisis, the regulatory treatment of the sovereign exposures of banks has remained unchanged. This is all the more difficult to explain, considering that the perverse effect of the preferential treatment, under the CRR, of euro-area sovereign debt extends to debt instruments issued by sovereign crisis-affected countries, the rating of which is poor (it is worth recalling that the core aim of sovereign ratings is, precisely, to reflect the probability of sovereign default, taking into account the economic fundamentals and fiscal performance of the rated sovereigns).[7] With the above considerations in mind, the inclusion of sovereign bonds within the family of RWAs, or some variation thereof,[8] would appear to represent a legitimate policy option if the link between ailing sovereigns and their banks is to be weakened. An alternative to the introduction of risk-weighting rules would be to introduce uniform, large exposure limits for the sovereign bonds held by banks: the effect on the sovereign–banks link of the capping, at a given level, of the permissible exposure of banks to a single sovereign would be similar to that of the holding, by a bank, of capital against its sovereign exposure; what is more, this alternative would appear to be more advantageous, both because its use would postulate a lesser degree of reliance on the (fallible) sovereign debt markets' price formation mechanism (which makes of risk-weights a pro-cyclical tool in stress situations, once sovereign ratings have fallen) and because it could reduce concerns around a possible 'flight to quality' to the bonds of the wealthier, more stable sovereign bond issuers.[9] However, the unwanted consequences of this option would also be significant in terms of their potentially serious destabilising effects, including higher funding costs for the weaker sovereigns, the creation of the need for banks to dispose, at short notice, of a large share of their sovereign bond holdings, and a reduction in available collateral.[10] A more sophisticated, 'mixed approach' would also be conceivable.[11]

7 Ad Van Riet, 'Government Funding Privileges in European Financial Law' (2016) *CentER Discussion Paper* 2016–045 <https://papers.ssrn.com/sol3/papers.cfm?abstract_id=2878841> accessed 30 September 2020. Also see Gaetano Gaballo and Ariel Zetlin-Jones, 'Bailouts, Moral Hazard and Banks' Home Bias for Sovereign Debt' (2016) 81 (C) *Journal of Monetary Economics* 70.

8 Some commentators have, for instance, proposed the imposition of a regulatory requirement for banks to hold sovereign debt in proportion to the issuing country's GDP, so as to benefit from zero risk-weighting (see Giancarlo Corsetti et al., 'A New CEPR Report: A New Start for the Eurozone: Dealing with Debt' (*VoxEU*, 15 April 2015) <https://voxeu.org/content/new-start-eurozone-dealing-debt> accessed 30 September 2020).

9 See Dion Bogaerts and Dirk Schoenmaker, 'A Call for Uniform Sovereign Exposure Limits' (*Bruegel*, 28 March 2017) <http://bruegel.org/2017/03/a-call-for-uniform-sovereign-exposure-limits/> accessed 30 September 2020.

10 Ángel Ubide, 'The Outlook for Sovereign Debt in the Euro Area' in Fernando Fernández Méndez de Andés (ed.), *Anuario del Euro 2015* (Fundación de Estudios Financieros 2015) (Ubide 2015), 264.

11 It has been argued that, '[T]here is some scope to take elements of the two options above to allow for a risk-free or low-risk-weight treatment of sovereign exposures under a certain limit, with a higher or increasing risk-weight applied to exposures exceeding that limit. While more sophisticated, this option would come with a more complex design requiring careful calibration that would determine its eventual effect on banks' (David Strachan and Scott Martin, 'Banking Union and Sovereign Expo-

The hitherto reluctance to revisit the issue of the risk-weighting of the sovereign debt that banks hold on the asset side of their balance sheet and, more broadly, the issue of the regulatory treatment of banks' sovereign exposures is, in many ways, understandable. For, the unwanted effect of penalising the large exposures of banks to their sovereigns could be to increase market volatility amidst the crisis, reduce the ability of banks to stabilise sovereign bond markets, and adversely affect the stability of both the domestic and the euro-area financial sector.[12] At the same time, it is only natural that there should be political resistance to the idea of de-privileging domestic sovereign bonds in banking regulation, and this resistance alone diminishes the likelihood of a change in their regulatory treatment in the short to medium term. The above notwithstanding, policy makers have, as of late, been more eager to engage with the idea of reform. Starting from the premise that '[E]levated levels of sovereign debt imply that such debt can no longer be regarded as having zero credit risk and may also not be liquid,' the ESRB assessed, in 2015, various options for a possible review of the current legal framework.[13] For its part, the Commission expressed the view that 'a reform [of the regulatory treatment of sovereign debt], if implemented wisely and gradually, could increase incentives for governments to reduce the risk profile connected to their own bonds.'[14] In January 2015, the Basel Committee on Banking Supervision initiated a review of the existing regulatory treatment of sovereign risk. Its work culminated, in December 2017, to the release for comments, until 9 March 2018 of a discussion paper assessing different policy options for a reform of the regulatory treatment of sovereign debt.[15] As no consensus had been reached, at that stage, for making concrete changes to the regulatory treatment of sovereign exposures, the paper explored a number of options for possible future action, including the (voluntary) disclosure by banks of their sovereign exposures.[16]

For an assessment of the likely economic implications of any of the various alternatives for dealing with sovereign risk exposures, and the complementarity between a change in the regulatory treatment of sovereign debt and

sures: Europe's Risk Averse Risk Sharing' (*Deloitte*, 23 March 2016) <http://blogs.deloitte.co.uk/financialservices/2016/03/banking-union-and-sovereign-exposures-europes-risk-averse-risk-sharing.html> accessed 30 September 2020).

12 See Victor Echevarria and Francisco J. Valero Lopez, 'Regulation on Banks' Sovereign Bond Holdings: Assessing the Impact of Potential Changes' (2016) 5 (2) *Spanish Economic and Financial Outlook* 75.

13 ESRB (2015), 57.

14 European Commission, 'Reflection Paper on the Deepening of the Economic and Monetary Union' COM(2017) 291 (European Commission (2017a)), 25.

15 Bank for International Settlements, Basel Committee on Banking Supervision, 'The Regulatory Treatment of Sovereign Exposures' (Discussion Paper, December 2017) <https://www.bis.org/bcbs/publ/d425.htm> accessed 30 September 2020.

16 Bank for International Settlements, Basel Committee on Banking Supervision, 'Voluntary Disclosure of Sovereign Exposures' (Consultative Document, November 2019) <https://www.bis.org/bcbs/publ/d485.pdf> accessed 30 September 2020.

the creation of a European safe asset, the reader is referred to our analysis in Chapter 3. Suffice it to say here that what the authors find striking is the patent discrepancy between two sets of rules currently applicable within the EU: those governing the regulatory treatment of bank exposures to sovereign debt, on the one hand, and those introduced in the aftermath of the Greek PSI to facilitate sovereign debt restructurings, on the other. In its current formulation, the core assumption underlying the legal regime governing the capital requirements of banks and, in particular, the zero risk-weighting attaching to sovereign bonds denominated and funded in the domestic currency of the issuing sovereign is that sovereign issuers *cannot* default. This assumption is flatly contradicted by the requirement to include standardised, two-limb collective action clauses ('CACs')[17] for all euro-area government bonds with a maturity exceeding one year issued after 1 January 2013, irrespective of their governing law (domestic or foreign) and their jurisdiction (competent court) clauses.[18] It is recalled that CACs are contractual provisions included in sovereign bond documentation to allow a majority of bondholders to agree on a restructuring of a particular series of bonds. Once agreed, such restructuring is binding on all remaining bondholders. Pre-crisis, most sovereign bonds in the EU contained no CACs and could not, as a result, be modified unless CACs were retroactively included in them by operation of law.[19] The obligatory inclusion of CACs in all euro-area government bonds signals the perception that a palpable risk of sovereign debt restructuring exists and suggests that also sovereign issuers pose certain default risks, which could warrant a possible restructuring of their debt. Squaring the conflicting assumptions that underlie the sovereign debt restructuring and banks' capital requirement regimes currently applicable within the euro area is genuinely difficult, if not downright impossible, and points to some of the

17 Details of the CACs were published on 26 March 2012 by a sub-committee of the Economic and Financial Committee on EU sovereign debt markets, and they are available at <https://europa.eu/efc/euro-area-model-cac-2012_en> accessed 30 September 2020.

18 This requirement is set out in Article 12(3) of the ESM Treaty. Two-limb CACs are those whose activation (and, by extension, also the debt restructuring itself) depends on a minimum threshold of bondholder support being reached *both in each bond series and across all series* subject to the restructuring. One of the lessons of the Greek PSI was that two-limb CACs can make it easier for holdout creditors to accumulate a sufficiently large share to block the activation of the CAC in a particular series. Thus, in the context of the euro area governance reform, the Eurogroup proposed the introduction in the debt documentation accompanying all government bonds with a maturity exceeding one year issued after 1 January 2022, of single-limb CACs (defined as those that provide for a single vote to be taken on all relevant debt, and for the restructuring of all relevant bonds to take place, provided a certain aggregate threshold is reached). This requirement, included in Article 12(4) of the draft revised text of the ESM Treaty (see below, Section 5.2.2.1), looks set to make the process of debt restructurings smoother and reduce the cost for the sovereign, who would no longer need to deal with holdout creditors.

19 This particular possibility, which exists only where sovereign bonds are governed by the issuer's domestic law, was exploited at the time of the Greek PSI (February–March 2012), when Greek law-governed GGBs that originally contained no CACs were 'retrofitted' with CACs so that they could be restructured.

contradictions that have found their way into the contemporary European regulatory framework following the start of the euro-area sovereign debt crisis.

One of the lessons of the euro-area sovereign debt crisis is that misguided regulatory incentives can bear the seeds of future crises or exacerbate their gravity once these have materialised. Whilst a review of the current EU rules on sovereign bond holdings would appear advisable in a bid to weaken the link between ailing sovereigns and banks, it follows from the foregoing analysis that neither risk-weights nor large exposure limits (nor, presumably, a combination thereof) would suffice to avert the re-emergence of a crisis similar to the one that affected the Greek banking sector, if unintended consequences are to be averted. Other policy options would (also) need to be considered and implemented in order to break the second channel of contagion. The remainder of this work will examine what some of the main options could be, with an emphasis on their legal advantages and shortcomings.

5.1.2 Other policy options

Of the various ideas ventilated since the onset of the crisis but not yet (or not fully) acted upon, two are worthy of particular attention, given their potential to help break the link between ailing sovereigns and their banks: first, the creation of an independent and credible euro-area-wide stability support mechanism, responsible for the provision of (mostly *ex post*) financial assistance to euro-area Member States beset by budgetary difficulties and featuring an appropriate bank-recapitalisation mechanism, and second the issuance of some form of common European asset. The remainder of this work explores these options from a legal perspective. Before proceeding with the substance of the analysis, the following observation is apposite: whatever their merits, these two options are not equivalent, as the former would apply mostly *ex post*, whereas the latter could, if implemented, avert a crisis from manifesting itself. Although it may be harder to generate political support for them, pre-emptive solutions are preferable, both as a matter of principle and because of the constant challenge for the EU and EMU to provide for efficient and effective crisis management.

5.2 A credible euro-area stability support mechanism: State of the debate

5.2.1 The European Stability Mechanism

On 16 and 17 December 2010, at the height of the euro-area sovereign debt crisis, the Council agreed to establish the ESM as a permanent financial crisis mechanism to replace the European Financial Stabilisation Mechanism ('EFSM').[20] The establishment of the ESM, which is a Luxembourg-based

20 The reference is to the emergency funding programme established by way of Council Regulation (EU) 407/2010 of 11 May 2010 establishing a European financial stabilisation mechanism [2010] OJ

public international law intergovernmental organisation, operating with the participation of, and for the benefit of, the euro-area Member States, was preceded by the Council's adoption, on 25 March 2011, of Decision 2011/199/EU,[21] based on the newly introduced 'simplified revision procedure' of Article 48(6) of the Treaty on European Union ('TEU'),[22] amending Article 136 TFEU to allow for the creation of a stability mechanism for Member States whose currency is the euro. The decision inserted the following new paragraph (3) to Article 136 TFEU:

> [T]he Member States whose currency is the euro may establish a stability mechanism to be activated if indispensable to safeguard the stability of the euro area as a whole. The granting of any required financial assistance under the mechanism will be made subject to strict conditionality.

The insertion of the above paragraph was deemed essential to overcome the obstacle of Article 125(1) TFEU (the 'no bail-out' clause), which, as the reader will recall, renders illegal the assumption, by the Union or any of its Member States, of the commitments of central governments of any Member State.[23]

The ESM itself was established by virtue of the ESM Treaty (which entered into force on 1 January 2013, following the notification to the Secretary General of the Council of the completion of the procedures for its approval in accordance with their respective constitutional requirements) with the task of granting financial assistance to euro-area countries with temporary financial problems. The ESM is an intergovernmental mechanism with a pro-rata guarantee structure, backed by a paid-in capital of €80 billion, and an unconditional and irrevocable obligation of its members (the euro-area Member States) to provide their contribution to the ESM's authorised capital stock of approximately €700 billion, that provides a minimum backstop of €500 billion, and which raises the funds necessary for the provision of financial assistance by issuing debt on the capital markets, with a maturity of up to 30 years. Pursuant to Article 12(1) of the ESM Treaty, if necessary to safeguard the financial stability of the euro area as a whole and of its Member States, the ESM may provide stability support to an ESM Member subject to strict conditionality, appropriate to the financial assistance instrument chosen. Decisions to grant stability

---

L118/1 (for which the legal basis was Article 122 TFEU), drawing on funds raised on the markets and guaranteed by the Commission, with the EU budget as collateral. The EFSM is not to be confused with the EFSF and the ESM.

21 European Council Decision 2011/199/EU amending Article 136 of the Treaty on the Functioning of the European Union with regard to a stability mechanism for Member States whose currency is the euro [2011] OJ L91/1.

22 Consolidated version of the Treaty on European Union [2016] OJ C202/13.

23 The provision of ESM assistance would, indirectly, amount to an assumption of a Member State's commitments, hence the perceived need to introduce a new paragraph (3) to Article 136 TFEU.

support are taken by unanimity (thus, Member States have a veto right).[24] Exceptionally, decisions may also be taken by a qualified majority of 85% of the votes cast (in terms of ESM capital key).[25] Upon receipt of a request for assistance, the Commission, in liaison with the ECB, have the task of assessing (a) the existence of a risk to financial stability; (b) debt sustainability; and (c) financing needs.[26]

Although stability support may be granted through six different financial instruments, two of these can be employed for the recapitalisation of financial institutions (these are the most relevant for the purposes of this work):

(1) The 'Indirect Recapitalisation Instrument' ('IRI') provided for in Article 15 of the ESM Treaty, the eligibility criteria for which are set out in Article 3 of the ESM Guideline on Financial Assistance for the Recapitalisation of Financial Institutions;[27] and
(2) The DRI that came into force on 8 December 2014 and is governed by the provisions of the Guideline on Financial Assistance for the Direct Recapitalisation of Institutions (hereinafter, 'the DRI Guideline').[28] By virtue of Article 8(1) of the DRI Guideline, this instrument should not be considered as a precautionary instrument, within the meaning of Article 32(4)(d)(iii) of the BRRD, and therefore, it should not be used to address capital shortfalls established in the national, EU or SSM-wide stress tests, asset quality reviews or equivalent exercises conducted by the ECB, the EBA or the NCAs (thus, precautionary public assistance in the form of participation in the equity of a solvent institution cannot take the form of the DRI, and should be dealt with at the national level). Crucially, the application of the DRI necessitates a contribution to loss absorption and recapitalisation equal to an amount of 8% of the total liabilities, including own funds (bail-in), of the target institution.[29]

The ESM could have a major role to play in breaking the second channel of contagion if it were to serve (as the intention was, at the time of writing) as a backstop for a future EDIS and, in particular, for the SRM/SRF. Funding deposit guarantee schemes and resolution funds are, ultimately, government tasks, which fiscally unsound sovereigns may be unable to perform if left to their own devices: the existence of a credible third party backstop to fund deposit guarantees and resolution measures would help ensure that the financial

24 ESM Treaty, Art. 4(3).

25 The reference is to the so-called 'emergency procedure' of Article 4(4) of the ESM Treaty.

26 Ibid., Art. 13.

27 Available at <https://www.esm.europa.eu/sites/default/files/esm_guideline_on_recapitalisation_of_financial_institutions_with_notice.pdf> accessed 30 September 2020.

28 Available at <https://www.esm.europa.eu/sites/default/files/20141208_guideline_on_financial_assistance_for_the_direct_recapitalisation_of_institutions.pdf> accessed 30 September 2020.

29 DRI Guideline, Art. 8(2).

challenges faced by ailing sovereigns will not prove fatal for their financial sectors, where the latter experience shocks, whether endogenous or attributable to spillovers from sovereigns to their banking sectors. The reader will recall that one of the major challenges standing in the way of the creation of a common European DGS, as a necessary component of the European Banking Union, is, precisely, the construction of a Treaty-compliant financial backstop. Similarly, as suggested earlier in this work, a solid public backstop, fiscally neutral over the medium term,[30] would be essential to ensure the credibility and proper functioning of the SRM/SRF. Could the ESM serve as a common financial backstop for EDIS and, perhaps more importantly, for the SRM/SRF, which, unlike EDIS, are a palpable reality?

At the time of writing, a direct bank recapitalisation by the ESM was possible if (a) the requesting ESM Member is unable to provide financial assistance to the institutions in full without very adverse effects on its own fiscal sustainability or if it is established that other alternatives would have the effect of endangering the continuous market access of the requesting ESM Member, and consequently require the financing of its sovereign needs via the ESM; and (b) providing financial assistance for the benefit of the requesting ESM Member would be indispensable to safeguard the financial stability of the euro area as a whole or of its Member States.[31] If it is to prove effective, a future ESM-based common backstop to the SRB should, in the authors' view, allow for the provision of solvency as well as liquidity support to institutions under resolution, either in the form of credit lines or in that of guarantees, allowing the maximum amount of flexibility to the SRB (see also Section 3.2). Besides, as a backstop to the SRF, the ESM should have critical mass so as to dispel any doubts regarding its adequacy in an emergency situation. Considering that the size of the backstop is to always be linked to the repayment capacity of the beneficiary banks (given the principle of fiscal neutrality over the medium term applicable to the decisions of the SRB), any discussion on the size of the backstop would need to be preceded by further analysis by the SRB, the SSM, the Commission and the ESM itself. The outcome of this analysis could form the basis for further negotiations among Member States and institutions, with the aim of increasing the funds available to the ESM so that it can fulfil its expanded mandate. The probability that these negotiations will prove less than easy in the largest EU Member State (and, quite possibly, also in other Member States) may have increased considerably following the ruling of the *Bundesverfassungsgericht* of 5 May 2020 in *Weiss*.[32] There, the *Bundesverfassungsgericht* declared both the Eurosystem's Public Sector Purchase

30 It is recalled that fiscal neutrality for the participating Member States is preserved because borrowings from the SRB are to be recovered through *ex post* contributions within the maturity period of the loan (24 months). Thus, the SRB is to fully recoup any financing from the financial sector within the medium term.

31 DRI Guideline, Art. 3(2).

32 Order of 5 May 2020 (Beschlüsse der EZB zum Staatsanleihekaufprogramm) 2 *BVerfGE* 859/15.

Program ('PSPP') and the 2018 ruling of the CJEU thereon to be ultra vires, citing the PSPP's (negative) socio-economic effects, mostly for (German) savers. Accordingly, the *Bundesverfassungsgericht* mandated the Federal Government and the *Bundestag* to take steps to ensure that the ECB conducts a comprehensive proportionality assessment of the PSPP to avoid the risk of its 'economic and fiscal policy effects' outweighing its monetary policy objectives.[33] To the extent that the effects of the provision, by the Member States, of (additional) funds to the ESM would be significant, from a socio-economic perspective, it is difficult to imagine that the authorities of a Member State subject to the edicts of a judicial instance as activist as the *Bundesverfassungsgericht* would not be reluctant to see the ESM provide the effective backstop that the SRM/SRF warrant. The above notwithstanding, the assumption by the ESM of the role of a financial backstop to the SRF should, in any event, not impinge on the competences of the SRB, its independence and the timely execution of its resolution tasks. In particular, it should be ensured that the ESM does not interfere with SRB decisions on the use of the SRF or on the activation of the SRF backstop for resolution cases.[34]

The eventual use of the ESM as a financial backstop for the SRM/SRF or for a common European DGS and, by implication, as a means of addressing the sovereign–banks nexus, would present a number of advantages. The ESM is an existing support mechanism, with experience in financial sector crises and a substantial (even if not adequate) capital cushion; it has interacted well with the ECB, and it has the trust of the Member States and financial markets (as reflected in its AAA credit rating); finally, it is accountable to the European Parliament (hereafter, 'the Parliament').

However desirable it may be, the use of the ESM as the SRM/SRF's and/or EDIS's fiscal backstop would also raise a number of concerns or difficulties.

A first difficulty with using the ESM as a fiscal backstop for the SRM/SRF and EDIS is linked to the differences between them in terms of their scope of application: the ESM only applies to the euro-area Member States, whereas

33 Significantly, the *Bundesverfassungsgericht* threatened to prevent the Deutsche Bundesbank from making any further asset purchases if the ECB failed to produce, within a period of three months, evidence on the basis of which the proportionality of the PSPP could be assessed by the *Bundesverfassungsgericht*, applying the methodology that it deems appropriate (and which, significantly, differs from that of the CJEU, which, unlike the *Bundesverfassungsgericht*, does not place the emphasis on the wider economic and social consequences of monetary policy). For an early, thought-provoking assessment of the *Bundesverfassungsgericht*'s ruling in *Weiss*, see Matthias Goldmann, 'Das BVerfG holt sich ein trojanisches Pferd ins Haus' (*Legal Tribune Online*, 6 May 2020) <https://www.lto.de/recht/hintergruende/h/bverfg-2bvr85915-ezb-anleihenkauf-eugh-europa-wirtschaft-geldpolitik-monetarismus-zentralbank-pspp-dialog-konfrontation/> accessed 30 September 2020.

34 To what extent new Article 18A of the draft revised ESM Treaty complies with these requirements is not entirely clear (see, in particular, Article 18A(5) thereof).

the SRM applies to all banks covered by the SSM, whilst EDIS would be pan-European in its scope.[35]

A second challenge in using the ESM as a backstop for the SRM/SRF and EDIS is that this would necessitate an amendment to the ESM Treaty to expressly include the SRM/SRF and EDIS as beneficiaries of ESM financing. Although such an amendment would appear legally unproblematic, as it would entail no additional transfer of national sovereignty but, merely, a widening of the scope of the ESM tools and of the eligible beneficiaries for ESM funding, and despite the fact that the draft revised ESM Treaty[36] caters, through a new Article 18A, for the backstopping of the SRF through the ESM, political support would be necessary for the actual activation of an ESM backstop to the SRF. It is recalled that the ESM operates on the basis of state guarantees, which, as part of the regular budgetary procedure at the national level, are subject to parliamentary assent. Should the ESM have to draw on those guarantees, in the future, Member States whose constitutions contain balanced budget provisions (so-called 'debt brakes') could run the risk of transcending them, especially if the drawings on those guarantees were to be substantial. Should such a situation materialise, delicate questions could arise with relevance to the relationship among constitutional, EU and public international law, and their normative hierarchy. Indeed, questions of a similar order have arisen before, not least in the jurisprudence of the *Bundesverfassungsgericht*, which is of particular relevance in this regard as, within the EU, debt brakes were, at the time of writing, a feature of German constitutional law only.[37] The *Solange* jurisprudence of the *Bundesverfassungsgericht*[38] and, in particular, its *Solange III* or '*Maastricht* judgment'[39] suggests that the *Bundesverfassungsgericht* has 'put itself in the position of supervising … any further European integration,'[40] and that

35 According to the ESM website, '[I]f non-euro area Member States join the Banking Union, the ESM and non-euro area Member States will together provide the common backstop to the SRF, through parallel credit lines' (see European Stability Mechanism, *Explainer on ESM Reform and Revisions to the ESM Treaty* (Press Release, 24 June 2019) <https://www.esm.europa.eu/press-releases/explainer-esm-reform-and-revisions-esm-treaty> accessed 30 September 2020).

36 On the draft revised ESM Treaty, see Section 5.2.2.1.

37 The reference is to Article 115(2) of the German Constitution, which stipulates that, as of 2016, the Federal Government's structural deficit cannot exceed 0.35% of Germany's GDP. Similar provisions already apply in Switzerland (Swiss Federal Constitution, Art. 126) and the US (US Constitution, 14th Amendment, s. 4). Close to the time of writing, the Austrian Parliament was set to vote in similar, constitutional budgetary restrictions, while France's lower house approved a bill to enshrine budget restraint rules in the French Constitution. If approved by the French Senate, the proposed change would need to be approved by referendum or by a three-fifths majority across both houses.

38 Order of 29 May 1974 (Solange I) 37 *BVerfGE* 271; and Order of 22 October 1986 (Solange II) 73 *BVerfGE* 339.

39 Order of 12 October 1993 (Maastricht) 89 *BVerfGE* 155.

40 Kevin D. Makowski, 'Sollange III: The German Federal Constitutional Court's Decision on Accession to the Maastricht Treaty on European Union' (1995) 16 *University of Pennsylvania Journal of International Business Law* 155, 171.

there is still room for 'a nationally assertive position,'[41] with all the uncertainties that these are bound to entail at so crucial a juncture.[42] This is without prejudice to the amendment of the German Constitution to conform to the principles enunciated by the *Bundesverfassungsgericht* in its *Maastricht* judgment.[43] Since then, Union law can only be subjected to constitutional review by the *Bundesverfassungsgericht*, where it is asserted that its evolution has fallen below the requisite standards of fundamental rights protection and democracy guaranteed by the German Constitution or is out of tune with the principles of subsidiarity and proportionality or the conferred powers doctrine. The *Bundesverfassungsgericht* has more recently applied much the same reasoning to the assessment of the compatibility of the Act Approving the Treaty of Lisbon with the German Constitution[44] as well as to the implementation, by the Deutsche Bundesbank, of some of the ECB's crisis-related asset purchase programmes.[45] From this perspective, despite openly contradicting the CJEU

41 Karl M. Meessen, 'Hedging European Integration: The Maastricht Judgment of the Federal Constitutional Court of Germany' (1993) 17 (13) *Fordham International Law Journal* 511, 512.

42 It is worth recalling that, according to the judgment of the *Bundesverfassungsgericht* in Solange III, '[T]he concept of the currency union as a "community based on stability" (*Stabilitätsgemeinschaft*) is the basis and subject matter of the German Act of Accession. If the monetary union should fail to deliver on a continuing basis the stability present at the beginning of the third stage of EMU within the meaning of the agreed mandate for stabilisation, it would be abandoning the Treaty conception and thereby fall outside the authority conferred in the Act of Accession' (para. 90). Moreover, '[U]nder the EU Treaty, monetary union is no more apt to give rise, automatically, to a political union than to an economic union. That would require an amendment of the Treaty, which could not happen without a decision of the national State institutions, including the *Bundestag*' (para. 93).

43 The reference is to Article 23(1) of the German Constitution, which provides for the participation of Germany in the development of an EU that is committed to democratic, social, and federal principles, to the rule of law, and to the principle of subsidiarity, and guarantees a level of protection of basic rights essentially comparable to that afforded by the German Basic Law (the German Constitution).

44 Order of 30 June 2009 (Lissabon) 123 *BVerfGE* 267. Interestingly, however, the *Bundesverfassungsgericht* found that the accompanying Act Extending and Strengthening the Rights of the *Bundestag* and the *Bundesrat* in European Union matters infringed Articles 38(1) and 23(1) of the German Basic Law, insofar as the *Bundestag* and the *Bundesrat* have not been accorded sufficient rights of participation in European law-making procedures and Treaty amendment procedures.

45 See Order of 21 June 2016 (Gauweiler) 2 *BVerfGE* 2728/13, 2 *BVerfGE* 13/13, 2 *BVerfGE* 2731/13, 2 *BVerfGE* 2730/13, 2 *BVerfGE* 2729/13. It is recalled that the validity of the ECB's purchases of government bonds under the Securities Markets Programme, and the announcement of the OMT Program was the object to a preliminary ruling request of the *Bundesverfassungsgericht* to the CJEU, which led to the judgment of the CJEU in *Gauweiler*. On the CJEU's ruling in *Gauweiler*, see Napoleon Xanthoulis and Takis P. Tridimas, 'A Legal Analysis of the Gauweiler Case' in Federico Fabbrini (ed.), *The European Court of Justice, the European Central Bank and the Supremacy of EU Law*, Special Issue (2016) 23 *Maastricht Journal of European and Comparative Law* 17; Paul P. Craig and Menelaos Markakis, 'Gauweiler and the Legality of Outright Monetary Transactions' (2016) 41 European Law Review; Dariusz Adamski, 'Economic Constitution of the Euro Area after the Gauweiler Preliminary Ruling' (2015) 52 *Common Market Law Review* 1485; and Federico Fabbrini, 'After the OMT Case: The Supremacy of EU Law as the Guarantee of the Equality of the Member States' (2015) 16 (4) *German Law Journal* 1004. The *Bundesverfassungsgericht* was to again approach the CJEU with one

in *Weiss* and although appearing methodologically rigid, the much-publicised ruling of the *Bundesverfassungsgericht* in *Weiss*[46] is largely consistent, in its core, with the earlier reasoning of the *Bundesverfassungsgericht*,[47] drawing attention to the legal risks of an increase in the ESM's envelope to cater for the needs of banks in anticipation of a crisis situation.

Related to the preceding point, a third, no less significant difficulty with the proposed extension of the remit of the ESM resides in the role that strict conditionality – explicitly referred to in Article 136(3) TFEU – has traditionally played as an inseparable part of the legal framework governing the terms for the provision, by the ESM, of financial support. Until the advent of the COVID-19 crisis, and the agreement by the Council of 23 April 2020, on the creation of an 'ESM Pandemic Crisis Support Facility,' the need for compliance with strict conditionality, as a condition precedent to accessing ESM financial support, was undisputed. Assuming that the advent of COVID-19 will not bring a lasting change in ESM practices, it is fair to wonder whether the price to pay for the ESM backstopping the SRM/SRF and EDIS is not too high, if it is to involve Member State commitments to a full macroeconomic adjustment programme and enhanced surveillance under Regulation (EU) 472/2013[48] and, inversely, what the effects would be on the fiscal and budgetary sovereignty and the constitutional orders of the Member States, as ESM guarantors, if no

more preliminary ruling request in the matter of the legality of the large-scale purchases of government bonds under the ECB's PSPP, leading to the judgment of the CJEU in *Heinrich Weiss and others v. Deutscher Bundestag* [2018] ECLI:EU:C:2018:1000. For an account of the *Weiss* ruling, and its relationship with *Gauweiler*, see Marijn Van der Sluis, 'Similar, therefore Different: Judicial Review of another Unconventional Monetary Policy in Weiss (C-493/17)' (2019) 46 (3) *Legal Issues of Economic Integration* 263; and Annelieke A.M. Mooij, 'The Weiss Judgment: The Court's Further Clarification of the ECB's Legal Framework: Case C-493/17 Weiss and Others' (2019) 26 (3) *Maastricht Journal of European and Comparative Law* 449.

46 See Order of 5 May 2020 (Beschlüsse der EZB zum Staatsanleihekaufprogramm) 2 *BVerfGE* 859/15.

47 'In several preceding decisions, the German Court had clearly expressed that … it reserves the right to have the "last word" in extreme cases; mainly when the acts in question would in effect imply an extension of competences which is reserved to the [Treaty] amending procedures. With its judgment of 5 May, the GFCC [the *Bundesverfassungsgericht*] has activated this reservation for the first time' (Helmut Siekmann and Volker Wieland, 'The Ruling of the Federal Constitutional Court concerning the PSPP: A Practical Way Forward' (2020) *Institute for Monetary and Financial Stability Working Paper* 140, 3–4 <https://www.imfs-frankfurt.de/fileadmin/user_upload/IMFS_WP/IMFS_WP_140.pdf> accessed 30 September 2020). In this regard, also see Order of 6 July 2010 (Honeywell) 2 *BVerfGE* 126/286, where the *Bundesverfassungsgericht* foreshadowed its ultra vires review of the actions of European institutions and bodies, where their impugned acts are manifestly in breach of their competences and lead to a structurally significant shift to the detriment of the Member States in the structure and division of competences between the EU and its Member States. Where the *Bundesverfassungsgericht*'s ruling breaks with past practice is in no longer treating a decision of the CJEU as authentic and binding upon it, on account of its assessment of it as being in conflict with recognised principles and methods of legal reasoning, and hence as arbitrary and ultra vires.

48 Regulation (EU) 472/2013 of the European Parliament and of the Council of 21 May 2013 on the strengthening of economic and budgetary surveillance of Member States in the euro area experiencing or threatened with serious difficulties with respect to their financial stability [2013] OJ L140/1.

such commitments were to be involved. However unreasonable it might seem to impose (blanket) conditionality requirements on the Member States in view of an extension of the remit of the ESM, it would take an imaginative reading of the ESM legal framework to strike out conditionality as an integral part of the process of its activation.

For the above reasons, it is legitimate to explore alternatives to the ESM, as it was at the time of writing. The most prominent alternative, to date, is discussed immediately below.

5.2.2 From the European Stability Mechanism to a European Monetary Fund?

5.2.2.1 Introductory remarks

One of the most prominent ideas advanced since the onset of the financial crisis, well before the Council's decision to create the ESM as a permanent financial crisis support mechanism, was that of the establishment of a 'European Monetary Fund' ('EMF') as an independent institution to address the solvency problems of EMU Member States in difficulty, through the provision of emergency loans or guarantees for the issuance of public debt. Although the analogy with the IMF (which, no doubt, underpins the term 'EMF') should not be stretched too far,[49] the idea of an EMU-internal sovereign support mechanism, originally proposed by Gros and Mayer,[50] reiterated, subsequently, by Sapir and Schoenmaker,[51] and supported by a number of leading political figures in Europe,[52] was an interesting and bold one, and early legal assessments of its

49 The suggestion to call a revamped ESM an 'EMF' is objectionable on several grounds. Unlike the IMF, the EMF would operate against the background of EMU, with its particular institutional and governance structure. Moreover, the use of the word 'monetary' as part of its nomenclature could unwittingly convey to the European public the erroneous impression that there are more than one 'monetary' authorities in the euro area, or that the EMF may be eligible to draw funds from the ECB. For these reasons, the term 'European Stability Fund' would suit better the mandate of such a fund.

50 Daniel Gros and Thomas Mayer, 'How to Deal with Sovereign Default in Europe: Towards a Euro(pean) Monetary Fund' (2010) *Centre for European Policy Studies Policy Brief* 202 <https://www.ceps.eu/wp-content/uploads/2010/02/No%20202%20EMF%20e-version%20update%2017%20May.pdf> accessed 30 September 2020.

51 André Sapir and Dirk Schoenmaker, 'The Time is Right for a European Monetary Fund' (*Bruegel*, 30 October 2017) <https://www.bruegel.org/2017/10/the-time-is-right-for-a-european-monetary-fund/> accessed 30 September 2020.

52 German Chancellor Angela Merkel, former German Finance Minister Wolfgang Shäuble and, more recently, French President Emmanuel Macron have supported the idea. That said, the German and the French conceptions of an eventual EMF differ: the former see in the EMF a tool through which to enforce strict compliance with fiscal rules (Bundesministerium der Finanzen, Wolfgang Schäuble, *Non-Paper for Paving the Way towards a Stability Union* (2017) <https://www.sven-giegold.de/wp-content/uploads/2017/10/17-10-10-Non-Paper-BMF-on-Reforming-ESM-09-10-2017.pdf> accessed 30 September 2020), the latter favour using an EMF as a stabilisation mechanism for the euro area. It is the latter conception of an EMF that these authors would subscribe to.

feasibility suggested that legal concerns would not represent the most significant barriers to its eventual creation.[53]

Despite the attention it originally attracted, the idea of creating an EU-law anchored sovereign support mechanism was to be abandoned until 6 December 2017, when the Commission published a proposal for a Council Regulation establishing an EMF (hereafter, 'the EMF Regulation'), derived from a revamped ESM.[54] At the Euro Summit of 15 December 2017, EU leaders threw their weight behind the idea of a reform of the ESM, which they considered necessary for the completion of the European Banking Union.[55] The salient features of the Commission proposal were as follows: first, the EMF would provide a common backstop to the SRF (in the form of a credit line or guarantees); second, in terms of governance, the EMF would decide by 'reinforced qualified majority' (rather than unanimity) in matters of relevance to the granting of stability support, disbursements and the deployment of the backstop; third, the EMF would be involved, more directly, in the management of financial assistance programmes, alongside the Commission; and fourth, the EMF would reserve the right to develop new financial instruments, to supplement and support other EU financial instruments and programmes.

Instead of bringing the ESM within the framework of the Treaties, the Eurogroup was to mandate, on 19 February 2018, a Task Force on Coordinated Action to work on the ESM's reform, maintaining its intergovernmental status. The mandate of the said task force was to work in EU-27 composition on a common backstop for the SRF, to review the ESM facilities, and to explore ways in which to ensure debt sustainability, with a view to avoiding PSI scenarios. Contrary to the original intention, the aim no longer is to incorporate the ESM into the EU legal framework by way of the EMF Regulation, as envisaged by the Commission in its proposal of 6 December 2017: instead, the focus of the discussion has shifted to reforming the role of the ESM in crisis management while maintaining its intergovernmental set-up under public international law. This change of direction has since been confirmed: on 14 December 2018, the Euro Summit instructed the Eurogroup to prepare the requisite amendments to the ESM Treaty with a view to achieving

53 In this regard, see Ulrich Häde, 'Legal Evaluation of a European Monetary Fund' (2010) 2 *Intereconomics: Review of European Economic Policy* 69 (Häde (2010)), 69–70; *cf.* Ansgar Belke, 'Reinforcing EU Governance in Times of Crisis: The Commission Proposals and Beyond' (2011) 44 (1) *Credit and Capital Markets*.

54 European Commission, 'Proposal for a Council Regulation on the Establishment of the European Monetary Fund' COM(2017) 827 (European Commission (2017b)). As the aim of the reform was to bring the ESM within the Treaty framework, transforming it from an intergovernmental into an EU law organisation, the legal basis for the Commission proposal was Article 352 TFEU (which, it is recalled, requires unanimity within the Council).

55 Euro Summit, *Statement* (15 December 2017) <http://www.consilium.europa.eu/en/meetings/euro-summit/2017/12/15/> accessed 30 September 2020.

the aforementioned objectives.[56] On 14 June 2019, the Eurogroup agreed on certain amendments to the ESM Treaty,[57] which the Euro Summit endorsed on 21 June 2019,[58] on the expectation that the necessary elements for the reform of the ESM Treaty would be finally agreed by the end of 2019. On 4 December 2019, the Eurogroup agreed, in principle and subject to the conclusion of national procedures, on the ESM reform elements.[59] At the time of writing, the revised ESM Treaty had yet to come into force, despite the fact that the text of the Agreement amending the ESM Treaty was agreed at the Eurogroup meeting of 30 November 2020:[60] the amendments to the ESM Treaty will only come into force once the amending Treaty had been ratified by all 19 ESM Member States.

If signed and ratified, the revised ESM Treaty will bring with it significant improvements in the ESM's ability to contribute to the resolution of future crises. Subject to their remarks, below, the authors view positively the ESM's newly attributed role as a backstop to the SRF – which promises to 'strengthen the SRF's ability to respond in resolution, thus strengthening the Banking Union'[61] – as well as the ESM's future contribution to the technical assessment of debt sustainability. At the same time, the authors see scope for improvement, both in terms of the institutional set-up of the ESM, where the idea of its incorporation into the EU legal framework deserves further consideration, and in terms of its powers, so that a revamped ESM can help break the channel of contagion moving from sovereigns to their commercial banks. We explore these and other issues below.

5.2.2.2 Choice of institutional set-up: An intergovernmental European Stability Mechanism or a supranational European Monetary Fund?

As a commentator cogently explained in an earlier work of legal scholarship,[62] two main options present themselves in terms of the institutional set-up of a revamped ESM: this can either continue to be intergovernmental (hence, existing outside the framework of the Treaties) or, instead, morph into an

56 Euro Summit, *Statement* (14 December 2018) <https://www.consilium.europa.eu/en/press/press-releases/2018/12/14/statement-of-the-euro-summit-14-december-2018/> accessed 30 September 2020.

57 Draft revised text of the Treaty establishing the European Stability Mechanism as agreed by the Eurogroup on 14 June 2019 <https://www.consilium.europa.eu/media/39772/revised-esm-treaty-2.pdf> accessed 30 September 2020.

58 Euro Summit, *Statement* (21 June 2019) <https://www.consilium.europa.eu/en/press/press-releases/2019/06/21/statement-of-the-euro-summit-21-june-2019/> accessed 30 September 2020.

59 See <https://www.esm.europa.eu/about-esm/esm-reform> accessed 30 September 2020.

60 See <https://www.consilium.europa.eu/media/47294/sn04244-en19.pdf> accessed 23 December 2020.

61 Aerts and Bizarro (2020), 174.

62 Alicia Hinarejos, 'A Possible European Monetary Fund and the Future of the Euro Area' (2019) 38 (1) *Yearbook of European Law* 119.

independent EU body. What militates in favour of the first option is continuity with the status quo. What speaks against, and in favour of the second, more revolutionary option, is the legitimate concern with the effectiveness of an intergovernmental EMF and with its ability to contribute towards closing the second channel of contagion.

Of the several arguments in favour of transforming a revamped ESM into an EU body, some are generic while others are of particular relevance to breaking the loop that connects sovereigns to their banks. One generic argument in favour of the proposed transformation can be derived from the key responsibility of the ESM, which is to ensure the stability of the euro area: this responsibility alone would appear to warrant its transformation into an EU body, accountable to the Parliament (and the Council).[63] Another generic argument is that, by bringing a revamped ESM within the framework of EU law, the Commission would be in a position to resort to the CJEU to challenge ESM decisions, on the basis of Article 263 TFEU.[64] However, it is the efficiency gains of the proposed transformation that would warrant undertaking it, from the perspective of the contribution that the ESM can make to breaking the sovereign–banks feedback loop. It is recalled that, currently, the euro-area Member States are the ESM's shareholders and, as shareholders, they enjoy the rights normally associated with shareholding. Accordingly, participating Member State parliaments are to be consulted before disbursement decisions, to align the assumption of financial liability by the ESM with democratic accountability and control. It is only by transforming the ESM into an EU body, with a paid-in capital derived from EU own resources (rather than Member State contributions), that its decision-making autonomy (and crisis management capabilities) can be decoupled from Member State control (which, at present, features *de facto* veto rights for each of the three largest euro-area Member States, each of which holds more than 15% of the ESM shares).[65] Arguably, the road to enhancing the effectiveness of a revamped ESM goes through lowering the voting threshold for the granting of stability support and ensuring the independence of its staff. In particular, consideration should be given to making the emergency procedure of Article 4(4) of the ESM Treaty

63 For an account of the related issue of the ECB's accountability to the Parliament in respect of the exercise of its supervisory tasks, see Adina Maricut-Akbik, 'Contesting the European Central Bank in Banking Supervision: Accountability in Practice at the European Parliament' (2020) *Journal of Common Market Studies*.

64 This argument is made in Tomi Tuominen, 'Mechanisms of Financial Stabilisation' in Federico Fabbrini and Marco Ventoruzzo (eds), *Research Handbook on EU Economic Law* (Edward Elgar 2020) (Tuominen (2020)), 104.

65 The veto powers of Germany, France and Italy are not commensurate with the euro area-wide mandate of the ESM, and their existence provides a core argument in favour of transforming the ESM into an EU body with autonomous decision-making capabilities.

the standard voting modality for decisions to grant financial stability support.[66] The above change in the ESM decision-making modalities should be accompanied by the introduction of adequate safeguards to enhance the leverage of the staff of a revamped ESM on the decision-making process (e.g. through the introduction of transparency and independence requirements similar to those of the IMF), to ensure that decisions are taken on the basis of independent, sound technical analyses of the ESM staff, acting free of political interference. ESM staff independence is key for ensuring the credibility and legitimacy of a revamped ESM and the credibility of its crisis management decisions (helpful guidance can be found, in both respects, in the rules of the IMF).[67]

The proposed transformation of the ESM into an EU body would necessitate achieving a consensus on the choice of legal basis for its integration into the EU legal order. The quest for an appropriate legal basis for an EMF involves a choice among the following Treaty provisions: Article 122(2), Article 136, Article 143, Articles 326–334, Article 352 or Article 114. We assess, below, the suitability of these provisions as a sound legal basis for the establishment of an EMF as an EU law body.

Starting with the 'rescuing clause' of Article 122(2) TFEU,[68] it is submitted that this cannot be meaningfully invoked to establish an institutionalised standing support mechanism, such as the one under consideration here, irrespective of whether this would only provide loans but no guarantees (a sustained sovereign or a banking crisis can hardly be compared to the 'natural disasters or exceptional occurrences beyond [a Member State's] control,' which are necessary to trigger the activation of this provision).[69]

Similarly, Article 143 TFEU could not be invoked, *de lege lata*, as a possible legal basis for establishing an EMF as a euro-area stability support mechanism: only Member States with a derogation (that is, those that have yet to adopt the

66 This would also be consistent with the Commission proposal, which was to make of the emergency procedure of Article 4(4) of the ESM Treaty (reinforced qualified majority of 85% of the votes) the standard voting modality for the granting of stability support to EMF Members (see draft Article 5(7) of European Commission (2017b)). The draft revised ESM Treaty proposes no changes to the voting rules of the original ESM Treaty (which, by default, require unanimity for most of the core ESM decisions).

67 It is worth noting in this regard the strong position of the IMF Managing Director and staff, and the well-defined and transparent IMF policies and procedures for financial programme work (e.g. procedures for entering into discussions, negotiations, and agreeing on a programme), which are particularly important for the operational efficiency and credibility of the IMF. In combination with the strong Independent Evaluation Office of the IMF, its rules of procedure and transparency requirements empower IMF staff, enabling it to push back on political interventions and giving it the necessary leverage in negotiations with the national authorities in the various programme countries.

68 This provides that, '[W]here a Member State is in difficulties or is seriously threatened with severe difficulties caused by natural disasters or exceptional occurrences beyond its control, the Council, on a proposal from the Commission, may grant, under certain conditions, Union financial assistance to the Member State concerned. The President of the Council shall inform the European Parliament of the decision taken.'

69 The CJEU was of the same view in *Pringle* (see the Court's ruling, para. 131).

single currency) can, at present, receive mutual financial assistance from the EU to deal with serious 'balance of payments' difficulties.

The idea of establishing an EMF under the 'enhanced cooperation' procedure of Articles 326–334 TFEU would also appear problematic, if only because EMU is, in and of itself, a special form of differentiated integration and is not, for that reason, amenable to (further) enhanced cooperation within the meaning of the Treaty.[70]

The closer 'coordination and surveillance' among the euro-area Member States contemplated in the newly introduced Article 136 TFEU[71] would appear to provide an acceptable legal basis for establishing a euro-area support fund, such as the EMF, and for laying down the conditions subject to which its support could be granted to Member States in need. Indeed, when the Council, on 16 and 17 December 2010, agreed to establish the ESM as a permanent financial crisis mechanism to replace the EFSM, as of June 2013, it declared its intention to do so by amending Article 136 TFEU, as Article 122(2) TFEU – the legal basis for the emergency-motivated EFSM – could not, in its view, provide an appropriate foundation for setting up a *permanent* ESM. Given its permanent nature and euro-area scope, the authors are of the opinion that reliance on Article 136 TFEU to establish the ESM would have been legally defensible, even if a fund providing assistance to Member States in need can only indirectly be said to be 'strengthening the coordination and surveillance of their budgetary discipline,' as per Article 136(1)(a) TFEU. The one major reservation to the suitability of Article 136 TFEU as a legal basis for a future EMF is that this provision only refers to the establishment of a fund *by the Member States* rather than by the EU: if the future EMF were to be established as an EU body (as it should, in these authors' view), use of Article 136 TFEU as its basis would not be uncontroversial.

A more promising legal basis for a future EMF can be found in Article 114 TFEU (the so-called 'internal market legal basis'), which forms part of Title VII, Chapter 3 ('Approximation of Laws') of the Treaty.[72] Article 114 TFEU has been the main legal basis for internal market harmonisation and the approximation of laws, and it has been invoked, in recent years, as the legal basis for

70 See Häde (2010).

71 Article 136 TFEU, one of three provisions belonging to a chapter entitled 'Provisions specific to Member States whose currency is the euro,' authorises the Council to adopt measures necessary to ensure the proper functioning of the EMU, acting in accordance with the procedures prescribed in Articles 121 and 126 TFEU. Voting rights are limited to those Member States only that participate in the third stage of EMU.

72 Article 114(1) TFEU provides that, '[S]ave where otherwise provided in the Treaties, the following provisions shall apply for the achievement of the objectives set out in Article 26. The European Parliament and the Council shall, acting in accordance with the ordinary legislative procedure and after consulting the Economic and Social Committee, adopt the measures for the approximation of the provisions laid down by law, regulation or administrative action in Member States which have as their object the establishment and functioning of the internal market.'

the establishment of the European System of Financial Supervision and the SRM. Although Article 114 TFEU does not, pursuant to the Court, vest in the Union legislature 'a general power to regulate the internal market,'[73] the jurisprudence of the Court is rich in instances where the creation of institutions or the enactment of harmonisation-motivated legal frameworks based on Article 114 TFEU were judicially upheld.[74] By the same token, the authors are only aware of one instance where a measure enacted on the basis of Article 114 TFEU was struck down by the Court.[75] It follows from the jurisprudence of the Court that the litmus test on the basis of which to determine whether the EU legislator can validly invoke Article 114 TFEU is whether the genuine object of the approximation or harmonisation measures adopted on its basis is 'the improvement of the conditions for the establishment and functioning of the internal market.'[76] Mere disparities among national laws are not adequate to meet the threshold for validly invoking Article 114 TFEU.[77] More recently, the Court held that

> the EU legislature, in its choice of method of harmonisation and, taking account of the discretion it enjoys with regard to the measures provided for under Article 114 TFEU, may delegate to a Union body, office or agency powers for the implementation of the harmonisation sought. That is the case in particular where the measures to be adopted are dependent on specific professional and technical expertise and the ability of such a body to respond swiftly and appropriately.[78]

This includes where the purpose of those measures is 'to ensure the proper functioning of the internal market and to improve the conditions of its functioning,

73 *Federal Republic of Germany v. European Parliament and Council of the European Union (Tobacco Advertising)* [2000] ECLI:EU:C:2000:544, para. 83.

74 See, for instance, *Federal Republic of Germany v. Council of the European Union (Product Safety)* [1994] ECLI:EU:C:1994:306; *United Kingdom of Great Britain and Northern Ireland v. European Parliament and Council of the European Union (Smoke Flavourings)* [2005] ECLI:EU:C:2005:743; and *ENISA*. The *ENISA* case is significant, for it was the first instance where the Court upheld the use of Article 114 TFEU as legal basis for the establishment of an EU body (until then, Article 114 TFEU had only been invoked for the adoption of harmonisation legislation).

75 *Federal Republic of Germany v. European Parliament and Council of the European Union (Tobacco Advertising)* [2000] ECLI:EU:C:2000:544. There, the Court struck down certain restrictions set out in Directive 98/43/EC of the European Parliament and of the Council of 6 July 1998 on the approximation of the laws, regulations and administrative provisions of the Member States relating to the advertising and sponsorship of tobacco products [1998] OJ L213/9 in various media, as the genuine object of that directive was not the improvement of the conditions for the establishment and functioning of the internal market but rather, the protection of public health.

76 Ibid., para. 84.

77 *The Queen, on the application of Vodafone Ltd and others v. Secretary of State for Business, Enterprise and Regulatory Reform* [2010] ECLI:EU:C:2010:321, paras 32–33.

78 *ESMA-short selling*, para. 105.

in particular with regard to the financial markets.'[79] Would the creation of an EMF (or, by the same token, the transformation of a revamped ESM, from an intergovernmental into an EU body) meet the Article 114 TFEU threshold? It is submitted that it would, for at least three reasons. First, pursuant to recital (6) to the ESM Treaty, the concern underlying the establishment of the ESM was 'the strong interrelation within the euro area,' as a result of which 'severe risks to the financial stability of Member States whose currency is the euro may put at risk the financial stability of the euro area as a whole': it follows that the provision, by the ESM, of stability support, could legitimately be viewed as a measure of economic coordination. Second, by providing funds for the direct recapitalisation of credit institutions (or, in the future, for the funding of the SRF), the ESM also has a key contribution to make to the functioning of the internal market, with its lending activities impacting on the prudential situation of the recipients of recapitalisation support (which is a matter of obvious euro-area and EU-wide interest). Third, the fact that the ESM Members are limited to the euro-area Member States does not mean that it only benefits them: by supporting the stability of euro-area Member States and their banks, the ESM pursues the interest of all EU Member States in averting spillovers apt to undermine the stability of the EU in its entirety.

Finally, the so-called 'flexibility clause' of Article 352 TFEU could provide a legal basis for a future EMF, as an EU body, but only as *ultima ratio*. It follows from the wording of Article 352 TFEU that a number of conditions must be fulfilled before Article 352 TFEU can be activated, namely, (a) certain action should be necessary to attain one of the Union's objectives; (b) no provision in the Treaty should provide for action to attain the objective; and (c) the envisaged action should not lead to the EU's competence being extended beyond those provided for by the Treaties.[80] In *Pringle*, the Court found that Article 352 TFEU conferred sufficient powers to the EU to adopt a system for the provision to Member States in need of financial support comparable to the ESM,[81] as there was no specific legal basis in the Treaties for its establishment, and as its creation belonged to economic policy, which, under Article 3(4) TEU, is an objective of the EU.[82] Moreover, the Court was of the opinion that the necessity of the creation of a body such as the ESM was based on factual elements and was confirmed by newly introduced Article 136(3) TFEU, as well as by recital (2) to the ESM Treaty, both of which stated that the ESM was 'to be activated if *indispensable* [emphasis is ours] to safeguard the stability of the

79 Ibid., para. 114.

80 Article 352(1) TFEU inter alia states that, '[I]f action by the Union should *prove necessary, within the framework of the policies defined in the Treaties*, to attain one of the *objectives set out in the Treaties*, and the Treaties have *not provided the necessary powers*, the Council, acting unanimously on a proposal from the Commission and after obtaining the consent of the European Parliament, shall adopt the appropriate measures [emphasis is ours].'

81 *Pringle*, para. 64.

82 Ibid., para. 60.

euro area as a whole.' Applying, *mutatis mutandis*, the reasoning of the Court in *Pringle* to the eventual creation of an EMF, it is considered that Article 352 TFEU could provide the legal basis for its establishment (provided the ESM were to fall out of the picture, so that the 'necessity' requirement built into Article 352 TFEU can be satisfied) and, interestingly, this was also the legal basis that the Commission opted for in its proposal, of December 2017, for a Council Regulation establishing an EMF.[83] The one reservation to the use of Article 352 TFEU as the legal basis for the eventual creation of an EMF relates to the last of the three conditions mentioned above for the valid activation of Article 352 TFEU (no extension of the EU's competences beyond those provided for in the Treaties):[84] an EU body, such as the EMF, that would provide financial assistance subject to conditionality, in pursuit of the EU economic policy objectives, could exceed the powers of the EU, which, in the field of economic policy, only has coordinating competences.[85]

To conclude, there is nothing to suggest that integrating the ESM into the EU legal order would be legally impossible, either on the basis of Article 114 TFEU or, alternatively, Article 136 TFEU or, as *ultima ratio*, on the basis of Article 352 TFEU. Our conclusion corroborates the earlier analysis of a commentator to the effect that 'the main obstacle against incorporating the ESM within EU law is one of resources, rather than legal bases.'[86] Moreover, as the COVID-19 crisis triggered European Recovery Fund-related discussions (still ongoing at the time of writing) suggest, an expansion of the EU budget is not out of the question, and it could be worth considering as a source of funding for a future EMF.

5.2.2.3 What powers for a credible European lender of last resort?

Without prejudice to the importance of further reflection on whether or not to transform the ESM into an EU body and, if so, on which legal basis, what is essential in order for a revamped ESM to be in a position to serve as a credible European LOLR and, at the same time, as an effective instrument through which to counteract the feedback loop between sovereigns and their banks is a review of its instruments. The eventual entry into force of the draft revised

83 European Commission (2017b).

84 'Article [352 TFEU] cannot be used as a basis for the adoption of provisions whose effect would, in substance, be to amend the Treaty without following the procedure which it provides for that purpose' (see Opinion 2/94 of the Court of 28 March 1996, para. 30).

85 Similar reservations have been expressed by Tuominen (2020), 104–105.

86 Federico Fabbrini, *Economic Governance in Europe: Comparative Paradoxes and Constitutional Challenges* (Oxford University Press 2016), 202, citing Alberto De Gregorio Merino, 'Legal Developments in the Economic and Monetary Union during the Debt Crisis: The Mechanisms of Financial Assistance' (2012) 49 (5) *Common Market Law Review* 1613, according to whom the main reason for opting for the intergovernmental model in the case of the ESM was the fact that the EU budget 'offered a quite small capacity of action, especially in a situation where the financial needs of the Member States... were so impressively high' (1635).

ESM Treaty would result in an overhaul of the ESM's approach to the direct recapitalisation of credit institutions, as well as in changes to its precautionary financial assistance instrument, whilst leaving unchanged its IRI. Are the proposed reforms to the ESM instruments apt to achieve the objective of turning a revamped ESM into a credible LOLR for euro-area banks?

Starting with direct recapitalisations, it is recalled that, at the time of writing, the relevant ESM instrument was the DRI (which was never activated). In many respects, the DRI seemed ill-adapted to the realities of the European Banking Union, as these had crystallised after its adoption. Of the several obstacles standing in the way of its eventual activation, the most notable included the (subsequent) establishment of the SSM and the SRM, the interplay between the conditions for the activation of the DRI and the BRRD's rules on precautionary recapitalisations,[87] the troubled relationship between the conditions for its activation and that of the activation of the SRF, and the likely severe impact of its activation for the ESM, from a financial risk perspective.[88] Moreover, two features of the DRI appeared likely to, however unwittingly, reinforce the vicious circle between sovereigns and banks. The first was the requirement for a mandatory contribution by the requesting Member State to the direct recapitalisation operation, alongside the ESM:[89] originally introduced to reduce moral hazard on the side of the requesting Member State, this requirement not only seemed of questionable utility following the introduction of the European Banking Union but, also, likely to reinforce the channel of contagion connecting banks to their sovereigns. The second was linked to the requirement for compliance, by the requesting Member State, with, *inter alia*, macroeconomic conditionality in order for it to have access to the DRI:[90] whereas the credit institution-specific and sector-specific conditionality to which the relevant ESM Guideline refer may have been legitimate, the same need not be true of macroeconomic conditionality, which, in a European Banking Union context, could unwittingly reinforce the feedback loop between sovereigns and banks. With these considerations in mind, the planned scraping of the DRI following the entry into force of the backstop facility provided for in new Article 18A of the draft revised ESM Treaty is, in principle, to be viewed positively. However, there is considerable scope for further improvements to reinforce the ESM's contribution to breaking the feedback loop between sovereigns and banks, while at the same time protecting the ESM from the risk of a depletion of its financial resources when backstopping the SRF. First, consideration

87 The combined reading of Article 32(4)(d)(iii) (Conditions for resolution) of the BRRD and Article 8 (Application of bail-in) of the ESM Guideline on Financial Assistance for the direct recapitalisation of institutions suggests that the bail-in requirements of the DRI are not aligned to those of the BRRD.

88 For an explanation, see Aerts and Bizarro (2020), 163.

89 See Article 9 (Contribution of the ESM Member to the Recapitalisation Operation) of the ESM Guideline on Financial Assistance for the Direct Recapitalisation of Institutions.

90 Ibid., Art. 1(4).

could be given to the ESM backstopping the SRF in respect of solvent SIs only, to the exclusion of LSIs: since the task of directly supervising SIs has been transferred to the European level, namely to the SSM, it would make sense if also the task of backstopping the funding of their resolution were to be transferred to the supranational level, namely to the ESM. Second, consideration should be given to the question of the adequacy of the ESM's backstop to the SRB for the SRF. It is recalled that although the entire lending capacity of the ESM is €500 billion,[91] the DRI was endowed with €60 billion, and that draft Article 19 of the Statute of the EMF[92] foresaw a ceiling of €60 billion in financial commitments for the direct recapitalisation of credit institutions. Although the legal documents released in connection with the ESM reform establish no explicit nominal cap for the backstop facility, it is understood that there is to be one[93] and that the size of the ESM credit line to the SRB for the SRF is to be aligned with the SRF's target level of €55 billion. This latter figure does not appear sufficient to cover the resolution funding needs of the SRF in the event of a generalised banking crisis affecting more than one SI in more than one euro-area Member States, questioning the financial capacity of the SRF but also the adequacy of the proposed ESM backstop.[94] Third, consideration should be given to removing national vetoes to the use of the backstop, which render its activation no less unlikely to a decision of the SRB to subject even a relatively small euro-area bank to resolution.

Turning to the IRI of Article 15 of the ESM Treaty (which the draft revised ESM Treaty leaves unchanged), it is submitted that this should also be adapted to the realities of the European Banking Union, as these have evolved since the adoption of the IRI. In particular, the IRI should be exclusively available for LSIs, which remain subject to the direct supervision of the NCAs (hence, the responsibility for their recapitalisation, including precautionary recapitalisation, should also be exercised at the national level, also in order to avoid reinforcing the bank–sovereign link). Precautionary recapitalisations would need to comply with the BRRD framework (in other words, they should only be available to solvent institutions, and burden sharing, under state aid rules, should apply to them). Besides, conditionality under the IRI should only be institution-specific and sector-specific, with macroeconomic conditionality appearing unsuitable in the context of the European Banking Union.

91 ESM Treaty, recital (6).

92 Annex to European Commission (2017b).

93 See Article 18A(1) of the draft revised ESM Treaty, read in conjunction with Article 3 of the draft Guideline on the Backstop Facility to the SRB for the SRF <https://www.consilium.europa.eu/media/41668/20191206-draft-backstop-guideline.pdf> accessed 30 September 2020.

94 For an account of the doubts expressed in this regard, see George S. Zavvos and Stella Kaltsouni, 'The Single Resolution Mechanism in the European Banking Union' in Matthias Haentjens and Bob Wessels (eds), *Research Handbook on Crisis Management in the Banking Sector* (Edward Elgar 2015), 146–147.

No less essential to the success of a revamped ESM in helping to close the second channel of contagion is the attractiveness and effectiveness of its precautionary instruments. It is recalled that the ESM Treaty includes two precautionary instruments: the precautionary conditions credit line ('PCCL'), for countries with sound fundamentals (assessed according to six criteria, including debt sustainability and compliance with the SGP and the Macroeconomic Imbalance Procedure) and with *ex ante* conditionality, and the enhanced conditions credit line ('ECCL'), available to countries with sound fundamentals which do not qualify for a PCCL, but which adopt measures to address the identified weaknesses. It follows from the Guideline on Precautionary Financial Assistance[95] that the objective of those instruments is to 'support sound policies and prevent crisis situations by allowing ESM Members to secure the possibility to access ESM assistance before they face major difficulties raising funds in the capital markets.' In their original formulation, the two ESM precautionary instruments were ineffective and unattractive, which helps to explain why they were never used. Starting with the PCCL, it is not obvious why euro-area Member States with strong fundamentals would wish to access that instrument if they are to avoid the stigma associated with its activation. Similarly, the stigma and the (unclear) conditionality associated with the ECCL instrument make it likelier than not that Member States would delay applying for it, with the risk that their situation will, as a result, have deteriorated so considerably that a precautionary line would no longer suffice to redress their situation, making of a fully-fledged ESM programme the only viable alternative. Conscious of the need to reform the ESM's precautionary instruments so as to make them more user-friendly, the Eurogroup agreed on certain changes, mostly to the PCCL, as part of the draft revised ESM Treaty.[96] In particular, access to the ECCL is to be preceded by the negotiation of an MoU, stipulating the conditionality attaching to it.[97] For its part, access to the PCCL is to be made independent of an MoU: instead, it is to be based on 'continuous respect of the eligibility criteria provided for in Annex III,' which include respect of certain quantitative fiscal benchmarks (general government deficit not exceeding 3% of GDP, a general government structural budget balance at or above the country-specific minimum benchmark and a general government debt to GDP ratio of below 60% or a reduction in the differential with respect to 60% over the previous two years at an average rate of 1/20 per year), the absence of excessive imbalances, a track record of access to international capital markets

95 See Guideline on Precautionary Financial Assistance (9 October 2012) <https://www.esm.europa.eu/sites/default/files/esm_guideline_on_precautionary_financial_assistance.pdf> accessed 30 September 2020.

96 See Article 14 of the draft revised ESM Treaty, read in conjunction with Annex III thereto.

97 Ibid., Article 14(3), read in conjunction with Annex III.

on reasonable terms, and the absence of severe financial sector vulnerabilities putting at risk its financial stability.[98]

Are the proposed reforms sufficient to make the ESM's precautionary credit instruments attractive, thereby encouraging ESM Member States to pre-emptively address, through them, incipient vulnerabilities and to undertake adjustments based on lighter conditionality? It seems difficult to answer this question in the affirmative. If the proposed ESM reform goes through, access to the PCCL will become harder than it was, at the time of writing, on account of the long list of stringent eligibility criteria, which closely mirror those applicable for the surveillance of compliance with the SGP.[99] By rendering access to the PCCL harder, the Eurogroup seems to be stressing the avoidance of moral hazard and the stigma effects attaching to precautionary financial assistance over its preventive rationale. That only a letter of intent would be required for access to the PCCL (instead of an MoU, as in the case of the ECCL) is, no doubt, a compensatory element, but how far it goes towards addressing the stigma effects of the PCCL remains to be seen. How could the revamped ESM's precautionary tools be improved? To start with, the difference between the ECCL and a standard ESM loan programme should be clarified: if both of them require an MoU and are subject to conditionality, it is not clear what distinct purpose, if any, the ECCL serves.[100] More generally, to avoid the stigma effects attaching to both the ECCL and the PCCL, it could be explored whether to provide standing access to a liquidity window for all euro-area Member States who fulfil the eligibility criteria of the current (or the future) ESM precautionary instruments. Moreover, the possibility should exist for the ESM to pro-actively approach a Member State in the wake of market turbulence or following a breach of the eligibility criteria, with a request to adopt specific reform policies in exchange for precautionary financial support. Similarly, to escape the conditionality trap, reflection could be given to introducing a permanent surveillance mechanism for euro-area Member States and

98 See Annex III to the ESM Treaty, Eligibility Criteria for ESM Precautionary Financial Assistance available at <https://www.consilium.europa.eu/media/39771/esmt-annexes.pdf> accessed 30 September 2020.

99 For the reasons explained in Grégory Claeys and Antoine Mathieu Collin, 'Does the Eurogroup's Reform of the ESM Toolkit Represent Real Progress?' (*Bruegel*, 13 December 2018) <https://www.bruegel.org/2018/12/does-the-eurogroups-reform-of-the-esm-toolkit-represent-real-progress/?utm_content=bufferb95db&utm_medium=social&utm_source=twitter.com&utm_campaign=buffer+(bruegel)> accessed 30 September 2020, the eligibility criteria for access to the revamped PCCL will be *stricter* than those applicable under the original PCCL, especially in respect of criteria concerning fiscal rules. These commentators also criticise the structural deficit eligibility criterion as impractical, on account of the difficulty of measuring it in a reliable way.

100 The point is aptly made in Shahin Vallée, Jérémie Cohen-Setton, Paul De Grauwe and Sebastian Dullien, 'The Proposed Reform of the European Stability Mechanism Must Be Postponed' (*LSE Blog*, 11 December 2019) <https://blogs.lse.ac.uk/europpblog/2019/12/11/the-proposed-reform-of-the-european-stability-mechanism-must-be-postponed/#Author> accessed 30 September 2020.

a requirement for credible commitment from the Member States to undertake the necessary policy adjustments within a given timeline, but short of *ex ante* conditionality, so as to remain eligible for access to ESM precautionary instruments. In the authors' view, only a genuinely independent ESM, elevated to the status of an EU body, can make the most of any reform to its precautionary instruments, to help prevent a sovereign debt crisis from arising and to ensure the calm that euro-area Member States and their banking sectors need, especially at turbulent times such as those pertaining at the time of writing.

5.2.2.4 Concluding remarks

For the reasons explained earlier in this chapter, the authors consider the existence of a credible euro-area support mechanism essential in order for progress to be made towards closing the second channel of contagion, and for financial stability in the euro area to be guaranteed without the need for recourse to other mechanisms through which to shield the banking sector from the consequences of sovereign debt crises. Neither the ESM, nor its precursor – the European Financial Stability Facility ('EFSF') – disposed of the material resources or the governance structure necessary for them to be in a position to perform swiftly, credibly and effectively the role of a credible LOLR in crisis situations.[101] In order for it to be in a position to act autonomously, a euro-area support mechanism should ideally be established within the framework of the Treaties, as an independent EU body.

Indeed, it is only if a revamped ESM were to be an EU body, with the primary task of providing stability support both *ex ante* and *ex post*, that it would stand a realistic chance of guaranteeing financial stability in the euro area, thereby helping to close the second channel of contagion. The EU-law character of an eventual EMF would need to be reflected in the choice of the legal basis for its establishment, in the full independence of its staff, and in its endowment with sufficient resources to fulfil its mission, drawn from the EU budget.[102] Transforming the intergovernmental ESM into an EMF should go

101 The creation of the EFSF and, thereafter, the ESM were largely motivated by the need to absolve the ECB of the assumption of an LOLR role for sovereigns, at a time when EMU was not equipped with alternative institutions to perform this role. There are solid arguments in favour of the ECB's performance of this role: as a commentator has aptly explained, '[F]ailure to play the lender of last resort role for government bond carries the risk of forcing the ECB to actualise their lender of last resort promise to banks in the countries hit by a sovereign debt crisis. And this sort of lending is almost certainly more expensive than backstopping the government debt. The reason is that typically the liabilities of the banking sector of a country are many times larger than the liabilities of the national government' (Paul De Grauwe, 'The European Central Bank as a Lender of Last Resort' (*VoxEU*, 18 August 2011) <https://voxeu.org/article/european-central-bank-lender-last-resort> accessed 19 September 2020).

102 An alternative financing mechanism proposed early into the crisis, which would entail a direct penalty payment for countries with an excessive debt or deficit ratio, would not be consistent with the conception of the EMF as a stability support mechanism, and would also be in conflict with

hand in hand with a reinforcement of its various funding instruments to ensure their consistency with the rationale of the European Banking Union, their effectiveness in combatting (or forestalling) sovereign crises, and their overall attractiveness to euro-area Member States facing fiscal challenges with a potential impact on the stability of their banking sectors. For the reasons explained earlier in this chapter, the recently agreed reforms to the ESM's arsenal of instruments are not sufficient, however positive, in several respects, and well-intended they may be.

5.3 Creation and issuance of a European safe asset: Eurobonds and other proposals

5.3.1 Eurobonds and other proposals

Already in the 1970s, the European Communities, as they then were, had contracted, in their name, 'Community loans' to assist Member States confronted with the fallout of the Oil Crisis.[103] The idea of the common issuance *by the EU Member States* (rather than by the Union itself) of some form of common European debt dates back to the late 1980s, when the then President of the Commission, Jacques Delors, floated 'Eurobonds' as a means through which to finance common infrastructure projects. For all its merit, this idea was to remain dormant until the outbreak of the European sovereign debt crisis.

5.3.1.1 Overview of proposals

The outbreak of the European sovereign debt crisis signalled the start of a new wave of interest in common (European) safe assets. The first proposal for their introduction was made by Boonstra who, in April 2010, suggested moving from national to central financing for all public debt, thereby abolishing the possibility for countries to separately raise debt on financial markets. An independent 'EMU fund' would issue Eurobonds and lend the funds raised to the participating euro-area countries at a premium over the Eurobond rate. While participation in the 'EMU fund' would be voluntary, Boonstra argued that the large liquidity and stability benefits of participating would ultimately convince all euro-area countries to participate.[104]

Article 126 TFEU, which exhaustively lists the conditions subject to which penalty payments are legally possible (and it should, also for that reason, be discarded (in this regard, also see Peter Bofinger and Stefan Ried, 'A New Framework for Fiscal Policy Consolidation in Europe' (2010) 45 (4) Intereconomics: Review of European Economic Policy 203)).

103 See Regulation (EEC) 397/75 of the Council of 17 February 1975 concerning Community loans [1975] OJ L46/1, the legal basis of which was Article 235 TEC, the precursor of Article 352 TFEU (the flexibility clause). Significantly, at the time of the adoption of the Regulation, the Treaties did not include any provision corresponding, in terms of content, to Article 125 TFEU.

104 Wim Boonstra, 'How EMU Can Be Strengthened by Central Funding of Public Deficits' (2010) 14 ELEC Cahier Comte Boël 3.

In December 2010, the Italian Finance Minister and the President of the Eurogroup also called for the issuance of Eurobonds, as a means of putting an end to the euro-area sovereign debt crisis.[105] Tremonti and Juncker conceived Eurobonds as a primary market, European (that is, common to all Member States) sovereign bonds, issued by an EDA[106] as a successor to the EFSF, the ESM's precursor. The EDA would finance up to 50% (in exceptional cases 100%) of new debt issued by its members, but never beyond 40% of their GDP (so as not to breach the Maastricht limits). The EDA could also stabilise the secondary market for national debt by offering Member States in difficulty the possibility to swap outstanding national bonds for Eurobonds at a discount, the size of which would depend on market conditions. Eurobonds would enjoy a higher priority than national debt and would qualify as eligible collateral for Eurosystem credit operations. As Eurobond interest rates would be lower than their national rates, at least in the case of Member States suffering from fiscal imbalances, the refinancing through Eurobonds of a large portion of their existing debt would improve both their solvency and their liquidity position.

For their part, Delpla and Von Weizsäker[107] proposed the creation of 'blue' and 'red' bonds. Their proposal suggested the mutualisation of euro-area debt up to 60% of GDP (the blue bonds), with the remainder being national bonds (red bonds). The 60% threshold would serve as an incentive for countries to reduce their debt levels towards the 60% of GDP target of the SGP. Blue bonds would be the more senior of the two, they would be issued by an EDA under a joint and several liability regime, and their risk-weighting would be zero, while the red bonds would be issued by the national treasuries, they would not be eligible for a bail-out, nor for use as collateral for Eurosystem refinancing operations, and they would be risk-weighted. The annual allocation of blue bonds for each country would be decided by an independent fiscal stability council. For their part, Philippon and Hellwig[108] proposed the issuance of 'Eurobills' as a way to introduce a safe and short maturity liquid asset that would foster further financial integration and stabilise government debt markets especially at

105 Juncker and Tremonti (2010). The idea of issuing some sort of 'Eurobonds' had earlier been considered by scholars, some of whom were against it. For instance, in favour, see De Grauwe and Moesen (2009) (Eurobonds to be issued through the European Investment Bank ('EIB'), based on a guarantee proportional to the Member States' participation in the EIB's capital, with the proceeds also allocated proportionately to their participation in the EIB's capital); and Delpla and Von Weizsäcker (2010) (separation of the Member States' debt in blue and red tranches – the former covering debt below 60% of GDP and the latter all debt in excess thereof – and pooling together of the blue tranches, to create a deep government bond market and reduced borrowing costs on the blue tranche, creating incentives for Member States to keep their debt to 60% of their GDP or below). Contra, see Wim Kösters, 'Common Euro Bonds – No Appropriate Instrument' (2009) 44 (3) *Intereconomics: Review of European Economic Policy* 135.

106 The idea of creating an EDA had been floated in March 2010 by the Belgian Prime Minister Yves Leterme.

107 Delpla and Von Weizsäcker (2010).

108 Philippon and Hellwig (2011).

times of stress. Eurobills would be intended as a short-term paper, the issuance of which would involve the joint and several liability of the Member States.

Alternative proposals have also been put on the table. In 2011, Brunnermeier et al.[109] proposed the creation of ESBies[110] as a pool of default risk-free tradable assets to serve as investment vehicles for global investors and as safe collateral for Eurosystem refinancing operations. Their issuance would be entrusted to an EDA, which would select and purchase, on the secondary market, a portfolio of euro-area government bonds, according to a fixed weight to reflect the size of the economies of the different euro-area Member States. The EDA would hold the bonds passively on its balance sheet and use them as collateral to issue securities in two tranches, one senior and one junior, and to provide cash flows for them. The success of ESBies, as SBBSs, would be conditional on two legal and regulatory changes: on the one hand, the ECB would need to grant preferential treatment to ESBies belonging to the senior tranche, accepting them as the main source of collateral for Eurosystem refinancing operations; on the other hand, bank regulators would need to apply a zero risk-weight to the senior tranche, which would make of it the preferred asset for banks (but, also, pension funds and other institutional investors).[111] In a more recent paper,[112] the same authors have suggested that restricting euro-area banks to holding ESBies only would effectively isolate those banks from sovereign risk, thereby defusing the sovereign-banks doom loop. The ESRB has also investigated the (very similar) idea of creating sovereign-backed securities ('SBSs'), comprising senior and junior claims on a diversified portfolio of government bonds.[113] The junior tranches would be the first in line to take losses in the event of sovereign default, while the senior ones would be liquid, low-risk assets with a senior claim on government bonds from across Europe. The issuance of these securitised financial instruments (i.e. SBBSs) would increase the diversification of banks' balance sheets, reduce systemic risk and mitigate fragmentation in the demand for low-risk sovereign assets, thereby reducing flights to quality and asymmetries in the euro-area sovereign bond markets.

109 Brunnermeier et al. (2012).

110 See, also, Section 3.4.2.

111 It is understood that demand for the junior tranche could come from hedge funds and other speculative investors.

112 Markus Brunnermeier et al., 'The Sovereign-Bank Diabolic Loop and ESBies' (2016) 106 (5) *American Economic Review, American Economic Association* 508.

113 See European Systemic Risk Board, High-Level Task Force on Safe Assets, *Survey on Sovereign Bond-Backed Securities* (2018) <https://www.esrb.europa.eu/pub/task_force_safe_assets/shared/pdf/esrb.report290118_sbbs_volume_I_mainfindings.en.pdf> accessed 30 September 2020. The survey builds on Brunnermeier et al. (2017). For an assessment of the SBSs proposal, see Markus Demary and Jürgen Matthes, 'An Evaluation of Sovereign-Backed Securities (SBSs) – Potentials, Risks and Political Relevance' (2017) *Institut der deutschen Wirtschaft Köln Policy Paper* 12/2017 <https://ideas.repec.org/p/zbw/iwkpps/122017.html> accessed 30 September 2020.

The concept of SBBSs was first[114] discussed by the Commission in a 2017 'Reflection Paper on the Deepening of the Economic and Monetary Union,' as a means of promoting the diversification of banks' balance sheets and helping to address the problem of interconnection between banks and their respective home countries.[115] In May 2018, the Commission espoused the idea of SBSs by putting forward a proposal for an EU Regulation laying down the framework for them (eligibility of sovereign bonds and composition of their underlying portfolio, issuance and tranching, regulatory treatment of SBBS held by banks and other financial operators, etc.).[116] The explanatory memorandum to the proposal cited the sovereign–banks nexus, the banks' tendency to concentrate their sovereign bond portfolios in their own sovereign and the need to facilitate the diversification of banks' sovereign portfolios as a means of reducing financial stability risks as the main rationale of the proposed regulation. The Parliament was to later endorse the Commission proposal, subject to relatively minor changes.[117] At the time of writing, no action was envisaged to be taken on the Commission proposal.

5.3.1.2 *Legal assessment of existing proposals*

As the reader will have surmised from the foregoing, although the Eurobond 'label' has been used for different types of instruments, serving different purposes,[118] the various Eurobond proposals fall into one of two groups: 'Eurobonds proper,' whose issuance would involve debt (or interest payment) mutualisation, joint and several liability and fiscal solidarity among the Member States ('blue' and 'red' bonds and Eurobills), and SBBSs, whose issuance would not (ESBies and SBSs).

The above distinction is of immediate relevance to an assessment of the legal feasibility of the issuance of Eurobonds or SBBSs. In particular, while it is clear that what lies at the heart of proposals for the issuance of Eurobonds proper is the common issuance of debt, what remains open for debate is the exact type of *common liability vis-à-vis* debt holders that would accompany such

114 Already in late 2011, the European Commission had discussed the feasibility of so-called 'stability bonds' (European Commission, 'Green Paper on the Feasibility of Introducing Stability Bonds' COM(2011) 818).

115 European Commission (2017a).

116 European Commission, 'Proposal for a Regulation of the European Parliament and of the Council on sovereign bond-backed securities' COM(2018) 339.

117 European Parliament, 'Legislative Resolution of 16 April 2019 on the "Proposal for a Regulation of the European Parliament and of the Council on sovereign bond-backed securities" COM(2018)339' C8-0206/2018 – 2018/0171(COD) P8_TA(2019)0373.

118 For a concise presentation and assessment of the key features of the main Eurobond-related proposals, see European Parliament, Directorate General for Internal Policies, 'Eurobonds: The Financial Equivalent of the Single Currency' IP/A/ECON/NT/2011-01.

common issuance of debt.[119] Three main options are conceivable: (a) pro-rata (i.e. proportionate) liability (which, whilst possible, is the least likely set-up, given the rationale for the issuance of Eurobonds); (b) joint and several liability or issuance under a state guarantee (as in the case of 'blue' and 'red' bonds or Eurobills); and (c) the absence of risk-sharing (as in the case of ESBies and SBSs). Each of these options raises different legal concerns, in respect of which the following general legal remarks can be made.

A first remark relates to the different types of liability backing the issuance of Eurobonds as opposed to SBBSs, whoever their obligor. A joint and several liability structure (entailing the provision by the participating Member States of a joint and several guarantee to back the issuance of debt) would mean that Eurobond holders can claim payment of the full guaranteed amount by the Member State of their choice (presumably the one with the deepest purse). A proportionate liability structure is one under the terms of which each participating Member State would only cover a fraction of the total Eurobond issuance in proportion to a predetermined benchmark (for instance, its GDP, the share of its contribution to the ECB's paid-up capital or another benchmark). This is, incidentally, the type of liability used in the context of both the EFSF[120] and the ESM[121] (although the particulars of their individual guarantee structures differ). For the reasons cogently explained by a commentator, although joint and several liability structures would raise more concerns than pro-rata guarantee structures, both would be legally problematic from an EU primary law perspective[122]. Contrary to Eurobonds, whose issuance would entail a measure of debt mutualisation, depending on their particular liability structure, the issuance of SBBSs would entail no element of mutualisation. Instead of being backed by a state guarantee, ESBies and SBSs would resemble 'federal treasuries' (devoid of the backing of a federal treasury),[123] the attraction of which would reside in their promise to serve as a common, low-risk synthetic asset accessible to all euro-area banks for use as an instrument of investment or collateral.

119 See Christian Scheinert, 'Eurobonds – One Word, Many Concepts, Boundless Expectations – Some Facts' (2011) *European People's Party Group Watching Brief* 16 (Scheinert (2011)), 5–7.

120 On the proportionate guarantees provided by the Member States to the EFSF, see Article 7 of and Annex 2 to the EFSF Framework Agreement of 7 June 2010 <https://www.esm.europa.eu/sites/default/files/20111019_efsf_framework_agreement_en.pdf> accessed 30 September 2020.

121 On the contribution key for the subscription of the ESM's authorised capital stock, see Article 11 of and Annex 1 to the ESM Treaty.

122 See Jörn Axel Kämmerer, 'How can Eurobonds be Legally Implemented into European Law?' (2016) 12 (3) *Review of Law and Economics* 585 (Kämmerer (2016)), 596–598 (explaining why pro rata liability Eurobonds, except for those carrying individual country interest rates at issuance, and where each participating country covers interest payments due on its other national bonds, would be inconsistent with Article 125 TFEU).

123 Markus Brunnermeier, Marco Pagano, Ricardo Reis, Stijn Van Nieuwerburgh and Dimitri Vayanos, 'A Safe Asset for Europe' (*Financial Times Alphaville*, 28 April 2017) <https://ftalphaville.ft.com/2017/04/28/2188024/guest-post-a-safe-asset-for-europe/> accessed 30 September 2020.

A second remark relates to the question of the legal basis for the issuance of Eurobonds, on the one hand, and SBBSs, on the other, and, connected to this, the choice of their obligor.[124] The choice of obligor is between the EU – presumably acting through the Commission or an EU vehicle, existing or new – and the EU Member States acting jointly. The former option would be relevant to Eurobonds proper and to SBBSs alike, whereas the latter would be of relevance to Eurobonds proper. If it is SBBSs that were to see the light of day with the EU acting as their issuer (through a dedicated securitisation vehicle), then the legal basis for their issuance would be Article 114 TFEU, conferring to the EU the competence to lay down appropriate provisions having as their objective the establishment and functioning of the internal market.[125] The choice of legal basis would be less straightforward if the EU or its Member States were to, instead, want to issue Eurobonds proper (rather than SBBS-type securitised assets). As a general proposition, the EU lacks a *general* competence either for sovereign borrowing, generally, or for the issuance of bonds, specifically.[126] The EU *has*, nevertheless, taken loans (see above) and provided support, including financial support (mostly for infrastructure projects), while the Member States *have*, for their part, established financial assistance facilities *and* issued bonds for their purposes (the reference being to the EFSM – which was created on the basis of Article 122(2) TFEU – and to the Balance of Payments Assistance facility[127] – which is destined for use by Member States with a derogation, and which is based on Article 143 TFEU – but, also, to the Macro-Financial Assistance to non-EU partner countries, under Article 212 TFEU). Should the instruments' obligor be the EU, the following legal bases could be considered for their issuance:

(1) Article 122(1) TFEU:[128] This provision, which was not activated during the European sovereign debt crisis, and which is not relevant to the provision of financial assistance from the EU to Member States that experience

124 On the question of the mechanics for their actual issuance process, see Section 5.3.2.

125 As an instrument through which to enhance financial stability and risk-sharing across the euro area, SBBSs would contribute towards deepening the internal market. Article 114 TFEU was also the legal basis for a Commission proposal for a Regulation of the Parliament and of the Council on sovereign bond-backed securities (see Section 5.3.1.1).

126 In this regard, see, in particular, Article 310 TFEU, which, by stating, inter alia, that '[T]he revenue and expenditure shown in the [annual] budget [of the Union] shall be in balance,' can be read to introduce in the Union legal order a balanced budget requirement, with an impact on the ability of the EU to borrow or to otherwise contract debt (in this regard, also see Federico Fabbrini, 'Il Pareggio di Bilanzio nelle Constituzioni Europee' (2011) Quaderni Constituzionali 933).

127 See Council Regulation (EC) 332/2002 of 18 February 2002 establishing a facility providing medium-term financial assistance for Member States' balances of payments [2002] OJ L53/1.

128 'Without prejudice to any other procedures provided for in the Treaties, the Council, on a proposal from the Commission, may decide, in a spirit of solidarity between Member States, upon the measures appropriate to the economic situation, in particular if severe difficulties arise in the supply of certain products, notably in the area of energy.'

or are threatened with severe financing problems,[129] could serve as the legal basis for the funding side of an eventual Eurobond structure, e.g. for the construction of the guarantee system through which the Member States would back an EU issuance of debt;

(2) Article 122(2) TFEU:[130] To invoke this provision (which provided the legal basis for the creation of the EFSM), certain conditions must be fulfilled. The first of those conditions is the existence of 'difficulties (or the serious threat thereof) caused by natural disasters or exceptional occurrences beyond a Member State's control.' The second condition is the provision, by the Union, of 'financial assistance,'[131] which, as the Court ruled in *Pringle*, can only be *temporary* (Article 122(2) TFEU cannot, in other words, be used to establish a more permanent assistance facility).[132] The third condition is the provision of such 'financial assistance' subject to 'certain conditions': judging by the precedent of the EFSM, this is a reference to so-called macroeconomic conditionality (or to the 'strong economic policy conditions' of Regulation (EU) 407/2010),[133] although the intensity of those conditions – which must depend on the circumstances – appears to be weaker compared to those required under Article 136(3) TFEU (there, the corresponding reference is to 'strict conditionality'). The suitability of this provision as the legal basis for the issuance of Eurobonds or SBBSs appears limited, except in a crisis situation and on a temporary basis;

(3) Article 136(3) TFEU:[134] This provision, inserted in the Treaty on the occasion of the establishment of the ESM,[135] could provide an alternative legal basis for a Eurobond issuance scheme. Significantly, its scope is limited to euro-area Member States, whereas, as suggested above, its conditionality standard appears to be more exacting compared to the one contemplated by Article 122(2) TFEU. Considering the rationale of

129 *Pringle*, para. 116.

130 'Where a Member State is in difficulties or is seriously threatened with severe difficulties caused by natural disasters or exceptional occurrences beyond its control, the Council, on a proposal from the Commission, may grant, under certain conditions, Union financial assistance to the Member State concerned. The President of the Council shall inform the European Parliament of the decision taken.'

131 This term has, so far, taken the form of repayable loans to the Member States. However, the natural meaning of the words 'financial assistance' does not a priori exclude other forms of financial assistance, such as grants.

132 *Pringle*, paras 104–105.

133 Recital (7) to Council Regulation (EU) 407/2010 of 11 May 2010 establishing a European financial stabilisation mechanism [2010] OJ L118/1.

134 'The Member States whose currency is the euro may establish a stability mechanism to be activated if indispensable to safeguard the stability of the euro area as a whole. The granting of any required financial assistance under the mechanism will be made subject to strict conditionality.'

135 Indeed, Article 136(3) was inserted into the Treaty after entry into force of Decision 2011/199/EU, following the procedure in Article 48(6) TEU.

Article 136(3) TFEU, this would not appear to represent an appropriate legal basis since the issuance of Eurobonds would bear no relation to the ESM's stability mechanism;

(4) Article 352 TFEU:[136] There are several precedents for the use of Article 352 TFEU as the legal basis for the adoption of EU legal acts or for the creation of EU legal structures. Three cumulative conditions are to be fulfilled before this provision can be activated, namely, (a) certain action should be necessary to attain one of the Union's objectives; (b) no provision in the Treaty should provide for action to attain that objective; and (c) the envisaged action should not lead to the EU's competences being extended beyond those provided for by the Treaties.[137] The circumstances of the deployment of Article 352 TFEU were the object of judicial scrutiny in *Pringle*.[138] There, the Court ruled that Article 352 TFEU conferred sufficient powers to the EU to adopt the ESM Treaty, as there was no specific legal basis in the Treaties for its establishment, despite the fact that its creation belonged to the sphere of economic policy, an objective of the EU under Article 3(4) TEU.[139] Applying, *mutatis mutandis*, the reasoning of the Court in *Pringle* to the eventual issuance of a Eurobonds, it is submitted that Article 352 TFEU could legitimately be invoked as the legal basis for the creation of an EU facility for their issuance. Legally speaking, this provision (used in conjunction with Article 122(1) TFEU) appears to be the most promising legal basis for the issuance of debt in the form of Eurobonds proper. However, its deployment requires unanimity at the level of the Council, suggesting that, politically speaking, it may not be a viable option.

Considering that the EU lacks a competence for sovereign borrowing, how would the issuance of debt by the EU be reconcilable with the EU budgetary rules in Articles 310 *et seq*. TFEU? Although this is not a question that lends itself to a straightforward answer, it is submitted that some comfort can be drawn from Article 311 TFEU. This *inter alia* states that '[T]he Union shall provide itself with the means necessary to attain its objectives and carry through its policies.' It follows that, despite the Union's lack of financing autonomy,

136 'If action by the Union should prove necessary, within the framework of the policies defined in the Treaties, to attain one of the objectives set out in the Treaties, and the Treaties have not provided the necessary powers, the Council, acting unanimously on a proposal from the Commission and after obtaining the consent of the European Parliament, shall adopt the appropriate measures.'

137 'Article [352 TFEU] cannot be used as a basis for the adoption of provisions whose effect would, in substance, be to amend the Treaty without following the procedure which it provides for that purpose' (see Opinion 2/94 of the Court of 28 March 1996, para. 30).

138 *Pringle*, para. 64. Moreover, the Court ruled that the necessity of the ESM's creation was based on factual elements, reflected in recital (2) to the ESM Treaty, both of which stated that the ESM was 'to be activated if *indispensable* (emphasis is ours) to safeguard the stability of the euro area as a whole.'

139 Ibid., para. 60.

if Article 311 TFEU is not to be hollowed out and lose its *effet utile*, it must be accepted that the EU is possessed of the inherent competence to resort to lending (*inter alia* through the issuance of debt) in order to be in a position to carry out its tasks.

If, on the other hand, the obligor of Eurobonds proper were to be the EU Member States acting jointly (either within the framework of the Treaties or on the basis of an intergovernmental agreement), identifying an appropriate legal basis for their issuance would be a less-than-straightforward exercise. Article 122(2) TFEU, which provided the legal basis for the EFSF, would not be an option, as Eurobonds proper are not a form of financial assistance but, instead, a form of collective borrowing (backed by joint and several liability). Article 136(3) TFEU would also not appear to be an option since the issuance of Eurobonds would bear no relation to the ESM's stability mechanism. The only remaining candidate would be Article 352 TFEU. However, it is recalled that this provision (the deployment of which requires unanimity at the level of the Council) cannot legitimately be invoked where its use would result in an extension of the EU's competences beyond those provided for by the Treaties, without the regular Treaty amendment procedure being complied with. As it happens, the Treaties are silent on the possibility of the issuance of joint debt for mainstream funding use. Thus, the better view is that a Treaty amendment (or amendments) would be necessary in order for the joint issuance of debt by the EU Member States. It is, of course, true that amendments to the Treaties have been negotiated before (of which the most recent example was the insertion of Article 136(3) TFEU into the Treaty to pave the way for the establishment of the ESM). As the recent COVID-19 pandemic crisis has confirmed,[140] reaching a consensus around any process leading up to the joint issuance of debt would be a challenge. What might, however, help is if consensus on the budgetary and labour market policy coordination necessary to make of certain types of Eurobonds a credible instrument can first be achieved at the political level.

A third and final remark relates to the legal obstacles to the issuance of collective debt. Since the ruling of the CJEU in *Pringle*,[141] it is accepted that

140 Motivated by concerns with mitigating COVID-19's severe economic impact, especially on some of the more fragile EU Member States that saw their bond yields rise sharply amidst the pandemic, Italian Prime Minister Giuseppe Conte urged EU leaders, on 17 March 2020, to consider issuing joint, EU level debt (referred to, by some, as 'coronavirus bonds'). The outcome of the European Council of 26 March was to quash the hopes of the advocates of the joint issuance of even a short-term, targeted Eurobond, to help alleviate the pandemic's immediate economic consequences, questioning the extent to which the COVID-19-triggered European economic crisis could provide the decisive impetus for the eventual issuance of Eurobonds.

141 There, the Court stated that, 'the activation of financial assistance by means of a stability mechanism such as the ESM is not compatible with Article 125 TFEU unless it is indispensable for the safeguarding of the financial stability of the euro area as a whole and subject to strict conditions' (para. 135), adding that, 'Article 125 TFEU does not prohibit the granting of financial assistance by one or more Member States to a Member State which remains responsible for its commitments

emergency bilateral loans or credit lines and ESM financial assistance *can* be compatible with EU law and, in particular, with the 'no bail-out' clause of Article 125 TFEU.[142] But the same would not necessarily be true of Eurobonds proper: their legality, as a matter of EU law, would greatly depend on the type of liability that the participating Member States would undertake for their issuance,[143] not least because Article 136(3) TFEU does not cover Eurobonds[144] and cannot, as a result, be invoked in defence of the validity of their issuance as a matter of EU law. Eurobonds, it is recalled, are not a form of financial assistance but, instead, collective borrowing, backed by joint and several liability (in the case of Eurobonds falling within the 'blue' and 'red' bond or the Eurobill mould). Such collective borrowing could give rise to legal concerns for two reasons: first, on account of its apparent incompatibility with Article 125 TFEU, and second, on account of its non-conformity with national law constraints (at least in some of the EU Member States). We explore each of these points below.

Starting with Article 125 TFEU, it is recalled that, in its assessment of the conformity of the ESM Treaty with the no-bail-out clause, the CJEU *inter alia* stated in *Pringle* that, 'Article 125 TFEU does not prohibit the granting of financial assistance by one or more Member States to a Member State which remains responsible for its commitments to its creditors.'[145] The Court also stated that 'the activation of financial assistance by means of a stability mechanism such as the ESM is not compatible with Article 125 TFEU *unless it is indispensable for the safeguarding of the financial stability of the euro area as a whole and subject to strict conditions* [emphasis is ours].'[146] It follows from the foregoing that, in order for the issuance of Eurobonds to be legally unobjectionable from the perspective of Article 125 TFEU, it is essential that the following three conditions be met: first, each of the beneficiary Member States should remain responsible for its commitments *vis-à-vis* its creditors; second, assistance should

---

to its creditors provided that the conditions attached to such assistance are such as to prompt that Member State to implement a sound budgetary policy' (para. 137).

142 Several commentators had, already before *Pringle*, supported the legality of the type of financial assistance eventually provided by the EFSF (and, thereafter, the ESM). See, for instance, Phoebus Athanassiou, 'Of Past Measures and Future Plans for Europe's Exit from the Sovereign Debt Crisis: What is Legally Possible (and What Is Not)' (2011) 36 (4) *European Law Review* 558; Jean-Victor Louis, 'The No-Bailout Clause and Rescue Packages' (2010) 47 *Common Market Law Review* 971 (Louis (2010)); and Ulrich Häde, 'Haushaltsdisziplin und Solidarität im Zeichen der Finanzkrise' (2009) *Europäische Zeitschrift für Wirtschaftsrecht* 399.

143 This is also the essence of the thesis of Kämmerer, who links the legality of Eurobonds to their underlying liability regime, and concludes that a Treaty amendment would be a prerequisite for most types of Eurobonds, the political feasibility of which appears questionable (see Kämmerer (2016)).

144 The issuance of Eurobonds would bear no relation to the ESM's Stability Mechanism (in this regard, also see Franz C. Mayer and Christian Heidfeld, 'Verfassungs- und europarechtliche Aspekte der Einführung von Eurobonds' (2012) 65 *Neue Juristische Wochenschrift* 422, 425).

145 *Pringle*, para. 137.

146 Ibid., para. 136.

be granted subject to strict conditionality; and third, the provision of financial assistance should be indispensable to safeguard the stability of the euro area as a whole.

The Court also had something to say on the *rationale* of Article 125 TFEU:

> It is apparent from the preparatory work relating to the Treaty of Maastricht that the aim of Article 125 TFEU is to ensure that the Member States follow a sound budgetary policy (see Draft Treaty amending the Treaty establishing the European Economic Community with a view to achieving economic and monetary union, *Bulletin of the European Communities*, Supplement 2/91, pages 24 and 54). The prohibition laid down in Article 125 TFEU ensures that the Member States remain subject to the logic of the market when they enter into debt since that ought to prompt them to maintain budgetary discipline. Compliance with such discipline contributes at Union level to the attainment of a higher objective, namely maintaining the financial stability of the monetary union.[147]

Although the Court did not use the term 'moral hazard' in its ruling, it clearly follows from the foregoing paragraph that the yardstick against which to assess the legality of financial assistance to Member States is the concept of 'moral hazard,' and the policy imperative of avoiding it, so as to discourage fiscal profligacy.[148] The collective issuance of debt, and the 'mutualisation' that this may entail, could give rise to 'moral hazard' by removing the incentives that some of the less fiscally disciplined euro-area Member States have to follow stability-oriented policies. Therefore, depending on its liability features, the collective issuance of debt could, however voluntary,[149] raise legal concerns from the perspective of its conformity with Article 125 TFEU.

The second reason why collective borrowing could give rise to legal concerns is linked to the decentralised nature of economic and fiscal policy and to the budgetary autonomy of the EU Member States. Unlike monetary policy (which, in the case of the EU Member States participating in the third stage of EMU is no longer a national competence), economic and fiscal policy remain the preserve of the Member States, whose constitutional courts (among them, the *Bundesverfassungsgericht*) have opposed the ceding of control over fundamental fiscal decisions or, *a fortiori*, the wholesale transfer

147 Ibid., para. 135.

148 In this vein, also see Vestert Borger, 'How the Debt Crisis Exposes the Development of Solidarity in the Euro Area' (2013) 9 *European Constitutional Law Review* 7, 13; Louis (2010), 77–78.

149 EU primary law does not explicitly regulate the provision of voluntary financial assistance to Member States in need. On the question of the legal compatibility of such assistance with Article 125 TFEU, see Helmut Siekmann, 'The Legal Framework for the European System of Central Banks' (2015) *Leibniz Institute for Financial Research, SAFE White Paper* 26 <https://econpapers.repec.org/paper/zbwsafewh/26.htm> accessed 30 September 2020.

of the budgetary responsibility of national parliaments to external actors.[150] Therefore, it is not only EU but also national (constitutional) law concerns that would need to be overcome before the common issuance of debt backed by *joint liability* becomes possible,[151] and this is despite (or, some have argued, because of) the fact that the Treaties do not preclude, as such, the setting up of a European vehicle for the issuance of bonds.[152] Even if the Treaty were to be amended (as Article 136 TFEU previously was) in order to overcome the barrier that Article 125 TFEU poses to the issuance of Eurobonds, national (constitutional) law obstacles would remain unresolved, only compounding the challenge of issuing Eurobonds the issuance of which would entail a measure of fiscal solidarity.

The foregoing legal concerns would not apply to SBBSs (the issuance of which would not involve any measure of debt mutualisation). Much the same, it is submitted, would also be true in a scenario involving the joint issuance by the Member States of debt intended to address the temporary economic fallout of exogenous shocks, such as a natural or man-made disaster or a public health emergency, e.g. the outbreak of a pandemic. For the reasons explained above, moral hazard risks would only materialise if the joint issuance of debt were to feature some form of debt mutualisation. Since moral hazard constitutes the yardstick against which to assess the legality of the provision of financial assistance to Member States in need, it logically follows that absent any moral hazard (as in the case of a natural disaster or a public health emergency), opposition to the provision of financial assistance, *including in the form of the joint issuance of debt*, can only legitimately[153] be motivated by reference to concerns that such assistance may

150 See, in particular, the *Bundesverfassungsgericht*'s Orders of (a) 7 September 2011 (Griechenland-Soforthilfe und Euro-Rettungsschirm) 2 *BVerfGE* 987/10 (on EFSF assistance to Greece); (b) 12 September 2012 (Stabilitätsmechanismus und Fiskalpakt) 2 *BVerfGE* 1390/12 (interim proceedings on the ESM Treaty and the amendment to Article 136 TFEU); (c) 18 March 2014 (Stabilitätsmechanismus und Fiskalpakt) 2 *BVerfGE* 1390/12 (in the same matter); (d) 21 June 2016 (Gauweiler) 2 *BVerfGE* 2728/13 (on the OMT case); (e) 30 July 2019 (Europäische Bankenunion) 2 *BVerfG* 1685/14; and (f) 5 May 2020 (Beschlüsse der EZB zum Staatsanleihekaufprogramm) *2 BVerfG* 859/15 (orders available at <www.bundesverfassungsgericht.de> accessed 30 September 2020).

151 Drawing on the jurisprudence of the *Bundesverfassungsgericht*, it has been argued that ways to help overcome constitutional law constraints in Germany (and, possibly, in other Member States) would be to define, a priori, the maximum liability incurred by the creditor Member States, to regularly seek parliamentary authorisation of relevant decisions, and to frame any bond-issuance scheme with strict safeguards, to ensure fiscal discipline in all Member States (see Expert Group on Debt Redemption Fund and Eurobills, *Final Report* (2014), 67 and Annex 7 <https://ec.europa.eu/economy_finance/articles/governance/pdf/20140331_report_en.pdf> accessed 30 September 2020).

152 'In accordance with Article 4(1) and Article 5(2)(2) TEU, stipulating that all competences not conferred on the Union remain with the Member States, the issuance of State bonds and the determination of its form and condition are, in principle, determined by constitutional law. The European Union is confined to some coordinating functions pursuant to Articles 5, 120, 121 TFEU' (Kämmerer (2016), 600).

153 As a commentator has aptly observed, '[E]ven if the obstacles on the legal path towards Eurobonds were removed, there would still be a great deal of political resistance to be overcome. Resistant

be in conflict with the letter (rather than the spirit) of Article 125 TFEU. This would only be the case if assistance were to involve the assumption by some of the Member States of the financial commitments of other Member States.

It could be argued that one way to help overcome (some of) the Article 125 TFEU-related legal concerns arising from the joint issuance of debt would be by establishing the Eurobond-issuing entity as a private institution (as in the case of the EFSF). However, it is questionable whether it is legitimate to draw analogies between the EFSF, on the one hand, and a future Eurobond-issuing entity, on the other. The EFSF was a private rather than a public institution, and its debt was therefore private rather than public debt, whereas the debt to be issued by a future Eurobond-issuing entity would presumably be public debt, guaranteed by the participating Member States.[154]

The conclusion to which the authors come is that only Eurobond proper proposals that would require no form of fiscal solidarity, and which would leave each of the euro-area governments responsible for its own solvency, would be legally viable, without raising the prospect of a breach of the 'no bail-out' clause and without the need to amend the Treaties. Considering that debt mutualisation is a decisive element of any Eurobond proper proposal, and that the credibility and effectiveness of Eurobonds is, perforce, dependent on the degree of their mutualisation, the above finding is tantamount to the exclusion of Eurobonds as a viable instrument through which to close the channel of contagion moving from sovereigns to banks. Inversely, proposals for the issuance of common safe assets (akin to SBBSs) would raise no obvious legal concerns, whether from the competence or from the conformity with primary and national law perspectives.

5.3.1.3 The European Central Bank as issuer of an alternative common safe asset?

As the reader will have gathered from the foregoing, the authors consider an auspicious path for closing the second channel of contagion to consist of two legs: on the one hand, reducing the level of public debt (faster, if possible, than budgetary prudence alone can), so as to mitigate (or eliminate) the latent source of instability for the banking sector that sovereign represent, and, on the other hand, to create a substantial amount of safe assets (which credit institutions can tender as collateral for the provision of central bank liquidity), without the process of their issuance and of the distribution of their proceeds involving a legally and politically problematic fiscal transfer from one Member State to another. In the authors' opinion, the creation of good quality collateral – other than sovereign bonds – which banks can tender in return for central bank liquidity, deserves to be *a policy goal in its own right*, rather than a mere positive side-effect of certain measures (such as, for instance, the issuance

politicians obviously tend to cherish the legal obstacles as arguments to hide behind' (ibid., 587).

154 Scheinert (2011), 6.

of Eurobonds), if decisive progress is to be made towards closing the second channel of contagion.[155]

It has been argued that one way to achieve this dual objective is through the issuance, by the ECB, of debt certificates ('DCs'), to substitute Member State-issued sovereign bonds as collateral for ECB credit operations, and to transform some of the liquidity created by the APP into DCs of different maturities.[156] Given that DCs would represent a liability of the ECB (which is default-free), it is not only credit institutions that would have an interest in their acquisition, as the safest asset available, but, also, other financial market actors, facilitating the transmission of the ECB's monetary policy.

Although they have not so far been issued, DCs – defined as debt obligations of the ECB in relation to the certificate holder – feature among the instruments at the ECB's disposal for conducting open market operations.[157] Moreover, under Article 10 of the Headquarters Agreement between the Government of the Federal Republic of Germany and the ECB,[158] debt instruments created by the ECB in its 'electronic debt register' are eligible for use in the banking business, and have the same status as other comparable debt instruments issued in Germany.[159] The exact modalities of the eventual issuance of DCs were not, at the time of writing, the object of ECB regulation.[160]

The creation of DCs would inevitably result in a novel, high credit quality instrument issued by a default-free debtor becoming available for use as collateral in Eurosystem credit operations (and beyond). However, it bears noting that, as a monetary policy instrument, DCs were intended for use as liquidity absorption instruments – superior to fixed-term deposits, on account

155 Commentators have tended to treat the creation of good collateral resulting from the issuance of a common safe asset as a positive side-effect thereof, rather than as its main policy justification.

156 See Mario Tonveronachi, 'European Sovereign Bond-Backed Securities: An Assessment and an Alternative Proposal' (2018) The Levy Economics Institute of Bard College Public Policy Brief 145 <http://www.levyinstitute.org/pubs/ppb_145.pdf> accessed 30 September 2020, and references therein). Under this proposal, sovereign bonds retained by euro area credit institutions would be subject to a less favourable regulatory treatment, thereby helping to put an end to the excessive exposure of banks to national debt.

157 See Articles 5, 9 and 13 of Guideline ECB/2014/60 of the European Central Bank of 19 December 2014 on the implementation of the Eurosystem monetary policy framework [2015] OJ L91/3.

158 Headquarters Agreement of 18 September 1998 between the Government of the Federal Republic of Germany and the European Central Bank concerning the seat of the European Central Bank, available at <https://www.ecb.europa.eu/ecb/legal/pdf/en_headquarters_agreement_final.pdf> accessed 30 September 2020.

159 Under Article 10(1) of the Headquarters Agreement, the ECB may act as a German CSD (*Wertpapiersammelbank*), exempt from any form of supervision and oversight by German competent authorities, whereas under Article 10(2) thereof, the ECB may maintain an 'electronic debt register' (*electronisch geführtes Schuldbuch*) under German law.

160 It is stated in Article 13(2) of Guideline ECB/2014/60 of the European Central Bank of 19 December 2014 on the implementation of the Eurosystem monetary policy framework [2015] OJ L91/3 that, 'ECB debt certificates shall be issued and held in book-entry form in securities depositories in Member States whose currency is the euro.'

of their marketability – through which to create a liquidity shortage and steer, more efficiently, short-term interest rates. It follows that, despite their obvious advantages from a 'safe asset' perspective, their issuance would mainly make sense in a blue skies environment, so that their issuance and subscription does not deprive markets of what they need the most at times of overall instability or outright crisis, namely liquidity.

5.3.1.4 Concluding remarks

As explained earlier, notwithstanding the moral hazards that their issuance would entail, Eurobonds have significant merits in terms of crisis prevention and management for sovereigns and credit institutions alike. However, for the reasons explained earlier in this chapter, their issuance would come up against significant legal obstacles, of which the most significant is that of Article 125 TFEU. These obstacles can only safely be surmounted through an amendment to EU primary law, which, even if not impossible, would certainly prove very challenging.

SBBSs would also present certain advantages, as explained earlier in this work. Besides, the issuance of SBBSs would not come up against the legal obstacles that the issuance of Eurobonds proper would give rise to. However, the success of SBBSs would also depend on at least two factors: the scale of their issuance (which would have to be very large) and their preferential regulatory and collateral treatment vis-à-vis the bonds of individual Member States: without them, SBBSs would struggle to achieve their aims.

It is not without interest that the prospect of the issuance of joint debt was to gain traction in the midst of the COVID-19 pandemic, initially garnering support or, at least, less opposition, including by some of the EU Member States that had previously been opposed to it, on the grounds of moral hazard.[161] Even if the outcome of the Council of 26 March[162] was to quash the hopes of the advocates of the joint issuance of even a short-term, targeted Eurobond, the resurfacing of proposals for the issuance of joint European debt – even if only in order to fight an exogenous shock, very different in nature to the one that triggered the European sovereign debt crisis – confirms the resilience of the idea of creating a European safe asset that Member States can draw on, if the challenge of overcoming an economic crisis threatening their finances or their banking sector were to prove superior to the potential of existing tools. Ironically, the 5 May 2020 ruling of the *Bundesverfassungsgericht* in *Weiss* – which, at its core,

161 Germany's traditional position to Eurobonds is encapsulated in a statement famously made by German Chancellor Angela Merkel who, in June 2012, famously declared that, '[T]here will be no full debt sharing as long as I live …' <www.spiegel.de/international/europe/chancellor-merkel-vows-no-euro-bonds-as-long-as-she-lives-a-841163.html> accessed 30 September 2020.

162 See European Council, *Joint Statement* (26 March 2020) <https://www.consilium.europa.eu/media/43076/26-vc-euco-statement-en.pdf> accessed 30 September 2020.

was all about preserving the fiscal and budgetary autonomy of the Member States in the face of (indirect) forms of debt mutualisation – could reinforce the case for Eurobonds and (direct) debt mutualisation: by torpedoing the 'whatever-it-takes' expectations of financial markets, and by undermining the public perception of the ECB as a restriction-free actor capable of releasing, ad infinitum, the pressure on national governments to coordinate their fiscal policies,[163] the ruling of the *Bundesverfassungsgericht* could breathe new life into the debate surrounding fiscal union, burden sharing (including some form of debt mutualisation) and, by extension, also Eurobonds, forcing national governments out of the shadows in which Eurosystem action had, conveniently, pushed them since 2015.[164]

As the prospect of the issuance of some form of safe European asset does not appear to be off the table, we consider, below, the mechanics of its issuance, from a securities law perspective, on the understanding that, unless worked out in advance, their absence could hamper the actual issuance of joint debt even after political opposition thereto has eventually been overcome.

5.3.2 A European Central Securities Depository for the issuance of common safe assets?[165]

The issuance of a safe asset, such as a Eurobond proper or an SBBS-type sovereign-backed asset, would be greatly facilitated by the creation of a common infrastructure, in the form of a 'European Central Securities Depository' ('ECSD'), responsible for managing the process of the issuance, across the EU, of same-ISIN, fully fungible debt instruments, at the instance of the instruments' obligor.

The EU law objective that the proposed issuance of common safe assets would serve is to promote financial stability – an established policy objective for internal market harmonisation[166] – and, more specifically, the stability of banks and financial markets at large, by breaking the dependence between

163 'The interpretation of the ECB's monetary policy mandate, as undertaken by the CJEU, encroaches upon the competences of the Member States for economic and fiscal policy matters. With few exceptions (*cf.* Arts 121, 122 and 126 TFEU), the competence of the European Union in economic policy matters is essentially limited to coordinating the policies of the Member States (Art. 119(1) TFEU). The ESCB is to merely *support* the general economic policies *in* the European Union (Arts 119(2), 127(1), second sentence, TFEU; Art. 2, second sentence of the Statute); it is not, however, authorised to pursue its own economic policy agenda' (Order of 5 May 2020 (Beschlüsse der EZB zum Staatsanleihekaufprogramm) 2 *BVerfGe* 859/15, para. 163).

164 See Gerald Braunberger, 'Ein weitreichendes Urteil' (*Frankfurter Allgemeine Zeitung*, 5 May 2020).

165 Section 5.3.2 draws heavily on Phoebus Athanassiou, 'Towards a More Integrated Primary Issuance Market for Securities in the EU: Legal and Policy Issues' (2020) 27 (2) *Maastricht Journal of European and Comparative Law* 137.

166 In this regard, see, for instance, *Private Equity Insurance Group SIA v. Swedbank AS* [2016] ECLI:EU:C:2016:851, paras. 23 and 42. For an account of financial stability as an EU law objective, see Jonathan Bauerschmid, 'Financial Stability as the Objective of the Banking Union' (2020) 17 (2) *European Company and Financial Law Review* 155, 179–182.

banks and sovereigns, and by making banks more resilient and better prepared to withstand future shocks triggered by challenges to the creditworthiness of sovereign issuers of debt. By facilitating the achievement of the above EU law objective, the creation of an ECSD would form an integral part of its pursuit. That this objective could not be achieved through market initiatives is relatively clear, both on account of the lack of market-driven proposals for the harmonisation of primary issuance processes, and because, as explained later in this chapter, such harmonisation would only make sense if accompanied by the introduction of a European private securities law, as a necessary complement to the eventual establishment and operation of the proposed ECSD, an ambitious enterprise that market actors are not legally equipped to bring forward.

However legitimate an objective for EU-level action the above may be, its pursuit through the creation of an ECSD would only be possible in the presence of an appropriate legal basis. We consider, below, the potential legal bases for the creation of an ECSD and assess the possible establishment of an ECSD against the principles of proportionality and subsidiarity.

5.3.2.1 Possible legal bases

It is submitted that Article 114 TFEU, the main legal basis for internal market harmonisation and the approximation of laws, could serve as legal basis for the creation of an ECSD (in much the same way as it has provided the legal basis for the establishment of the European System of Financial Supervision and the SRM). It is recalled that the rationale for establishing an ECSD is to contribute to financial integration through an infrastructure that would not only bridge differences in national primary issuance rules and practices but also improve the functioning of the internal market by removing some of the obstacles to primary issuance market integration, helping attain the goal of a Capital Markets Union. The establishment of an ECSD would seem to squarely fall within the remit of Article 114 TFEU (which, apart from providing its legal basis, could also provide the legal basis for the adoption of the accompanying 'European private securities law,' discussed in Section 5.3.2.4).

Alternatively, it is submitted that a fall-back legal basis for the creation of an ECSD could be sought in the so-called 'flexibility clause' of Article 352 TFEU.[167] The conditions to be fulfilled before this provision can be activated were explored earlier in this chapter. Applying, *mutatis mutandis*, the reasoning of the Court in *Pringle* to the eventual creation of an ECSD, it is considered that Article 352 TFEU could legitimately be invoked as the legal

167 Article 352(1) TFEU inter alia states that, '[I]f action by the Union should *prove necessary, within the framework of the policies defined in the Treaties*, to attain one of the *objectives set out in the Treaties*, and the Treaties have *not provided the necessary powers*, the Council, acting unanimously on a proposal from the Commission and after obtaining the consent of the European Parliament, shall adopt the appropriate measures … [emphasis is ours].'

basis for its establishment, without resulting in an extension of the EU's competences beyond those provided for in the Treaties. This is notwithstanding the fact that the business of a future ECSD (i.e. the centralised provision of EU-wide primary issuance services to the issuers of transferable securities) would be unprecedented for the EU: it is not the novelty of Union action that determines its legitimacy but, rather, the extent to which such action is consistent with attaining one of the Union's objectives. The objective to which the creation of an ECSD would contribute (i.e. the establishment of an internal market in cross-border securities issuance services) is a Union objective, which could legitimately be pursued through EU action.

5.3.2.2 Proportionality considerations

It follows from Article 5(4) TEU that 'the content and form of Union action shall not exceed what is necessary to achieve the objectives of the Treaties.'[168] What lies at the heart of the principle of proportionality is the idea that EU action should match, in terms of means, the objective it pursues, without going beyond what is necessary to achieve those objectives.[169] One of the more recent, high-profile instances of the application of the principle of proportionality was in the context of the Court's scrutiny, in *Gauweiler*,[170] of the Eurosystem's OMT Program. Following its established practice, the Court split its proportionality analysis into two parts: first, it assessed the *appropriateness* of OMTs to attain their declared monetary policy objectives, and second, it examined the compliance of OMTs with the *necessity* requirement.[171] In addition, the Court confirmed that the ESCB weighed up the various interests in play to prevent disadvantages from arising, which would be manifestly disproportionate to the OMTs' objectives.[172]

The proportionality analysis to which the Union's decision to create an ECSD would be subject is bound to consist of the same two legs as in *Gauweiler*: one appropriateness and one necessity leg. In terms of *appropriateness*, the Union would need to demonstrate that the policy decision to create an ECSD is backed by an adequate statement of reasons, that it is based on a substantiated analysis of the state of the EU and euro-area primary issuance markets, and that the analysis in question is not vitiated by manifest errors of assessment. In terms of *necessity*, the Union would need to demonstrate that the decision to create an ECSD does not go beyond what is necessary to achieve the objective of establishing an internal market in cross-border securities issuance services: this could be achieved in a number of ways such as, for instance, by the Union demonstrating that, notwithstanding the importance

168 TEU, Art. 5(4).

169 See, for instance, *United Kingdom of Great Britain and Northern Ireland v. Council of the European Union* [1996] ECLI:EU:C:1996:431, para. 57.

170 *Peter Gauweiler and others v. Deutscher Bundestag* [2015] ECLI:EU:C:2015:400.

171 Ibid., paras 67, 72 and 81.

172 Ibid., para. 91.

of the public interest in the creation of a pan-European securities issuance infrastructure, adequate and effective Member State or market-led initiatives have yet to be taken to overcome fragmentation in primary issuance processes across the EU or, even if taken, would be less effective than EU-level action.[173] Finally, even if one looks into the question of the *weighing up* of interests, it is difficult to see what adverse effects (i.e. costs) the creation of an ECSD would entail, especially for third parties;[174] at the same time, the benefits of its creation seem clear, not least from the perspective of facilitating a break in the dependence of banks from their sovereigns. Considering that primary issuance activity is fragmented along national borders, that no national or market-lead initiatives are in place to overcome fragmentation, and that the issuance of certain types of transferable securities can only be undertaken, *de lege lata*, by licensed central securities depositories ('CSDs'),[175] we consider it likelier than not that any eventual EU decision to establish an ECSD would pass the proportionality test.

5.3.2.3 Subsidiarity considerations

It follows from Article 5(3) TEU that

> [U]nder the principle of subsidiarity, in areas which do not fall within its exclusive competence, the Union shall act only if and in so far as the objectives of the proposed action cannot be sufficiently achieved by the Member States, either at central level or at the regional and local level, but

173 A case in point is *The Queen v. Minister of Agriculture, Fisheries and Food and Secretary of State for Health, ex parte: Fedesa and others* [1990] ECLI:EU:C:1990:391, where the Court ruled that the reason why the outright prohibition of the use of hormones in the rearing of livestock was proportionate is because other measures (such as consumer information) would be a less effective means of achieving the overriding objective of public health protection. A similar proportionality analysis is conceivable here, on the understanding that, (a) the creation of a pan-European securities issuance infrastructure is a matter of public interest; and (b) such individual Member State or market initiatives as there have been in this area would be less effective at overcoming fragmentation in primary issuance processes across the EU or the euro area.

174 The obvious concern here is with competition. However, provided the contractual agreements to be entered into between a future ECSD, on the one hand, and securities issuers and participating (investor) central securities depositories, on the other hand, are not unduly restrictive, it is difficult to see how the establishment of an ECSD could lead to the 'foreclosure' normally associated with a breach of Article 101(1) TFEU. Indeed, the establishment of an ECSD should be expected to *promote* rather than to restrict competition, since its objective would be to facilitate the development of a genuine single market for the pan-European issuance of securities, free of the national structures to which the securities issuance and distribution processes are currently subject.

175 Regulation (EU) 909/2014 of the European Parliament and of the Council of 23 July 2014 on improving securities settlement in the European Union and on central securities depositories and amending Directives 98/26/EC and 2014/65/EU and Regulation (EU) 236/2012 [2014] OJ L257/1 stipulates that, '[W]here a transaction in transferable securities takes place on a trading venue, the relevant securities shall be recorded in book-entry form in a CSD on or before the intended settlement date' (Article 3(2) thereof).

> can rather, by reason of the scale or effects of the proposed action, be better achieved at Union level.

Applied in an EU context, the principle of subsidiarity seeks to govern the use of competences allocated to the Union (rather than, strictly speaking, their delineation) by ruling-out Union action in areas of shared competence unless the criteria of Article 5(3) TEU are met (first, the objectives of the proposed action cannot be sufficiently achieved by the Member States – 'necessity' criterion – and second, the action can more successfully be undertaken at the Union level – 'added value' criterion). Unlike in the case of the proportionality principle, which applies to all Union actions, subsidiarity only applies in areas *not* falling within the Union's exclusive competence. The internal market – that the establishment of a future ECSD would contribute to – is among the areas of shared competence (see Article 4(2) TFEU), to which the principle of subsidiarity applies.

EU institutions enjoy wide discretion in applying the principle of subsidiarity. However, pursuant to Article 8 of Protocol (No 2) to the TFEU on the application of the principles of subsidiarity and proportionality, the consistency of legislative measures with the principle of subsidiarity can be the object of *ex post* judicial review by means of an action for annulment.[176] Notwithstanding its 'constitutional' importance, the principle of subsidiarity has yet to feature conclusively in the jurisprudence of the Court.[177] In its ruling in the *Deposit Guarantee* case (an action brought by Germany against Directive 94/19/EC[178]), the Court found that a legislative measure's consistency with the principle of subsidiarity can be ascertained on the basis of its recitals and the reasons stated in them for its adoption, in line with the requirement of Article 296 TFEU for the EU to state the reasons for its legislative acts.[179] Although some of the more recent jurisprudence of the Court reveals a judicial tendency to engage with

176 Article 8 of Protocol (No 2) to the TFEU on the application of the principles of subsidiarity and proportionality states that, '[T]he Court of Justice of the European Union shall have jurisdiction in actions on grounds of infringement of the principle of subsidiarity by a legislative act, brought in accordance with the rules laid down in Article 263 of the Treaty on the Functioning of the European Union by Member States, or notified by them in accordance with their legal order on behalf of their national Parliament or a chamber thereof. In accordance with the rules laid down in the said Article, the Committee of the Regions may also bring such actions against legislative acts for the adoption of which the Treaty on the Functioning of the European Union provides that it be consulted.'

177 For a comprehensive overview of the Court's jurisprudence in this area, see Gabriël A. Moens and John Trone, 'The Principle of Subsidiarity in EU Judicial and Legislative Practice: Panacea or Placebo?' (2015) 41 (1) *Journal of Legislation* 65.

178 Directive 94/19/EC of the European Parliament and of the Council of 30 May 1994 on deposit-guarantee schemes [1994] OJ L135/5.

179 *Federal Republic of Germany v. European Parliament and Council of the European Union* [1997] ECLI:EU:C:1997:231, paras 22–29.

the principle of subsidiarity not only procedurally but also substantively,[180] the Court's overall approach remains deferential and non-activist. What probably explains the Court's deference is the fact that deciding which objectives can be better achieved at the Union level can be politically sensitive. This is particularly so in the context of measures intended to contribute to the establishment and functioning of the internal market, where the Court has been reluctant to substitute its own assessment to that of the Union legislator in complex matters of economic policy, where the EU legislator's leeway is, understandably, greater. How would the Court view, from a subsidiarity standpoint, the establishment of an ECSD? Without prejudice to the difficulty of risking predictions over the outcome of future litigation, it stands to reason that the Court should favourably approach any EU action which, as in the case of the establishment of an ECSD, would aim to remove barriers to the effective functioning of the internal market. The likelihood of a Union-friendly judicial interpretation of an eventual Union decision to create an ECSD is, therefore, greater than that of its rejection on subsidiarity grounds.

5.3.2.4 Legal regime governing a European Central Securities Depository and the instruments issued through it

Regarding the legal regime governing the proposed ECSD, it is submitted that this can legitimately deviate from the one laid down in Regulation (EU) No 909/2014[181] ('CSDR'), given the ECSD's public (Union) ownership and the public interest rationale of its establishment. It is worth recalling in this context that, in accordance with Article 1(4) of the CSDR, many of its provisions

> do not apply to the members of the European System of Central Banks, other Member States' national bodies performing similar functions, or to other public bodies charged with or intervening in the management of public debt in the Union in relation to any CSD which the aforementioned bodies directly manage ... and which is not a separate entity.

In the interest of legal certainty, Article 1(4) of the CSDR could be revisited to expressly bring within its scope of application CSDs operated by EU

180 Referring to the requirement to state reasons (the basis for the Court's subsidiarity analysis), the Court has recently stated that compliance with it 'must be evaluated not only by reference to the wording of the contested act, but also by reference to its context and the circumstances of the individual case' (*Philip Morris Brands SARL and others v. Secretary of State for Health* [2016] ECLI:EU:C:2016:325, para. 225).

181 Regulation (EU) 909/2014 of the European Parliament and of the Council of 23 July 2014 on improving securities settlement in the European Union and on central securities depositories and amending Directives 98/26/EC and 2014/65/EU and Regulation (EU) 236/2012 [2014] OJ L257/1.

institutions or dedicated EU agencies.[182] CSDR provisions that, on the above understanding, would not bind the eventual operator of the proposed ECSD would include, notably, the CSDR's rules on CSD authorisation, supervision, capital requirements, and outsourcing.[183]

Turning to the law of issuance of ECSD-issued securities, and the content of the legal entitlement evidenced by their crediting to their holders' investor accounts, it is legitimate to posit that, *de lege lata*, the former will typically be the law of the Member State of the eventual establishment of the ECSD, which would, then, also determine the latter. It is only in the presence of a body of substantive 'European private securities law,' currently not in existence, that the law of issuance and the content of the legal entitlement in ECSD-issued securities could be determined by reference thereto, instead of being a function of purely national law concepts of property law in transferable securities, in the jurisdiction of the eventual establishment of the ECSD. Does the EU possess the legal competence to establish such a body of law, and, if so, what should its minimum content be?

Although there is no across-the-board EU competence to regulate private law matters, several Treaty provisions already grant-specific competences to the Union over selected private law aspects. These include, notably, Article 50 TFEU (which empowers the EU to harmonise certain aspects of company law in order to attain freedom of establishment), Articles 114 and 115 TFEU (which empower the Union to approximate both public and private law in pursuit of the establishment of the internal market and the removal of obstacles to its functioning) and Article 118 TFEU (which, 'in the context of the establishment and functioning of the internal market' empowers the EU to create 'European intellectual property rights'). It is also recalled that the so-called 'flexibility clause' of Article 352 TFEU allows the EU to adopt, under certain circumstances, secondary legislation through which to regulate areas of public or private law not falling within the remit of a specific conferral, to the EU, of legislative powers.[184] Finally, it bears noting that the object of the Treaty's

182 As a member of the ESCB, the ECB would fall, as CSD operator, within the scope of Article 1(4) of the CSDR.

183 Applying, mutatis mutandis, Article 1(4) of the CSDR to an ECSD, the following CSDR provisions would not apply to it: (a) CSD authorisation (Arts 10–20); (b) supervision of CSDs and provision of services in other Member States (Arts 22–24); (c) organisational provisions concerning senior management, management body and shareholders (Art. 27); (d) duty to inform the relevant NCA and the user committee of the CSD management body's decision not to follow the user committee's advice (Art. 28(6)); (e) no need to seek national competent authority's authorisation before outsourcing a core service (Art. 30(4)); (f) investment policy and capital requirements (Arts 46–47); and (g) provisions of Title IV of the CSDR for the provision of banking-type ancillary services for CSD participants (Arts 54–60).

184 Article 352(1) TFEU inter alia states that, '[I]f action by the Union should *prove necessary, within the framework of the policies defined in the Treaties*, to attain one of the *objectives set out in the Treaties*, and the Treaties *have not provided the necessary powers*, the Council, acting unanimously on a proposal from the Commission and after obtaining the consent of the European Parliament, shall adopt the

anti-trust framework are also private law relationships, with the relevant Treaty provisions conferring rights and imposing obligations on undertakings.[185] In light of the above, the better view is that, however substantial the challenge of establishing a body of European private securities law (*inter alia* from the perspective of its harmonious interplay with relevant national law),[186] the EU is already possessed of the primary law competence to adopt secondary legislation in this field. What is less clear is what the *minimum content* of such secondary legislation should be, a question explored below.

In deciding on the minimum content of a European private securities law necessary to complement the eventual establishment and operation of the proposed ECSD (effectively, a '27th regime,' specifically intended for ECSD-issued securities), inspiration can usefully be drawn from the work of the Legal Certainty Group ('LCG') on securities holdings with a cross-border dimension. It is recalled that the mission of the LCG was to explore the legal position (effectively, the property rights) of account holders in respect of securities credited to their account, and their legal effects (effectively, how these, or an interest in them, can be validly acquired and disposed of), rather than to harmonise basic legal concepts of relevance to the fundamental nature and core attributes of 'securities.'[187] Thus, the (modest) ambition of the LCG was to achieve clarity in terms of the legal effects of entries made in securities accounts rather than to devise a fully-harmonised body of 'EU securities law' since to tamper with the fundamental nature of 'securities' (an integral part of the legal system of each Member State) would be to open Pandora's box in an area of great complexity and interconnectedness with other areas of the law. It is submitted that the same approach should also be followed in charting the minimum content of a European private securities law: the aim of EU legislation to be introduced in support of a future ECSD should be to harmonise only those aspects of securities law that are essential for the holders of ECSD-issued securities to be in a position to put their securities into the economic uses that these were intended

---

appropriate measures … [emphasis is ours].' It is recalled that, in accordance with the principle of 'conferral of powers' (Art. 5(2) TEU), the EU can only exercise regulatory powers where provided for in the Treaties.

185 Richard Whish and David Bailey, *Competition Law* (8th edn, Oxford University Press 2015), 227.

186 In his analysis of the EU competences in the field of private law, and his assessment of the challenges posed by the hitherto piecemeal EU-level initiatives in that field, a commentator has astutely observed that, '[T]he clash between, on the one hand, coherent national systems of private law and, on the other hand, the EU functionalist approach, leads inevitably to a fragmentation of EU legislation regarding private law. This poses a challenge to the coherence of national systems of private law, with adverse effects not only on consistency, but also transparency and legal security' (Rafał Mańko, 'EU Competence in Private Law – The Treaty Framework for a European Private Law and Challenges for Coherence' (2015) *European Parliamentary Research Service* PE 545.711 <https://ssrn.com/abstract=2553945> accessed 30 September 2020).

187 The advice of the LCG is available at <https://ec.europa.eu/info/publications/advice-legal-certainty-group-2006-2008_en> accessed 30 September 2020.

to serve.[188] It follows that legislation to be introduced in support of a future ECSD should, as a minimum, aim at the following:

(1) Declare ECSD-issued instruments to be, functionally, on a par with 'dematerialised securities' issued on any of the EU Member State CSDs, in terms of their legal effects and attributes, i.e. prescribe that they enjoy the same legal status as dematerialised securities in any and all EU Member State jurisdictions, regardless of the status and location of the ECSD as the relevant securities account-providing intermediary;
(2) Exempt the issuers of ECSD-issued instruments from compliance with specific, issuance-related national law formalities, before those securities can enter, for trading and settlement, into CSDs governed by the laws of any of the EU Member States;
(3) Render the primary acquisition and subsequent disposition of ECSD-issued securities conditional on the crediting and debiting of a securities account held with the ECSD, and dispense with the need for additional national law-mandated requirements to be complied with in order for their primary acquisition or subsequent disposition to be legally valid and effective throughout the EU;
(4) Declare the securities settlement system operated by a future ECSD to automatically benefit from protection under Directive 98/26/EC,[189] without the need for 'designation' or the fulfilment of any additional formalities but subject to compliance with the said directive; and
(5) Harmonise the taxes payable by the buyers and/or sellers of securities at the time of the purchase and/or sale of ECSD-issued securities.[190]

By ensuring that all existing EU Member State CSDs have access, under the same objective and non-discriminatory terms, to the proposed ECSD, as investor CSDs, it should be possible to facilitate cross-border secondary market trading in ECSD-issued securities even without a full network of links among all existing EU Member State CSDs.

188 In this vein, also see Philipp Paech, 'Chapter 2 – Market Needs as Paradigm – Breaking Up the Thinking on EU Securities Law' in Pierre-Henri Conac, Ulrich Segna and Luc Thévenoz (eds), *Intermediated Securities – The Impact of the Geneva Securities Convention and the Future European Legislation* (Cambridge University Press 2013), 30–36 and 60–62.

189 Directive 98/26/EC of the European Parliament and of the Council of 19 May 1998 on settlement finality in payment and securities settlement systems [1998] OJ L166/45.

190 It bears noting that Article 115 TFEU provides for the Council, 'acting unanimously in accordance with a special legislative procedure and after consulting the European Parliament and the Economic and Social Committee, to issue directives for the approximation of such laws, regulations or administrative provisions of the Member States as directly affect the establishment or functioning of the internal market.' Both recommendations and legislation have been adopted on this basis, in the areas of personal tax, company tax and capital duty.

Concluding remarks

The EU was unprepared for large-scale sovereign debt derived banking crises, and the EMU had no tools in place to deal with them. This lack of preparedness and paucity of tools was to challenge the cohesion of the euro area after several of the EMU participating Member States were hit, starting in 2010, by sovereign debt crises, some of them caused by ailing banking sectors and others triggered by the woes of banks that fell victim to downgrades in the ratings of their sovereigns. What exacerbated the effects of these crises on euro-area banks was their interconnectedness to their sovereigns: encouraged by regulatory incentives and following settled practices, euro-area banks had invested heavily in sovereign debt, mostly that of their own sovereigns, becoming vulnerable to sovereign debt crises. And yet, as suggested in this work, it will take more than a shift in regulatory incentives and hitherto practices to avert a repetition of a sovereign-driven banking crisis: by forcing banks to significantly reduce their stock of (mostly domestic) government bonds, an eventual change in the Basel III framework, however well intended, could have adverse effects, both for the sovereign issuers concerned and for the commercial banks that hold their debt. If what we have referred to in this work as the second channel of contagion is to be closed, and if the institutional and other reforms introduced in the form of the European Banking Union are to achieve their financial stability objectives, two main reforms are, in the authors' view, necessary: first, the creation of a permanent euro-area stability support mechanism, to mitigate the effects of sovereign debt crises on sovereigns (and, indeed, to avert them, through the option to recapitalise, on a precautionary basis, troubled commercial banks), and second, the issuance of some form of common, euro-area sovereign debt, which, by being more liquid, would represent a safer investment for commercial banks compared to debt issued by individual euro-area issuers.

Europe has already taken some steps in the direction of creating a permanent euro-area support mechanism, but obstacles remain ahead *inter alia* in terms of identifying an appropriate legal basis for its establishment as an EU body, aligning its mission to that of the SSM, and ensuring that its mandate includes the provision of solvency and liquidity support to credit institutions under resolution, either in the form of credit lines or in the form of guarantees, to facilitate the fulfilment, by the SRB, of its tasks. The ESM would be a good candidate to assume the role of precisely such a euro-area support mechanism, provided that (a) it is transformed into an EU body equipped with human and material resources commensurate with its mission; (b) its governance and staff rules are such as to ensure its operational efficiency and independence from external influence; and (c) its financial tools are revisited, to improve their efficiency and attractiveness. An intergovernmental structure, with no own budget, with limited independence from the Member States and with inefficient or unattractive financing instruments is unlikely to prove successful in tackling the task of combatting sovereign crises or, a fortiori, in preventing them from emerging.

Where progress is, in the authors' view, also needed is on the collective debt issuance front. As explained earlier in this work, proposals that do not require any form of fiscal solidarity, and which leave each of the euro-area governments responsible for its own solvency are legally viable without raising the prospect of a breach of the 'no bail-out' clause and without the need to amend the Treaties. In the authors' view, the merits of those proposals cannot be stressed strongly enough: by mitigating the risks to which banks are exposed by holding domestic debt, and by generating a larger volume of safe assets in the euro area, which commercial banks can pledge to their NCB in return for Eurosystem liquidity, these proposals, if acted upon, would have a significant contribution to make towards preserving financial stability and mitigating the risk of future euro area crises. The issuance of collective debt would greatly be facilitated by the creation of a common infrastructure, in the form of an ECSD, for the issuance, across the euro area and the EU, of same-ISIN, fully fungible debt instruments, in which commercial banks could more safely invest.

Are these the only available policy options or are there alternatives to them capable of breaking the second channel of contagion and contributing to the preservation of financial and systemic stability? Much has been made in the literature of the benefits of setting up a euro-area Member State sovereign debt restructuring mechanism in terms of increasing legal certainty and predictability, reducing the costs of debt workout negotiations, averting contagion risks, fostering fiscal discipline and doing away with the need for costly sovereign bail-outs.[1] Moreover, the establishment of such a mechanism would appear

1 See, *ex multi*, Sebastian Grund and Mikael Stenström, 'A Sovereign Debt Restructuring Framework for the Euro Area' (2019) 42 (3) *Fordham International Law Journal* 795; Clemens Fuest, Friedrich Heinemann and Christoph Schröder, 'A Viable Insolvency Procedure for Sovereigns (VIPS) in the Euro Area' (2014) *Leibniz-Zentrum für Europäische Wirtschaftsforschung Discussion Paper* 14-053 <https://ideas.repec.org/p/zbw/zewdip/14053.html> accessed 30 September 2020; and François Gianviti, Anne O. Krueger, Jean Pisani-Ferry, André Sapir and Jürgen von Hagen, 'A European Mechanism for Sovereign Debt Crisis Resolution: A Proposal' (*Bruegel Blueprint Series*, 2010) <https://www.bruegel.org/2010/11/a-european-mechanism-for-sovereign-debt-crisis-resolution-a-proposal/#:~:text=Blueprint-,A%20European%20mechanism%20for%20sovereign%20debt%20crisis%20resolution%3A%20a%20proposal,%2C%20Francois%20Gianviti%2C%20Anne%20O.> accessed 30 September 2020.

to be legally possible, whether by relying on the flexibility clause of Article 352 TFEU or by building upon the example of the intergovernmental ESM Treaty. Whatever its merits, and even if its establishment were to raise no legal concerns, the most serious shortcoming of a euro-area Member State sovereign debt restructuring mechanism is that its operation would be detrimental to commercial banks as sovereign debt holders. Most of the euro-area sovereign debt was, at the time of writing, held either by euro-area commercial banks or by euro-area central banks. Considering that the latter cannot actively participate in debt restructuring processes if they are not to breach the monetary financing prohibition of Article 123 TFEU,[2] it is commercial banks that would bear the brunt of a sovereign debt restructuring process, with the balance sheet losses they would sustain risking to be very substantial.[3] Far from helping address the sovereign–banks doom loop, a euro-area Member State sovereign debt restructuring mechanism would likely have the effect of shifting to commercial banks the burden of sovereign debt restructurings, with unpredictable consequences for financial and systemic stability. Besides, the introduction of two-limb CACs in all euro-area debt with a maturity exceeding one year issued as of 1 January 2013, and of single-limb CACs in all euro-area debt with a maturity exceeding one year issued after 1 January 2022 already cater for the orderly restructuring of sovereign debt, if and when necessary, obviating the need for any other, dedicated restructuring mechanism.[4] Significantly, there is one more, this time *political*, objection to the establishment of a euro-area sovereign debt restructuring mechanism: the euro area has invested a great deal of capital, over the last several years, to avoid any restructuring of the debts of sovereigns within the euro area. It is difficult to imagine a sudden change of course, where the euro area would espouse a policy option that it has so persistently avoided to pursue.

As the outbreak of the COVID-19 pandemic and the resulting economic slowdown have demonstrated, Europe's recovery from the ravages of the euro-area sovereign debt crisis of 2010–2015 remains fragile, and this is despite the fact that euro-area banks in 2020 were in a better position to withstand shocks than they had been in 2010 (as reflected in their significantly higher levels of capital and liquidity), as a result of which there is every hope that they can be part of the solution to the problems that the pandemic has visited on the Member State economies. The COVID-19 pandemic once again saw sovereign bond yield spreads increase between the Member States of the periphery and those of the core, not only questioning the ability of some of the less robust euro-area Member States to come to the aid of their banks, should that prove necessary amidst the crisis triggered by the outbreak of COVID-19 but, more

2 This is despite the fact that, under the PSPP, the NCBs have accepted (passively) the same (*pari passu*) treatment as private investors in respect of securities they have purchased under that programme.

3 Ubide (2015), 264.

4 This point is aptly made in Aerts and Bizarro (2020), 174.

importantly, raising concerns with regard to a possible spillover to Europe's banking sector of sovereign fragility, accentuated by the higher deficits that many euro-area Member States will have to run in response to the crisis.

The collective issuance of euro-area debt, in conjunction with the establishment of an independent EMF, are, in the authors' view, the most reliable avenues through which to effectively address the sovereign–banks doom loop from the side of the sovereigns, complementing the SSM and the SRM and the contribution that the latter have had in closing the first channel of contagion. What is necessary for progress to be made in the direction of pursuing these two avenues is for the euro-area Member States to muster the requisite political will. The authors are aware that the obstacles to reform are legion. At the same time, they can only hope that the resolve to act on proposals such as those made in this work can, eventually, be mustered. In this respect, they draw some comfort from the decisions taken by the Council, on 21 July 2020, which paved the way for the creation of the European Recovery Fund, the first-ever attempt by the EU to jointly raise debt on the capital markets.[5] What is in any event clear is that a continuation of the *status quo* does not appear to be a viable option: for, what is at stake is nothing short of the success of the European Banking Union, the ability of commercial banks in the euro area and the EU to withstand a future sovereign debt crisis, whether or not attributable to endogenous factors, and, ultimately, the prosperity of Europe and its people.

5 The authors also draw comfort from the German Constitutional Court's rejection, close to the time of publication of this work, of a legal challenge to the adoption of national legislation ratifying the European Recovery fund. The continuing opposition to the joint issuance, within the EU, of short-term, targeted debt, to help alleviate the pandemic's immediate economic consequences, would not have augured well for the future. Legally speaking, such opposition would be difficult to motivate by reference to any compelling moral hazard argument: if it was possible, on earlier occasions, to invoke the culpability of individual Member States for the weak state of their public finances, and as a principled argument against the joint issuance of debt – which could disincentivise them from pursuing a stability-oriented policy – no such argument could plausibly be made where public debt pressure and higher financing needs are attributable to an uncontrollable exogenous factor, such as a pandemic.

Bibliography

Law

Books

Almhofer M., *Die Haftung der Europäischen Zentralbank für rechtswidrige Bankenaufsicht* (Mohr Siebeck 2018).

Athanassiou P., *Κρίση Δημοσίου Χρέους και Τραπεζικό Σύστημα στη Ζώνη του Ευρώ* [*The Sovereign Debt Crisis and the Euro Area Banking System*] (Nomiki Bibliothiki 2018).

Bassani G., *The Legal Framework Applicable to the Single Supervisory Mechanism* (Wolters Kluwer 2019).

Fabbrini F., *Economic Governance in Europe: Comparative Paradoxes and Constitutional Challenges* (Oxford University Press 2016).

Fairgrieve D., *State Liability in Tort: A Comparative Law Study* (Oxford University Press 2003).

Gortsos C.V., *The Single Supervisory Mechanism (SSM), Legal Aspects of the First Pillar of the European Banking Union* (Nomiki Bibliothiki 2015).

Grundmann S. and Micklitz H.-W. (eds), *The European Banking Union and Constitution* (Hart Publishing 2019).

Jefferson T., *The Works of Thomas Jefferson*, Vol. 11: Correspondence and Papers 1808–1816 (G.P. Putnam's Sons 1905).

Lackhoff K., *Single Supervisory Mechanism, A Practitioner's Guide* (Beck – Hart – Nomos 2017).

Lo Schiavo G. (ed.), *European Banking Union and the Role of Law* (Elgar Financial Law 2019).

Reinhart C.M. and Rogoff K.S., *This Time is Different: Eight Centuries of Financial Folly* (Princeton University Press 2009).

Smits R., *The European Central Bank* (Kluwer Law International 1997).

Whish R. and Bailey D., *Competition Law* (8th edn, Oxford University Press 2015).

Contributions to Edited Books

Acharya V.V. and Steffen S., 'Analyzing Systemic Risk of the European Banking Sector' in Fouque J.-P. and Langsam J. (eds.), *Handbook on Systemic Risk* (Cambridge University Press 2013).

Athanassiou P., 'The Institutional Architecture and Tasks of the ECB' in Fabbrini F. and Ventoruzzo M. (eds.), *Research Handbook on EU Economic Law* (Edward Elgar 2019).

Binder J.-H., 'Cross-Border Coordination of Bank Resolution in the EU: All Problems Resolved?' in Haentjens M. and Wessels B. (eds.), *Research Handbook in Cross-Border Bank Resolution* (Edward Elgar 2019).

Gleeson, S. 'The Single Resolution Mechanism and the EU Crisis Management Tools' in Lo Schiavo G. (ed.), *The European Banking Union and the Role of Law* (Elgar Financial Law 2019).

Marafioti G., 'The Trasta Komercbanka Cases: Withdrawals of Banking Licenses and Locus Standi' in Zilioli C. and Wojcik K.-P. (eds.), *Judicial Review in the European Banking Union* (Edward Elgar 2021).

Paech P., 'Chapter 2: Market Needs as Paradigm: Breaking Up the Thinking on EU Securities Law' in Conac P.-H., Segna U. and Thévenoz L. (eds.), *Intermediated Securities: The Impact of the Geneva Securities Convention and the Future European Legislation* (Cambridge University Press 2013).

Scouteris B. and Athanassiou P., 'National Central Bank Tasks and the Boundaries of the ECB Governing Council's Powers under Article 14.4 of the Statute: State of Play and Future Prospects' in Tzouganatos D., Kotsovilis V., Kontovazainitis T. and Voglis E. (eds.), *Commemorative Volume in Memory of Professor Dr. Leonidas Georgakopoulos* (Bank of Greece, Centre for Culture, Research and Documentation, August 2016).

Sérgio A. and Rebelo De Sousa A., 'The Impact of the Financial Crisis on Portuguese Banks: The Problem of Portuguese Sovereign Debt' in Sérgio A. (ed.), *Banking in Portugal* (Palgrave Macmillan 2016).

Singh D., 'Should Member States Join the Banking Union?' in Grundmann S. and Micklitz H.-W. (eds.), *European Banking Union and Constitution* (Hart Publishing 2019).

Smolenska A., 'Single Resolution Board: Lost and Found in the Thicket of EU Bank Regulation' in Grundmann S. and Micklitz H.-W. (eds.), *European Banking Union and Constitution* (Hart Publishing 2019).

Tridimas T.P., 'The Constitutional Dimension of Banking Union' in Grundmann S. and Micklitz H.-W. (eds.), *European Banking Union and Constitution* (Hart Publishing 2019).

Tuominen T., 'Mechanisms of Financial Stabilisation' in Fabbrini F. and Ventoruzzo M. (eds.), *Research Handbook on EU Economic Law* (Edward Elgar 2020).

Ubide Á., 'The Outlook for Sovereign Debt in the Euro Area' in Méndez de Andés F. (ed.), *Anuario del Euro 2015* (Fundación de Estudios Financieros 2015).

Wymeersch E.O., 'The Single Supervisory Mechanism for Banking Supervision: Institutional Aspects' in Busch D. and Ferrarini G. (eds.), *European Banking Union* (2nd edn, Oxford University Press 2019).

Xanthoulis N. and Tridimas T.P., 'A Legal Analysis of the Gauweiler Case' in Fabbrini F. (ed.), *The European Court of Justice, the European Central Bank and the Supremacy of EU Law* Special Issue (2016) 23 Maastricht Journal of European and Comparative Law (Intersentia).

Zavvos G.S. and Kaltsouni S., 'The Single Resolution Mechanism in the European Banking Union' in Haentjens M. and Wessels B. (eds), *Research Handbook on Crisis Management in the Banking Sector* (Edward Elgar 2015).

Conference Papers

Af Jochnick K., 'Banking Performance, Competition and Financial Stability: A Supervisory View' (Speech at the 7th Frankfurt Conference on Financial Market Policy entitled

'European Banking – Too Much Competition?,' organised by the Research Centre SAFE, Frankfurt am Main, 15 November 2019).

Draghi M., 'The Interdependence of Research and Policymaking' (Speech given at the Lindau Nobel Laureate Meeting, Lindau, 23 August 2017).

Hakkarainen P., 'The Future of European and Global Banking' (Panel intervention to Panel 1 at the 25th Dubrovnik Economic Conference, Dubrovnik, 15 June 2019).

Stournaras Y., 'The Impact of the Greek Sovereign Crisis on the Banking Sector: Challenges to Financial Stability and Policy Responses by the Bank of Greece' (Keynote speech given at the London Business School Greek Alumni Association and Stanford Club of Greece Event entitled 'Breaking the Bottlenecks – Steps Towards Sustainable Growth,' American School of Classical Studies, Athens, 8 June 2016).

Whelan K., 'Ireland's Economic Crisis: The Good, the Bad and the Ugly' (Paper presented at the Bank of Greece Conference on the Euro Crisis, Athens, 24 May 2013).

Journal Articles

Acharaya V.V. and Steffen S., 'The "Greatest" Carry Trade Ever? Understanding Eurozone Bank Risks' (2015) 115 *Journal of Financial Economics* 215.

Adamski D., 'Economic Constitution of the Euro Area after the Gauweiler Preliminary Ruling' (2015) 52 (6) *Common Market Law Review* 1451.

Aerts J. and Bizarro P., 'The Reform of the European Stability Mechanism' (2020) 15 (2) *Capital Markets Law Journal* 159.

Alter A. and Schüler Y.S., 'Credit Spread Interdependencies of European States and Banks during the Financial Crisis' (2012) 36 *Journal of Banking and Finance* 3444.

Andenas M. and Fairgrieve D., 'Misfeasance in Public Office, Governmental Liability and European Influences' (2002) 51 *International and Comparative Law Quarterly* 757.

Angeloni C., Merler S. and Wolff G.B., 'Policy Lessons from the Eurozone Crisis' (2012) 47 (4) *The International Spectator: The Italian Journal of International Affairs* 17.

Athanassiou P., 'Non-Contractual Liability under the Single Supervisory Mechanism: Key Features and Grey Areas' (2015) 30 (7) *Journal of International Banking Law and Regulation* 382.

Athanassiou P., 'Of Past Measures and Future Plans for Europe's Exit from the Sovereign Debt Crisis: What is Legally Possible (and What Is Not)' (2011) 36 (4) *European Law Review* 558.

Athanassiou P., 'On the Legal and Economic Treatment of Bank Deposits as Investments: Some Reflections' (2014) 29 (12) *Journal of International Banking Law and Regulation* 717.

Athanassiou P., 'Towards a More Integrated Primary Issuance Market for Securities in the EU: Legal and Policy Issues' (2020) 27 (2) *Maastricht Journal of European and Comparative Law* 137.

Avgouleas E. and Goodhart C., 'Critical Reflections on Bank-Bail-Ins' (2015) 1 (1) *Journal of Financial Regulation* 3.

Battistini N., Pagano M. and Simonelli S., 'Systemic Risk, Sovereign Yields and Bank Exposures in the Euro Crisis' (2014) 29 (78) *Economic Policy* 203.

Bauerschmid J., 'Financial Stability as the Objective of the Banking Union' (2020) 17 (2) *European Company and Financial Law Review* 155.

Belke A., 'Reinforcing EU Governance in Times of Crisis: The Commission Proposals and Beyond' (2011) 44 (1) *Credit and Capital Markets* 1.

Bofinger P. and Ried S., 'A New Framework for Fiscal Policy Consolidation in Europe' (2010) 45 (4) *Intereconomics: Review of European Economic Policy* 203.

Boonstra W., 'How EMU Can Be Strengthened by Central Funding of Public Deficits' (2010) 14 *ELEC Cahier Comte Boël* 3.

Borger V., 'How the Debt Crisis Exposes the Development of Solidarity in the Euro Area' (2013) 9 *European Constitutional Law Review* 7.

Brunnermeier M. et al., 'The Sovereign-Bank Diabolic Loop and ESBies' (2016) 106 (5) *American Economic Review*, American Economic Association 508.

Brunnermeier M., Langfield S., Pagano M., Reis R., Van Nieuwerburgh S. and Vayanos D., 'ESBies: Safety in the Tranches' (2017) 32 (90) *Economic Policy* 175.

Chamon M., 'EU Agencies: Does the Meroni Doctrine Make Sense?' (2010) 17 (3) *Maastricht Journal of European and Comparative Law* 281.

Craig P.P. and Markakis M., 'Gauweiler and the Legality of Outright Monetary Transactions' (2016) 41 *European Law Review* 4.

De Grauwe P. and Moesen W., 'Gains for All: A Proposal for a Common Euro Bond' (2009) 44 (3) *Intereconomics: Review of European Economic Policy* 132.

De Gregorio Merino A., 'Legal Developments in the Economic and Monetary Union during the Debt Crisis: The Mechanisms of Financial Assistance' (2012) 49 (5) *Common Market Law Review* 1613.

Dermine P. and Eliantonio M., 'Case Note: CJEU (Grand Chamber), Judgment of 19 December 2018, C-219/17, Silvio Berlusconi and Finanziaria D'investimento Fininvest SpA (Fininvest) v. Banca D'Italia and Istituto per La Vigilanza Sulle Assicurazioni (IVASS)' (2019) 12 (2) *Review of European Administrative Law* 237.

Echevarria V. and Valero Lopez F.J., 'Regulation on Banks' Sovereign Bond Holdings: Assessing the Impact of Potential Changes' (2016) 5 (2) *Spanish Economic and Financial Outlook* 75.

Fabbrini F., 'After the OMT Case: The Supremacy of EU Law as the Guarantee of the Equality of the Member States' (2015) 16 (4) German Law Journal 1003.

Fabbrini F., 'Il Pareggio di Bilanzio nelle Constituzioni Europee' (2011) 4 *Quaderni Constituzionali* 933.

Gaballo G. and Zetlin-Jones A., 'Bailouts, Moral Hazard and Banks Home Bias for Sovereign Debt' (2016) 81 (C) *Journal of Monetary Economics* 70.

Galliani C. and Zedda S., 'Will the Bail-In Break the Vicious Circle between Banks and Their Sovereign?' (2015) 45 (4) *Computational Economics* 597.

Gortsos C.V., 'Competence Sharing between the ECB and the National Competent Supervisory Authorities within the Single Supervisory Mechanism (SSM)' (2015) 16 (3) *European Business Organization Law Review* 401.

Grund S., 'The Quest for a European Safe Asset: A comparative Legal Analysis of Sovereign Bond-Backed Securities, E-bonds, Purple Bonds, and Coronabonds' (2020) 6 *Journal of Financial Regulation* 223.

Grund S. and Stenström M., 'A Sovereign Debt Restructuring Framework for the Euro Area' (2019) 42 (3) *Fordham International Law Journal* 795.

Häde U., 'Haushaltsdisziplin und Solidarität im Zeichen der Finanzkrise' (2009) *Europäische Zeitschrift für Wirtschaftsrecht* 399.

Häde U., 'Legal Evaluation of a European Monetary Fund' (2010) 2 (45) *Intereconomics: Review of European Economic Policy* 273.

Hardouvelis G.A., 'Overcoming the Crisis in Cyprus' (2014) 9 (1) *Eurobank Research* 225.

Hinarejos A., 'A Possible European Monetary Fund and the Future of the Euro Area' (2019) 38 (1) *Yearbook of European Law* 119.

Kämmerer J.A., 'How can Eurobonds be Legally Implemented into European Law?' (2016) 12 (3) *Review of Law and Economics* 585.

Kösters W., 'Common Euro Bonds: No Appropriate Instrument' (2009) 44 (3) *Intereconomics: Review of European Economic Policy* 64.

Lane P.R.R., 'The Real Effects of European Monetary Union' (2006) 20 (4) *Journal of Economic Perspectives* 47.

Louis J.-V., 'The No-Bailout Clause and Rescue Packages' (2010) 47 (4) *Common Market Law Review* 971.

Maarand M., 'The Impact of the Judgment in Case C-219/17, Berlusconi and Fininvest, on Court Jurisdiction regarding Legality of Acts by Institutions of Single Resolution Mechanism' (2019) 5 (2) *International Comparative Jurisprudence* 149.

Makowski K.D., 'Sollange III: The German Federal Constitutional Court's Decision on Accession to the Maastricht Treaty on European Union' (1995) 16 *University of Pennsylvania Journal of International Business Law* 155.

Maricut-Akbik A., 'Contesting the European Central Bank in Banking Supervision: Accountability in Practice at the European Parliament' (2020) *Journal of Common Market Studies* 1199.

Mayer F.C. and Heidfeld C., 'Verfassungs- und Europarechtliche Aspekte der Einführung von Eurobonds' (2012) 65 *Neue Juristische Wochenschrift* 422.

Meessen K.M., 'Hedging European Integration: The Maastricht Judgment of the Federal Constitutional Court of Germany' (1993) 17 (13) *Fordham International Law Journal* 511.

Merler S. and Pisani-Ferry J., 'Hazardous Tango: Sovereign-Bank Interdependence and Financial Stability in the Euro Area' (2012) 16 *Banque de France Financial Stability Review* 201.

Moens A.G. and Trone J., 'The Principle of Subsidiarity in EU Judicial and Legislative Practice: Panacea or Placebo?' (2015) 41 (1) *Journal of Legislation* 64.

Mooij A.A.M., 'The Weiss Judgment: The Court's Further Clarification of the ECB's Legal Framework: Case C-493/17 Weiss and Others' (2019) 26 (3) *Maastricht Journal of European and Comparative Law* 449.

Pizzolla A., 'The Role of the European Central Bank in the Single Supervisory Mechanism: A New Paradigm for EU Governance' (2018) 43 (1) *European Law Review* 3.

Singh M.K., Gómez-Puig M. and Sosvilla-Rivero S., 'Sovereign-Bank Linkages: Quantifying Directional Intensity of Risk Transfers in EMU Countries' (2016) 63 *Journal of International Money and Finance* 137.

Uhlig H., 'Sovereign Default Risk and Banks in a Monetary Union' (2014) 15 (1) *German Economic Review* Special Issue: Special Issue on Government Debt in Democracies: Causes, Effects and Limits 23.

Van der Sluis M., 'Similar, Therefore Different: Judicial Review of Another Unconventional Monetary Policy in Weiss (C-493/17)' (2019) 46 (3) *Legal Issues of Economic Integration* 263.

Wissink L., 'Challenges to an Efficient European Centralised Banking Supervision (SSM): Single Rulebook, Joint Supervisory Teams and Split Supervisory Tasks' (2017) 18 (3) *European Business Organization Law Review* 431.

Institutional Reports, Working Papers and other Publications

Abascal M., Alonso T. and Mayordomo S., *Fragmentation in European Financial Markets: Measures, Determinants and Policy Solutions* (2013) Banco Bilbao Vizcaya Argentaria Working Paper 13/22.

Bank for International Settlements, Basel Committee on Banking Supervision, *Regulatory Consistency Assessment Programme (RCAP): Analysis of Risk-Weighted Assets for Credit Risk in the Banking Book* (July 2013).

Bank for International Settlements, Basel Committee on Banking Supervision, *The Regulatory Treatment of Sovereign Exposures* (Discussion Paper, December 2017).

Bank for International Settlements, Basel Committee on Banking Supervision, *Voluntary Disclosure of Sovereign Exposures* (Consultative Document, November 2019).

Bank for International Settlements, Committee on the Global Financial System, *The Impact of Sovereign Credit Risk on Bank Funding Conditions* (2011) Committee on the Global Financial System Paper 43.

Bank of Canada, European Central Bank, Bank of Japan, Sveriges Riksbank, Swiss National Bank, Bank of England, Board of Governors Federal Reserve System, Bank for International Settlements, *Central Bank Digital Currencies: Foundational Principles and Core Features* (2020).

Bank of England, *Financial Stability Report, June 2010* (2010).

Bank of Greece, *The Chronicle of the Great Crisis: Bank of Greece 2008-2013 – Public Interventions and Institutional Actions to Safeguard Financial Stability and Overcome the Crisis* (2014).

Berger H., De'Ariccia G. and Obstfeld M., *Revisiting the Economic Case for Fiscal Union in the Euro Area* (2018) International Monetary Fund Research Department Departmental Paper 18/03.

Bogaerts D. and Schoenmaker D., *A Call for Uniform Sovereign Exposure Limits* (Bruegel, 28 March 2017).

Brunnermeier M. et al., *European Safe Bonds (ESBies)* (2012).

Brunnermeier M., Pagano M., Reis R., Van Nieuwerburgh S. and Vayanos D., *A Safe Asset for Europe* (Financial Times Alphaville, 28 April 2017).

Bundesministerium der Finanzen, Schäuble W., *Non-Paper for Paving the Way towards a Stability Union* (2017).

Bundesregierung, *A French-German Initiative for the European Recovery from the Coronavirus Crisis* (Press Release 173/20, 18 May 2020).

Central Bank of Cyprus, *Annual Report* (2013).

Claessens S., Mody A. and Vallée S., *Paths to Eurobonds* (2012) International Monetary Fund Working Paper WP/12/172.

Claeys G. and Collin A.M., *Does the Eurogroup's Reform of the ESM Toolkit Represent Real Progress?* (Bruegel, 13 December 2018).

Clemens F., Heinemann F. and Schröder C., *A Viable Insolvency Procedure for Sovereigns (VIPS) in the Euro Area* (2014) Leibniz-Zentrum für Europäische Wirtschaftsforschung Discussion Paper 14-053.

Commission of Investigation into the Banking Sector in Ireland, *Misjudging Risk: Causes of the Systemic Banking Crisis in Ireland* (2011).

Committee of Central Bank of Governors, *Monetary Financing of Budget Deficits in Stage* Three (1991).

Corsetti G. et al., *A New Start for the Eurozone: Dealing with Debt* (VoxEU, 15 April 2015).

Council of the European Union, Economic and Financial Affairs, *Outcome of the Council Meeting* 10324/16 (17 June 2016).

Council of the European Union, Economic and Financial Affairs, *Outcome of the Council Meeting* 15068/15 (8 December 2015).

Council of the European Union, Economic and Financial Affairs, *Outcome of the Council Meeting* 16603/14 (28 January 2015).

De Grauwe P., *Governance of a Fragile Eurozone* (2011a) Centre for European Policy Studies Working Document 346.

De Grauwe P., *The European Central Bank as a Lender of Last Resort* (VoxEU, 18 August 2011b).

De Marco F. and Macchiavelli M., *The Political Origin of Home Bias: The Case of Europe, Finance and Economic* (2016) Board of Governors of the Federal Reserve System, Finance and Economic Discussion 2016-060.

Delpla J. and Von Weizsäcker J., *The Blue Bond Proposal* (Bruegel, 5 May 2010).

Demary M. and Matthes J., *An Evaluation of Sovereign-Backed Securities (SBSs) – Potentials, Risks and Political Relevance* (2017) Institut der deutschen Wirtschaft Köln Policy Paper 12/2017.

Eschenbach F. and Schuknecht L., *The Fiscal Costs of Financial Instability Revisited* (2002) European Central Bank Working Paper 191.

Euro Area Summit, *Statement* (29 June 2012).

Euro Summit, *Statement* (14 December 2018).

Euro Summit, *Statement* (15 December 2017).

Euro Summit, *Statement* (21 June 2019).

European Banking Authority, *Potential Impediments to the Cross-Border Provision of Banking and Payment Services* (2019).

European Central Bank, *Annual Report* (2014).

European Central Bank, *Convergence Report* (2012).

European Central Bank, *ECB Announces €750 Billion Pandemic Emergency Purchase Programme (PEPP)* (Press Release, 18 March 2020).

European Central Bank, *Monetary Policy Decisions* (Press Release, 12 September 2019).

European Central Bank, *Monetary Policy Decisions* (Press Release, 4 June 2020).

European Central Bank, *Opinion of the European Central Bank of 2 July 2012 on the Recapitalisation of the Cyprus Popular Bank* (2012) CON/2012/50.

European Central Bank, *Opinion of the European Central Bank of 8 October 2008 at the request of the Belgian Ministry of Finance on a Preliminary Draft Law on Measures Promoting Financial Stability and in particular Establishing a State Guarantee for the Provision of Credit in the context of Financial Stability* (2008a) CON/2008/46.

European Central Bank, *Opinion of the European Central Bank of 10 September 2008 at the request of the Banque centrale du Luxembourg on Amendments to the Draft Law Improving the Legislative Framework for Luxembourg as a Financial Centre and Amending the Law of 23 December 1998 on Monetary Status and on the Banque centrale du Luxembourg* (2008b) CON/2008/42.

European Central Bank, *Report on Financial Structures* (2017).

European Commission, *Communication to the European Parliament, the Council, the European Central Bank, the European Economic and Social Committee and the Committee of the Regions on completing the Banking Union* (COM 2017) 592.

European Commission, *Economic Adjustment Programme for Cyprus* (2013) European Economy Occasional Paper 149.

European Commission, *Green Paper on the Feasibility of Introducing Stability Bonds* (COM 2011) 818.

European Commission, *Proposal for a Council Regulation on the Establishment of the European Monetary Fund* (COM 2017) 827.

European Commission, *Proposal for a Regulation of the European Parliament and of the Council on Sovereign Bond-Backed Securities* (COM 2018) 339.

European Commission, *Reflection Paper on the Deepening of the Economic and Monetary Union* (COM 2017) 291.

European Commission, The President, Juncker J.-C., in Close Cooperation with Tusk D., Dijsselbloem J., Draghi M. and Schulz M., *Completing Europe's Economic and Monetary Union* (2015).

European Council, *Conclusions* (n.d.) EUCO 205/12 (14 December 2012).

European Council, *Joint Statement* (26 March 2020).

European Council, Special Meeting of the European Council, *Conclusions* (17–21 July 2020) EUCO 10/20.

European Council, The President, Van Rompuy H., *Towards a Genuine Economic and Monetary Union* (n.d.) EUCO 120/12.

European Parliament, *Legislative Resolution on the "Proposal for a Regulation of the European Parliament and of the Council on Sovereign Bond-Backed Securities" COM(2018)339'* (16 April 2019).

European Parliament and Committee on Economic and Monetary Affairs, *Report on the Council Recommendation on the Appointment of the President of the European Central Bank* N9-0023/2019 – C9 0048/209 - 2019/0810(NLE) (9 September 2019).

European Parliament and Directorate General for Internal Policies, *Eurobonds: The Financial Equivalent of the Single Currency* IP/A/ECON/NT/2011-01 (March 2011).

European Stability Mechanism, *Explainer on ESM Reform and Revisions to the ESM Treaty* (Press Release, 24 June 2019).

European Systemic Risk Board, *ESRB Report on the Regulatory Treatment of Sovereign Exposures* (2015).

European Systemic Risk Board, High-Level Task Force on Safe Assets, *Survey on Sovereign Bond-Backed Securities* (2018).

Expert Group on Debt Redemption Fund and Eurobills, *Final Report* (2014).

Financial Stability Board, *Key Attributes of Effective Resolution Regimes for Financial Institutions* (2011).

Fleming S., Brunsden J., Arnold M. and Chazan G., *German Eurozone Banking Plan Wins Cautious Backing* (Financial Times, 6 November 2019).

Gardella A., Rimarchi M. and Stroppa D., *Potential Regulatory Obstacles to Cross-Border Mergers and Acquisitions in the EU Banking Sector* (2020) European Banking Authority Staff Paper 7.

Gerald Braunberger, *Ein weitreichendes Urteil* (Frankfurter Allgemeine Zeitung, 5 May 2020).

Gianviti F., Krueger A.O., Pisani-Ferry J., Sapir A. and Von Hagen J., *A European Mechanism for Sovereign Debt Crisis Resolution: A Proposal* (Bruegel Blueprint Series, 2010).

Goldmann M. et al., *The Case for Corona Bonds: A Proposal by a Group of European Lawyers* (Verfassungsblog, 5 April 2020).

Gopinath G., *The Great Lockdown: Worst Economic Downturn Since the Great Depression* (International Monetary Fund Blog, 14 April 2020).

Gros D. and Mayer T., *How to Deal with Sovereign Default in Europe: Towards a Euro(pean) Monetary Fund* (2010) Centre for European Policy Studies Policy Brief 202.

Hofmann H.C.H., *Multi-Jurisdictional Composite Procedures: The Backbone to the EU's Single Regulatory Space* (n.d.) University of Luxembourg Law Working Paper 003-2019 (4 June 2019).

Independent Commission on the Future of the Cypriot Banking Sector, *Interim Report* (June 2013a).

Independent Commission on the Future of the Cyprus Banking Sector, *Final Report and Recommendations* (October 2013b).

Juncker, J.-C. *Completing Europe's Economic and Monetary Union* (22 June 2015).

Juncker J.-C. and Tremonti G., *E-Bonds Would End the Crisis* (Financial Times, 5 December 2010).

Kirschemann K., Korte J. and Steffen S., *The Zero Risk Fallacy? Banks' Sovereign Exposure and Sovereign Risk Spillovers* (2017) Leibniz-Zentrum für Europäische Wirtschaftsforschung Discussion Paper 17-069.

Korte J. and Steffen S., *A 'Sovereign Subsidy' – Zero Risk Weights and Sovereign Risk Spillovers* (VoxEU, 7 September 2014).

Lackhoff K., *The SSM Framework as a Source of ECB Administrative Procedural Law* (European System of Central Banks Legal Conference, 2016).

Laeven L. and Valencia F., *Systemic Banking Crises: A New Database* (2008) International Monetary Fund Working Paper WP/08/224.

Lefterov A., *The Single Rulebook: Legal Issues and Relevance in the SSM Context* (2015) European Central Bank Legal Working Paper 15.

Lenarčič A., Mevis D. and Siklós D., *Tackling Sovereign Risks in European Banks* (2016) European Stability Mechanism Discussion Paper 1.

Mańko R., *EU Competence in Private Law: The Treaty Framework for a European Private Law and Challenges for Coherence* (2015) European Parliamentary Research Service PE 545.711.

Matthias Goldmann, *Das BVerfG holt sich ein trojanisches Pferd ins Haus* (Legal Tribune Online, 6 May 2020).

Mody A. and Sandri D., *The Eurozone Crisis: How Banks and Sovereigns Came to Be Joined at the Hip* (2011) International Monetary Fund Working Paper WP/11/269.

Nelson R.M., Belkin P. and Mix D.E., *Greece's Debt Crisis: Overview, Policy Responses, and Implications* (2011) Congressional Research Service R41167.

Nouy D., *Statement of 22 February 2018* (Press Release, 22 February 2018).

Olaf Scholz, *Germany will Consider EU-wide Bank Deposit Reinsurance* (Financial Times, 5 November 2019).

Organisation for Economic Co-operation and Development, *Sovereign Borrowing Outlook for OECD Countries 2020* (Special COVID-19 Edition).

Parliamentary Committee on Institutions and Commissioner for Administration, *The Operation of the Cypriot Financial Sector Institutions, Joint Report* (May 2014).

Patrick Jenkins, *Scholz's Secret Motive: Why Germany Needs Full Banking Union* (Financial Times, 11 November 2019).

Philippon T. and Hellwig C., *Eurobills, not Eurobonds* (VoxEU, 2 December 2011).

Sandbu M., *How a Pan-EU Insolvency Regime Could Advance Banking Union* (Financial Times, 19 November 2019).

Sapir A. and Schoenmaker D., The Time is Right for a European Monetary Fund (Bruegel, 30 October 2017).

Sarmiento D., *Resolution Litigation, Standing of Credit Institutions and the Iccrea Banca Judgment of the Court of Justice* (Banking and Finance, Institutional Law, Justice and EU Litigation, 5 December 2019).

Scheinert C., *Eurobonds: One Word, Many Concepts, Boundless Expectations: Some Facts* (2011) European People's Party Group Watching Brief 16.

Siekmann H., *The Legal Framework for the European System of Central Banks* (Leibniz Institute for Financial Research, 2015), SAFE White Paper 26.

Siekmann H. and Wieland V., *The Ruling of the Federal Constitutional Court Concerning the Public Sector Purchase Program: A Practical Way Forward* (2020) Institute for Monetary and Financial Stability Working Paper 140.

Strachan D. and Martin S., *Banking Union and Sovereign Exposures: Europe's Risk Averse Risk Sharing* (Deloitte, 23 March 2016).

Tonveronachi M., *European Sovereign Bond-Backed Securities: An Assessment and an Alternative Proposal* (2018) The Levy Economics Institute of Bard College Public Policy Brief 145.

Triparty Committee, *Report of the Investigation Committee on the State of the Cypriot Banking System and the Cypriot Economy* (2013).

Vallée S., Cohen-Setton J., De Grauwe P. and Dullien S., *The Proposed Reform of the European Stability Mechanism Must Be Postponed* (LSE Blog, 11 December 2019).

Van Riet A., *Government Funding Privileges in European Financial Law* (2016) CentER Discussion Paper 2016-045.

Véron N., *A Better European Union Architecture to Fight Money Laundering* (Bruegel, 25 October 2018).

Véron N., *Taking Stock of the Single Resolution Board* (Document requested by the European Parliament's Committee on Economic and Monetary Affairs, March 2019).

Waysand C., Ross K. and De Guzman J., *European Financial Linkages: A New Look at Imbalances* (2010) International Monetary Fund Working Paper WP/10/295.

Economics

Books

Brunnermeier M., James H. and Landau J.-P., *The Euro and the Battle of Ideas* (Princeton University Press 2016).

Dang T.V., Gorton G. and Holmström B., *The Information Sensitivity of a Security* (unpublished manuscript 2015).

Honohan, P., Donovan, D., Gorecki, P., and Mottiar, R., 'The Irish Banking Crisis: regulatory and financial stability policy 2003-2008' (Central Bank of Ireland 2010).

Keynes J.M., *A Treatise on Money* (Macmillan 1930).

Mueller R.C., *The Venetian Money Market Banks, Panics and the Public Debt, 1200–1500* (Johns Hopkins University Press 1997).

Reinhart C.M. and Rogoff K.S., *This Time is Different: Eight Centuries of Financial Folly* (Princeton University Press 2009).

Regling, K. and Watson, M., 'A preliminary report on the sources of Ireland's banking crisis' (Dublin: Government Publications Office 2010)

Schumpeter J.A., *Business Cycles* (McGraw-Hill 1939).

Sinn H.W., *The Euro Trap. On Bursting Bubbles, Budgets, Beliefs* (Oxford University Press 2014).

Contributions to Edited Books

Alogoskoufis S., Giuzio M., Kostka T., Levels A., Molestina L. and Wedow M., 'How Could a Common Safe Asset Contribute to Financial Stability and Financial Integration in the Banking Union?' in *Financial Integration and Structure in the Euro Area* (European Central Bank 2020).

Baudino P., Murphy, D., and Svoronos, J., 'The banking crisis in Ireland' (Financial Stability Institute 2020).

Goodhart C., Romanidis, N., Tsomocos, D., and Shubik, M., 'Macromodelling, default and money' in Mayes, D., Siklos, P. and Sturm J. (eds), *The Oxford Handbook of the Economics of Central Banking* (Oxford Handbooks 2019).

Krugman P., 'Revenge of the Optimum Currency Area' in Acemoglu D., Parker J. and Woodford M. (eds), *NBER Macroeconomic Annual* (University of Chicago Press 2012).

Leandro A. and Zettelmeyer J., 'A Safe Asset for the Euro Area? Evaluating Alternative Proposals' in Andritzky J. and Rocholl J. (eds), *Ideas from the 'Future Europe' Forum* (Centre for European Policy Studies, European School of Management and Technology, German Council of Economic Experts 2018).

Matthes D. and Rocholl J., 'Breaking the Doom Loop' (2018) in Andritzky J. and Rocholl J. (eds), *Ideas from the 'Future Europe' Forum* (Centre for European Policy Studies, European School of Management and Technology, German Council of Economic Experts 2018).

Otero-Iglesias M., 'Explaining the Resilience of the Euro: What the Political Economy Says' in Hishow O. (eds), *The Euro Paradox: Explaining the Resilience of the Single Currency* (German Institute for International and Security Affairs 2018).

Pagano M., 'The Sovereign-Bank Nexus and the Case for European Safe Bonds' in *European Economy, Banks, Regulation and the Real Sector* (Associazione Centro Studi Luca d'Agliano 4 July 2016).

Schoenmaker D., 'How Should the Euro Area Build a Stable Deposit Insurance System?' in Andritzky J. and Rocholl J. (eds), *Ideas from the 'Future Europe' Forum* (Centre for European Policy Studies, European School of Management and Technology, German Council of Economic Experts 2018).

Veron N., 'Bank Crisis Management and Resolution: What Is Missing?' in Andritzky J. and Rocholl J. (eds), *Ideas from the 'Future Europe' Forum* (Centre for European Policy Studies, European School of Management and Technology, German Council of Economic Experts 2018).

Conference Papers

Barroso J.M., 'State of the Union 2012 Address' (Speech at the Plenary Session of the European Parliament, Strasbourg, 12 September 2012).

Bean C., 'The Great Moderation, the Great Panic and the Great Contraction' (Speech at the Annual Congress of the European Economic Association, Barcelona, 25 August 2009).

Cœuré B., 'Why the Euro Needs a Banking Union' (Speech at the conference 'Bank Funding: Markets, Instruments and Implications for Corporate Lending and the Real Economy, Frankfurt am Main', 8 October 2012).

Cœuré B., 'Sovereign debt in the euro area: too safe or too risky?' (2016) Keynote address at Harvard University's Minda de Gunzburg Center for European Studies in Cambridge MA, 3 November 2016.

Constâncio V., 'European Financial Architecture and the European Safe Asset' (Speech at the Conference on 'European Financial Infrastructure in the Face of New Challenges,' Florence, 25 April 2019).

Garicano L., 'Two Proposals to Resurrect the Banking Union: The Safe Portfolio Approach and SRB+' (Paper prepared for European Central Bank Conference on 'Fiscal Policy and EMU Governance,' Frankfurt, 19 December 2019).

Haldane A.G., 'Constraining Discretion in Bank Regulation' (Paper given at the Federal Reserve Bank of Atlanta Conference on 'Maintaining Financial Stability: Holding a Tiger by the Tail(s),' Federal Reserve Bank of Atlanta, Atlanta, 9 April 2013).

Issing, O., 'One Size Fits All! A Single Monetary Policy for the Euro Area' (Speech at the International Research Forum, Frankfurt am Main, 20 May 2005).

Praet P., 'The ECB and Its Role as Lender of Last Resort During the Crisis' (Speech at the Committee on Capital Markets Regulation Conference on the Lender of Last Resort: An International Perspective, Washington, DC, 10 February 2016).

Schnabel I., 'The Shadow of Fiscal Dominance: Misconceptions, Perceptions and Perspectives' (Speech at the Centre for European Reform and the Eurofi Financial Forum on 'Is the Current ECB Monetary Policy Doing More Harm than Good and What Are the Alternatives?,Berlin 11 September 2020).

Journal Articles

Acemoglu D., Ozdaglar A. and Tahbaz-Salehi A., 'Systemic Risk and Stability in Financial Networks' (2015) 105 *American Economic Review* 564.

Acharya V.V. and Mora N., 'A Crisis of Banks as Liquidity Providers' (2015) 70 *Journal of Finance*, 1.

Acharya V.V. and Steffen S., 'The "Greatest" Carry Trade Ever? Understanding Eurozone Bank Risks' (2015) 15 *Journal of Financial Economics* 215.

Acharya V.V., Drechsler I. and Schnabl P., 'A Pyrrhic Victory? Bank Bailouts and Sovereign Credit Risk' (2014) 69 *Journal of Finance* 2689.

Alesina A., Azzalini G., Favero C., Giavazzi F. and Miano A., 'Is it the "How" or the "When" that Matters in Fiscal Adjustments?' (2018) 66 *International Monetary Fund Economic Review* 144.

Allen F. and Gale D., 'Financial Contagion' (2000) 108 *Journal of Political Economy* 1.

Almeida H., Cunha I., Ferreira M.A. and Restrero F., 'The Real Effects of Credit Ratings: The Sovereign Ceiling Channel' (2017) 72 *Journal of Finance* 249.

Andritzky J., Gadatsch N., Körner T., Schäfer A. and Schnabel I., 'Removing Privileges for Banks' Sovereign Exposures: A Proposal' (2016) 2016.1 *European Economy* 139.

Anginer D., Demirgut-Kunt A. and Zhu M., 'How Does Deposit Insurance Affect Bank Risk? Evidence from the Recent Crisis' (2014) 48 Journal of Banking and Finance 312.

Armingeon K., Guthmann K. and Weisstanner D., 'How the Euro Divides the Union: The Effect of Economic Adjustment on Support for Democracy in Europe' (2016) 14 *Socio-Economic Review* 1.

Augustin P., Boustanifar H., Breckenfelder J. and Schnitzler J., 'Sovereign to Corporate Spillovers' (2018) 50 *Journal of Money, Credit and Banking* 857.

Ayres J., Navarro G., Nicolini J.P. and Teles P., 'Sovereign Default: The Role of Expectations' (2018) 175 *Journal of Economic Theory* 803.

Benzoni L., Collin-Dufresne P., Goldstein R.S. and Helwege J., 'Modeling Credit Contagion via the Updating of Fragile Beliefs' (2015) 28 *Review of Financial Studies* 1960.

Blanchard O.J. and Leigh D., 'Effects of Fiscal Policy in Deep Recessions: Simple and Hopefully Credible Empirical Evidence' (2013) 103 *American Economic Review* 117.

Blanchard O.J., 'On the future of macroeconomic models' (2018) 34 *Oxford Review of Economic Policy* 117.

Bodellini M., 'Greek and Italian "Lessons" on Bank Restructuring: Is Precautionary Recapitalisation the Way Forward' (2017) 19 *Cambridge Yearbook of European Legal Studies* 144.

Bonner C., 'Preferential Regulatory Treatment and Banks' Demand for Government Debt' (2016) 48 *Journal of Money, Credit and Banking* 1195.

Brancati E. and Macchiavelli M., 'The Information Sensitivity of Debt in Good and Bad Times' (2019) 133 *Journal of Financial Economics* 99.

Broner F., Didier T., Erce A. and Schmukler S., 'Gross Capital Flows: Dynamics and Crises' (2013) 60 *Journal of Monetary Economics* 113.

Broner F., Martin A. and Ventura J., 'Sovereign Risk and Secondary Markets' (2010) 100 *American Economic Review* 1523.

Broto C. and Molina L., 'Sovereign Ratings and Their Asymmetric Response to Fundamentals' (2016) 130 *Journal of Economic Behavior and Organization* 206.

Brunetti C., Harris J.H., Mankad S. and Michailidis G., 'Interconnectedness in the Interbank Market' (2019) 133 *Journal of Financial Economics* 52.

Brunnermeier M., Langfield S., Pagano M., Reis R., Van Nieuwerburgh S. and Vayanos D., 'ESBies: Safety in the Tranches' (2017) 32 (90) *Economic Policy* 175.

Caballero R. and Farhi E., 'The Safety Trap' (2017) 85 *Review of Economic Studies* 223.

Caballero R., Farhi E. and Gourinchas P.-O., 'Safe Asset Scarcity and Aggregate Demand' (2016) 106 *American Economic Review: Papers and Proceedings* 513.

Caccioli F., Catanach T.A. and Farmer J.D., 'Heterogeneity, Correlations and Financial Contagion' (2012) 15 *Advances in Complex Systems.*

Calvo G.A., 'Servicing the Public Debt: The Role of Expectations' (1988) 78 (4) *American Economic Review* 647.

Chari V.V. and Kehoe P.J., 'Bailouts, Time Inconsistency and Optimal Regulation: A Macroeconomic View' (2016) 106 *American Economic Review* 2458.

Cooper R. and Nikolov K., 'Government Debt and Banking Fragility: The Spreading of Strategic Uncertainty' (2018) 59 International Economic Review 1905.

Cronin D. and Dunne P.G., 'How Effective Are Sovereign Bond-Backed Securities as a Spillover Prevention Device' (2019) 96 *Journal of International Money and Finance* 49.

De Grauwe P. and Ji Y., 'Self-Fulfilling Crises in the Eurozone: An Empirical Test' (2013) 34 *Journal of International Money and Finance* 15.

De Santis, R., 'Redenomination risk' (2018) 51 *Journal of Money, Credit and Banking* 2173.

Demary M. and Matthes J., 'Can a Reliable Framework for Sovereign-Backed Securities Be Established?' (2017) 5 *Intereconomics* 308.

Dermine J., 'Banks' Home Bias in Government Bond Holdings: Will Banks in Low-Rated Countries Invest in European Safe Bonds (ESBies)?' (2020) *European Financial Management* 841.

Diamond D.W. and Dybvig P.H., 'Bank Runs, Deposit Insurance and Liquidity' (1983) 91 *Journal of Political Economy* 401.

Ericsson J. and Renault O., 'Liquidity and Credit Risk' (2006) 61 *Journal of Finance* 2219.

Farhi, E., and Tirole, J., 'Collective moral hazard, maturity mismatch, and systemic bailouts' (2012) 102 *American Economic Review* 60.

Farhi E. and Tirole J., 'Deadly Embrace: Sovereign and Financial Balance Sheets Doom Loops' (2018) 85 *Review of Economic Studies* 1781.

Fischer L., 'Determinants of the Risk Premiums on Corporate Bonds' (1959) 67 *Journal of Political Economy* 217.

Fratianni M. and Spinelli F., 'Italian City-States and Financial Evolution' (2006) 10 *European Review of Economic History* 257.

Fratzscher M. and Rieth M., 'Monetary Policy, Bank Bailouts and the Sovereign-Bank Risk Nexus in the Euro Area' (2019) 23 (4) *Review of Finance* 745.

Gabor D. and Ban C., 'Banking on Bonds: The New Links Between States and Markets' (2015) 54 *Journal of Common Market Studies* 617.

Gennaioli N., Martin A. and Rossi S., 'Sovereign Default, Domestic Banks and Financial Institutions' (2014) 69 *Journal of Finance* 819.

Greenwald B.C. and Stiglitz J.E., 'Financial Market Imperfections and Business Cycles' (1993) 108 *Quarterly Journal of Economics* 77.

Groll D. and Monacelli T., 'The Inherent Benefit of Monetary Unions' (2020) 111 *Journal of Monetary Economics* 63.

Habermas J., 'The Crisis of the European Union in the Light of the Constitutionalization of International Law' (2012) 23 *European Journal of International Law* 335.

Haltenhof S., Lee S.J. and Stebunovs V., 'The Credit Crunch and Fall in Employment during the Great Recession' (2014) 43 *Journal of Economic Dynamics and Control* 31.

He Z. and Xiong W., 'Rollover Risk and Credit Risk' (2012) 67 *Journal of Finance* 391.

Hubrich K. and Tetlow R., 'Financial Stress and Economic Dynamics: The Transmission of Crises' (2015) 70 *Journal of Monetary Economics* 100.

Issing O., 'On the Relation of Monetary and Political Union' (2016) 1 *Intereconomics* 16.

Jordà O., Schularick M. and Taylor A.M., 'Leveraged Bubbles' (2015) 76 *Journal of Monetary Economics* 1.

Krishnamurthy A. and Vissing-Jorgensen A., 'The Aggregate Demand for Treasury Bills' (2012) 120 *Journal of Political Economy* 233.

Louzis D.P., Vouldis A.T. and Metaxas V.L., 'Macroeconomic and Bank-Specific Determinants of Non-Performing Loans in Greece: A Comparative Study of Mortgages, Business and Consumer Loan Portfolios' (2011) 36 *Journal of Banking and Finance* 1012.

Lutz B., Molloy R. and Shan H., 'The Housing Crisis and State and Local Government Tax Revenue: Five Channels' (2011) 41 *Regional Science and Urban Economics* 306.

Markowitz H., 'Portfolio Selection' (1952) 7 *Journal of Finance* 77.

McLeay M., Radia A. and Thomas R., 'Money Creation in the Modern Economy' (2014) 54 *Bank of England Quarterly Bulletin* 14.

Michaelides, A., 'Cyprus: from boom to bail-in' (2014) 29 *Economic Policy* 639.

Minetti R., 'Bank Capital, Firm Liquidity and Project Quality' (2007) 54 *Journal of Monetary Economics* 2584.

Mishkin F.S., 'Over the Cliff: From the Subprime to the Global Financial Crisis' (2011) 25 *Journal of Economic Perspectives* 49.

Modigliani F. and Miller M.H., 'The Cost of Capital, Corporation Finance and the Theory of Investment' (1958) 48 American Economic Review 261.

Monfort A. and Renne J., 'Decomposing Euro-Area Sovereign Spreads: Credit and Liquidity Risks' (2014) 18 *Review of Finance* 2103.

Mundell R., 'A Theory of Optimum Currency Areas' (1961) 51 *American Economic Review* 657.

North D.C. and Weingast B.R., 'Constitutions and Commitment: The Evolution of Institutions Governing Public Choice in Seventeenth-Century England' (1989) 49 *Journal of Economic History* 803.

Pagano M. and Von Thadden E.-L., 'The European Bond Markets under EMU' (2004) 20 *Oxford Review of Economic Policy* 531.

Pancotto L., ap Gwilym O. and Williams J., 'The European Bank Recovery and Resolution Directive: A Market Assessment' (2019) 44 *Journal of Financial Stability*, https://doi.org/10.1016/j.jfs.2019.100689.

Prati A. and Sbracia M., 'Uncertainty and Currency Crises: Evidence from Survey Data' (2010) 57 *Journal of Monetary Economics* 668.

Rochet J., 'Solvency Regulations and the Management of Banking Risks' (1999) 43 *European Economic Review* 981.

Ryan, J., and Loughlin, J., 'Lessons from historical monetary unions – is the European monetary union making the same mistakes?' (2018) 15 *International Economics and Economic Policy* 709.

Sarmento J., 'The Determinants of Value Added Tax Revenues in the European Union' (2016) 21 *European Journal of Management Studies* 79.

Shin H.S., 'Securitisation and Financial Stability' (2009) 119 *Economic Journal* 309.

Stein J.C., 'An Adverse-Selection Model of Bank Asset and Liability Management with Implications for the Transmission of Monetary Policy' (1998) 29 *RAND Journal of Economics* 466.

O'Sullivan, K., and Tom Kennedy, T., 'What caused the Irish banking crisis?' (2010) 18 *Journal of Financial Regulation and Compliance* 224.

Summers P.M., 'What Caused the Great Moderation? Some Cross-Country Evidence' (2005) 90 *Federal Reserve of Kansas Economic Review* 5.

Sussman N. and Yafeh Y., 'Institutional Reforms, Financial Development and Sovereign Debt: Britain 1690–1790' (2006) 66 (5) *Journal of Economic History* 906.

Taleb N., 'Errors, Robustness, and the Fourth Quadrant' (2009) 25 *International Journal of Forecasting* 744.

Thygesen N., 'Why Did Europe Decide to Move to a Single Currency 25 Years Ago?' (2016) 1 *Intereconomics* 11.

Vouldis A.T. and Louzis D.P., 'Leading Indicators of Non-Performing Loans in Greece: The Information Content of Macro-, Micro- and Bank-Specific Variables' (2018) 54 *Empirical Economics* 1187.

Wendorff K. and Mahle A., 'Staatsanleihen neu ausgestalten: Für eine stabilitätsorientierte Währungsunion' (2015) 95 *Wirtschaftsdienst* 604.

Wyplosz C., 'Fiscal Policy: Institutions versus Rules' (2005) 191 *National Institute Economic Review* 64.

Yiangou, J., O'keefe, M., and Glöckler, G., '"Tough love": How the ECB's monetary financing prohibition pushes deeper euro area integration' (2013) 35 *Journal of European Integration* 223.

Institutional Reports, Working Papers and other Publications

Admati A. and Hellwig M., *Bank Leverage, Welfare and Regulation* (2018) Rock Center for Corporate Governance at Stanford University Working Paper 235.

Adrian T. and Shin H.S., *Liquidity and Leverage* (2009) Federal Reserve Bank of New York Staff Report 328.

Ali Abbas S.M., Blattner L., De Broeck M., El-Ganainy A. and Hu M., *Sovereign Debt Composition in Advanced Economies: A Historical Perspective* (2014) International Monetary Fund Working Paper WP/14/162.

Alogoskoufis S. and Langfield S., *Regulating the Doom Loop* (2018) European Systemic Risk Board Working Paper 74.

Andreeva D. and Vlassopoulos T., *Home Bias in Bank Sovereign Bond Purchases and the Bank-Sovereign Nexus* (2016) European Central Bank Working Paper 1977.

Baldwin R. et al., *Rebooting the Eurozone: Step 1: Agreeing a Crisis Narrative* (VoxEU, 20 November 2015).

Bank for International Settlements, Basel Committee on Banking Supervision, *Regulatory Consistency Assessment Programme (RCAP): Assessment of Basel III Regulations: European Union* (Implementation Report, December 2014).

Bank of England, *Financial Stability Report* (December 2011).

Barrios S. and Fargnoli R., *Discretionary Measures and Tax Revenues in the Run-Up to the Financial Crisis* (2010) European Commission Economic Paper 419.

Bellia M. et al., *The Sovereign-Bank Nexus in the Euro Area: Financial and Real Channels* (2019) European Economy Discussion Paper 122.

Bénassy-Quéré A. et al., *Reconciling Risk Sharing with Market Discipline: A Constructive Approach to Euro Area Reform* (VoxEU, 17 January 2018).

Bindseil U., Corsi M., Sahel B. and Visser A., *The Eurosystem Collateral Framework Explained* (2017) European Central Bank Occasional Paper 187.

Bini-Smaghi L. and Marcussen M., *Strengthening the Euro Area Architecture: A Proposal for Purple Bonds* (2018) SUERF Policy Note 35.

Brunnermeier M. et al., *European Safe Bonds (ESBies)* (2012).

Buiter W. and Sibert A., *How the Eurosystem's Treatment of Collateral in Its Open Market Operations Weakens Fiscal Discipline in the Eurozone (and What to Do about It)* (2005) Centre for Economic Policy Research Discussion Paper 5387.

Carmassi J., Dobkowitz S., Evrard J., Parisi L., Silva A. and Wedow M., *Completing the Banking Union with a European Deposit Insurance Scheme: Who is Afraid of Cross-Subsidisation?* (2018) European Central Bank Occasional Paper 208.

Chari V.V., Dovis A. and Kehoe P., *On the Optimality of Financial Repression* (2018) Federal Reserve Bank of Minneapolis – Research Department – Staff Report 1000.

Claessens S. and Kose M.A., *Frontiers of Macrofinancial Linkages* (2018) Bank for International Settlements Paper 95.

Clayes G. and Raposo G., *Is the ECB Collateral Framework Compromising the Safe-Asset Status of Euro-Area Sovereign Bonds?* (Bruegel, 8 June 2018).

Committee for the Study of Economic and Monetary Union, *Report on Economic and Monetary Union in the European Community* (1989).

D'Agostino A. and Ehrmann M., *The Pricing of G7 Sovereign Bond Spreads: The Times They are A-Changin* (2013) European Central Bank Working Paper 1520.

De Grauwe P., *Governance of a Fragile Eurozone* (2011) Centre for European Policy Studies Working Document 346.

De Grauwe P. and Ji Y., *Financial Engineering Will Not Stabilise an Unstable Euro Area* (VoxEU, 19 March 2018).

De Grauwe P. and Moesen W., 'Gains for All: A Proposal for a Common Euro Bond' (2009) 44 (3) *Intereconomics: Review of European Economic Policy* 132.

De Groen W.P. and Gros D., '*Estimating the Bridge Financing Needs of the Single Resolution Fund: How Expensive Is It to Resolve a Bank?*' (2015) Centre for European Policy Studies Special Report 122

De Jong J. and Gilbert N., *Fiscal Discipline in the EMU? Testing the Effectiveness of the Excessive Deficit Procedure* (2018) De Nederlandsche Bank Working Paper 607.

De Marco F. and Macchiavelli M., *The Political Origin of Home Bias: The Case of Europe* (2016) Board of Governors of the Federal Reserve System Finance and Economics Discussion Paper 2016–060.

Dell'Ariccia G., Martinez Peria M.S., Igan D.O., Addo Awadzi E., Dobler M.C. and Sandri D., *Trade-Offs in Bank Resolution* (2018) International Monetary Fund Discussion Note 18/02.

Delpla J. and Von Weizsäcker J., *The Blue Bond Proposal* (Bruegel, 5 May 2010).

Disyatat P., *The Bank Lending Channel Revisited* (2010) Bank for International Settlements Working Paper 297.

Domingues Semeano J. and Ferdinandusse M., *The Fiscal Impact of Financial Sector Support Measures: Where Do We Stand a Decade on From the Financial Crisis?* (2018) European Central Bank Economic Bulletin 6.

Eberl J. and Weber C., *ECB Collateral Criteria: A Narrative Database 2001–2013* (2014) IFO Institute, Leibniz Institute for Economic Research at the University of Munich Working Paper 174.

Erce A. and Mallucci E., *Selective Sovereign Defaults* (2018) Board of Governors of the Federal Reserve System, International Finance Discussion Paper 1239.

European Banking Authority, *Guidelines on Methods for Calculating Contributions to Deposit Guarantee Schemes* (2015).

European Central Bank, *Collateral Eligibility Requirements: A Comparative Study across Specific Frameworks* (2013).

European Central Bank, Banking Supervision, *Risk Assessment for 2020* (2019).

European Commission, 'One Market, One Money: An Evaluation of the Potential Benefits and Costs of Forming an Economic and Monetary Union' (1990) 44 *European Economy* 9.

European Commission, The President, Juncker J.-C., in Close Cooperation with Tusk D., Dijsselbloem J., Draghi M. and Schulz M., *Completing Europe's Economic and Monetary Union* (2015).

European Systemic Risk Board, *Annual Report 2018* (2019).

European Systemic Risk Board, *Report on the Regulatory Treatment of Sovereign Exposures* (2015).

European Systemic Risk Board, High Level Task Force on Safe Assets, *Sovereign Bond-Backed Securities: A Feasibility Study* (2018).

Eyraud L., Gaspar V. and Poghosyan T., *Fiscal Politics in the Euro Area* (2018) International Monetary Fund Working Paper 17/18.

Financial Stability Board, *Key Attributes of Effective Resolution Regimes for Financial Institutions* (2014).

Financial Stability Board, *Principles for Reducing Reliance on CRA Ratings* (2010).

Fitch Wire, *Proposed Reforms Could Boost ESM's Intrinsic Risk Profile* (Fitch Ratings, 5 July 2018).

Frey R. and Weth M., '*Banks' Holdings of Risky Sovereign Bonds in the Absence of the Nexus – Yield Seeking with Central Bank Funding or De-Risking?*' (2019) Deutsche Bundesbank Discussion Paper 19/2019.

German Council of Economic Experts, *Annual Report 2017–18* (2017).

German Council of Economic Experts, *Annual Report 2018–19* (2018).

Gourinchas P.-O. and Jeanne O., *Global Safe Assets* (2012) Bank for International Settlements Working Paper 399.

Gourinchas P.-O., Philippon T. and Vayanos D., *The Analytics of the Greek Crisis* (2016) National Bureau of Economic Research Working Paper 22370.

Gros D., *A Simple Model of Multiple Equilibria and Default* (2012) Centre for European Policy Studies Working Document 366.

Gros D. and Roth F., *Do Germans Support the Euro?* (Centre for European Policy Studies, 15 December 2011).

Heipertz M., *The Stability and Growth Pact: Not the Best but Better than Nothing. Reviewing the Debate on Fiscal Policy in Europe's Monetary Union* (2003) Max Planck Institute for the Study of Societies Working Paper 03/10.

House C.L., Proebsting C. and Tesar L.L., *Austerity in the Aftermath of the Great Recession* (2019) Research Seminar in International Economics, University of Michigan, Working Paper 672.

Jan Mallien, *Die Bundesbank sollte bei Corona-Bonds nicht rumeiern* (Handelsblatt, 2 April 2020).

Ji K., *A Review on ESBies: The Senior Tranche of Sovereign Bond-Backed Securities* (CPB Netherlands Bureau for Economic Policy Analysis Background Document, June 2018).

Jokivuolle E. and Pennacchi G., *Designing a Multinational Deposit Insurance System: Implications for the European Deposit Insurance Scheme* (2019) 17 (1) ifo Institute, Leibniz Institute for Economic Research at the University of Munich 21.

Juncker J.C. and Tremonti G., *E-Bonds Would End the Crisis* (Financial Times, 5 December 2010).

Kenny G. and Morgan J., *Some Lessons from the Financial Crisis for the Economic* (2011) European Central Bank Occasional Paper 130.

Kopf C., *Restoring Financial Stability in the Eurozone* (2011) Centre for European Policy Studies Policy Brief 237.

Kraemer M., 'How S&P Global Ratings Would Assess European "Safe" Bonds (ESBies)' in *Standard & Poor's Ratings Direct* (25 April 2017).

Lane P.R., *Capital Flows in the Euro Area* (2013) European Economy Economic Paper 497.

Larch M. and Santacrose S., *Numerical Compliance with the EU Fiscal Rules: The Compliance Database of the Secretariat of the European Fiscal Board* (2020).

Leandro A. and Zettelmeyer J., *The Search for a Euro Area Safe Asset* (2019) Peterson Institute for International Economics Working Paper 18-3.

Lenarčič A., Mevis D. and Siklós D., *Tackling Sovereign Risks in European Banks* (2016) European Stability Mechanism Discussion Paper 9.

Macchiarelli C. and Monti M., 'The ECB Collateral Policy beyond Conventional Policy Stimulus' in *In-depth analysis requested by the European Parliament's Committee on Economic and Monetary Affairs, Monetary Dialogue* (July 2018).

Matthes D. and Rocholl J., *Breaking the Doom Loop* (2017) European School of Management and Technology White Paper 17-01.

Mongelli F., *European Economic and Monetary Integration and the Optimum Currency Area Theory* (2008) European Commission Economic Paper 302.

Muellbauer J., 'Resolving the Eurozone Crisis: Time for Conditional Eurobonds' (2011) *Centre for Economic Policy Research Policy Insight* 59.

Nyborg K., *Central Bank Collateral Frameworks* (2015) Swiss Finance Institute Research Paper 15-10.

Otero-Iglesias M., Steinberg F. and Tokarski P. (eds), *The Euro Paradox: Explaining the Resilience of the Single Currency* (2018) German Institute for International and Security Affairs Working Paper 1.

Paret A.-C. and Weber A., *German Bond Yields and Debt Supply: Is There a 'Bund Premium'?* (2019) International Monetary Fund Working Paper WP/19/235.

Pasche M., *ESBies as a Basis for a TARGET2 Settlement Mechanism* (2017) Munich Personal RePEc Archive Paper 83012.

Perez D., *Sovereign Debt, Domestic Banks and the Provision of Public Liquidity* (2015) Stanford Institute for Economic Policy Research Discussion Paper 15-016.

Philippon T. and Hellwig C., *Eurobills, not Eurobonds* (VoxEU, 2 December 2011).

Philippon T. and Salord A., *Bail-Ins and Bank Resolution in Europe: A Progress Report* (VoxEU, 22 March 2017).

Poghosyan T., *Long-Run and Short-Run Determinants of Sovereign Bond Yields in Advanced Economies* (2012) International Monetary Fund Working Paper WP/12/271.

Regling K., *The Time for European Solidarity is Now* (Kathimerini, 2 April 2020).

Reinhart C. and Rogoff K., *The Forgotten History of Domestic Debt* (2008) National Bureau of Economic Research Working Paper 13946.

Roberds W. and Velde F., *Early Public Banks* (2014) Federal Reserve Bank of Chicago Working Paper 2014-03.

Sachverständigenrat zur Begutachtung der gesamtwirtschaftlichen Entwicklung, *Verantwortung für Europa wahrnehmen* (2011) Statistisches Bundesamt, Wiesbaden Jahresgutachten 2011/12.

Sandbu M., *The Landing Zone for Europe's Banking Union* (Financial Times, 16 January 2020).

Schnabel, I., and Véron, N., 'Breaking the stalemate on European Deposit Insurance' (Bruegel blog, 5 March 2018).

Schneider Y.M. and Steffen S., *Feasibility Study: Transition to a New Regime for Bank Sovereign Exposure?* (Study provided at the request of the European Parliament's Committee on Economic and Monetary Affairs, November 2017).

Singh M., *Velocity of Pledged Collateral* (2011) International Monetary Fund Working Paper WP/11/256

Single Resolution Board, *SRF Grows to €33 Billion after Latest Round of Transfers* (Press Release, 17 July 2019).

Snyder F., *EMU Revisited: Are We Making a Constitution? What Constitution Are We Making?* (1998) European University Institute Working Paper 98/6.

Stolz S.M. and Wedow M., *Extraordinary Measures in Extraordinary Times: Public Measures in Support of the Financial Sector in the EU and the United States* (2010) European Central Bank Occasional Paper 117.

Tordoir S., Carmassi J., Hauptmeier S. and Jahning M., *The State of Play Regarding the Deepening Agenda for Economic and Monetary Union* (2020) European Central Bank Economic Bulletin 2.

Van Riet A., *Addressing the Safety Trilemma: A Safe Sovereign Asset for the Eurozone* (2017) European Systemic Risk Board Working Paper 35.

Veron N., *Precautionary Recapitalisations: Time for a Review* (In-depth analysis provided in advance of the European Parliament's Committee on Economic and Monetary Affairs, Public Hearing with the Chair of the Single Resolution Board, July 2017).

Whelan K., Wolff G. and Belke A., *Eurosystem Collateral Policy and Framework* (Compilation of notes provided at the request of the European Parliament's Committee on Economic and Monetary Affairs, Monetary Dialogue, November 2014).

Index

www.ingramcontent.com/pod-product-compliance
Lightning Source LLC
LaVergne TN
LVHW021123300926
849160LV00010B/835
9781032030555